William Safire is a political columnist and the author of the "On Language" column of *The New York Times*, as well as a winner of the Pulitzer Prize for distinguished commentary. His books include *Safire's Political Dictionary*, *What's the Good Word?* and the best-selling novels *Freedom* and *Full Disclosure*.

YOU
COULD
LOOK IT UP

YOU
COULD
LOOK IT UP

MORE *ON LANGUAGE* FROM

WILLIAM SAFIRE

𝕿𝖎𝖒𝖊𝖘 BOOKS

Library of Congress Cataloging-in-Publication Data
Safire, William, 1929–
You could look it up.

Includes index.
1. English language—Usage. I. Title.
PE1421.S234 1988 428'.00973 87-40595
ISBN 0-8129-1234-8

Manufactured in the United States of America
9 8 7 6 5 4 3 2
First Edition

Designed by: Mary Beth Kilkelly/Levavi & Levavi

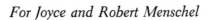

For Joyce and Robert Menschel

Forewords March

As a brief prolegomenon to today's discourse, be warned: nobody reads *prefaces*. An *introduction* is considered part of a text and is the piece of *front matter* closest to the first chapter; it usually gets skimmed, rarely perused. A *preface* comes before that and is most often a personal comment by the author apologizing for writing the work, or for being alive; in fact, a couple of centuries ago, the *preface* was often called the *apology*. Even before the *preface* comes the most ignored part of what publishers call the *prelims:* the selling job on why the reader is obligated to read the rest of the book, usually by a famous name willing to shill for his buddy, the author, and it is called the *foreword*.

We have not yet truly begun to probe the subject of prefaces. Forget the preceding prolegomenon, pronounced *pro-luh-GOM-e-non*, a deliciously pretentious word meaning "a preliminary explanation prefixed to a scholarly work." I don't read prolegomena, as Leona Helmsley would say, so why should you?

Now start. I have a copy of a letter here from James A. Michener, the author of *Texas* (a best-selling page-turner and terrific flower-presser), to his agent, Owen Laster of the William Morris Agency in New York.

"I've been receiving a constant stream of appeals," Mr. Michener writes, "perhaps ten a year, for me to write *forewords* to books about to be published. There seems to be a misconception about the value of such puffery. . . .

"What fascinates me is that of fifty such requests in recent years fully seventy percent of the applicants have spelled the word *forward*, and I have had two wonderful secretaries who not only spelled the word this way but also corrected me when I spelled it my way. . . .

"I have tried during these years to fight a battle in defense of the proper spelling of this useful word, but I have failed. . . . This morning I received the crowning humiliation. My own agent, one of the finest and a man of unusual sophistication, forwards to me the information that I am to be paid a modest fee for my latest *forward!*"

This has caused Jim to abandon the ramparts. "Maybe the most effective spelling for the device under question *is* 'forward.' Maybe what it signifies is 'Into battle for the good, the beautiful and the true!' "

Jim sent me a copy of his missive to his agent because he does not really want to surrender. *Forward*, meaning "onward, ahead," is not the same as *foreword*, "a word that comes before."

For-, without the *e*, is a prefix meaning "prohibiting, refusing, neglecting, failing." That's what gives the stern look to *forbear, forbid, forfend*, and twists the meaning of the last syllable in *forgive, forget* and *forgo*. (So many people have been misspelling *forgo* recently that some dictionaries accept *forego* as a variant, but I forswear such permissiveness.)

Fore-, with the *e*, is a combining form, giving a meaning of "occurring earlier" or "out front" to the word attached aft. That's how we get *foreclose, foregone, foreground, forewarn, forearm, forerunner* and—slap my *forehead*—*foresight*.

Maintaining the distinction is useful. *Forbear* is a verb meaning "to refrain from"; *forebear* is a noun meaning "ancestor." The *for* denies; the *fore* looks to an earlier time.

The forward-foreword confusion has taken us, with malice aforethought, into the land of homonyms, in which order-followers mistakenly *tow the line* (no, *toe the line*) and financiers find themselves in dire *financial straights* (no, *straits*, more narrow than straight). I am sitting on my *softwear* and writing on my *software*.

Words that sound the same need not mean the same, and the clue we should cling to is the spelling, which at least helps us with the written words. Jim Michener, therefore ("consequently; that which follows the point that has gone before"), should stick to writing *forewords* and leave the *forwards* to generals leading a charge. That is the way to make a mint on a book while avoiding a gilt complex.

YOU
COULD
LOOK IT UP

Aboard the Zoo Plane

There are no good seats on the *zoo plane*.

It was the presidential campaign of 1968 and, aboard Richard Nixon's plane, press aide Ronald Ziegler faced a "pool" reporter who had written a piece criticizing the candidate. Ziegler joked, "You'll never get off the *zoo plane* after this."

Five years later, the phrase appeared in print: Jules Witcover, writing in the *Washington Post* of a Republican with reporter's credentials aboard the Democrats' campaign plane, defined the term: "She was shunted to the *zoo plane*—the No. 2 plane in the McGovern entourage."

"It was so named by reporters," he continued, "because it mostly carried television cameramen and technicians—'the animals' in the quasi-affectionate, quasi-snobbish parlance of political campaigns."

The phrase remains with us, burrowing deeper into the political-journalistic lingo. "On *Air Force One*," writes Jacob Lamar in *Time* magazine in the 1984 campaign, "an eleven-member press pool sits in the back, well behind President Reagan's closed-off cabin . . . with the rest of the press traveling on a separate *zoo plane*."

The press likes to zap politicians, but appears to be saving the meanest derogations for itself. Zoos? Animals? I asked my *New York Times* colleague Steven R. Weisman if the writing press really dumped this way on the photographic press.

His answer: "The lighting, camera and sound operators work the longest hours of anyone. Generally, they have the most reason to carry on at the end of the day on their plane: throwing food, drinking, partying, etc. Hence their nicknames as *animals* or even as *The Visigoths* or *The Goths*. (Honest.)"

The origin of *animals*? "It would seem to go back to fraternity talk," speculates Weisman, "as in 'Animal House.' "

"An *animal*," he continues, "is fraternity lingo for 'happy-go-lucky slob.' And where do animals live? Sample phrase: 'This place is like a zoo.' "

Time's account of the press's cross-flagellation went on: "Life on a campaign plane can lead to a curious sociological hierarchy, which ranges from the *big feet*, top national correspondents who come aboard for a few days and figuratively step on the toes of regular reporters, to the *roaches*, local newsmen who travel only on one leg of a trip."

Readers of this space already know the origin of *Big Foot*; when Hedrick Smith of *The New York Times*, with his foot in a cast, joined the press plane in the 1980 campaign, his *Times* colleague on the regular beat, Drummond Ayres, good-humoredly dubbed him that. (I say "good-humoredly" because I like to keep peace in the family.)

But *roaches* is mean. Dave Beckwith, the *Time* magazine reporter who first caught the term being used, says the term is not as pejorative as it sounds: "Say you're on a plane, an intrastate flight from one part of Illinois to another, and all of the Chicago reporters fill up the seats on the flight; then you might hear the word *roaches* to describe them. I think it's fairly new."

Narcotics agents know that *roach* is a 1938 slang term for the butt of a marijuana cigarette. Perhaps that is all that is meant by this latest derogation of local reporters by the national press corps, and there is no intention of comparing local newsies to crawling insects. If not, from *Air Force One* to the *zoo plane*, it's going to be war to the knife.

Your column about "zoo planes" reminded me of a summer I spent working at a hotel on Cape Cod as a waiter. At this hotel the staff was given free room and board, and there was a very specific graduation of privileges. Bell captains, headwaiters, the chef, and other middle-management types were served their meals in small dining rooms known as "side halls."

The rest of us were required to pass through a chow line at the back of the kitchen and carry our trays into a crowded and greasy room that was known as the "zoo." While this wouldn't be worthy of your notice if there had been only one "zoo," I thought you might like to know that this is (or was) the accepted term for the staff dining room on the whole resort circuit.

Perhaps the term "zoo plane" is related to the "zoos" of resort hotels. They both seem to refer to a place of exile and rowdy behavior. Also, a great deal of personal

pride was felt by those veterans who worked enough seasons to gain "side hall"
status. Of course, the lowliest job in the hotel was that of the poor "zoo girl" who
didn't wait on guests, middle management, or anyone human. She had to clean up
after the animals.

Richard Stanton
Salem, Massachusetts

Abort the Correction!

When economic jargonauts talk, everybody falls asleep.

"Will rising deficits *abort* the recovery?" Conventional wisdom on Wall Street holds that big deficits mean heavy government borrowing, which in turn drives up interest rates and threatens to—here comes the verb on the lips of every security analyst—*abort* the recovery.

A few lonely economic seers at the Treasury Department argue that interest rates fell last year as deficits rose, contrary to all the prognostications of abort-talkers. These pro-choice economists have no verb to fit with *recovery* like *abort*, which is wedded to the rebound as *four-footed* is to *friend*, or *diametrically* is to *opposed*, or *greasy* is to *kid stuff*. (Those are not precisely parallel; I should choose word weddings of verb and noun to compare with *abort* and *recovery*. Try *cast* and *aspersion, harbor* and *grudge,* or the latest television news favorite, *claim* and *responsibility*.)

Who got in on the ground floor of *abort* as applied to business? According to Fred Mish, top man at Merriam-Webster, the earliest user on record is Henry Kaufman, superseer for Salomon Brothers. In 1971, he told the New York Society of Securities Analysts that "a further increase in interest rates . . . will eventually abort the current economic recovery." (Henry does keep saying that.) Four years later, William Simon, then secretary of the Treasury, said that "Oversize Federal deficits . . . would drive up interest rates and abort the process of recovery." (Bill is consistent, too.)

The Safire Surefire Make-A-Killing Econoclastic Contrarian Vogueword Market-letter advises: Sell *abort* at the high—which is now—and invest in a 1950's word that has a minimum downside risk with strong upside potential. What would an aborted recovery lead to, marketwise? You've heard it a thousand times—not a *slide, downturn, dip, selloff, nosedive, plummet* or *falling out of bed*, but a vogue word that all the forecasters, ballgazers, seers and touts have conspired to use: *correction*!

That word, from the Latin *corrigere*, "to make straight," has in nonmarket terminology become a euphemism for *incarceration:* A "correctional facility" is a jail, where they attempt to encourage the crooked to go straight. However, on Wall Street, a correctional facility is the ability of the Dow Jones average to drop about 10 percent before marching upward again.

The earliest citations for *correction* in that sense come from the financial reporting of Burton Crane in *The New York Times* in 1953: "When they make up their minds that the wiggly lines have signaled a decline or a 'reaction' or a 'correction,' their trading can make it happen." A few months later, he wrote: "They felt . . . that overcapacity was beginning to appear, that a business 'correction' was overdue."

The meaning is now "a drop in the stock market after a sharp or prolonged advance"; unlike the other words for *decline* listed three paragraphs back, *correction* carries a connotation of comeback: Like a prodigal investor after a speculative binge, a short time in a correctional facility will enable the market to get on the straight and narrow, headed back upward. Unless it all aborts.

Apostrophe Catastrophe

Does prose that appears on a television screen make a lasting impression on the mind? Put another way—in dealing with catastrophes, do apostrophes count?

Evidently not. In 1983, when the Mobil Oil Corporation presented the television version of a novel by Charles Dickens, the series of four programs—produced by Colin Callender—was begun by these words on the screen: "Charles Dicken's 'The Life and Adventures of Nicholas Nickleby.' "

Edward Burke of Walpole, New Hampshire, wrote to me about the misplaced apostrophe: "Who the dicken's is responsible? I await your response with no small expectation's." I did not respond; no mass of Dickensians or apostrophiliacs wrote in; the mistake went unremarked. Perhaps the audience was too small.

No such excuse could be offered by ABC-TV for *The Day After*, which reportedly was watched by 100 million people. (That is almost as many viewers as saw the last episode of *M*A*S*H*, which obviously ranks with the first Joe Louis–Billy Conn fight as the most significant American entertainment event of the century.)

"Of all the millions watching television that evening," writes Norman Bunin, circulation manager of *Parents Magazine*, "I wonder how many noted the errant apostrophe in the text that came on the screen at the end of the program."

I was the other one. These were the words that appeared on the screen soon after the end of the world: "In it's presentation, ABC has taken no position as to how such an event may be initiated or avoided."

Slamming a hundred million impressionable people in the teeth with *it's* as a possessive is a grammatical event of such magnitude that no responsible language maven can avoid taking (or initiating) a position.

Apostrophes do two things: They form the possessive *(This missile is Henry's)*, and they substitute for little letters that are not there *(Don't play with that button, Nancy)*.

In the case of *its* and *it's*, we have a confusion: *Its* is a possessive but has no apostrophe, and *it's* is not a possessive but has an apostrophe. That throws a great many people, especially writers of prose for television graphics, because they forget the second function of the apostrophe: substituting for left-out letters. In *it's*, the apostrophe substitutes for the second *i* in *it is*.

To prevent confusion, the language over the centuries has worked out this rule: The word *its* will handle the possessive of "it," and the contraction *it's* will handle "it is." It's its best rule. The job of clarification gets done, and not even the most round-heeled permissivist argues that the mistake when made should be left uncorrected.

Was ABC deluged with complaints from irate grammarians after the show? "We received a handful of calls," reports Jeff Tolvin, a network spokesman. "To my knowledge, we've had no letters yet."

Moral: Not every bomb has a fallout.

I read your article concerning the unnecessary apostrophe which appeared in the concluding paragraph of ABC-TV's The Day After. *I NOTICED IT!! I was furious! I called my husband into the living room and asked him to watch the paragraph on videotape. He didn't notice anything wrong; by the way, he's chairman of our English Department. I called another English teacher on the phone; had she been aware of the gross error? No. What is this world coming to? How am I justified in correcting my students' errors when they can go home and watch television only to be mesmerized by double negatives and lack of subject-verb agreements?*

Anne MacLeod Weeks
Pennsburg, Pennsylvania

I'm surprised that my scream of anguish did not reach you all the way from Columbus, Ohio, where I was visiting, following the plight of IT'S *on the screen. Having been educated in the 20's and 30's, I am something of a grammatical purist, much to the annoyance of friends and family, who often claim that my concern for form far exceeds that for content.*

While we're at it, how about the "20's and 30's" vis-à-vis the apostrophe? And how does it affect you when you encounter the apostrophe preceding an s in a simple plural: boy's *and* toy's *and* girl's *and* joy's *merely evoke my repeated "oi's"!*

Carol Lowenstein
Bayside, New York

There was one apostrophic catastrophe that you didn't mention, and that was omitting the apostrophe in using the plural form, such as in "There are three n's *in Cincinnati," "The terrible 60's," or "There are three* and's *in that paragraph."*

Then again, do we say "6 SATs" or "6 SAT's"? I have worked with the SAT exams for many years. I've come to the conclusion that, with periods, S.A.T. reads as "ess-ay-tee" but without periods SAT should read as the word sat. *Thus, I would say that both "6 SATs" or "6 S.A.T.'s" are correct. Unfortunately, the word* SAT *is usually spelled out. The incorrect result is "6 SAT's." Truly the English language and its usage is a most fascinating business.*

Stanley H. Kaplan
Chief Executive Officer,
Stanley H. Kaplan Educational Center, Ltd.
New York, New York

I am still puzzled over the manner in which none other than the Times *often misuses the apostrophe. I edit a music magazine, so I always read the record reviews in the* Times. *As you are probably aware, the record album, abbreviated as LP (Long-Play), is a singular item. According to my sense of language that would make two record albums LPs. Yet according to the* Times *they are considered LP's. I can't understand this use of the apostrophe. Since when does the apostrophe denote that a plural is being referred to? LP's does not refer to either a possessive or a contraction. They are not saying that something belongs to the record or that the "record is." So isn't LPs the correct spelling? And if so, why does the* Times *continue to misspell that and many other similar abbreviations?*

> Jeff Tamarkin
> Editor, Goldmine Magazine
> New York, New York

On Charles Dickens's apostrophe problems, there is another aspect that might be discussed. In the wonderful Elements of Style *(Get this little book!), Strunk and White say that articles ought to be dropped in titles when they follow the artist's, composer's or author's name as a possessive. I don't have the book with me today, but my recollection is their example was: Dickens's* Tale of Two Cities, *not Dickens's* A Tale of Two Cities. *That may be a good device for the ear. My own example would be: Write* The Ring *by Wagner, but write Wagner's* Ring.

On its vs. it's, I have always taught my students this way of never getting it wrong: The rule is that personal pronouns never take an apostrophe in possessive, such as hers, theirs, his (a derivation of him's?). You'll probably get mail on this one.

> Irv Molotsky
> Washington, D.C.

I see that your column on apostrophes has inspired a correspondent to resurrect the old theory that the mark of the possessive 's is a contraction of his; that Safire's book derives from Safire his book.

This is an old theory (it dates back at least as far as 1634) and a popular one, but it was exploded in the mid-eighteenth century by both Samuel Johnson and Bishop Lowth. Both pointed out that in expressions like Juno's unrelenting hate *or the rabble's insolence, his could not be understood where her or their was required. Lowth identified the source of 's as the Old English genitive ending es (often spelled -is).*

The apostrophe itself, however, is probably traceable to the mistaken theory. George H. McKnight in Modern English in the Making *points out that in the late seventeenth century, when 's began to be used as a sign of the possessive, the apostrophe was used only to indicate the omission of letters. Since the his theory*

was then current, he opines that printers began using the apostrophe because they
supposed they were marking the omission of hi.

E. W. Gilman
Springfield, Massachusetts

Attaboy, Adamant

John J. Louis, our ambassador to the Court of St. James's (pronounced *JAME-ziz*), was replaced in 1983. In wishing the bounced envoy a fond farewell, President Reagan wrote: "The alliance today between the United States and Great Britain is adamantine and for that you are in no small part responsible."

Adamantine is not what you would call a typical Reagan word, such as *ratcheting*; it is not a word bandied about at the White House Mess, either; in fact, nobody at the White House will come forward and claim authorship of that hifalutin encomium.

The word means "firm, unyielding," from the Greek words for "not to subdue." The best political use of *adamant* was Winston Churchill's oxymoronic blast at an irresolute politician as "adamant for drift." However, I can find no recent diplomatic use of *adamantine*; some writer must have asked, "What's a good word for 'too tough to break'?" And out went the presidential letter with *adamantine*.

Away With You, Nosy Parker

It all began with *Claire Voyant*. She was the heroine of a cartoon strip of the 1940's by Jack Sparling, and the obsession to change words or phrases into a woman's name has afflicted me since. Readers of this space will recall the infinitely detailed *Vera Similitude* and the damsel too often used by common usage, *Norma Loquendi*.

Norma slipped past a few people because her name is taken from the Latin and made part of the linguist's jargon for "everyday speech." Olympics fans made the acquaintance of Sarah Yayvo, who used to pal about with the Archduke Ferdinand. One of these days I will find a use for *Natalie Attired, Lolly Gagging* and *Sally*

Forth—also the name of a comic-strip heroine—because names not only make news but make language.

Take, for example, *Nosy Parker*. My longtime colleague Sally Cutting had the habit of replying to every query about her private life with a crisp "What are you, a Nosy Parker?" In a card game in the 1940 film *My Little Chickadee*, W. C. Fields called one of the players "a Nosy Parker" for daring to question what he claimed to have in his hand. That name was the embusybodiment of the pruriently curious; in these times of necessary resistance to intrusions upon privacy, civil libertarians apply the name *Nosy Parker* to anyone who pries for purposes of gossip or salacious titillation. Where did that fellow come from?

"In England, beginning in the 14th century," reports Stuart Flexner, keeper of the reference flame at Random House, "*parker* originally meant a park keeper, especially the keeper of a game park. By the late 19th century it was occasionally used to mean any nature lover, bird watcher, etc., who frequented parks."

But what about the specific *Nosy* Parker? "That is a 1907 term, originally applied to one who loitered in London's Hyde Park for the vicarious, voyeuristic thrill of watching lovemaking couples." Mr. Flexner sounded a bit dubious about this derivation, but it is the standard explanation for *Nosy Parker* in the slang-etymology trade. (Somewhat puckishly, Mr. Flexner suggests I put forward an outrageously false etymology, like "a man who constantly drove the streets looking for a parking place"; he also wishes I would put out the canard that *posh* is derived from "Port out, Sherry home"; my friend Stu has been fighting off too many false etymologies.)

Another name in the language is *Nutsy Fagan*. "Would you have any idea," asks Michael Bronson Leach of Thonex, Switzerland, who lives on a street with the intriguing name of Impasse de Mon-Idée, "about the origin of the name Nutsy Fagan? The context in which I have for some years heard it is to denote an eccentric sort of person who does or has done things which don't meet with someone's approval. A specific reference was a play on words in the 1968 movie 'The Producers' ('Nazi Fagan'). One source tells me that the name was in circulation at least around 1910–20 in the New York area."

No, it's not the Dickens character of Fagin in *Oliver Twist*, nor is it likely to be rooted in the narcotic *fagine*, made from beechnut hulls. My sources and I are stumped. Where are you, Nutsy Fagan? What we need is help from Lexicographic Irregulars or a good steer from Nosy Parker.

When we were high school kids, years ago, we had a favorite, Lena Genster, later supplanted by Ophelia Pratt, and still later by Rhoda Gravure.

More recently, in playing with the idea, I produced several that seem to ring true—Anita Rangement, Barbie Khan, Candy La Bras, Dinah Sowers, Isolde Carr, and my favorite, Jennie Sequa.

I have a total of over two hundred that have some appeal and I think I hit bottom when I found the frightening Godiva Payne.

John A. Ferner
Medford, New Jersey

Please don't forget Natalie Attired's good friend, that rising young realtor, Joyce Lotz.

Emery Meschter
Kennett Square, Pennsylvania

For starters: Aida Biglunch, Eileen Slightly, Diane Tomeetcha, Ella Gant (women's shirts), Leah Tard, Emma Sar, Bessie Mae Mucho, Clara Fie, and Abdi Kate. God only knows where—or when—this will end.

Albert Komishane
Elizabeth, New Jersey

You failed to check with Notes & Queries, *which considered the origin of "Nosy Parker" with a query and some answers in 1932. Briefly, one replier explained that "Nosey Parker" was applied to the chief figure in a magazine story and became popular during World War I for a prying person. A second replier described a woman named Parker and thought that the term was used in music halls before World War I for prying female characters.*

David Shulman
New York, New York

Philip Howard, on page 85 of A Word in Your Ear, *says, "Who was the first Nosey Parker? Dr. Matthew Parker (1504–75), Archbishop of Canterbury, and notorious for his zeal in poking his nose into anything remotely concerned with church business."*

Richard M. Lederer, Jr.
Scarsdale, New York

Well-known vaudeville comedian. Born around 1880 and still alive in 1955, when I last visited him. A Jersey City native, snappy dresser, colorful local character.

William J. Bell
Huntington, New York

According to "The Cue" 1924 Class Book of the Albany Academy, Albany, New York, Willard Lee Ulcher was characterized as the "class roué." In "Class Humoresque" there is no mention of Ulcher, except at the very end—"Ulcher, 24"—so it was he who composed it.

Probably in the spring of 1924, during a Friday Chapel, the upper school was entertained with a short program of popular music by a student band. This kind of infrequent activity replaced the more customary singing of college songs and those of a bygone day, such as "The Anvil Chorus," "Upidee, Upidah," etc.

Striking, even at this distance in time, was Ulcher's laying aside his musical instrument (or did he leave his drums?) to sing at least a rousing chorus of (at last we get to it) "Nutsy Fagan."

> *Nutsy Fagan, Nutsy Fagan,*
> *He's the guy for me;*
> *Nutsy Fagan, Nutsy Fagan,*
> *Lives up in a tree.*
> *When the party's getting good,*
> *He recites Red Riding Hood.*
> *Nutsy Fagan, Nutsy Fagan,*
> *He's the guy for me!*

Alex McKenzie
Eaton, New Hampshire

I write in response to your appeal regarding the origin of "Nutsy Fagan." I have no specific source to allege, but I can offer an aside that may be of some interest. In the Navy, as you probably know, it's ironclad tradition to show a movie every night at 8 p.m. This film is announced from the quarterdeck sometime in the afternoon, more or less as follows—"Now hear this, the movie on the mess deck tonight is 'Dark Victory' starring Bette Davis." Now and again, the messenger or petty officer will add the name Nutsy Fagan to the list of actors. This was a mildly exasperating way of teasing junior officers who hadn't spent much time yet on the quarterdeck. This practice implies that Nutsy Fagan was someone who had the habit of appearing in

*places where he wasn't expected, clearly a tendency that would be compatible with
the general notion of unpredictable behavior.*

> Thomas L. (Nosy) Parker
> Oklahoma City, Oklahoma

Womenclature

I thought my habit of turning words into women's names—from *Natalie Attired*
to *Vera Similitude* and *Helen Highwater*—was off-beat, but it turns out that others
have been doing this for years, too often without a print outlet or a kindred soul
with whom to share their womenclature.

A writer of religious news in Baldwinsville, New York, uses a nom de plume of
Delores Mae Shepherd, and I am informed by Barbara Machell of Glens Falls, New
York, that the local newspaper features tongue-in-cheek fiction by *Shirley Eugeste*.

Eugene Kaplan of Great Neck, Long Island, suggests that the offspring of
statesman Henry Clay and an unidentified gypsy woman was named *Romana Clay*
and has become the most novelized real-life heroine. Ira Avery of Stamford,
Connecticut, relishing the punch lines of the old "Knock, knock" gags, unveils
Marian Haste, who, repenting in leisure, turned for legal services to *Marcia Law*,
who also represents the androgynous *Eunice X*. Morton Siegel of Scarsdale, New
York, recalls with sweet nostalgia the days with his thankful Italian friend, *Millie
Grazie*.

My most prolific correspondent in this endeavor, which causes us to listen more
closely to hackneyed phrases and to re-examine long words, is Donald Marks of
Kew Gardens, New York, who has known the crass *Phyllis Teen* and the multifac-
eted *Polly Glott*, the slightly inebriated *Sherry D. Cantor* and the diffident *Moira
Less*; he has seen *Anna Mossity* square off against *Bella Kose* and watched *Minna
Skewel* make *Maude Lynn* burst into tears when teased by the French chick, *Coco
Vann*.

If this sort of thing grabs you, explain that you're not just horsing around; you're
building a vocabulary. As for me, all this name stuff is prelude to the good news
about names in language: *Nutsey Fagan* has been found!

Toby Lelyveld of New York reports that "I'm either one of your *Nosy Parkers*
or a snapper-up of unconsidered trifles, but your *Nutsey Fagan* struck an almost
lost chord. It was a popular song in 1923 with words by Billy Rose and Mort Dixon
and music by Ernest Breuer, the same team that shared the dubious honor for such
other masterpieces as 'Barney Google' and 'You Tell Her, I Stutter.' "

Despite the vague recollections of many readers, *Nutsey Fagan* is not a comic-strip character. On May 16, 1926, Billy De Beck, creator of "Barney Google" (the comic strip, not the song), originated the strip "Parlor, Bedroom and Sink." The main character was Bunker Hill. In May of 1927, Bunker and his wife, Bibsy, had a baby and they named him Bunker Hill Jr., or "Bunky" for short. Another character in the strip, Fagin, attempted to train Bunky in a life of crime (à la Dickens). Bunky would often remark, "Fagin, youse is a viper," and Fagin became known as Fagin the Viper. That is not *Nutsey*.

The music division of the New York Public Library is notoriously unhelpful, but the Library of Congress confirms the copyright date (July 23, 1923) and adds the hyphenated spelling of the first name: *Nut-sey*. With a salute to my old friend Billy Rose, here is a snippet from the lyric:

> *When his ears are standing up,*
> *He looks like a loving cup,*
> *Nut-sey Fagan, Nut-sey Fagan,*
> *He's the guy for me!*

Dear Bill:
Your column reminded Marilyn and me of the staff we have been assembling for our newspaper.
Rome correspondents . . . Al Fresco and Al Dente.
Weather editor . . . Mozely Fair.
Night life columnist . . . Betty Bigh.
Horse racing . . . Thayer Off.
Boxing . . . Kayo Pectate.
Baseball . . . Hi Hopper.
Food . . . Sue Flay.
Gardening . . . Rose Blight.
Diet . . . Anna Rexia.
Exercise . . . Aileen Dover and Ben Dover.
Our photographer is F. Stop Fitzgerald and we plan to publish the paper in Elizabeth, New Jersey, and call it The Elizabethan Times.

> *Don [Hewitt]*
> *60 Minutes*
> *New York, New York*

Your pieces on womenclature set off a frenzy of remembering. There was Sarah Nade, who sang so sweetly; Dee Ceptive, the one I couldn't trust; my comfortable

Irish friend Patti O'Furniture; the hard-hearted Ada Mantine; Sal Monella, delectable but deadly; Gerry Mander of the peculiar figure; the intoxicating Marie Juana; and Rachel Prejudice, who was a hopeless bigot.

Were there others? You bet. I'm sure their names will come to me.

Douglas A. Ramsey
Los Angeles, California

A few suggestions for your Womenclature list:

Tanya Hyde
Ginger Vitis
Tamara Knight
Helena Handbasket

Vernon D. MacLaren
Augusta, Maine

Back in my undergraduate days of not too long ago, I enjoyed playing a word game with other school-employed tutors in between hourly tutoring sessions. Your "Womenclature" reminded me of it. The idea of the game is to take an occupation and couple it with an associated first name in the following phrase: "So, I said to the [occupation], '[name] . . . .'" For example: "So, I said to the geologist, 'Rocky, ...'" Before I give my favorite, here are a few I recall: 'So, I said to the lawyer, 'Sue, ...' "; "So, I said to the meteorologist, 'Gale, ...' "; As Dr. Frank Field must have said to his meteorologist son, "Storm, ..."

And now for my favorite: "So, I said to the nervous hooker, 'Hortense. . . .' " In perpetuity I bequeath this to you, Will.

Paul Bridgwood
Astoria, New York

Your venture into "womenclature" was fascinating and thoroughly enjoyable, and I'm sure your correspondents have enlivened your mailbox with scores of examples.

But others have gone before, and used men's names as well. The most notable practitioner, I think, has been Norton Juster, the author of The Dot and the Line, *who published* Stark Naked: A Paranomastic Odyssey, *around 1969 (Random House), in which he introduced us to the denizens of Emotional Heights, where Emilio Rate is the welfare commissioner, Hiram Cheap is a leading manufacturer, and Peter Asta is a scoutmaster.*

New York *magazine a while ago (in competition 197) asked its readers to invent* similar fractured names for up to three affinitive persons. Among the charming entries was

Jenny Saitqua—Broadway star who couldn't make her mind up (submitted by David Pearlman of White Plains).

My favorite trio:

W. Price Glory—Southern powerbroker.

Mourning Glory—His wife, who walks the plantation grieving for

Glory B.—Their son, recently turned in to the Atlanta draft board by W. Price in exchange for a future draft choice. (That was from Stuart A. Segal of Yonkers.)

That sort of thing can be very contagious, and I've found myself scribbling little addenda in the margins of Stark Naked, like

Ida Claire—town gossip

Owen Moore—perpetual debtor

Won Lump Sum—Chinese mathematician

Jacques Cuze—French revolutionary

Quincy Dental—defendant

Anya Toze—ballet teacher

Ilsa Pell—French teacher

Some of these probably originated elsewhere, with the author lost (conveniently).

> Hal Davis
> White Plains, New York

In your words-and-phrases-as-women's-names piece, you neglected that advocate of library censorship, Helen A. Handbasket and that femme fatale, Heddy Wein.

And why only feminine names? What about Chester Droars? (He's with the Bureau.) Or that German militarist, Helmut Leiner?

How about those two Nashville record producers, E. Odle Leahy, and his brother, O. Leo Leahy? Or the hillbilly fascist, Goober Mensch? Or the incisive Gordie N. Knott?

And don't forget those two ingenious inventors, Albert and Bernard Weevil. (That's right, the pair that devised the laser of two Weevils.)

> Noah Count
> (a.k.a., G.J.A. O'Toole)
> Mount Vernon, New York

For years my wife and I have played with people's names, whiling away vacation time on the road by matching them with occupations. I started dropping a few of the names into a talk show I host (METZ HERE!) and before I knew it, callers contributed a flock of their own.

At any rate, we were pleased to know we aren't the only ones who are on to this kind of nonsense, and so I am sending you my female list:* (Among my male favorites are the mortician, Paul Bearer; the gardener, Pete Moss; and the artist of another era, Art Deco).

> Milton W. Metz
> Louisville, Kentucky

*Alma Mater (teacher)
Barb Wire (prison guard)
Carrie On (playboy)
Charity Case (orphan)

You inspired an interesting game in your column. The attached results may be of some interest and/or amusement to you.

Tanya Hyde	Lily Livered
Sonya Buttons	Farrah Naceous
Wanda Lust	Gladys Seeya
Connie Lingus	Della Catessen
Kay Pasa	Angie O'Gramm
Lana Lynn	Dinah Mite
Flora Dation	Molly Coddle
Fran Chise	Ann Soforth

> Richard U. Gaudier
> New York, New York

My fascination with language has prompted me to collect lists of Anna Litical's, and I now have about 1000 of them, some on neatly typed pages, and some just scribbled on scratch paper—in fact, slightly over a thousand (I know, I just counted them).

So, here for your amusement (and, in a small way, to thank you for years of great columns) are some from my mammoth list of names:

Rhonda Laye	Faye Daway
June Yerprom	Gay Community
Cara Sell	Stella Object
Molly Coddle	Mala Propp
Bea Flatte	Kami O'Appearance
Ella Mosnerry	Erna Fortune

> Bella D'aball   Ann Tithesis
> Mia Culpa   Paige Turner

> Mona Moore
> Rego Park, New York

P.S. The second reason, of course, why I'm fascinated with "Anna Litical's," is that my own name is the equivalent of a French Anna Litical: mon amour = *Mona Moore.*
P.P.S. (My band even performs a song called "The Further Adventures of Rhonda Laye.")
  Isn't English Marva Luss?!?!!

How about these girls' names?

> Ellie Mosinary   May Pole
> Kay Nable   Bea Tiffik
> Belle Weather   Nan Tucket
> Dulcie Merr   Terrie Hoot
> Emma Blue   Polly Morfuss

> Emma P. Goldfrank
> Mamaroneck, New York

It was unkind of you to cut me in your column. I hope it was unintentional. I don't want to think you could be so cruel after all we have meant to each other.
> Etta Mology
> Northampton, Massachusetts

Banned Words

"Fascist," reported the Associated Press from London, "joined the list of words that members may not call each other in the House of Commons. Following an acrimonious debate . . . Speaker Bernard Weatherill ruled that the word was taboo from now on."

What other words are too strong to be used in the Mother of Parliaments? I sent this query to the Speaker, whose aide replied: "Erskine May did, in fact, once list banned words and, once a word was banned, it was added to that list and remained banned. However, with the latest edition . . . this list has been done away with, and a definition of the type of word or expression which should not be used is given instead."

What a pity; the delicious specificity of a list of banned words is of much greater interest than general instructions to avoid calumny. Eschewing the sanitized edition of Erskine May's *Treatise on the Law, Privileges, Proceedings and Usage of Parliament*, I went to an early edition and found the old proscribed list.

This candid and unexpurgated guide included nouns like *blackguard* (from the most menial servant, who cleaned the blackened pots), *cad* (from *cadet*, an underling who was the object of scorn at British universities), *coward, dog* (along with the even more insulting *cheeky young pup*), *guttersnipe, hooligan, humbug, hypocrite, jackass, murderer, pharisee* (originally a member of an ancient Jewish order that advocated the democratization of religion, but later one who observed the letter rather than the spirit of laws, and hence one who is sanctimonious and hypocritical), *rat, stool pigeon* (from the decoy bird used by hunters, which was usually attached to a stool to attract other pigeons into a trap), *swine, traitor* and the comparatively mild *villain.*

The more general rules in today's Parliament warn against "the imputation of false motives . . . the accusation of misrepresentation . . . charges of uttering a deliberate falsehood . . . abusive and insulting language." On the last item, the meaning is: try it, and we'll tell you whether it's out of order or not.

However, "expressions which are unparliamentary when applied to individuals are not always so considered when applied to a whole party." Thus, the *guttersnipe party* might get through. And the usage book notes that "the word *calumnious* has generally been held to be in order." You are thus permitted to denounce an opponent as a *calumniator*, one who maliciously utters falsehoods intended to blacken another's reputation, which strikes me as rougher than *cheeky young pup.* Shakespeare used that word in a way that should be remembered by legislators everywhere, in an observation by Hamlet to Ophelia: "Be thou as chaste as ice, as pure as snow, thou shalt not escape calumny."

In the United States, the House of Representatives operates on the same we'll-tell-you-later basis when it comes to specific words. When a member calls another a *demagogue*, for example, the attacked member may ask that "the words be taken down"; the House parliamentarian, William Holmes Brown, or one of his assistants then opens a little green box on his desk to see if the word is among the banned.

A few years ago, Speaker Thomas P. O'Neill Jr. said that Representative Marga- ret Heckler, now U.S. ambassador to Ireland, had been "duped"; it turned out that *dupe* is among the no-nos in the little green box, and the Speaker was punished by not being permitted to speak for the rest of the day.

In the United States Senate, Rule 19 protects senators from the hot words of their colleagues; the presiding officer's opinion decides if language impugns mo- tives or is generally unbecoming. The parliamentarian of the Senate, Robert Dove, exhumed a few records for me. In 1937, Senator Tom Connally of Texas lit into Senator Bennett Champ Clark of Missouri with "I protest against the Senate being made a sewer by the vaporings of the Senator from Missouri," and he was shut up for that. Thirteen years later, as presiding officer, it was Connally who slapped down Senator William Jenner of Indiana for unfairly blasting Senator Millard Tydings of Maryland for "the most scandalous and brazen whitewash of a treason- able conspiracy in our history, who would continue to cover up these termites and vermin who, even as I speak, are gnawing at the foundations of our freedom." (This was not the earliest use of *cover up*, which had become a noun in 1927.)

Since the 1950's, however, records of the offensive phrases are not kept to guide the presiding officers, as such terms are now expunged from the record and do not officially exist. Old-timers remember Senator Homer Capehart of Indiana when he was savaged as "a rancid tub of ignorance," which was considered then, and would be considered now, beyond the pail.

Parliamentarians here are as reluctant as their brothers in Britain to reveal the lists of banned words or even to point to the precedents that guide them in deciding what is out of order, but I am told that the newest addition to the secret lists is *sleaze*.

The inherent danger in compiling a list of acceptable and unacceptable expressions is obvious when one considers that the context in which a word is used may well determine its propriety in debate. In this regard, I note an extract from the 19th edition of Sir Erskine May, pages 434 and 435. The author quite correctly states that the use of the term "Hear, hear" in one instance may be quite in order, but out of order when used to express dissent, derision or contempt.

It is also delightful to note in the same excerpt that on March 19, 1972, the noise of the crowing of cocks proceeding from Members behind the Chair caused the Speaker some considerable "pain."

E. George MacMinn, Q.C.
Victoria, British Columbia

In your piece on banned words, specifically in the House of Commons, you describe "villain" as comparatively mild. I think you're sticking yourself with the watery American usage, if any.

To my knowledge, the English use "villain" to describe top criminals of the most vicious nature. With reference to your May proscription list, I'd say "villain" is more calumnious than virtually all the others, excepting the likes of "traitor" and "murderer."

I'm sorry I can supply no roll of specific sources. Generally, the English detective novel is a good one. Doyle describes Moriarty as an arch villain, and perhaps Colonel Moran qualifies without the prefix; but as opprobrium the word doesn't descend to pickpockets or car thieves or other relatively mild offenders.

For a reason that eludes me, in American English "villainous" carries considerably more bite than does the noun. Perhaps this is because "villain" is a little archaic on these shores, except in the categorization of dramatic roles.

Carl Jellinghaus
Westport, Connecticut

You have fallen into the trap of characterizing the Pharisees the way their Christian opponents characterized them. It is because of the Christian use of the word that it has become a term of opprobrium. In fact, the Pharisees never called themselves by that name. The word comes from a Hebrew root (P-R-SH) which means "to separate"; hence, separatists. Scholars are divided in their explanation of the name. One group argues that it is a nickname given to them by the Sadducees, who were the "Old Guard" of religious interpreters (see S. Zeitlin, Rise and Fall of the Judaean State, *vol. I). Others explain that they separated themselves from the* am ha-aretz, *the ignorant farmers who did not know or observe the law in its detail, particularly the laws of tithing (see L. Finkelstein,* The Pharisees, *vol. I). In either event, the idea that the Pharisees observed and valued the letter but not the spirit of the law is a Christian, pejorative one. Your definition is of the same genre as calling the God of the Hebrew Bible (not the Old Testament, as you have chosen to call it in the same column) as being the God of strict judgment and vengeance, compared to the God of the New Testament as the God of love and forgiveness.*

Samuel Tobias Lachs
Professor, History of Religion
Bryn Mawr College
Bryn Mawr, Pennsylvania

Paleontology

"Old-timers remember Senator Homer Capehart of Indiana," I wrote in a piece on banned words, "when he was savaged as 'a rancid tub of ignorance,' which was considered then, and would be considered now, beyond the pail."

A sensitive copyreader (copyreaders are not assigned to this column; they are sentenced to it) called to my attention the following facts: "beyond the pale" was the way the phrase was properly spelled and that while she was fully aware of the play on words intended by "tub" and "pail," others—perfectly innocent readers—might be drawn into the correction business. The copyreader was particularly fearful of the "Gotcha!" gang, the shock troops of the Nitpicker's League, who take special glee in exposing errors in this space.

I could not be dissuaded and now have fifty-four letters explaining the spelling and derivation of "beyond the pale." A *pale* is a stake or picket used to mark off territorial boundaries; the *English Pale* was the country around Dublin held by the English conquerors of Ireland before Cromwell's victories, and the *Jewish Pale* was the zone in Russia and eastern Poland established by Catherine II beyond which Jews were not permitted to travel. To venture "beyond the pale" was to go to a perilous and forbidden place, and the phrase has been metaphorically transformed into any forbidden area or subject.

Members of the Gotcha! gang need fear no embarrassment; your names are safe with me. Try again, but beware of puns.

Bark Off

More explication (a word that has a more learned and profound connotation than the plain *explanation*) of my Americanism-laden prose is needed. "Reading your column this morning," writes Richard Helms, a man of intelligence and recipient of the Medal of Freedom, "reminded me that for some time I have wanted to know the origin of the saying 'Let's have it *with the bark off.*' Is that correct? Or should you have written, 'Let's have it *with the bark on*'? President Johnson used this phrase frequently and, as I recall, he favored your choice of words."

President Johnson and I had it wrong. Mitford Mathews, in his *Dictionary of Americanisms*, traces *with the bark on*—meaning "plainly, in an unpolished natural state"—to an 1839 use: "I see Long has 'spoke the word with the bark on.'" The use of quotes around the expression indicates an earlier use, in a time of log cabins and taking kids out to woodsheds for discipline. In Mark Twain's 1872 book *Roughing It*, the Mormon leader Brigham Young is quoted on polygamy and concludes, "That is the word with the bark on it."

Seems simple enough: With the bark *on* is the natural state. So how did the bark *off* get started, tripping up both President and pundit? Probably not from the expression *to take the bark off*, meaning "to chastise, lambaste, flog the skin off a man or beat the bark off a tree." More likely, the expression that led to the confusion was *to talk the bark off a tree*, a talent for persuasion no less effective than charming the birds out of the trees, but with the use of profanity at the top of one's lungs.

Let's straighten this metaphor out here and now, once and for all: If "plain talk" is meant, leave the bark *on*. Any other way is barking up the wrong tree.

If you're right about the bark, then Franklin D. Roosevelt was wrong. According to Robert Caro's absorbing biography of Lyndon Johnson, The Path to Power, *when Roosevelt wanted plain talk from his vice president, John Nance Garner, Roosevelt wanted the bark* off. *Here's the quote:*

> *When . . . the subject turned to the court fight [in Congress], Garner asked him, "Do you want it with the bark on or off, Cap'n?" Roosevelt threw back his head and, with a hearty laugh, said he would have it with the bark off. "All right," Garner said. "You are beat. You haven't got the votes." (p. 562)*

Caro cites two sources for the quote.

Marie Shear
Brooklyn, New York

The Beltway Bandits

"Trying to get a piece of the action," said the hero of David Wise's spy thriller, *The Children's Game*, in giving a cover story to another former member of the C.I.A. "No reason the beltway bandits should get it all."

The novelist, who in real life is a correspondent covering the cosmos of the clandestine, goes on to explain what his character means: "The beltway bandits were the dozens of research and development firms scattered around Washington in northern Virginia and Maryland. Staffed mostly by former Government officials, the bandits lived off Government contracts, performing research on weapons, electronic warfare, antiterrorism and similar subjects for the Pentagon, the C.I.A., N.S.A. and other agencies."

The first citation I can find of *Beltway bandit* is from a story by Jerry Knight in the *Washington Post* on January 25, 1978: "Some 'Beltway bandit' ought to be hired to put one team of computer experts to work designing crime-proof defenses. . . ." The use of quotation marks suggests that the phrase was coined earlier.

Writers covering the growth of the nation's capital, and its spillover into the city's suburbs, took up the phrase: *The New York Times* reported in 1982 that "well-paying jobs in electronics and at national corporate headquarters are filled by 'Beltway Bandits'—scientists and consultants adept at securing Government contracts" and in 1983 described "the complex of consulting concerns called 'the Beltway bandits.' "

In late 1983, Under Secretary of the Navy James Goodrich suggested to the Naval War College that such reliance on outsiders stultified the intelligence of the

Defense Department: "The long, sad trend of passing our requirements for thinking onto . . . 'think tanks' and 'beltway bandits' must end," said the in-house Mr.
Goodrich, "if we are to have naval leaders who have fully developed their minds,
just as athletes do their muscles."

From this analysis of the phrase on historical principles, we can determine that
the words began as an alliterative description of consultants who worked near the
Capital Beltway. (*Beltway* was coined in 1951 to denote a highway skirting or
circumnavigating an urban area; in England, such a road enabling motorists to
bypass town traffic is a *ring-road*.) The *bandit* was jocular, usually connoting
grudging admiration for the way consultants get and keep their business, but lately
it has taken on a harder note: Newsmen are suspicious of *revolving doors*, in which
Defense employees give contracts to firms and later join them at higher salaries,
and evidently the top brass at the Navy wants to curb the spinoff of projects to
think tanks, a phrase coined in the late 1960's that is less geographically specific
than *Beltway bandits*.

As can be seen, a capitalization problem exists, both for raising money for the
consultants and uppercasing the first letter of their sobriquet. Since *Beltway* in this
case refers to a specific beltway, I capitalize the word, but do not capitalize the
bandits, because such a description of individuals would embroil the writer in a
lawsuit.

A related phrase, *inside the Beltway*, means "of interest to tea-leaf readers of
Washington goings-on but strictly a yawner to the World Out There." On *Meet
the Press*, Vice President George Bush sought to minimize the dispute between
economist Martin Feldstein and Treasury Secretary Donald Regan by calling it "an
inside-the-Beltway thing that nobody really cares about." In further deriding talk
of disarray, the Vice President, who might have spent some time stalled in traffic
on the crowded highway, urged his interlocutors to listen to the President rather
than "the who's-up, who's-down, inside-the-Beltway stuff." A few minutes later,
columnist Joseph Kraft deftly picked up on the Bush usage with a question that
began: "Mr. Vice President, you are known, at least within the Beltway here, as
the czar of deregulation. . . ."

The coinage of *Beltway bandits* should not be derogated as a nonce phrase,
because it fills a need. We need a term to perform as an effective antonym to
in-house, and the obvious opposite won't do.

*As a resident of Montgomery County in the early 1970's I remember news articles
about a new kind of house thief who hit neighborhoods with ready access to the
Beltway where husband and wife were usually away during the day. The Beltway*

bandit would start from a jurisdiction further around the Beltway, make a swift heist, and put easy miles between himself and the police on his getaway.

From this literal definition seems to have come the extension of the term to include business firms clustered along the Beltway who "raid" government for contracts.

John P. Richardson
Washington, D.C.

Beware the Basher

"The latest [interest] rate increases," wrote the *Wall Street Journal*, "have already driven the Administration to attack the Federal Reserve Board. . . . Reagan aides hope their *'Fed-bashing'* will pressure the central bank to ease its tight grip on the nation's credit."

Commented economist Jerry Jordan: "I don't think they're going to help inflationary psychology by bashing the Fed like that."

Bashing, particularly as a hyphenated suffix, is bigger than ever. Columnist Mary McGrory wrote about "scandalized conservatives who never thought they would see the day the world's premier *Commie-basher* would sit down with the conquerors of Gen. Chiang Kai-shek."

Commie-basher is a coinage of *The Economist*, a weekly published in London that has popularized the *bashing* suffix worldwide. French Gaullist leader Jacques Chirac was tagged in 1975 as an "articulate *Commie-basher*" and United States Senator Henry Jackson was "a veteran *Russia-basher.*" *The Economist* labeled editor Conor Cruise O'Brien a "well-known *I.R.A.-basher*" in 1977, described demonstrators in Belfast as *"bin-lid bashers"* in 1978, reported that automaker "Peugeot wants to launch its own *Granada-basher*" in 1979, and wrote that parliamentarian Willie Hamilton "labors unfortunately under his media image of *Crown-basher*" in 1982. To this publication, auctioneers are *gavel-bashers* and steelworkers are *metal-bashers*. I don't want to be an *Economist*-basher, but it seems that this publication has *bashing* on the brain.

Eric Partridge, the British slanguist, speculated that *bash* was either of echoic origin or blended *bang* and *smash* and meant "to strike with a crushing blow." He reported that, in English slang, a *basher* in the nineteenth century was a prizefighter or a professional thug. Partridge, a student of lingo in the armed services, noted that Royal Air Force mechanics were frequently called *instrument-*

bashers, and that the once-dreaded word now means "little more than fellow, chap." The *Oxford English Dictionary* later found the earliest use of the suffix *-bashing* in the most elemental of army occupations: Potato-peeling was cited in 1940 as *spud-bashing*.

In Australia, a *bash* was a drinking spree, a usage similar to its meaning as "a wild party" in the United States. The superb *Macquarie Dictionary* defines the colloquial *bash one's brains out* as "to expend a great deal of effort in intellectual activity" and *give it a bash* as "to make an attempt."

The combining form *-bashing* has traveled to the United States in recent years, thanks largely to the readership here of *The Economist*. The intention is to derogate by metaphoric exaggeration; *bashing* is the use of excessive rhetorical force to attack an object, person, principle or organization, usually for the demagogic purpose of changing the subject or passing the buck.

Today's *Fed-bashing* is a relatively mild form of finger-pointing. *Commie-bashers* remember the cold war with fondness; that was a real bash.

As further evidence that bash, basher, bashing *are of British derivation, we noticed during a recent trip through England that* piano-bashing *is a popular fete activity. The objective is for two teams of sledgehammer-wielding men to bash their respective upright pianos into small enough pieces to fit through the hole of a tire. The team that gets all the piano pieces through the hole first wins. One such event we witnessed followed a cricket match and was, in turn, followed by some heavy stout drinking on the part of the exhausted participants. So much more significant than either* Commie-bashing *or* Crown-bashing *for citizens of a fallen empire.*

Richard F. Hixson
Clinton, New Jersey

Beware the Virtuallies

Newspaper writers have a new and invidious aphorism: *"Virtually* is its own reward."

A few years ago, we had a rash of the *reportedlies*. Writers too lazy to look up the clips, or unwilling to take a chance on what might not be a fact, hedged their bets with their favorite don't-blame-me adverb. (Hamlet: "Seems, madam? Nay, it is; I know not 'seems.' ") Under ridicule here and elsewhere, *reportedly* is now as suspect as *allegedly* and is on the way out, apparently.

This year's advogue is *virtually*. Nobody can knock the use of qualifiers per se (although I would knock overly used *per se* in itself), but what has happened to *almost*? Is *nearly* nearly dead? As the British say, "Very nearly."

Practically every user of *virtually* assumes a pseudo-intellectual expression, both in print and on the face, as the vogue word tumbles forth. No, that's not quite right; *practically* means "for all practical purposes" and should not be a substitute for *almost*. That sentence should start "Almost every user . . . ," or "All but a couple of linebackers for the Redskins. . . ." Hold *practically* for "Chances are practically nil."

The meaning of *virtually* is best denoted in an illuminating definition in *Webster's New World Dictionary:* "in effect although not in fact." (Occasionally a dictionary's editor gets off a beauty and deserves a salute: a T-shirt stenciled "Lexicographers Never Lose Their Meaning" to you, David Guralnik.) The word is rooted in the Latin for "strength" and "power" and from its possession of those physical virtues gained its meaning of "in essence" and "as good as in fact." In the church, Virtualism was the Calvinist doctrine of the virtual presence of Christ in the Eucharist.

In advertising, *virtually* has become a sneaky word to slip an announcer past the legal eagles, to be downplayed to the point of disappearance: In "Virtually every dress in stock on sale!" the first word is melded into the first syllable of "every," spoken with the same speed as "member F.D.I.C." or "Use only as directed."

Meg Greenfield, the *Newsweek* columnist who conducted the successful campaign to stamp out *watershed*, is leading the anti*virtually* crusade. Victory is almost certainly, all but surely, assured.

Blow 'Em Away

"It was a good, solid fire fight," said Vice Admiral Joseph Metcalf 3d, describing our early military action on Grenada, "and then we blew them away."

After White House aides had an advance viewing of an antiwar film, one anonymous confidant told columnists Evans and Novak: "This can blow us away."

"We dominated them the first half," a Redskins fan said, in describing the early-season loss to the Dallas Cowboys, "and then they blew us away."

Whence comes this thunderous metaphor for "defeat decisively"? How come nobody ever moans, "They kicked our teeth in," or boasts, "We beat their pants off"? Who sold short on "smithereens"?

The answer is going to blow your mind. During the Revolutionary War, when cannons were firing, they were said to be *blowing away*; a common command to fire was "Blow away!" Then a quaint method of execution came to the fore: A traitor or spy was tied to the mouth of a cannon and with the roar of the explosion was described as having been "blown away."

"The first use of *to blow away a person*," says lexicographer Stuart Flexner, "was in this rather gory sense. The term then reappeared, or perhaps appeared anew, in street-gang use of the 1950's, referring to killing a rival gang member or stool pigeon. From that street-gang use, it entered—re-entered, really—the military in the Vietnam War, where our soldiers used it in referring to killing an enemy or destroying a village."

Other uses of blowing are still in the wind; we all still blow our stacks, tops, fuses and gaskets. And it still exists as an archaic euphemism for "damned": In Dickens's *Our Mutual Friend*, Fledgely shouts, "Holiday be blowed!" expressing a feeling many people have in January.

In Dickens's Our Mutual Friend, *when Fledgeby (not Fledgely) says, "Holiday be blowed!", he is not expressing the feeling of exhaustion, annoyance, let-down, depression, ennui, or whatever else many people feel in January about the recent holiday season. Fledgeby is scolding the Jew, Riah, for not coming to the door promptly. Riah protests that "it being holiday" he expected no one. "Holiday be blowed!" says Fledgeby and continues with anti-Semitic wrath, "What have you got to do with holidays?" This is an attitude that I hope is less common now than it was in Dickens's time.*

> *Wendy Dellett*
> *Alexandria, Virginia*

You missed the commonest usage for blow away. *It's somewhat similar to "knock out," e.g., "saw the latest Bergman flick and it blew me away" (or "knocked me out"); def.: "to impress to the point of speechlessness." Also similar to "knock their socks off."*

> *Jack Friend*
> *Burbank, California*

Bluestocking Desperadoes

The appearance of a serious new dictionary is always good news, and its emergence as a bookstore-chain best-seller is evidence that the business of looking it up is looking up.

Webster's II New Riverside University Dictionary is an unwieldy name for the latest lexicographical effort of Houghton Mifflin, but some of senior editor Anne Soukhanov's short essays on etymology have the light touch of original scholarship: Under *desperado*, for example, we find that sixteenth-century Spain had a powerful influence on English life and language. The *-ado* suffix "was added to words that were not borrowed from Spanish to form words that did not exist in Spanish." "*Desperado*," the entry continues, "is simply a refashioning of the English word *desperate*." Spanish-influenced words with the *-ado* ending include *bravado* and *tornado*.

Bluestocking is a "pedantic woman" (not to be confused with *bluenose*, which is found in the superb Merriam-Webster's Ninth Collegiate, to mean "one who advocates a rigorous moral code," and which most of us would call a "prude" or, as the Riverside says, "a puritanical person").

The Riverside word history: "The term *bluestocking* seems always to have been one of contempt and derision, for it originally signified one who was informally and unfashionably dressed in blue worsted rather than black silk stockings." Bluestocking Societies were female literary clubs of eighteenth-century London, scorned by idler ladies. "Since the literary gatherings were organized and attended primarily by women, the term *bluestocking* was transferred, sneer and all, to any woman with pretensions or aspirations to literature and learning."

That "sneer and all" is good to see in a dictionary, which need not be a repository of abbreviations and symbols. Also of interest are the current expressions that lexicographers think might be more than nonce words, and thus deserve definition: Miss Soukhanov and associates considered but held back on the unproven *yuppie* and *breakdancing*, but went ahead with *byte* and *floppy disk*.

A place was found for *golden parachute*, business slang for "a lucrative termination agreement with an executive who is fired or demoted following a corporate takeover" and *fast-track*, an adjective defined as "very high-powered and aggressive."

This may be nit-picking, but it seems to me that *fast track* is more often used in its noun form, meaning (1) "a place or situation of intense competition," as in "New York is the *fast track*," and (2) "a career path of unusual opportunity," as in "She was placed in Strategic Planning, known to be a *fast track* to the top." At any rate, credit the Riverside for getting on lexicography's *fast track* by spotting the term and defining it as an adjective at least as deserving as the verb *fast-talk*.

Which sent me to *nit-picking* and its back-formed verb, *nitpick*. In Riverside, to *nit-pick* is "to be concerned with or critical of insignificant details." In Merriam-Webster's Ninth Collegiate, that useful noun *nit-picking* is dated as entering the language in 1956 and defined as "a minute and usually unjustified criticism"; *Webster's New World* defines *nit-picking* as an adjective and noun meaning "paying too much attention to petty details; niggling."

Lexis Magnificus:
I can agree wholeheartedly with your high opinion of the etymology essays in Webster's II *without any fear of being accused of immodesty because, in fact, I didn't write 'em! The essays were written by Marion Severynse, the etymologist at Houghton Mifflin, who has currently been working with Professor Calvert Watkins of Harvard University to update the Indo-European roots which were such an outstanding feature of the first edition of* The American Heritage Dictionary. *The publication of* The American Heritage Dictionary of Indo-European Roots *is scheduled for the first part of 1985 [now available in hardcover and paperback]. And for all who are interested in the historical development of English words, I would like to point out that this work, which incorporates advances in the field that have taken place in the past two decades, will be the only dictionary of its kind in English. Marion is the person to consult, should you have questions about the origins of English words and phrases, incidentally. Things like* lynch *as in "lynch atmosphere . . ." and so on.*

Anne [H. Soukhanov]
Boston, Massachusetts

Your paragraph on the suffix -ado *as an ending for non-Spanish words overlooks the Spanish* esper *(to hope) and the older English* desperado *(one without hope). Brava and* Torna *are equally Spanish and likely all Latin derived—long before the English stopped dyeing blue.*

Another niggle—your references to nit-picking—*failed to note that the activity described goes way back to the grooming practices of primates.*

Daniel Green
Sarasota, Florida

With reference to your paragraph on fast-track, *I thought both definitions referred back to "fast-lane," not "fast-track."*

You fail to note the meaning of fast-track *as I know it best: A recent approach to building construction has certain parts of a building under construction before other parts are even designed on paper. Steel can be erected to the top of the skyscraper before the mechanical engineers have even begun to design the piping and equipment for the toilets and such. They just leave a 3-foot space between floors and figure that's enough room in which to install the piping and electrical and air-conditioning ducts.*

That's called "fast-track construction," and it's an absolute mess for everyone involved in it except the accountants, who say it's cheaper in the end.

Jerry D. Moore
San Rafael, California

The construction industry has a very popular and specific use for "fasttrack" (normally without a hyphen and sometimes without the second "t"). It is a procedure for soliciting early construction bids for less than a full set of the subcontracts needed for a total building, on the basis of incomplete drawings and specifications, in order to get a jump on escalating costs during inflationary times. The word, if not the procedure, is generally considered to have been coined by Frank Matzke, an architect with the New York State University Construction Fund in the 60's.

Robert F. Gatje, FAIA
New York, New York

Dear Bill:
May I pick a nit? You say Merriam-Webster's Ninth Collegiate dates nit-picking *from 1956. But the Supplement to the Oxford English Dictionary traces* nit-picker *to 1951, when it appeared in the following passage from* Collier's*:*

> *Two long-time Pentagon stand-bys are fly-speckers and nit-pickers. The first of these nouns refers to people whose sole occupation seems to be studying papers in the hope of finding flaws in the writing, rather than making any effort to improve the thought or meaning; nit-pickers are those who quarrel with trivialities of expression and meaning, but who usually end up without making concrete or justified suggestions for improvement.*

So nit-picker *(and if* nit-picker, *then surely* nit-picking) *was already a "long-time Pentagon stand-by" five years prior to 1956. And though memory may well be failing me (after all, I'm two months older than Ronald Reagan), my strong impression is that I have been nit-picking, and calling it that, since before World War II.*

Willard [R. Espy]
New York, New York

Booming the Babies

Gary Hart, according to Lance Morrow in a *Time* magazine essay, tried in his campaign "to tap into the underground wells of memory and longing in the souls of the baby-boom generation."

That was a richly evocative metaphor (although there are no wells above ground) and the use of *baby-boom generation* deserves a closer look.

After World War II, the soldiers came home and their wives started having babies like crazy. This caused a bulge in the population, with the cohort born between 1947 and 1961 attracting attention as the tribulation of colleges and the salvation of new-product salesmen.

In the 1970's, this bulge—traveling through the demographic graphs like a small pig being digested by a large snake (to use a favorite metaphor of morbid statisticians)—became known as *the baby boom*, its members *baby-boomers*.

Many of them have fared well, as their name has been clipped in familiarity to *boomers*. "By the end of the decade," wrote *People* magazine in a 1984 advertisement, "married boomers will account for 50 percent of America's superaffluent households. . . . Quite simply, the boomers are booming."

The word *booming*, an imitation of the sound of a cannon, blasted off in extended use in the 1870's, probably about the political candidacy of General Ulysses S. Grant. Now it has come to mean any activity that mushrooms or explodes excitingly.

Where did *baby boom* originate? Thanks to the ever-vigilant citation-filers at Merriam-Webster, we have the earliest use in print that anyone has yet found. "We are now using the potential female labor force almost as fully as we did at the height of World War II," reported the President's Commission on Immigration and Naturalization in 1953, "a fact all the more remarkable since the 'baby boom' of the past few years has greatly increased the number of young mothers."

One generation—the Lost Generation—was named by Gertrude Stein. A later generation was named, appropriately enough, by the unknown writer of an obscure government document. If the anonymous coiner still lives, he or she should come forward: phrasemaking immortality awaits.

Can you imagine the headline, LIFE GIVES BIRTH TO BABY BOOM, *in one of your columns? Even if it is not the earliest recorded use of* baby boom, *it is better than the date Merriam-Webster provided you, 1953. Yes,* Life *magazine in its issue of*

1941, Dec. 1, page 73, uses baby boom: *"But, whatever the reasons, the U.S. baby boom is bad news for Hitler."*

David Shulman
New York, New York

Baby Boom *is the title of a play I wrote in 1982.* Baby Boom *seems to be a bust, but many of my acquaintances have begun to use my word from it:* biopanic. Biopanic *refers to the physiological process of a woman's biological clock insisting that she start having babies. Specifically, it is hormones overruling both cognitive and discriminatory capabilities, simply known as the body ruling the brain. Men can have* biopanic *as well, usually referred to as* male biopanic. *I've seen single men, closing in on 40, who note with alarm and self-loathing that they have no children. In either sex, the panic is the desire to grab for the most available and fertile member of the opposite sex. The antidote for* biopanic, *as for any panic, is to keep calm.*

My other word is part of the title of my latest play, Convulsions: A Neurocomedy. *I am hoping that* neurocomedy *will become a new literary genre. Neurocomedy is simply a comedy that takes place within the memory or imagination of a character. The neurocomedy will be somewhat Surrealistic in structure, since it will imitate the brain's mechanisms for the shifting illogic of dreams and memory as well as the enforced logic of conscious thought.*

Wendy-Marie Goodman
Charlottesville, Virginia

Coin Collecting

Why, Republicans asked for years, should we allow the Democrats to get away with the adjective *democratic?* As a result, partisan Republicans, especially those who had been head of the Republican National Committee, called the opposition "the Democrat party."

Who started this and when? Acting on a tip, I wrote to the man who was campaign director of Wendell Willkie's race against Franklin Delano Roosevelt.

"In the Willkie campaign of 1940," responded Harold Stassen, "I emphasized that the party controlled in large measure at that time by Hague in New Jersey, Pendergast in Missouri and Kelly Nash in Chicago should not be called a 'Democratic Party.' It should be called the 'Democrat party.' . . ."

Mr. Stassen, who is only four years older than President Reagan, is remembered as a moderate Republican; his idea is still used by the most partisan members of the G.O.P. Democrats once threatened to retaliate by referring to their opponents as Publicans, but that was jettisoned. Despite the urge to clip, Democratic and Republican the parties remain.

On the subject of historic coinages, we have the coiner of *baby boom*, described here as having originated in a 1953 report to President Harry S. Truman by his Commission on Immigration and Naturalization. "I wrote the report," asserts Harry Rosenfield, now a lawyer in Washington for the National Safety Council. He lays no claim to originating the term, but nobody can find an earlier citation, and as he says, "I think the term *baby boom* was not in general use at the time."

The Build-Down Buildup

A new arms-control plan has been proposed: to destroy two old land-based missiles for every new one deployed. This idea, when originally put forward by Senator William Cohen of Maine, was dubbed a *build-down:* "This guaranteed build-down, while not offered as a panacea, would raise the nuclear threshold to a higher, safer level. . . ." The headline over Senator Cohen's Op-Ed article in the *Washington Post* underscored the *down* in *build-down* for readers who might suspect a misprint.

Senator Cohen, the only published poet in Congress, had reason to believe he had coined not only a good idea but a good word. His was the first attractive term in a lexicon that sports such sinister acronyms as *MAD* (for "Mutual Assured Destruction").

However, the word was used before in another context. *Buildup* (originally hyphenated, but the hyphen wore out) was first spotted in a 1927 *Collier's* magazine—"That's the old build-up for the Patsys"—and meant the accumulation of publicity for a person or product. Playing on that word with a reversal of meaning, somebody somewhere will be found using *build-down* to mean the reverse of "publicity buildup." Sure enough, the earliest citation of *build-down* that Sol Steinmetz at Barnhart Books can find is by British journalist William Rees-Mogg, writing about the rise and fall of the reputation of public figures. On November 13, 1966, the economist John Kenneth Galbraith was quoted as saying, "The autonomous buildup always strikes someone who is already in the public eye. . . . In a common case he has just assumed public office. . . . Then comes the buildup. He is a man transformed, indeed he is no longer a man but a superman."

Commented Mr. Rees-Mogg: " 'The autonomous buildup' is followed by the autonomous build-down. Precisely because the image makers exaggerate, they expose their hero-victims to the resentment of public disappointment." The writer made a syntactic compound out of a verb used earlier that year by Irving Kolodin, writing in *The Saturday Review* about a new Balanchine ballet: "The impression from this viewpoint was that it 'built down' from the first to the last treatment."

But what of *build-down* (hyphenated, unlike *buildup*, to separate the two *d*'s) in its current nuclear sense? Just as the primary application of *buildup* shifted from "publicity campaign" to "arms race," the application of its opposite changed. Fred Mish at Merriam-Webster is on top of that. On April 2, 1976, *The New York Times* reported the answer of Senator Henry Jackson, in a debate-format Q. and A. with Jimmy Carter, to a question about Soviet relations: "I would have as my immediate objective a program to build down in strategic and conventional forces instead of building up."

Therefore, the hawkshaws of the Phrase Detection Brigade give the first use of the noun to journalist William Rees-Mogg, the first use of the metaphor to music critic Irving Kolodin, the first use of the verb in its nuclear context to Scoop Jackson, and the first use of the noun in its current nuclear meaning to Senator William Cohen. That's the current state of play; new information may turn up showing that Shakespeare said it in an argument with Ben Jonson over plagiarism.

Word coiners often find, to their dismay, some earlier use of their baby in a different context. *Meltdown* was an important new term in 1963, referring to the ultimate accident in a nuclear reactor and the fear that it could sizzle its way through the earth clear down to China. It is used metaphorically today throughout the language: In *Dismantling America: The Rush to Deregulate*, by Susan and

Martin Tolchin, a chapter title is "Political Meltdown." However, the first use of the word was in March 1937, in *The Ice Cream Trade Journal:* "Due to the clean meltdown . . . a cooler sensation results in the mouth than with gelatin ice cream."

The alert reader is probably wondering: "If *buildup* led to *build-down*, why hasn't *meltdown* led to *melt-up?*" Good question, alert reader, because in linguistics, just about everything that goes up has come down. However, the word formed by substituting a *down* for an *up*, or vice versa, is seldom opposite in meaning.

For example, you can get a *rundown*, or summary, on a stock that has had a *run-up*, or sudden surge. You can have a *shake-up*, or reorganization, in a police department whose leaders participated in *shakedowns*, or extortions. Similarly, a married couple practicing psychiatry could undergo a *breakup* while studying *breakdowns* (breaking down is hard to do), and auto-safety engineers could call for a *crackdown* on *crackups*.

For every word ending in *up* or *down*, there is—or soon will be—another word created ending in *down* or *up*. A *sit-down* is a strike; a *sit-up*, an exercise. A *touchdown* is a score; a *touch-up* is the removal of warts and all from Oliver Cromwell's portrait. A *windup* is a quick ending; a *wind-down*, a slow ending.

Melt-up is troublesome, however. An accident in a nuclear reactor in China?

You exhaust every use and meaning of build-down *but fail to address the basic absurdity of combining* build *and* down. *Compounding the additive action of* build *with the detractive aura of* down *results in nonsense or, at best, a sneaky euphemism which attempts to put a positive light on the destruction of missiles on which a lot of taxpayer money has been spent. If this hidden motivation were not present, then why not use the quite adequate* dismantle?

Incidentally, if one must *use this piece of gobbledygook, it should, indeed, be hyphenated to separate the two consonant d's. Just this week I was reading an article and was stopped in my tracks by an unhyphenated* upphase.

                                                        Robert O. Vaughn
                                                        West New York, New Jersey

You listed William Rees-Mogg's 1966 use of the term "build-down" as the first of which you were aware. Consequently, you may find it interesting that this expression was used as a verb in 1949 in the addendum to a book by John T. Flynn entitled The Road Ahead. *There it is suggested on page 204 that we "build down Washington's swollen bureaucratic Big Government."*

                                                        Douglas Heckathorn
                                                        Kansas City, Missouri

From Timon of Athens, *Act IV, sc. iii:*

> *Had'st thou . . . proceeded the sweet degrees that this brief world affords
> . . . thou wouldst have (plunged thyself in general riot and) melted down
> thy youth in different beds of lust and never learned the icy precepts of
> respect.*

*Though never one for frigidity, Shakespeare is shaking a finger at indiscriminate
acts. Anti-nukers have obviously taken up the banner.*

> *Irregularly,*
> *Eric Conger*
> *New York, New York*

Add roundup *to the incomparable* meltdown. *The Meltdown Roundup would be
a good name for a journal.*

The word formed by substituting down *for* up, *or vice versa, is often opposite in
meaning when it begins with* up *or* down: upturn, downturn; upwind, downwind;
upstairs, downstairs, *etc. But watch out for* upright, downright.

It's hard to be upright *when the language is so* downright *quirky.*

> *Malcolm Stone*
> *Stanstead, Quebec*

Dear Bill,
*For at least 38 years I've heard Fred Schuberth of Paterson, N.J., describe the process
of raising the temperature of various waxy chemicals he's preparing to mix as "I've
got to melt up a batch."*

I'm not certain how the hyphen might be pronounced.

> *Curtis [Michel]*
> *New York, New York*

Two things to bring to your attention:

1. *You discussed the use of* up *and* down *when attached to various
    words. In at least one instance the use is just not to make the words
    to which they are attached mean the opposite of each other. Thus*
    knock-down *and* knock up *have very different meanings.*

2. *In an article in the Business section of the* Times, *use is made of*
    knockoffs. *Knockoffs are copies, usually much cheaper than the
    original. There is also* knock off, *which means "to quit doing some-*

thing, to terminate the action." Is there anything like a knock on
or knockon?

Donald M. Kirschenbaum
Brooklyn, New York

Cantonlike

"I reckon it is an attempt to really partition Lebanon," said an adviser to Druse chieftain Walid Jumblat, "on a cantonlike basis."

Of course, I nodded: chopped up like Canton, China. But then sober second thought intruded: China's Canton is neither a divided city nor even especially known for its sections. For weeks, as reports of the threatened *cantonization* of Lebanon came in, I kept trying to figure out what the Chinese connection was.

There is none. In Old French and Middle English, a *cant* is a corner. The French took *canton*, a corner or a portion of a country, and made it into a verb, *cantonner*, "to chop into portions." In France, a *canton* came to mean a division of an arrondissement containing several communes. In English, it became obsolete—occasionally used to describe the top inner portion of a flag—but popped up again in diplomatic usage in a verb form: to *cantonize*, "to make cantonal by agreeing to break up territory." In 1949, Arthur Koestler wrote of "a scheme of Cantonization prepared by the Colonial Office."

From his capitalization of the word, we may infer that Mr. Koestler thought it had something to do with the Chinese city. Not so; forget it. Drop the capital letter. A *canton* is a portion, like a neighborhood or the dexter region of a heraldic field. (*Dexter*, the right-hand side, is opposed to *sinister*, the left. I didn't know that; I just looked it up with great dexterity because I know my readers get lazy.)

So why did the Chinese name their city Canton (now spelled Guangzhou)? Because people there were right-handed? Wrong. The Chinese called their province *Guangdong*; Portuguese explorers who arrived there in 1517 found that hard to say and corrupted the sounds into *Canton*.

But what about Canton, Massachusetts, or Canton, Ohio? Did those names come from the French meaning or from the Chinese city? According to George Stewart in *Names on the Land*, by the turn of the nineteenth century, when Ohio was being settled, Yankees in the China trade were familiar with the port of Canton; legend has it that one Yankee trader from Massachusetts maintained that his New England town was antipodal to the Chinese city—drill a hole, he told his friends, and out you would come amidst the Cantonese and their delicious cooking. This theory was 1,300 miles in error, but who knew? Some dismiss that legend as folk etymology and argue that the French influence underlies the American Cantons, but the story has had the virtue of persistence.

While we're in Canton, China, we can find the origin of *gunboat diplomacy*. "President Reagan's dramatic resort to gunboat diplomacy" were the words that led Jack Anderson's column after the invasion of—incursion into, or rescue mission concerning (pick one)—Grenada.

In 1839, the Chinese in Canton burned 20,000 cases of opium to protest its importation; the British, in a punitive expedition, launched the First Opium War, taking over Hong Kong and humiliating the Chinese in a way that Maggie Thatcher would now deplore. A few years later, American ships wrested from the Chinese similar trade concessions, in what was then called *gunboat diplomacy*, though no citation earlier than 1927 has been found.

The German name for this activity was *Panthersprung*, after the name of a gunboat *(Kanonenboot)* that intimidated the Moroccans in Agadir in 1911. In United States usage, *gunboat diplomacy* was replaced by *dollar diplomacy* at the turn of the twentieth century and by *shuttle diplomacy* in the 1970's. Back to the gunboats!

I'm not sure whether you were saying that a canton is "like . . . the dexter region of a heraldic field," or that it is *the dexter region of a heraldic field. A canton actually is a rectangle placed in the "dexter chief" of a heraldic field, but that does* not *mean that it is on the right side of the field as viewed. In heraldry, the terms* dexter *and* sinister *refer to the right and left side, respectively, of the shield* from the standpoint of the shield's bearer: *thus, it is a classic "my right, your left" situation. If you've ever looked at a shield with a bend sinister (which, contrary to popular belief, is not always a mark of bastardy) and wondered why it starts on the upper right of the shield, you now know why: The sinister side of the field is the right of the field as viewed. Thus a canton, located in the "dexter chief," is found in the upper left.*

Michael J. O'Shea
Meadowbrook, Pennsylvania

I am surprised you did not notice that the word "cantonize" had nothing to do with the Chinese town of Canton. As applied to Lebanon, it is aptly used, since it refers to semi-autonomous political subdivisions in a multi-racial country.

Obvious cases that come to mind are the cantons of the federal state of Switzerland with their French, Italian and German population. Also, two German-speaking

*areas, Eupen and Malmédy, returned to Belgium after World War I, are known as
the "redeemed cantons."*

José de Vinck
Allendale, New Jersey

*If you ever saw a Swiss-owned car being driven on the roads of Europe you would
have noticed that it bore a plaque marked "CH"—that stands for "Cantons Hel-
vetii" the ancient name for Switzerland.*

Ernest S. Heller
New York, New York

*I'm sure you've already had batches of letters about "canton," but I'll add my two
bits, because I was writing about it from Beirut, without using the word.*

*You were on the right track to start with, citing medieval French, but you went
astray with China. The reference is thoroughly modern—to Switzerland, which has
achieved national solidity, prosperity, and enduring peace in a small country with
great communal diversity of language as well as religion. The Helvetic Confederation isn't loose, it's quite firm, but the confederated cantons have a great degree of
local autonomy and the central government is quite weak. I don't know how it
compares with the Articles of Confederation before adoption of the U.S. Constitution. My hunch is that it's weaker in some ways, stronger only in the existence of
a central bank and banking laws.*

*There's a lot of talk now about trying the Swiss model for Lebanon, and the reason
I wrote about it was to say that it's an illusion, it won't work. First, the communal
geography is much more checkerboard and hard to define. More important, the Swiss
made it work by resolute neutrality, the opposite of the Lebanese tradition of calling
in stronger forces to tip the balance in local factional fighting. Furthermore, they
achieved this neutrality in times when the maximum range of a weapon was the flight
of an arrow. Even now, their topography is a great deterrence to invasion by land,
but planes and missiles make defense of a small country's proclaimed neutrality very
difficult.*

*As for "gunboat diplomacy," the U.S. had gunboats patrolling the Yangtze for
"diplomatic" purposes in the 1930's. It got us into a quarrel with Japan, which
attacked and sank one. Under the Platt amendment, which gave the U.S. a right
of intervention in Cuba, gunboats were often sent to "show the flag" off Havana
and thus, without firing, to force both diplomatic concessions and internal political
decisions which the U.S. favored.*

Flora [Lewis]
Paris, France

In sports parlance, Sunday's column about "cantonization" might be called making the easy play look hard. Need we look any further than the cantons of Switzerland to find a current and illustrative use of the word?

Jay Branegan
Washington, D.C.

Culpa for Mayor

A sin of omission was committed in this space during a discussion of the origin of *cantonization*. "Canton, beyond the Chinese connection and when defining a governmental or territorial division," writes Alfred Stern of New York, "is certainly most prevalent as applied to the Swiss Confederation of states. There each of the cantons from Aargau to Zurich has its own distinctive flag. . . ." Lyman Hamilton, also of New York—a place that, according to my mail, is a hotbed of Swiss-canton expertise—writes: "In the fourth grade (1935 or thereabouts) in Los Angeles, we studied Switzerland: the Alps, edelweiss and the cantons. In fact, at the age of 9 I was reciting from memory the names of all the Swiss cantons, alphabetically." He adds wistfully: "The only one I can recall now is Uri."

I do not stand corrected, however, on the assertion of several readers that *to gin up* comes from the cotton gin or is rooted in *engine*. Until a printed citation comes along, that will be airily dismissed as folk etymology. (Anybody know where *to cotton to* comes from?)

Nor will I waver in the use of *stood in bed*; a phalanx from the Nitpicker's League came crashing through with demands that it be written "stayed in bed." My only error in using that Yiddishism was to couple the idiomatic *stood* with the standard *should have*; the phrase is best presented as "shoulda stood in bed."

And anybody who takes pen in hand to complain about "committing a sin of omission" is afflicted with oxymoronphobia.

Is "I should have stood in bed" a Yiddishism? It represents a confusion of the verbs stay *and* stand; *but this construction is not peculiar to Yiddish. The only Yiddish connection I know of for the expression is that it seems to have achieved currency after Jewish boxing manager Joe Jacobs ("Yussel the Muscle") declaimed it when one of his fighters was defeated.*

Matthew J. Bruccoli
Columbia, South Carolina

For at least the past two years, I have been sending some of your columns on words to an English friend of mine, Miss J. M. Bosdet. She sent me the enclosed clipping I thought might amuse you and in the accompanying letter wrote:

Cotton *derives from the Arabic* gutton, *the fleecy outer covering of a Middle Eastern plant with which they stuffed jerkins to wear under their chain-mail. These were brought home by Crusaders and called* actons (alquton), *and their stuffing was obviously cotton. The French began to cultivate the plant in the Midi and to get a sufficiently long staple thread to knit; and we began to import the raw materials in the Tudor period but mainly to stuff breeches. Because of its closeness to the body and the difficulty of brushing off loose strands,* to cotton *or* cotton on to *someone or something meant "to get on together" and later "to understand" (first literary allusion according to the OED is 1560).*

Forrest Alter
Ann Arbor, Michigan

Cardinal Is My Middle Name

The *Washington Post*'s lead was: "A dramatic grass-roots challenge to Polish Primate Cardinal Jozef Glemp . . . ," while *The New York Times* reported "a challenge to the authority of the Polish Primate, Jozef Cardinal Glemp."

Where does the title *Cardinal* fit in a cardinal's name?

The New York Times Manual of Style and Usage says: "John Cardinal Manley." The *Washington Post Deskbook on Style* agrees: "*Cardinal* precedes the surname." The Chicago *Manual of Style* straddles: "Francis Cardinal Spellman, *or, less formally,* Cardinal Francis Spellman."

On the other hand, *The Associated Press Stylebook* advises: "*Cardinal Timothy Manning.* The usage *Timothy Cardinal Manning,* a practice traceable to the nobility's custom of identifications such as *William, Duke of Norfolk,* is still used in formal documents but otherwise is considered archaic." The United Press International and *Los Angeles Times* stylebooks also take this modern, or more informal, view.

But wasn't the *Washington Post* breaking its own rule? Yes, says Dan Griffin, top wordsman at the newspaper: "The *Post* has consciously varied from the stylebook. We altered our style to conform with common wire-service usage." The next edition of its stylebook will reflect this decision.

How do cardinals feel about all this? "The way it is still done on official documents from the Holy Father," replies Joseph Zwilling at the Archdiocese of New York, "is Christian name, Cardinal and surname. That is the proper way." Softening, Mr. Zwilling adds: "Cardinal, then Christian name and surname is becoming more and more used, probably because it sounds more natural than the traditional way."

One man's traditionalism is another man's archaism. In matters ecclesiastical or in texts of constitutions, there is much to be said for clinging to tradition even when the informal seems so much more "natural." It stimulates children to ask why the text looks so funny or the title seems out of whack, thereby providing teachers and parents with a good opening to explain the way things came to be. Don't knock vestiges of the past in our present.

Welcome to New York, John soon-to-be-Cardinal O'Connor. (But how come no comma after the Christian name?)

First, I disagree with Mr. Joseph Zwilling's claim that official documents from the Holy Father use "Christian name, Cardinal and surname." I am enclosing copies of two letters from Pope John Paul II addressed to "Cardinal Terence Cooke."

Cardinals are likewise listed that way in the Annuario Pontificio, *the official Vatican yearbook, and in* L'Osservatore Romano, *the semi-official Vatican newspaper.*

Second, while cardinals may be addressed in that fashion by the Vatican, they do not seem to have adopted it in their own correspondence. I have a large collection of autographed pictures and letters from cardinals all over the world. Every one of the items I have, without exception, is signed "Christian name, Cardinal and surname." From that, I might conclude that they wish to be addressed that way.

Finally, there is one curious element in all this. One may be tempted to think that when prelates have waited as long as most cardinals have to receive this great honor, they would make use of the full word "Cardinal" without abbreviation. Alas, only a handful do. The vast majority simply sign "Card." between their Christian and surnames.

Monsignor Francis R. Seymour
Newark, New Jersey

I think a better case would have been made for "Cardinal John O'Connor" had you explained the reason for "William Duke of Norfolk."

Placing the title before the surname in that instance is not merely a custom of the British peerage. It establishes the descendability of the title. There will be a Duke of Norfolk unless and until the male line dies out. He may be a William or a Charles or have any other given name, but he will always be the Duke of Norfolk. Consider Lord Laurence Olivier. He is not Laurence Lord Olivier since his title is honorary, not inherited. He sits in Lords by courtesy of the Crown.

While some lords (and occasionally stars) are born, cardinals are always elected. It makes no more sense to refer to the soon-to-be-promoted Archbishop as "John Cardinal O'Connor" than it does to call our leader "Ronald President Reagan."

Linda S. Rein
New York, New York

Claim to Fame

Somewhere up high in today's harangue, a wedding of words was observed. (I refer back this way to keep editors alert; nobody can cut this column without reading it.) The verb-noun combo now so prevalent on television is *claim responsibility*. Soon after a terrorist bomb goes off, a sobersided rip-and-reader intones that some underground outfit or lone lunatic had called to *claim responsibility*.

This is a slight improvement over *claim credit*, which was the operative phrase until somebody pointed out that credit for a terrorist act was hardly deserved.

Occasionally, a newspaper attempts to get away from the current cliché. A caption writer for *The New York Times* tried: "There was no immediate assertion of responsibility . . ."—but the bit of jargon has reached the jugular of journalism.

"*Responsibility*, to me," writes Richard DeLia of New York, "is much too fine a word to continue to rub elbows with murderers, mutilators and other megalomaniacs. The use of such a positive word to report incontestably base behavior smacks to me of glamorizing violence. . . ."

What to do? How about *holds itself accountable*? No, that's not what the terrorist organization is doing at all. *Confessed*? No, that suggests contrition. *Takes the blame*? That's closer to the truth, imputing guilt, but the verb is too passive.

Claims blame has a nice rhyme as well as a defiant verb; also, *blame*, with its attendant fury and possibly repressive reaction, is what the terrorist seeks—not cool responsibility. The jury is still out on the best phrase to describe the call from a defiant terrorist seeking fair notoriety for his foul deed. Responsible suggestions will be accepted; credit need not be claimed.

Clause Wits

"Abraham Lincoln wrote the Gettysburg Address while traveling from Washington on the back of an envelope."

That is a famous example of a misplaced clause. Presidents do not travel on the backs of envelopes—only stamps do, and when so traveling they belong on the fronts of envelopes.

A Lexicographic Irregulars regiment that calls itself the Clause Wits—after the famed Prussian military strategist who habitually misplaced his clauses—stays on permanent alert for this specimen of solecism.

James Drake of New York took a hard look at an advertisement for the Hilton International Trinidad hotel that boasts: "The only hotel with tennis courts, a health club and TV in every room." He observes: "Jumping over the net to leave the room must be inconvenient." The copy might have been improved by placing the "TV in every room" phrase ahead of the tennis courts.

I have awarded leadership of the regiment to William R. Hutchison, who is Charles Warren Professor of the History of Religion in America at the Harvard Divinity School, for spotting the best recent example: a heart-rending appeal for the end of capital punishment of annoying *paparazzi*.

Professor Hutchison found it on the introductory panel for an art exhibit at the Dartmouth College Hopkins Center. The text read: "This exhibition . . . consists of nearly 90 works by American photographers executed between 1850 and 1980."

"Presidents do not travel on the backs of envelopes—only stamps do, and when so traveling they belong on the fronts of envelopes."

Should this not read: "Presidents do not travel on the back of envelopes—only stamps do, and when so traveling they belong on the front of envelopes"?

Even though "envelopes" is used collectively, envelopes still have only one front and one back.

> Clarence R. Warrington
> Rochester, New York

Clause Witless

In a piece in this space labeled "Clause Wits," I showed how some unthinking writers twisted their meanings by misplacing clauses. The famous example was "Abraham Lincoln wrote the Gettysburg Address while traveling from Washington on the back of an envelope."

The trouble with my exposition was that I identified *on the back of an envelope* as a clause. That was an error; a clause, writes Professor Robert M. Isaacs of Housatonic Community College in Bridgeport, Connecticut, "is defined as a group of words that contains a subject and a predicate. It may be dependent or independent." (I will point out a dependent clause if I can: It is the *if I can* leaning dependently on the main, independent clause at the beginning of that sentence and pleading for the keys to its car.) Adds Mike Hindman of Effingham, Illinois: "Not one of your examples of misplaced modifiers was a clause. *On the back of an envelope* is a prepositional phrase. Here is an example of a misplaced clause: *The man with the wooden leg that has an I.Q. of 160 will speak at the meeting.*

One wonders about the I.Q. of his real leg. The clause, which includes a subject, *that*, and a verb, *has*, should modify *man*, not *leg*."

If you can't tell a phrase from a clause, go with hooting at "misplaced modifiers." The best example to come in (of a misplaced phrase, not a clause) was from Laraine R. Fergenson of Tenafly, New Jersey: " 'Midnight Express' is a movie about a man who escaped from a Turkish prison where he had been mistreated with the help of his girlfriend."

Dead Again

To aid our campaign against misplaced modifiers, Margrett McFadden of Fairport, New York, sends along the obituary on the United Press International wire of cartoonist George Lichty: "He was recovering at the hospital when he suffered a second fatal attack."

Appropriately, it was Lichty who popularized the expression "Grin and Bear It."

Your campaign against misplaced modifiers is indeed a worthy one, but the contribution that appeared in your column was, I am afraid, a diversion.

The "second fatal attack" suffered by George Lichty is transformed from a logical impossibility to a sad but everyday occurrence by the simple addition of a comma—"a second, fatal attack." The two meanings nicely illustrate the difference between coordinate and qualifying pairs of adjectives.

Burton Lasky
New York, New York

Cloud Seven Plus Two

Cloud 9 is the title of a British comedy by Caryl Churchill that played Off Broadway in 1982 and at Arena Stage in Washington in 1984. The meaning of the phrase is clear—"off on a transport of joy"—but where does it come from?

Some have suggested a root in the National Weather Service's classification of nine cloud types, the ninth type being the cumulonimbus cloud that can reach way up there in the wild blue yonder. Others prefer the explanation of Merriam-Webster that the phrase is "perhaps from the ninth and highest heaven of Dante's Paradise, whose inhabitants are most blissful because nearest to God."

More likely, it began with *cloud seven*, associated with *seventh heaven* and influenced by *Cloud-Cuckoo-Land*, a translation of the Greek *Nephelokokkygia*, the imaginary realm built by the title characters in Aristophanes' play *The Birds*.

"Oh, she's off on cloud seven," says a character in Osborn Duke's 1956 novel *Sideman* about the music business, "—doesn't even know we exist." Within a few years, the escalation of the numbers of cloudy ecstasy began, and *cloud nine* is now the phrase for ignorant bliss. This should hold for a while, then—cloud 11, anyone?

Colon Cognoscenti

Consider this: Why should you and I, both busy people, clutter up our brains with information about the difference between a phrase and a clause? The answer: It will tell us when to capitalize the first word after a colon.

For years, I have flunked one test: capitalizing after colonizing. That is a problem I share with the following: other colon-happy writers, copy editors who hate to end any sentence, and undeveloped nations. But now that I know that a clause has both a subject and a verb while a measly phrase does not, I can write this rule with confidence: Always capitalize the first word after a colon if the words following the colon stand as an independent clause or otherwise look like a complete sentence. Here's how to treat dependent clauses: like phrases, with no capitals after the colon.

If all you have to offer is a phrase or a list of words, what follows the colon is a lowercase letter: one like this, or that, or whatever.

I suppose there are those who will say: "Who cares whether the first letter after a colon is a capital or not?" To them, those of us who have taken the trouble to commit this rule to memory can smirk knowledgeably and reply: most grammarians, elegant writers and the elite colon cognoscenti.

To me, "elite colon cognoscenti" suggests a group of Harley Street physicians specializing in gastroenteritis.

Joan Henzell de Ley
Baltimore, Maryland

Bill,

Some years ago, in response to entreaties by Dick Eder (whose ear is golden), we changed our rule on capitalization after a colon.

I think—still think, after reading your column—that our rule is right: sometimes, as in this sentence, you need to introduce a second complete clause with a fanfare slightly louder than a semicolon. In that case, you use a colon, and lowercase what follows.

> Al [lan M. Siegal]
> News Editor
> The New York Times
> New York, New York

Hurray for your rule in "Colon Cognoscenti."

As I see it, it is just a matter of logic (Snob School) over being arbitrary (Slob School). Nevertheless, I give you my corollary to your rule ("Always capitalize the first word after a colon if the words following the colon stand as an independent clause or otherwise look like a complete sentence."): Otherwise, do not use a colon—use a dash. Exception: When what follows is a list, keep the colon.

> David Bernklau
> Brooklyn, New York

P.S. Furthermore, if a list, then serial commas follow each particular (except, of course, the last), such as in one W. Safire's "most grammarians, elegant writers(,) and the elite colon cognoscenti."

P.P.S. You see—logic warrants that last serial comma!

Dear Pops,

You sham grammaturge! Methinks your column suffers from a colonitis of the most pernicious sort—it threatens to infect your readers. A properly used colon ogles at you from between two independent clauses: The second clause expands upon or clarifies the first. A postpunctuational fragment (a dependent clause or object, alone or in a list) cries for another antephrasal symbol—the dash. In all of your examples, except one, you incorrectly used a colon to do a dash's work: the one correct usage (". . . Always capitalize the first word after a colon . . .") erred only in its capitalization of the first word after the colon—a no-no.

> Humbly,
> Your dependent clause,
> Mark [Safire]

P.S.: Hi Mom!

Comes the Evolution

"The amendment was written in such a way," said Howard Baker, the Senate majority leader, at a subcommittee hearing in 1981, "that it could be changed through the process of evolution. But unfortunately, we don't let it evolute."

That citation of a curious verb was sent to me by David Mann of Kinnelon, New Jersey. It went into a file labeled "Suspicious Sightings." More recently, a former White House aide sent along this quotation, which appeared in *Advertising Age*, of Katharine Graham, chairman of The Washington Post Company, discussing the format of *Newsweek:* "With anything that works, you may want to evolute it and let it grow, but you don't want to mess with the format."

Evolute is a bastard verb back-formed from the noun *evolution*, which is a back-formation of the verb *evolve*. (The legion of parameter-crazed mathematicians about to write me that *evolute* is a noun meaning "a curve that is the locus of the center of curvature of another curve" can just lay off.) We can assume *evolute*, from the Latin for "to unroll," was used by Senator Baker jocularly, but evidently it was catching, and now our media moguls are willing to mess with the verb's format.

So what's wrong, say the permissivists? If *convolve* can lead to *convolution* and then to *convolute*, why can't *evolve* evolve in a similar fashion?

Because there are those of us who man the ramparts, taking our weapons from the Georgetown Molotov Cocktail Circuit and heaving them with attendant ridicule at the imaginative verbifiers of nouns.

At present (I would have written "presently," but hordes of nitpickers still think that means "soon"), the verb *evolute* is a mistake; in time, it may become accepted as an unmistakably transitive form of *evolve*. We may let something *evolve* by itself, but when we *evolute* it, we switch a few genes around and give it some evolutionary help. Personally, I'd use *develop*, or if I wanted to dazzle 'em with education, *educe*.

This is not to say that all verbification of nouns is beyond the pale. It has been happening all along in the language, from the long established *to telephone* and *to map* to the more recent *to party* and *to guest-host*. (E. J. Kahn Jr. of *The New Yorker* wrote to say that he no longer uses "authored" as a verb, since it led to an East Side weekly's usage of "She has authorized more than 40 articles and books.")

Here's a stirring verbification from the *San Francisco Examiner* sent along by Gene Marine of Berkeley, California: "Economists Say Reagan Silverlines Job

Outlook." In that imaginative headline, the message comes across succinctly that the President is being overly optimistic. I am reminded of the pessimist's credo: "For every silver lining, there's a cloud."

Commander in Thief

Anastasio Somoza Jr., who took power in Nicaragua in 1966, was given a very hard time in the Kissinger Commission's report on Central America. "His rule was characterized by greed and corruption so far beyond even the levels of the past," the blue-ribbon panel concluded, "that it might well be called a kleptocracy."

That is a satisfying kick in the teeth by some anonymous intellectual polemicist. The word *kleptocracy*—from the Greek *klepto-*, "theft," and *-cracy*, "government"—has been in use since 1819, predating the more familiar *kleptomania*, or "compulsion to steal." (I am still looking for the *biblioklept* who made off with my copy of *Studs Lonigan* with the hot parts marked.) The *Oxford English Dictionary*'s original definition—"a ruling body or order of thieves"—has been updated in the current supplement to "government by thieves," and *The Barnhart Dictionary of New English Since 1963* pinpoints a 1971 use in the *Manchester Guardian Weekly* about an author's description of the Federal Republic of Cameroon, "which he seems to regard as one of the less wicked kleptocracies."

Whenever a zestful word appears in the usually turgid product of a commission, the ghostly author deserves a pat on the head. My own belief is that the Somoza regime was followed by a kakistocracy.

Bravo for kakistocracy, *"government by the worst men in the country." This is the opposite of* aristocracy, *which means "government by the best," but unfortunately became confused with the hereditary nobility.*

Arthur J. Morgan
New York, New York

Condone

The language of cartoon captions can be instructive. In *The New Yorker* of August 1983, Joe Mirachi showed a relaxed congressman dictating the following straddle to his secretary: "And close with the usual—'I neither condemn nor condone it, but suspend judgment pending further study.' "

In that instance, *condone* is used as the opposite of *condemn*—that is, as a synonym for *approve*.

Doris Weller of New York City sends in the following citation from *The Hite Report*, a book on sensuality by Shere Hite: "Heterosexual intercourse . . . is the only form of sexual pleasure really condoned in our society." Miss Weller notes: "Ms. Hite evidently has been hearing the word as I have and went ahead very forthrightly to use it, without the negative, to mean *approved of* or *accepted*."

If that meaning is taking hold, a word is changing its meaning before our very eyes. *Condone* means "to forgive, pardon, excuse"; it has not meant "approve" or "accept," nor has it been a synonym for *endorse, sanction* or *certify*.

To *condone* is to overlook; to *approve* is to see and reward with a pat on the back. The meanings are different; although not antonyms, they are surely not synonyms.

"Are the politicians and professors really using the word correctly?" asks Miss Weller. "That is—are they consciously using it to mean *pardon, forgive*, or *excuse*—when they say, 'I cannot *condone*'? Or has the accepted (condoned?) definition changed over the years, even though I haven't yet found it in the newer dictionaries?" She adds slyly, "Please condone me if I'm mistaken."

As that last little fillip indicates, *condone* is used mainly in the negative: You *do forgive*, but you *do not condone*. Although *condone* can be used accusingly— "My opponent condones horse thievery"—the answer to "Do you really condone stealing horses?" will always be "I do not condone it." The average respondent will add, "Indeed, I condemn it." The respondent who understands the language would add, "Even less do I approve it."

As the fumblerule goes, "Eschew obfuscation": Let us resist creeping fuzziness. Climb those ramparts, English teachers, and maintain the difference: *Condone* means "overlook"; while such indulgence may be construed as tacit approval, the word is not synonymous with *approve*. (And close with the usual—"Some passively *condone* the fuzzification of the language, while some actively *approve* it; I *condemn* it.")

I have a bone to pick with you about your column on the word "condone." Have your prejudices so ossified that you cannot imagine that Ms. Hite may have been using the word quite correctly, to imply that in our repressive Christian society even the most traditional expression of sexuality is only condoned, not approved? To overlook the possibility seems the sheer depth of boneheadedness.

Richard W. Taylor
Chatham, New Jersey

Counting Olympiads

"Isn't the *Olympiad* the years between the Olympic Games?" asks Michael Antebi of Brooklyn. "If so, there are millions of coins with the error engraved on them."

The original meaning of *Olympiad* is "the time between Olympic Games" and, in this sense, an Olympiad would be equivalent to a United States presidential term. But most people, and all television announcers, take the Olympiad to mean "the quadrennial celebration," a meaning that has a lineage of five centuries. This newer meaning gets the gold medal.

The organizers of the 1984 Games pushed an odd amalgam of Roman numerals and English words in styling their event "the XXIIIrd Olympiad."

Sports columnist Dave Anderson of *The New York Times* reacted: "Notice that the organizers have added a blob of California culture, putting 'rd' after Roman numerals. That's like putting guacamole on pizza. In L.A., you can get guacamole on pizza."

The New York Times style is "the XXIII Olympiad," which is an improvement over the nerd's *rd* but is not a complete representation of the spoken term. Upon deliberation, I would write "Olympiad XXIII," in the style of the Super Bowls, or "the Twenty-Third Olympiad," or "the 23d Olympiad." Who ever heard of the XXIIIrd Psalm? Or the XXIII Psalm? The eye should see what the internal ear hears.

Not true that "The organizers of the 1984 Games pushed an odd amalgam of Roman numerals and English words in styling their event 'the XXIIIrd Olympiad.'"

As a former copy editor (now reporter) at the Boston Globe, I wondered about our style on this matter when I saw "The XXIIIrd Olympiad" at the top of our sports pages. I searched all through my language books, from Fowler to Bernstein (and

Safire, of course) and could find no reference to the transformation of cardinal Roman numerals into ordinal ones. Only when I recalled that there is a wonderful section on language number usage in the front of Webster's Third New International Dictionary *(unabridged) did I come upon an answer.*

Not precisely there but some 1500 pages later, under the word "number," is a chart of Roman and Arabic numbers, both cardinal and ordinal. Footnote No. 10 says: "... The Roman numerals are sometimes read as ordinals (Henry IV = Henry the Fourth; *the* Argonaut II = *the* Argonaut the Second*); sometimes they are written with the ordinal suffixes (XIXth Dynasty, XXth Dynasty)."*

Incidentally, one thing that called my eye to this was an idiosyncrasy of Globe *style under which we add only a "d," not an "rd," to the ordinal of a number ending in a 3. Our editors decided that "XXIIId Olympiad" was so aesthetically unacceptable that they would violate style and make it "XXIIIrd."*

Presumably, this will not be done again until the "XXXIIIrd Olympiad."

> Tom Cruise Palmer, Jr.
> Dedham, Massachusetts

Although "the XXIIIrd Olympiad" is awkward, "the 23d Olympiad," one of your three alternatives, should not be acceptable without the r: *"the 23rd Olympiad."*

What next? Many New York subway riders already know. For example, what was once "42nd Street" is now "42 Street," both on the station's pillars and out of a few conductors' mouths. (Even "Street 42," although silly, would at least be justifiable.)

Language will deteriorate further if people no longer differentiate between ordinal numbers and cardinal numbers. Furthermore, your wise concluding sentence, "The eye should see what the internal ear hears," would become meaningless.

So, let us get back to the first square (a.k.a. Square One): 1st, 2nd, 3rd, ...

> David Bernklau
> Brooklyn, New York

Cover Me

"Liberalism has no integument of courage," the comedian-philosopher Mort Sahl told Lawrence Christon of the *Los Angeles Times*, "because liberalism now is the product of rednecks who think the currency is tolerance. . . ."

I know what a *redneck* is—a bigoted rural white—first used in 1830 against Presbyterians in Fayetteville, North Carolina, but what is an *integument*?

It is a word snatched from anatomy and zoology by writers who want a punchy term for "outer covering."

Edmund Wilson, the critic, used the word in the 1940's, writing about a visit to George Santayana. He described the philosopher as lying on a chaise longue (that's *longue*, not *lounge*, if you're a purist) with "all the philosophies through which he has passed making an iridescent integument about him."

Soon after that quotation appeared in a 1983 review of Wilson's *The Forties*, the word began popping up: "Under the clothed she seeks out the naked," wrote Helen Vendler in a review of the poetry of Jorie Graham, "over the soil, the air; inside the integument, the kernel. . . ."

The word's new popularity was not limited to the world of belles-lettres. In a piece about luggage, David Eames wrote: "A small fortune may be paid for the more exotic integuments of lizard or ostrich." In a political column about punishment, George Will wrote of the "superstition that causes us to feel that the skin is in some way the boundary of the self. When the state may violate an individual's integument, it may disregard his individuality."

The word is rooted in the Latin *tegere*, "to cover," and was most often used by anatomists and zoologists to describe hides, skins, shells and husks and other boundaries of the body. Now, however, the word is shedding its scientific skin to emerge in the land of metaphor.

In Mr. Sahl's use, the meaning is clearly "outer skin" or "covering"; if this keeps up, the psychological term *persona*, meaning the "image one presents to the world," will have a new synonym. If I am wrong in this prediction, keep your eye on advertising copy for new suntan oils.

"Integument" as used in anatomy is all that covers the body, including the nails, the hair and the skin. In medical and anatomical terminology this has not changed.
Heskel M. Haddad, M.D.
New York, New York

A Czar Is Not a Tsar

A leak from the Justice Department landed on my desk, staining the walnut veneer and infuriating the washer-person. The document, rapidly melting into a puddle of hot, inside skinny, was from Edward C. Schmults, acting attorney general (that's how Ed signs his memos when the A.G. takes a long lunch) to President Reagan. The subject: "Administration Response to 'Drug Tsar' Legislation."

The key word in the hush-hush intra-Administration memo, the leakage of which in this space will cause fourteen prosecutors to pop Miltown pills to help them get past the new lie-detector tests, was repeated in the first sentence of the memo: "The Administration must determine its response to continuing efforts by Congress to establish a 'drug tsar' to oversee all federal drug enforcement efforts."

I shall not go into the substance of the leak, because this column deals with language policy, not policy policy; nor have I passed on or written about the information vouchsafed to me in the memo in another forum because the subject is a MEGO (My Eyes Glaze Over). But the spelling caught my eye; in American usage, the word for "overseer" or "person in complete charge" is spelled *czar*. The word is rooted in the Latin *Caesar* and probably came to the Russians via the German *Kaisar*.

Its first use in United States politics was in 1832; according to *American Political Terms*, by Hans Sperber and Travis Trittschuh, the director of the United States Bank, Nicholas Biddle, was known as "Czar Nicholas." Petroleum V. Nasby—a humorist named David Ross Locke, whose work was beloved by Lincoln—used that spelling against Andrew Johnson in 1866: "There wuz a immense crowd, but the Czar uv all the Amerikas didn't get orf his speech here." (That might have been the first use of America with a *k*, adopted later by demonstrators in the 1960's.) At the turn of the century, Julius Chambers, a copy editor for *The New York Times*, was searching for a shorter word than *autocrat* to apply to House Speaker Thomas Reed, which is the way, some say, "Czar" Reed got his title.

Note that the word always used was *czar*, pronounced with a *z* at the start, not *tsar*, pronounced with a *ts*, as the Russians do. This anglicization is reflected in a frank admission in *The New York Times Manual of Style and Usage* (once stylishly known as "the stylebook"): "Czar, czar, czarist. These more familiar spellings are to be used in preference to the *tsar* form—an exception to *The Times*'s usual system of transliteration." In other words, *we* know the correct Russian pronunciation should be spelled *tsar*, but we go with the widely used American mispronunciation, *czar*, with *zzz*.

So why is the acting attorney general out of step? Don't Cabinet members check for spelling in the memos they send to the President?

"We've been using the *tsar* spelling since midsummer," explains Tom DeCair, who is both real and acting spokesman for the acting attorney general. "Bob McConnell, in our Office of Legislative Affairs, devised it and we continue to use the outdated spelling as a small, symbolic gesture—because the concept of 'drug tsar' is one whose time has come and gone. Because it is an outdated idea, we use the antiquated spelling to express that point in a subtle way."

Could the spokesman be spoofing, in the most skillful cover-up of the year? ("Are you pulling my leg?" a woman once asked Groucho Marx, who replied, "Just trying to make 'em even.") Or is he trying to divert attention from the dreary information in the leaked memo that nobody is interested in anyway? As they say in Russian: "Czk, czk."

Don't you realize that the lately popularized "Amerika" comes from Franz Kafka's Amerika?

And didn't it ever occur to you that "Czar" is pronounced by many in the Polish manner (CHAR)?

> Jan L. Czarnowski
> Philadelphia, Pennsylvania

I don't think the suggestion of continuity from Nasby's creation of "Amerika" to protestors' use of that spelling quite fits. Rather, my sense is that, instead of a cute attempt at vernacular or churlish misspelling, today's use of a "k" for the "c" seeks to link our nation with totalitarian ones. Both Slavic and Teutonic languages unambiguously use a "k" for our hard "c" sound (there is also, of course, the KKK connotation). Note, too, that Kafka (definitely a "k" name, and Czech-German to boot) wrote a novel with the name "Amerika." By the way, a well-known pun and semi-clandestine protest phrase in prerevolutionary Russia was Ne bog a ne tsar, updating the Babylonian king's name as the slogan: Not God and Not Tsar.

Thomas A. Reiner
Philadelphia, Pennsylvania

You suggest that Tsar "probably came to the Russians via the German Kaisar."

The Germans never had a Kaisar. They had a Kaiser, the last of whom was Kaiser Wilhelm, affectionately known to the doughboys of the First World War as "Kaiser Bill."

I have heard a number of language experts using the same sobriquet for you.

Arthur J. Morgan
New York, New York

Dear Bill:

Regarding the Russians picking up "Tsar" from German Kaiser: no, no, my friend.

Ivan III, grand prince of Moscow, was married in 1505 to Sophia Paleologue, niece of the last Byzantine emperor who died when Byzantium (Constantinople) fell to the Moslems. Sophia had been raised in Rome by the Catholics, but when she went to Moscow she returned to the Greek Orthodox side. Ivan himself adopted the title of Tsar informally and clothed himself in the regalia of the Basileus of Constantinople, as did those of his court in formal functions.

Ivan's grandson, Ivan IV (the Terrible), was officially crowned under the title of Tsar and his coronation ritual was Byzantine. Thereafter the court—pushed, of course, by the clergy—took upon itself the attributes of what it called "the Third Rome."

In short, Russia adopted "Tsar" by deliberate reference to Rome and the original word, Caesar, not through any influence of German Kaiser. The ruler of Russia was in the 1500's addressed as a "Tsar"—i.e., as one of the Caesars (this having become a term covering the leader of a country attached to the Christian church). The same title, Tsar, was used for a Bulgar in the 14th century. I doubt that the German word Kaiser even existed then. Karl der Grossel (Charlemagne) was a koenig—but then all the western princes styled themselves as Caesars in their own pronunciations.

The role that Russia attempted—as a successor to Byzantium—is pretty well *forgotten in modern times because of the effort to suppress religion there. The Tsar, after all, was considered a holy man.*

> Bill [Higginbotham]
> Fort Worth, Texas

Very good.
*	The real story is that I cannot spell any word of any difficulty. All the best.*

> Ed [C. Schmults]
> Deputy Attorney General
> Washington, D.C.

Dash It All

The dash is running away with itself.

Too many writers—who ought to know better—are using dashes—which God knows we could not do without—too often.

Let us now repunctuate that sentence, using the tools of insertion—the comma, the parentheses and the dash—in a way that does not require a mainframe computer to count cadence: Too many writers, who ought to know better, are using dashes (which—God knows!—we could not do without) too often.

Use *commas*, my friends, to slip in a phrase like "my friends" without making it a big deal.

Use *parentheses* (which should be plural, because you would be open-ended in saying "use a parenthesis") when you have some information to add, like the foregoing "(which should be plural, etc.)," and when you want to downplay the insertion instead of letting it overpower the rest of the sentence.

Use *dashes*—hey, are you listening? If you get this wrong, you could flunk!—when you want to grab the reader by the throat with the interjection of a sudden aside or sentence-dominating phrase.

Use commas to count, parentheses to calculate, dashes to compute. Put in olive-sizing terms, commas are large, parentheses giant and dashes supercolossal. (I am getting carried away by metaphor. *Commas* are neutral and rarely cause trouble; *parens*—we can shorten the name now that we know them—are effective devices to simulate a clear whisper, and *dashes* are the crowbars of punctuation, used to force in a raised voice.)

That was easy, because it dealt with insertions in the middle of a sentence. Now we come to a harder part: handling afterthoughts or fragments at the end of a sentence. (I may join Sentence Enders, a close-encounter group that breaks members of the fragmented-ending habit.) When do you use a dash and when a colon?

If you are being tricky and want to change grammatical construction in the middle of a sentence for dramatic effect (as in the jerky writings of Anna Coluthon, *viz*. "I told you if you didn't vote—what'll happen to the country?"), then a dash is called for.

If you have an afterthought, or leftover phrase that can be flippantly chucked in at the end, the dash is the answer. Indeed, a student at Brown University who signs himself as my "dependent clause" argues that I frequently misuse the colon: "A properly used colon ogles at you from between two independent clauses: The second clause expands upon or clarifies the first. A postpunctuational fragment (a dependent clause or object, alone or in a list) cries for another antephrasal symbol—the dash."

I dunno what they're teaching those kids in Providence, but I do know that— what? My time is up? A final word: Go easy on the dashes, especially when the clause on this end of the punctuation is independent and looks like a separate sentence. As for the fragment-introducing dash—what the hell.

The curved dividers are indeed parentheses, but the entire phrase or clause, including the dividers, is a parenthesis, * *as illustrated by the pseudo-Shakesperian verse describing a bowlegged man:*

> *What ho, what ho, what manner of man is this*
> *who carries his balls within a parenthesis?*

Arthur J. Morgan
New York, New York

* *(Literally, an insertion.)*

Your "Dash It All" said it all. However, if your noteworthy statement to "use commas to count" is to be heeded, then that last serial comma is called for! Otherwise, my friend, you would be counting one fewer thing in the series, unless you believe "and" is used to supersede the last serial comma, instead of its correct concurrent usage as an auxiliary conjunction in order to tip off the reader that the last thing to count is about to come.

David Bernklau
Brooklyn, New York

Dash it all! The dash may be running away with itself, but folks are running away from the comma. You write that "the comma, the parentheses and the dash" are the tools of insertion. Right there in that sentence, you—even you!—neglect the comma: there should be a comma between "parentheses" and "and." Or is the-parentheses-and-the-dash, as it were, one tool of insertion? Whatever the source of this error, it is rampant, and spreading like wildfire. It may even be too late for individual actions to have an effect, but if anyone can stem the tide, it is you. Defend the comma!

> Peter Saint-André
> Readfield, Maine

I enjoyed your "Dash It All" observations . . . but there's at least one punctuation device you did not comment on . . . how come?

> Edward C. Cohen
> New York, New York

Dash of Grenadine

"On the *NBC Nightly News*," worried a caller, "John Chancellor talked about our invasion of *Gren-A-da* and then about our invasion of *Gren-AH-da*. Which is it?" He then hummed the song "Granada," which is spelled with three *a*'s and pronounced with an *AH*.

At the start, I went along with the Chancellor Straddle, alternating my pronunciation. This is the way that most of us deal with words we have to use and hate to have to look up. Faced with the query, however, and recognizing my responsibility as a news-hip language maven, I hit the etymological beach.

It all started with the Latin *granum*, "seed," from which grew the English *grain*. Then there was a city in Spain named after that grain, Granada, and we all know the song: "The dawn in the sky greets the day with a sigh/For Granada. . . ." For Spanish Granada, say *AH*.

Meanwhile, the French latched onto the Latin *granum* to describe a seedy fruit: the pomegranate. This fruit struck French farmers as similar to an apple with many seeds and was spelled in Old French *pome grenate*. This spelling with an *e—gre—* led to *grenade*, a small bomb thrown by hand, which was about the size of a pomegranate and sprayed its seeds of destruction; infantrymen who carried them were called *grenadiers*. Getting back to the fruit, we know that a syrup made from the juice of the pomegranate was called *grenadine* and is used today to add color to Shirley Temples, if they still use that name for jazzed-up soft drinks.

Over to the island in the Caribbean (pronounced *Cari-BE-an*, after the Carib Indians, but *Ca-RIB-ean* isn't wrong): It was originally a French island, with the French spelling—*Grenada* with an *e*, like *grenade* and *grenadine*. When the English took it over in the late eighteenth century, they kept the spelling and changed the pronunciation. The Angles anglicized everything.

Therefore, here's the drill: If you're talking about the city in Spain or you're serenading a *señorita* on a balcony, it's *Gran-AH-da*. If you're denouncing a band of "leftist thugs," you are talking about *Gren-A-da* with a long *a*; Grenadians rhyme with Canadians. There never was a connection between the Old French *grenate* and the Latin/English form *granate* until the current unpleasantness: Now we have seen grenades thrown on Grenada.

Shame on you, William! You wrote, "Grenadians rhyme with Canadians." I'll bet that those two groups don't get together very often. When they do, do they jointly write poetry? What a fascinating trivia item!

I believe you should have written, "The word Grenadians rhymes with the word Canadians." Maybe you're just testing your readers to see if they're awake. Here's one who is.

> Don Naples
> West Springfield, Virginia

You wrote a column on the pronunciation of Grenada in which you rhymed Grenadian and Canadian. Obviously, while you may be an expert on lexicography, you are not a poet or even a versifier. I quote from The Complete Rhyming Dictionary *by Clement Wood, p. 25. "Rhyme is the identity in sound of an accepted vowel in a word, usually the last one accented, and of all consonantal and vowel sounds following it; with a difference in the sound of the consonant immediately preceding the accented vowel." It is the last phrase of the definition that trips you up. You could have used "Barbadian," or, if your heart is set on Canada, you could have used "Acadian." "Canadian," however, is a bad rhyme.*

> Arthur H. Carver
> Poughkeepsie, New York

Dear Mavin (Expert) (1),

We members of the communis vulgus *(ordinary people) (2), who speak English as our* mama lush'n *(native tongue) (3), take the* pronunciamentos *(pronunciamen-*

tos) (4) of all you mavinim *(plural of* mavin*) (1) on our language,* cum grano salis *(with a grain of salt) (2).*

Hochachtungsvollst *(Most respectfully) (5),*
Arthur J. Morgan
New York, New York

(1) Hebrew (The Yiddish is usually transliterated "maven.")
(2) Latin
(3) Yiddish
(4) Spanish
(5) German

Dearest Computer

A piece of electronic mail has come my way. That means that a colleague in New York has dumped a message in my directory, or file, and when I sit down at my word-processing terminal in Washington to bang out these lines, the message suddenly appears before me. No muss, no fuss, no tearing open envelopes, no stamps, no singing-telegram delivery boy.

The question arises: As this wave of the future slams into our sandbags, what is communications etiquette? Do you begin a piece of electronic mail with the letterly salutation *Dear colleague*—or the businesslike, telegraphic *Metrodesk to Safire*? Do you conclude with *regards*, or *answer soonest collect* or *over and out*? This is a worry we never knew we had.

Somehow, *dear* seems out of place when written in green letters on a black screen. Yet *Memo to* is strictly business; what about those notes that executives send to each other (F.Y.I.) that are informal? Peeling that onion right down to where the tears are—is electronic mail a new form of letter or a quicker way of sending a telegram?

I'm stumped. We need electronic etiquette for the post-*Post* era. Those with ideas for electriquette are urged to communicate with this department. Regards, Roger Wilco.

While on this subject, I have received a written communication that looks as if it came out of a typewriter from Peter McWilliams, author of *The Word Processing Book*, a happily helpful work in the field. Included is an advertisement for "The McWilliams II Word Processor," which has this unique set of features: "Portable; prints characters from every known language; graphics are fully supported; gives off no appreciable degree of radiation; uses no energy; memory is not lost during a power failure; user friendly; no moving parts; silent operation; occasional maintenance keeps it in top condition."

A picture of the amazing technological breakthrough is attached: It's a pencil.

I was brought up to believe that the abbreviation for for your information *is the lower-case f.y.i.*

Richard L. Williams
Unadilla, New York

Hold it, friend Safire! Stop! Desist! While I selftype this message.

You are encouraging a method of communication—wrongly—that springs from movies of the 30's . . . for instance, Test Pilot *with Clark Gable and Spencer Tracy. (Not to imply that your age is showing.)*

Any former or present naval aviator worth his salt will tell you there is no such thing as "over and out" or "roger wilco." When your message is completed and you are looking for an answer, the word to use is "over." When you have completed a message and you are not *looking for a reply, the word to use is "out."*

When you have heard a message and understand it, the response is "roger." When you have heard a message, understand it and will comply, the response is "wilco."

Never, ever, is it "over and out" or "roger wilco." Can we please deep-six this one along with knots per hour.

OUT.

Jim [Gorman]
Public Information, Census Bureau
Washington, D.C.

Debating Words

Debates reveal the living language. The carefully phrased answers suggested in briefing books cannot all be committed to memory; in actual debate, the prompting devices are stripped away, and the words that tumble off the screen are often made up in the speaker's head.

In the three national debates of the 1984 campaign, several of the candidates' formulations were instructive. Should a politician be held to what he said or what he meant to say? Can you make an issue out of a deliberate misinterpretation of what you say? Down to specifics:

For Shame

The hottest item in 1984's series of debates was a phrase used by Vice President Bush in his debate with Geraldine A. Ferraro. "For somebody to suggest, as our two opponents have," he said about the deaths of United States Marines in Beirut, "that these men died in shame—they better not tell the parents of those young Marines."

Representative Ferraro came back with an angry, "No one has ever said that those young men who were killed through the negligence of this Administration and others ever died in shame."

The headline in *USA Today* read: " 'Shame': New War Over Word." When Mr. Bush could not produce a "died in shame" quote, he relied on his verb *suggest*, a slippery term that permits the almost-quoter to interpret and sometimes twist what his target has said. (Another good way of exaggerating or making ridiculous your opponent's statement is by saying "in effect" and then carrying his position to an extreme.) Seizing the shame issue, Walter F. Mondale then said the Vice President "doesn't have the manhood to apologize," an equally low blow suggesting that Mr. Bush lacked manliness.

Stung by the counterattack, Mr. Bush turned to a dictionary, always a sign that the user of a word is in trouble. He cited his opponents' use of *humiliated* in connection with the United States and terrorists, and quoted an unnamed dictionary's definition of that word: " 'Humiliation: shame, disgrace and degradation.' *Webster's* equates humiliation with abase—deep shame. . . . Accusing young men of dying without a purpose and for no reason is, in the lexicon of the American people, a shame." (*Webster's* is the name of any number of different dictionaries; quoting *Webster's* is like saying "The dictionary says," as if there were only one dictionary. In this case, Mr. Bush was using the *American Heritage Dictionary*, which admirably makes no claim to being Noah Webster's work.)

Mr. Mondale raised the "shame" remark in his second debate with President Reagan, who wisely ignored it. That is because the Bush remark was indefensible, even with a stack of dictionaries.

Died in shame implies that Administration critics are attacking the honor of the men who died; that is a distortion of the criticism, which attacks the policy that led to the humiliation of the country by terrorists. Mr. Bush chose to misinterpret the charge that his Administration's policy was shameful, pretending that the critics were blaming the marines instead; in so doing, he imputed a lack of patriotism to the critics, which is generally considered beyond the pale of political debate. *Died in vain*, a common phrase attaching no dishonor to the dead, would not have raised a storm.

Nights at the Round Table

"Well, I can't say that I have roundtabled that and sat down with the Chiefs of Staff," Mr. Reagan began an answer. *Roundtable* as a verb? Yes; it cannot be derogated as the latest Pentagon jargon. King Arthur's legendary table, designed without a head to avoid jousting over precedence, has been used as a verb since 1887 to mean "to take part in a round-table conference." The original political use was at the Round Table Conference of a century ago in England, when the squabbling Liberals tried to reconcile their differences. In the United States, the verb has gained a Madison Avenue connotation like "to run it up the flagpole."

Recall Those Missiles

"When a President doesn't know that submarine missiles are recallable," said Walter Mondale, ". . . these are things a President must know to command."

"You've been all over the country," Mr. Reagan snapped back, "repeating . . . that I believe that nuclear missiles could be fired and then called back. I never conceived of such a thing. I never said any such thing."

The President may not have had the mistake in his head, but he seemed to have had the mistaken words on his lips. In 1982, he had been talking at a news conference about the impossibility of recalling land-based missiles after they had been launched from their silos in the ground. Then he said: "Those that are carried in bombers, those that are carried in ships of one kind or another, or submersibles, you are dealing there with a conventional type of weapon or instrument, and those instruments can be intercepted. They can be recalled. . . ."

His first *those* is a pronoun referring to missiles; his second *those* is also a pronoun referring to missiles; but his third *those*, an adjective in "those instruments can be intercepted," is ambiguous. *"Those* instruments" and the subsequent pronoun *"they"* could refer either to the missiles again or to the weapons from which the missiles are launched, such as a bomber or submarine. There is a big difference; the air and submarine carriers of missiles can be recalled, but their missiles, once fired, cannot be recalled. A close rereading of the Reagan answer tends to lead the objective reader to accept the President's later explanation and to assume he shifted gear from missiles to carriers in the middle of his sentence.

That is what grammarians call *amphibology*, which is defined in the *Oxford English Dictionary* as "ambiguous discourse; a sentence which may be construed in two distinct senses" because of uncertain sentence construction. Try this: "Joe and Mike took his sister and her friend to the disco, but they didn't want to dance." Who does *his* refer to, Joe or Mike? And who are *they*, the two girls or all four of the confused wallflowers?

This issue should persuade young voters to make certain their pronouns clearly refer to their antecedents. Lest Mr. Mondale make hay by calling the President an unreconstructed amphibologue, let the reader reconsider the Mondale charge at the beginning of this entry. It's totally botched. What he meant to say was, "When a President doesn't know that submarine missiles are *not* recallable. . . ." The technical term for saying the opposite of what you mean is yet to be invented.

That Smarts

"Strength must also require wisdom and smarts in its exercise," said Walter Mondale. That is a nice distinction. *Smarts* is a plural slang noun, which means that you say *"smarts* are"; the word means "intelligence, brains, know-how," and differs from *wisdom*, which combines knowledge with judgment.

Usages in the context of a formal national debate help move a word from slang to colloquialism, from substandard to informal. Mr. Mondale did not do for *smarts* what the abdicating King Edward VIII did for *radio* (substituting that word for *wireless*), but he helped.

Indeed, the use of roundtable *as a verb is not the latest Pentagon jargon. Rather than being around a mere hundred years, the verb* roundtable *was in vogue centuries ago as the hottest Pendragon jargon.*

> *Eleanor Cook*
> *Brooklyn, New York*

The minute I heard RR say ". . . I have roundtabled that . . ." I turned to a friend and said, "That will turn up in Safire's column." And so it did!

> *Anne Jones*
> *Riverdale, New York*

In your New York Times *column you write: ". . . The technical term for saying the opposite of what you mean is yet to be invented."*

I quote from my dictionary: "LITOTES—a figure of speech in which an affirmative is expressed by negation of its opposite. 'This is no small problem.' "

> *S. George Greene*
> *New York, New York*

In your pre-election column, you said there was no word for the accidental negation of one's intended utterance. There are many medical terms ending in "-phasia" which refer to speech disorders. "Heterophasia" is close to what you want; it refers to the situation in which what comes out of one's mouth is different from what one intended; the two words are usually quite unrelated. The mixup usually results from a confusion in the lexicon caused by a stroke or other brain damage.

For accidental negation, I suggest a similar word: "contraphasia." I have used this word for weeks to refer to those confused utterances resulting from a hidden double negative, like Elizabeth Holzman's "I'll miss not being in Congress," or the news report on the Southern ski season, which said, "There's something missing here besides the lack of snow."

Dana Walker
Montgomery, Alabama

Dental Deceit

In his "Letter from America" on the BBC (why do we say "the BBC" when we never say "the ABC"?), Alistair Cooke spoke about an Administration official caught "lying in his teeth."

"Both my wife and I jumped at that," writes Donald Woodrow of Geneva, New York, who gets his news from listening to the BBC World Service, on shortwave, "since we thought the official had lied *through* his teeth. Which is it: *in* or *through*? Both imply an absurdity: to speak with your mouth closed and teeth gritted. Or it might mean that a lie spoken in such a way is an especially serious one."

That was the first correction in my file. Then Doreen Moore of St. Albans, New York, writes that in a recent essay "you speak of 'lying *in* his teeth.' Isn't the correct metaphor 'lying *through* his teeth'?"

No, I thought; when talking nonsense, one talks *through* one's hat, but when speaking falsely, one lies *in* one's teeth.

"I think that 'to lie *in* one's teeth' must be older," agrees John Algeo, professor of English at the University of Georgia, "because I haven't found the preposition *through* used in that phrase in any lexicographic source."

The first clear use was in the fourteenth century's *The Romance of Sir Guy of Warwick*, in which the hero says, "Thou lexst amidward thi teth." The Middle English *amidward* meant "inside" or "in the middle of," not "through." An earlier citation, in a 1300 Northumbrian poem, cautions, "Sal yee na leis here o mi toth," which seems to advise against "lies here in my tooth," but scholars cannot be sure if the old *o* means "in" or "through."

In my teeth is an intensifier. When Shakespeare wanted to emphasize the dirtiness of a lie, he preferred the throat to the teeth: "I had lied in my throat if I had said so," says Falstaff, and "Even in his throat . . . I return the lie," says Pericles. "Who . . . gives me the lie i' the throat, as deep as to the lungs?" demands Hamlet. However, Shakespeare on occasion used the preposition *through* in this metaphor, explaining its meaning quite clearly in *Richard II:* "Then, Bolingbroke, as low as to thy heart, Through the false passage of thy throat, thou liest."

For about five hundred years, then, *in* was generally preferred over *through* in this metaphor; the *Century Dictionary*, published at the turn of the twentieth century, cites *lie in one's teeth*.

But times are changing, and common usage crosses transcendental *t*'s. "To lie *through* one's teeth is more commonly heard nowadays," states Professor Algeo, and my correspondents evidently agree.

Although it is likely that the confusion comes from "talking through one's hat," which first surfaced about a century ago, both uses are now common, and it is mistaken to call either one incorrect. Those of us who have worked in politics and appreciate the brazen beauty of a baldfaced, double-dyed prevarication still say, "He lied in his teeth."

Dear Bill,
Apropos lying in one's teeth—or through—*I notice that nobody suggested the picture that comes to me, not of clenched jaws and grinders but of spread lips and a grin, which the gullible take as a smile, accepting the lie. May not this bit of intended deception be part of the whole action?*

> Frederic *[G. Cassidy]*
> *Director-Editor,* DARE
> *Madison, Wisconsin*

Your antepenultimate paragraph could have begun "For about five hundred years, then, users of this metaphor have generally preferred in over through." (That's the preposition hat trick: ending a sentence with three prepositions.)

> Henry T. Gayley
> Ithaca, New York

Bergen Evans and Cornelia Evans' A Dictionary of Contemporary American Usage *gives some insight to* the's usage: The *is dropped from certain prepositional phrases, such as* at church, on campus, in jail. *The rule is that the* the *is retained when one is thinking about the actual place, object, or institution, and omitted when what is uppermost in the mind is the thing's purpose or function. If so, Englishmen must be more function-minded than Americans, because they drop a great many* the*'s that we keep. They say* she is in hospital, we were at table, he looked out of window.

Since foreign languages have different rules from English regarding the use of articles, I thought a look at language instruction books might help. One French grammar indicates that nouns in French taken in a general sense require the use of the definite article. English nouns used this way, however, require the omission of the definite article. For example, La viande est chère *(Meat is expensive).*

Many (all?) other Romance languages follow this rule. It's curious to note that Spanish writer Calderón de la Barca's work, La vida es sueño, *is translated into English as* Life Is a Dream; *the English translation requires dropping the definite article before one noun and adding an indefinite article before the other noun!*

Books which teach English to non-English speakers would be the ideal place to find the answer to our question, since they would have to explain when and why to use or omit articles. A Russian English-teaching book would be the best source, since the Russian language doesn't have any articles at all, and would require a rigorous explanation of usage of articles. Unfortunately, none of these books are within easy access to me.

I'm reminded of something that happened to me on a visit to the Soviet Union a few years ago. I was talking about langauge with my Intourist guide and her friend, an English teacher. They asked me which was correct: "I'm going to Red Square" or "I'm going to the *Red Square." I told them that* the *should be omitted and mumbled something about Red Square being the name of a well-known location and therefore not requiring an article. (I really didn't know the reason, but I thought I did, and I wanted so much to be helpful.) Then they asked if "Lenin Library" would require* the *in the same sentence, and I had to admit that in this case,* the *should be included. But the Lenin Library is also the name of a well-known location, so my explanation/theory was invalidated.*

I suppose the best answer to this question of when and why to use the *is stated by Roy H. Copperud in* American Usage and Style: The Consensus: *"It is a tortuous business to generalize about places where* the *is or is not normally required. The matter is governed by idiom, which does not yield to rules anyway." In other words, we use or omit definite articles because one way "sounds better" than the other.*

Frank Vlastnik
New York, New York

I was struck by your parenthetical under "Dental Deceit," asking why we say "the BBC" and not "the ABC."

Here's something that caught my fancy for a long time. When one gets sick in England, he is taken to hospital, not to the hospital. I used to think this was strange, but it occurred to me that it's we Americans who are inconsistent. In other usage of this sort, we do as the English do—i.e., drop the the: "going to camp," "going to prison." So, why not "going to hospital"? I think the British have us on this one.

James P. Jimirro
Los Angeles, California

Detritus

Detritus is in vogue. This word, meaning "debris" or "product of disintegration," was used in *Time* magazine in 1983 in the scientific sense: "It was in 1822 that an English fossil hunter first identified some newly discovered teeth as the detritus of extinct reptiles." Columnist William Buckley, writing about archivists, used it metaphorically: "He will ask you, if he is collecting your opera, to save for him everything. Literally everything. Even what you'd have thought of as detritus."

When the word was misspelled in the *Times* last year—"Defunct phone numbers are not the only detritis in the memory"—Aran Safir, the only member of my clan who is an ophthalmologist, wrote to point out a mnemonic: *itis* frequently means "inflammation of," but *detritus* is dead.

When reaching for a phrase to enliven *debris*, I turn from the voguish toward that favorite vaudeville team: Flotsam and Jetsam (floating wreckage and jettisoned cargo).

In your column on "detritus," you refer to "that favorite vaudeville team: Flotsam and Jetsam. . . ." Actually, the team is not a duo, but a trio, including Lagan, which is anything sunk in the sea but attached to a buoy, so that it may be recovered by its rightful owner. But not once in a hundred is lagan mentioned—I hope you will be able to do so in a future column.

Charles Steir
Bronx, New York

Doing Pragma

"A new note of pragmatism" has been observed in Democratic speeches of late, mainly by Republicans who have forgotten the voguishness of that word in the Kennedy era. The word is rooted in the Greek *pragma*, meaning "deed" or "business."

In the Reagan White House, two camps have emerged in all foreign strategy and economic planning: the *pragmatic* camp vs. the *principled* camp. Pragmatists see the principle-peddlers as a pack of rigid ideologues, while principlians view the pragmatists as a sanhedrin of sell-out artists with a weather vane for a moral compass.

Among the Republican pragmatists are Chief of Staff James Baker, Deputy Chief Michael Deaver and *éminence grise* Richard Darman; all are leaning now toward the principled supply-side economics, and their conversion is derided by old ideologues as an example of pragmatists going with principle when the wind shifts that way. Democratic pragmatists include Walter Mondale, who told delegates, "We know that government must be as well managed as it is well meaning."

The man who established pragmatism in American thought was William James. The foremost expert on that philosopher is Jacques Barzun, the usagist who shores up my occasional erosions, and who wrote *A Stroll with William James*. Here is Barzun on pragmatism:

"Pragmatism is not a philosophy but an attempt to explain how the mind ascertains truth. If correct, the explanation supplies a means of testing truths. The pragmatic test, as it is called, consists in seeing whether an idea, a hypothesis or even a mere hunch is borne out by the concrete experiences that occur when one acts on the given hunch or hypothesis. In simplest form, if one thinks the umbrella has been left in the kitchen, one must go to the kitchen in order to find it or fail to find it. The proof is by consequences.

"In more complex matters—in science or ethics or social policy—the test must be based on a very large number of consequences, including careful comparison with truths previously established. The pragmatic question always is: If this is indeed true, what will follow—in life, thought, feeling and our earlier stock of knowledge?

"As commonly *mis*used, pragmatism stands for the exact opposite of what William James intended it to mean. It stands for rough-and-ready methods of pushing things through, *regardless* of consequences; or again, it is used for readiness to compromise instead of sticking to one's principles. These attitudes are so common and obvious that it is a pity to debase for their description a term which is important in the history of thought."

Dear Bill:

I imagine you would agree with me that the word pragmatism *is past rescuing. Like* puritan, romantic, *and a few others, it is needed by those who won't make up their minds about their likes and dislikes and use epithets to hide their waffling.*

But the world would be a terrible place if it were full of definite people like you and me.

> *Jacques [Barzun]*
> *New York, New York*

Although William James and later John Dewey did much to develop and popularize pragmatism, it was Charles Sanders Peirce (rhymes with verse) who founded the movement and established it in American thought.

Some of Peirce's writings were written so turgidly that they still serve as effective soporifics for hyperactive sophomores. However, his earliest contributions—particularly the articles on his new theory of "pragmaticism" that he wrote for Popular Science Monthly *in 1877–78—are still the most lucid and powerful statements of the theory yet to appear in print.*

Peirce's greatest mistake, endowing the name of the theory with too many syllables, was corrected by James, who was a witty, practical man. But James, alas, brought the movement into some disrepute by his occasional careless writing and by making such absurd claims as that truth is whatever works. Early critics of pragmatism, among them Bertrand Russell, had a field day with that one.

> *Burton M. Leiser*
> *Professor of Philosophy*
> *Pace University*
> *New York, New York*

I pride myself on the depth of my vocabulary, but today you sent me scurrying to the dictionary with sanhedrin *(which I discovered was "a great council in Jerusalem destroyed in 70* AD*"). Much to my surprise, however, it is one of the very few words in Hebrew that is derived from the Greek, viz.* synedrion, *"an assembly." Perhaps one of your Irregulars can recall a few more.*

> *Steve A. Demakopoulos*
> *New York, New York*

Dominating the Momentum

It's fourth and inches. (If you do not instantly tense with the knowledge that this is football shorthand for "fourth down and inches to go for a first down," skip hurriedly to the next item; the vocabulary for the Super Bowl is not for you.) The worried quarterback looks over to the sidelines for the perfect verb to call. The coach sends in a tight end (a lineman woozy from doing too many beer commercials) with the pro-bowl predicate of the year.

The meaning sought is "to be winning decisively." Two wide receivers, *control* and *command*, line up on the right; the tight end, *intimidate*, hiccuping noisily, is on the left; the tailback, *rule*, is ready to cooperate in a play-fake to freeze the linebackers; the offensive linemen are worried about being penalized for *holding sway*. In the stands, a couple of old-timers, *in the driver's seat* and *have the upper hand*, are yelling "AH-fense!"

Which verb gets the call? You go with that action-packed part of speech that has been smashing steadily into our eardrums, standing tall over all the words used in sportscasting this year. The unanimous choice is considered unstoppable in its race for Most Valuable Vogue Verb in the linguistic super bowl.

It's a give to the fullback! There goes *dominate*!

PAT: We just have a moment to wrap up. John, what do you think was the turning point of the game?

JOHN: It was when *dominate* began to dominate. That was their game plan, to

dominate on the ground and force the other side to change their strategy, permitting them to dominate in the air.

PAT: Whatever happened to *get momentum*?

JOHN: Got too old, I guess, happens to all of us. *Get momentum* this year has
been totally dominated by *dominate*.

PAT: Was *dominate* this good in college? He wasn't even a first-round draft pick.

JOHN: In those days, he was *predominate*, which was too long and intellectual.
In the past few years with the pros, *dominate* shed that extra poundage, that
baby-fat prefix of his, and came into his own this year. The game can't do without
him.

PAT: Nobody else comes close to being verb of the year. I see they're helping
intimidate off the field. Do you suppose *dominate* will ever be replaced?

JOHN: Keep your eye on that kid on the bench, *domineer*—he's even more
arrogant and push-'em-around than *dominate* and just needs a break to get in there
and dominate *dominate*.

PAT: Well, they all come from the same house, or domicile, and are accustomed
to ruling the roost. I expect they'll blow 'em away. Our hang-time is up—over to
you, Brent.

Don't Bug Me

Calling long-distance from Chicago, Robert Jacobs asks, "Do you remember what
the operator says whenever you call long-distance?" I put him on hold, dialed a
long-distance number, and heard the voice with the snarl say, "Thank you for
calling A.T.&T."

I told Mr. Jacobs what I remembered, and he responded, "Yes, but did you call
A.T.&T.? Or did you call some other number?"

He's right. A.T.&T. is a company with a telephone number to dial if you want
to discuss the philosophy of long-distance competition. Theirs is not the number
you call when you call your kids at college to demand to know why they never
write.

All across this land, thousands of times a minute, a solecism is being committed.
To the voice that says, "Thank you for calling A.T.&T.," the answer is: "No
offense, madam, but I didn't call you at all." One of these days, the operator will
say, "Thank you for *using* A.T.&T.," and I will revert to my normal, gracious
mumble.

Dear Bill:

I entirely agree with you about the smarmy gratitude expressed by A.T.&T. and other corporations for their customers' patronage. But on the plane of language, don't you suppose that "Thank you for calling A.T.&T." really means "calling by means of"? The parallels: "Thank you for traveling Amtrak, for flying Delta" suggest this phrasal apocope (hum!).

> *Jacques [Barzun]*
> *New York, New York*

Hasn't it all been said already? I remember Fibber McGee's reaction to having a conversation with the phone company, instead of the conversation he wanted to have with the phone company's help, from about 40 years ago—"Oh, is that you, Myrt? How's every little thing, Myrt?" That was before you could dial long-distance calls yourself, and you really had to call *(address or speak to) a person in order to be put through.* Call *here was transitive, while the intransitive* call *meant "visit."*

Haven't you noticed that, in today's direct-dial world, your correspondent Robert Jacobs used call *long-distance as an intransitive verb and omitted the implied connective* by *or* through*? AT&T's newly competitive voice that thanks you for calling AT&T is doing exactly the same thing. Is that really a solecism? The implied connecting word the writer (or speaker) omits is usually quite clear to the reader (or listener). However, in AT&T's case (decided by Judge Harold Greene only 1 1/2 years ago) the usage is new enough to offend you, while you've probably been thanked for flying _____ airlines and urged to go such railroad and yea bus line so much that you don't notice the implied connective isn't expressed. That usage goes back at least to the London Transport posters of the early 1930's that said* Go Underground. *Do you remember* Fly Me, I'm _____? *I recall complaints that this was sexist, but no complaint that it was wrong grammatically.*

> *Otto Kauder*
> *New York, New York*

Surely you understand about calling AT&T. It's like flying United. Sure, "calling" is usually a transitive verb, so you might expect the word after "calling" to be a direct object, but you can hardly insist upon it. Sometimes, all you get is a noun-used-as-an-adverb. In this case, you tried running AT&T, but you ended up running amok.

> *Lawrence J. Kramer*
> *Philadelphia, Pennsylvania*

Mulling over your comments on "Thank you for calling A.T.&T.," I realized suddenly that you had hit on a new phenomenon in the English language—the adverbial noun. *"Calling A.T.&T."* is indeed not a solecism, any more than is *"fly United"*: in each case the name of the company serves as an adverb that modifies the corresponding verb. *("How are you calling?"* The response is *"A.T.&T.")*

> Jacob E. Goodman
> Professor, City College
> New York, New York

Calling AT&T is equivalent to flying Eastern or going Greyhound. It is not "a solecism" but an ellipsis.

> Paul Arons
> Old Town, Florida

Another of their mistakes aggravates me even more: the recorded message that "The number you have reached is not in working order." If it were, I would have reached it; "reached" is the single wrongest verb they could have chosen.

> Paul L. Klein
> New York, New York

Downsurging Uptick

"No satisfactory reason," said President Reagan, exists for the "recent *upticks*" in interest rates. *The New York Times* quoted Roger Brinner, an economist, on the reason for the President's concern: "The economy will pay a price before the election for each *uptick* in interest rates."

The word's roots are in Wall Street, home of what old-timers remember as the stock ticker and ticker tape. At a cocktail party for stock traders, I asked Gilbert Kaplan, publisher of *Institutional Investor* magazine, for his definition of *uptick*. "An eighth of a point up" was his first answer. Upon reflection, he added, "The only legal short sale, except for a zero-plus tick." By law, a short sale—the selling of a security at one price before actually buying it, hopefully at a lower price—cannot be executed by a trader unless the price is an eighth of a point or more higher than the last transaction; that guards against the rapid fall of the security's value. After an *uptick*, if the next sale is at the same price, that is called a *zero-plus tick*, which tells the trader that the sale was made at no change, but the last change was plus, or up. Now you can make a fortune in puts and calls.

That original meaning of a slight rise in the price of a share has been metaphorically extended to an increase in anything. The term is replacing *pickup*, as in "a pickup in economic activity"—that's an *uptick* now. *Newsweek*, as far back as 1975, was describing "a recent uptick in applications," while *U.S. News & World Report* was hailing "business spending, production, profits—all on *uptick*."

The word now means "a noticeable increase in frequency" or "small rise." Its use, as the presidential comment demonstrates, is picking up.

Lest Mr. Reagan be accused of intemperate optimism, let the record show that on May 14, 1984, he used another directional compound: "There was a downsurge recently." I like that one. As the Irish say—"Up the downsurge!"

Dear Bill:

Your "uptick" item could be expanded into something about the prepositionality of English and a curious modern trend to switch prepositions from the rear to the front of verb forms. "Upcoming," which I believe is AP-ese, is the most annoying example. "Downplay" is another. Also "input." There are plenty of ancient examples that have acquired respectability, of course. "Outgoing," "overseer," "income," "downcast," etc. But the present trend could create a nightmare for song lyricists. Who could make music to "outget and underget"?

Russell [Baker]
New York, New York

Dust Heaps of History

"Those who encroached on the integrity of our state," thundered Soviet leader Yuri Andropov in the fall of 1983, ". . . found themselves on the garbage heap of history." That was the official Tass translation: *garbage heap*.

Speaking in London more than a year before, President Ronald Reagan blazed forth with his belief that "the march of freedom and democracy . . . will leave Marxist Leninism on the ash heap of history." That was the official White House text: *ash heap*.

Well, gentlemen, which is it? What kind of heap does history offer?

The phrase was popularized by Leon Trotsky, who told the Mensheviks departing from the 1917 Congress of Soviets, "Go to the place where you belong from now on—the dustbin of history!" That was the way his phrase, transliterated as *musornyi yashchik*, was translated in the English edition of Trotsky's autobiography; in reviews of the movie *Reds*, Trotsky was quoted as saying of the faction opposing the Bolsheviks, "They are just so much refuse which will be swept into the garbage heap of history."

A third translation is *trash heap*, which rhymes with *ash heap* and compounds the confusion. "The transliteration for *trash heap* . . . is closer to *trash can*," says Professor Carl Linden of the George Washington University's Institute of Sino-Soviet Studies. "In old Russia—and probably still—there would be a courtyard . . . with a big box for all the tenement trash." That was probably the *trash can, ashcan, ash heap, dustbin, dust heap* or *garbage heap* Trotsky meant.

The most accurate translation would be *dust heap*. That is what the original English phrase was, stolen by Trotsky in its metaphoric form. In 1887, the English essayist Augustine Birrell coined the term in his series of essays, *Obiter Dicta:* "that great dust heap called 'history.' "

I will returneth to *dust* in a minute, but first to the meaning of *ashes* when they appear in a *heap:* An *ash heap*, which is written as two words because of the adjacent *h*'s, was a collection of household refuse, including but not limited to the contents of stoves. The present-day definition would be *garbage*, which is rooted in the Middle English word for chicken's innards. (Where is this taking me?)

In the Bible, when Job announced he would "repent in dust and ashes," according to the 1611 King James translation, he meant he would sit ignominiously amidst the refuse. In British usage, *dust* retains its secondary meaning of garbage: A *dustbin* is what Americans would call a garbage pail, and a *dustman*—

immortalized in Shaw's *Pygmalion* in the character of Alfred Doolittle—was until recently a *garbage collector*, when he became a *sanitation worker*.

Thus, while the translation offered by Tass—"garbage heap of history"—is accurate and up-to-date, it loses its historical evocation of Trotsky. Mr. Reagan's choice of words—"ash heap of history"—is close, but does not win the cigar. I would go with Birrell's original *dust heap*, until this phrase winds up in the waste-disposal unit of oratory.

Perhaps Russian is just not your forte. Yes, musornyi yashchik *means "trash box/ bin," and the official Tass translation is imprecise if not plain wrong. But you missed a more important point. Whether or not Trotsky stole the phrase from Augustine Birrell, these two writers used their respective phrases with decidedly different meanings. Trotsky meant that there is a place in history for the chronicling of historical events where those of no significance are to be consigned (analogous to a* musornyi yashchik*); Birrell, on the other hand, meant that* all *of history is one giant dust heap (= garbage can).*

Andropov's use of the Russian word gumanizm *(humanism) is not idiosyncratic, as you imply. In contemporary Russian, one of the meanings of* gumanizm *is something like both "morality" and "humanitarianism"; the word is related directly to the adjective* gumannyi *(humane), which is in turn equivalent (in Russian) to* gumanitarnyi *(humane, humanitarian).*

Michael Shapiro
New York, New York

Re: "An ash heap, *which is written as two words because of the adjacent* h's, . . ."
And what about fishhook *and* withholding tax?

Ruth B. Roufberg
Kendall Park, New Jersey

Ash heap *two words because of the adjacent* h's? *You mean because of the consonants? So what have you got against adjacent* k's? *Take the word* bookkeeper. *You could look it up—in the Help Wanted pages of the* NYT.

Jerome Meyer
Rye Brook, New York

Euph Will Be Served

In a snarling disquisition on euphemisms this past summer (*This past* shows it was backward in time but not too far back; *this summer* could mean "this coming summer," and *last summer* could mean "summer of last year"; only *this past summer* removes all ambiguity. I pause to recall my original subject). . . .

Euphemisms are words that prettify; euphemists are people who mistake words for things and think by renaming unpleasant things they can render them pleasant. In a snarling disquisition in July of this year (being specific is best), I called for help in naming the category of euphemism that renames something not intrinsically unpleasant—like *limbs* for *legs* in olden times, or *full figured* for *bosomy*.

"*Figleafism*," suggests Rita Newberry of Hilton Head Island, South Carolina; I'll buy that coinage for treating the natural as embarrassing. Bill McCullam of New York City offers a correlative word: *dysphemism*, little-known but in use for a century.

"*Dysphemism* means a verbal uglification as opposed to a prettying up," he writes, "since the Greek prefix *dys*—'ill' or 'bad'—is the opposite of *eu*, 'good.'" Thus, for the plain statement *He died*, the euphemism is *He passed away*, but the dysphemism is *He croaked*. If the euphemism for *pimpled* is *blemished*, the dysphemism is *crater-faced*. In my own files, I have held *entry-level position* to be the euphemism for *trainee slot*; M. Mallahy of New York suggests a term that can only be described as its dysphemism: *slob job*.

Other Lexicographic Irregulars have put forward *upscalism*, celebrating the linguistic marketing that turns the mundane into the worldly (using *mundane*, from the Latin word for "world," in its sense of "ordinary," and *worldly* to mean "sophisticated"). An example is some Pentagonese submitted by the writer Paul Hoffman of New York, in which a bureaucrat reports the capsizing of a ship due to "loss of hull integrity." He envisions a classy kid, whose mother is wondering why soda has been spilled all over the floor, replying, "Loss of bottle integrity."

The most imaginative case of upscalism I have found recently is the marketing move to rise above *health food*, a term coined a century ago, when *lactovegetarians* and *fruitarians* held faddist sway. *Health food* is a phrase that has long been regarded with suspicion by the Squad Squad, but now is accepted by redundancy guardians because it provides a balance to *junk food*. However, its proponents aimed at a wide audience, pushing alfalfa sprouts, wheat germ, acidophilus milk, middlings, yogurt and peanut flour to hoi polloi. Newer phrases, like *diet food, natural food, unprocessed food* and *organic food*, have been ingested by the language, but never replaced *health food*. (However, the soybean-and-tiger's-milk blueplate luncheon leads to a state called *wellness*, which is the opposite of *sickness* but somehow more chic than *health*.)

Comes now The Four Seasons, the high-style New York restaurant, with a way of lifting dreary old health food out of the ordinary. According to a missive just received from owners Tom Margittai and Paul Kovi, a "timely addition to our menu . . . is the result of a happy collaboration between our esteemed Chef Seppi Renggli and the Director of the Institute of Human Nutrition at Columbia University, Dr. Myron Winick."

The happy upscalism: *spa cuisine*. *Spa* is the name of the mineral-water resort in Belgium and has become a word for "watering place" associated with the weight-conscious affluentials around the world. And what goes into *spa cuisine*? Whole-wheat linguine! Vegetable platter with peanut sauce! None of the house-salad health foods we get at Mel Krupin's or Duke Zeibert's in Washington. We may laugh at the pretensions of the euphemists and declensions of the dysphemists, but we salute the upscalists who make us feel that dieting is something to hunger for.

Your help would be appreciated in promoting a dysphemism I like to use: "people warrens" for "apartment houses."

> Paul Lewinson
> Arlington, Virginia

My colleague Professor Adrienne Lehrer, a linguist, has done a study of wine terms in which she finds a double set of terms for the characteristics of wines, depending on whether the traits are viewed positively or not. A wine may be light or watery, full-bodied or heavy, fruity or green. The only contrast in meaning seems to be whether the trait is considered good or bad.

Kenneth S. Goodman
Tucson, Arizona

Your essay on "the upscale euphemism" was top-flight.

". . . dysphemism, little-known but in use for a century."

Probably incorrectly used. If "little-known" were an adjective modifier of a noun, then it should be hyphenated. But standing alone, probably should be "little known but in use," etc.

Richard Wilson
Mobile, Alabama

You have used the phrase "to hoi polloi." *Hoi polloi* is the masculine plural, nominative case. In classical Greek, the preposition *to* requires the use of the accusative case. Properly speaking, you should have written "to tous pollous." *If you had, not one in a myriad of your readers would have known what in Hades you were referring to. My solution to this problem is to rearrange the sentence so that* hoi polloi *becomes the subject.*

Hugh O'Neill
New York, New York

I must disagree with you and Paul Hoffman; the phrase "loss of hull integrity" is hardly bureaucratese. It's eminently correct usage of the word integrity *in its engineering sense. Ships' hulls, bridge support structures, pressure containers and scores of other mechanical structures possess (or unhappily, sometimes do not possess) structural integrity or soundness. In a ship's hull, integrity is a watertight condition. The usage has a long history.*

Raphael Paganelli
New York, New York

Eurolingo

"There is no way out." That lugubrious conviction, supposedly rampant among many important European businessmen and politicians, was described by *Washington Post* ecolumnist Hobart Rowen on April 8, 1984, as *Europessimism*.

"The first person to use *Europessimism* to my knowledge," reports Mr. Rowen, "was Anthony Solomon, president of the Federal Reserve Bank of New York, in a speech given in Geneva in 1983. To the best of his recollection, he was the first to use it."

The Solomonlike gnomenclature caught on in Switzerland and spread throughout meetings of undercollateralized bankers. Not surprisingly, when time came for preparation for 1984's economic summit conference, it was seized upon by the sherpa-watching community. (A *sherpa* is a bureaucrat who works on the preparations for a summit meeting, the name taken from the Tibetan tribesmen who assist mountain climbers. *Watcher* has replaced *observer* in jargonic description of an outsider who is an authority; it is derived from *China-watcher*, which has been replaced by *Pekingologist* now that observations of China by Westerners can take place from inside the capital. *Community* is a warmhearted way of saying *in-group*, which can also be derogated by being called an *establishment*. Thus, the *sherpa-watching community* is a phrase embracing the set of journalistic insiders who look over the shoulders of the advance men as they pave the way for agreement-signing sessions at summits.)

The preceding paragraph went off on what is known as a *tangent* (from the Latin *tangere*, "to touch," and used in geometry to describe a line that touches but does not intersect a curve; from the same root we derive *tact*, the lightness of touch of diplomats as they get ready for summiteers. And you thought this column was running out of material. Where are we?)

Europessimism will be the inescapable vogue word for the first week of June. Take an intangible mood (just touched old *tangere* again), slap on a new label that raises it to the level of a mini-*Weltschmerz*, and you have the headiness of longheadedness—especially if the new word is the product of a familiar and popular combining form.

Euro- rivals *mini-* and *mega-* as the favorite combining form of our time. In some ways, they are interchangeable—we may soon see *mini-Communists* wearing *Euro-skirts* and suffering from *megapessimism*—but of the three, *Euro-* has become too much of an *idée préfixe*.

It all began with *Euro-Asian*, says Fred Mish of Merriam-Webster, who has the first citation in the Smithsonian Institution Annual Report published in 1898. Then the *New International Encyclopedia* of 1903 described the word *nabob* this way: "In the United Kingdom it is applied derisively to Euro-Indians who, having amassed fortunes in India, returned to make an ostentatious display of their wealth." (Not until much later did the nabobs natter negatively.)

In the early 1950's, *European* began being used in the title of Western European defense and economic organizations, and the *Euro-* prefix exploded as the Common Market idea advanced. "It is the Eurobusinessmen who . . . are helping to create 'Europeanism,' " wrote *The Saturday Evening Post* in 1963, in a citation supplied by Ruth Kent at Webster's New World. "The prefix *Euro-* appears on every conceivable commodity—from Euroraincoats and Eurobeer to Euro-Union (a mutual fund) and Eurovision (the television link-up between a dozen European nations)." (O.K., the Satevepost writer used *between* when he meant *among*, but he was sensitive to prefixes.)

Eurocommunism blossomed in the 1970's to describe a tendency of some European Communists to act independently of Moscow. This coinage was often attributed to Arrigo Levi of Italy's *La Stampa*, but he credited the word to Franj Barberi in Milan's *Il Giornale*. It has faded, but we still have *Eurodollars*, also called *Euromoney* and *Eurocurrency; Eurocrats*, who sit on piles of paper as other bureaucrats do, and the adjective *Euro-centric*, which has taken over from *Europocentric* as a variation of *ethnocentric*.

In the spring 1984 issue of *American Speech* magazine, the invaluable "Among the New Words" section includes *Euromark* and *Euroyen* (sorry, no *Eurorubles*), *Euromissile* and a city planned to be permanent headquarters of the European Economic Community, *Euroville*, where presumably every pre-teen-age girl will be leered at as a potential *Euronymphet*.

With *Euro-* turned into a prefixture, it was only a matter of time until someone looked at the gloomy Gustavs and labeled the general down-in-the-mouth demeanor as *Europessimism*.

At this point, the prefix deserves a megarest. Here, however, is the opportunity for the reader of this column to coin a word that is sure to be seized upon next fall or winter as the perfect description of the mood of what we used to call the Continent:

Assume that Maggie Thatcher will patch up her quarrel with the Common Market over payments due, the Germans and French regain their creative fire, and the economic recession lifts. What word will then burst upon the scene as descriptive of the new, buoyant, smiling ebullience of the Europeans?

You got it. Now, quick, rush into print with the antithesis of *Europessimism*. That's how neologicians make it into word history.

Dear Bill—
   The only thing you missed here is the new expression

   Eurotrash

to describe Europeans who live and play between there *and New York. I just encountered this very expressive description in Takis' column in* Esquire *and* The Spectator, *but I don't know if he invented it.*
                                                            Liz [Smith]
                                                            New York, New York

Eurocurrencies, Euromarks, Euroyen, Eurosterling *are all spin-offs from* Eurodollars; *the generally accepted financial mythology has Eurodollars beginning in the mid-1950's. It is defined as a U.S. dollar deposited in a banking office outside the U.S. This apparently began when, for political safety, British banks got the Soviets to move their dollars from the U.S. into British banks. The whole concept exploded in the ensuing 30 years.*

   Today it no longer refers to Europe. Eurodollars are traded, deposited and lent in Hong Kong and Singapore (where they are called Asian dollars), the Bahamas, Cayman Islands, Panama, some spots in the Middle East, as well as in Europe. Thus the term Euro *has come to mean "international" or "external" rather than European. There has even been the expression* petro dollars, *which meant Eurodollars owned by oil-producing countries. And we even have them in the U.S. (remember the definition!). Lawyers, bankers and the federal banking regulators created an entity called an International Banking Facility, which can be set up in a U.S. bank so it can trade Eurodollars, take deposits, and make loans, and which everyone pretends is outside the U.S.(!) Eurodollars today never even touch Europe in many cases.*

Thus, when European bankers want to refer to a European currency, they have to use that word. A European Currency Unit is made up of currencies of European countries and is completely different from a Eurocurrency, which now means the international use of any of these currencies.

You mentioned Euromoney. *That's a British-based financial magazine which surveys the entire world financial scene, not just Europe.*

Peter K. Oppenheim
San Francisco, California

To me, as a gynecologist, only one word suffices to describe, not a mood, but the entire coterie of people who observe the European scene. (Is "of people" redundant?) This would be Eurologist. *I'm sure they are checking on the plumbing too.*

Donald R. Reisfield, M.D.
Somerset, New Jersey

Europropitious?
Eurobonheur?

M. B. Dolinger
Cleveland, Ohio

Surely, when the Europtomists win, they will chorus a Euro-paean!

Mary P. Caughey
Moorestown, New Jersey

European Anti-Pessimists

Europessimism was reported here to be the hottest new word for 1984's Continental malaise. I asked readers to make the obvious next coinage, using the ever-popular *Euro-* combining form.

The word I had in mind was *Euro-optimism*, but a passel of Lexicographic Irregulars sent in a far zingier alternative: *Europhoria*.

The new word is a godsend to neo-isolationists. Try this: "If the Eurocrats at NATO headquarters in Brussels think that United States forces are going to be stationed over there forever, then they're afflicted with an acute case of *Europhoria*."

Forgive Me, But . . .

"Forgive me," President Reagan began, "but judging from the record of those who are philosophically or constitutionally opposed to what we are doing, we might be better off consulting astrologers about what the deficit will be in 1989."

So much for the Dr. Gloom economists. Earlier in the campaign, he said about the Democratic candidates: "Forgive me, but their 'new realism' seems to begin right where their old ideas left off."

Again, in rebutting critics of the volunteer Army, the insistently apologetic President began, "Forgive me, but those are the same people who were wrong on inflation, wrong on unemployment . . . and there they go again."

Students of the presidency like Steven R. Weisman of *The New York Times*, who called this pattern to my attention, are wondering what Mr. Reagan is getting at. Why is he constantly seeking forgiveness beforehand? Didn't conservative Barry Goldwater entitle his latest book *With No Apologies*? Or is Mr. Reagan's repeated plea for permission merely a meaningless introductory phrase, a form of throat-clearing, like the famous Reagan *we-e-ell*, which the President stopped using after it was analyzed exhaustively in this space?

The answer is that Mr. Reagan is a *parrhesian*. No, this does not mean that our President comes from Paris; *parrhesia*, emphasis on the *he*, is a word rooted in the Greek for "frankness, free-speaking," and its general meaning is "boldness in speech."

In rhetoric, however, *parrhesia* has a specialized meaning: "warning of potential offense, and asking pardon in advance." It is similar to the announcement by the television anchor, "Portions of the following may be offensive to children" (though the kids lap it up and the only offense taken is by adults).

The technique has long been used by skillful orators and studied by rhetoricians. (I use *rhetoric* in its old sense, "the art of effective persuasion," rather than in its new meaning of "showy and empty oratory; bloviation.") In 1586, *parrhesia* was described in this way: "when by winning of curtesie to our speech we seeke to avoide any offence therein, as thus: Pardon if I be tedious." A better definition was offered by Edward Phillips in his 1678 *New World of English Words:* "in Rhetorick it is a figure in which we speak boldly, and freely, in things displeasing. . . ."

In Henry Peacham's 1577 *The Garden of Eloquence* (not to be confused with Willard Espy's book of the same title that reprints portions of Peacham's work), the Reagan technique was presaged in this denotation of the word: *"Parrhesia,* when speaking before them whom we ought to reverence and fear, & having something to say which either toucheth themselves or their friends, we do desire them to pardon our boldness. . . ."

The example given is from the Roman orator Cicero, who began a speech with: "I speak with great peril, I fear, Judges, after what sort you will take my words. . . . I pray and beseech you that if my speech be either bitter or incredible unto you at the first hearing, yet that you would accept it without offense, neither that you will reject it before I have plainly opened it unto you."

Or, in modern dress, *"Forgive me, but. . . ."*

Forgive me, but saying that parrhesia *has "emphasis on the* he" *is almost like making a similar assertion for* rhetoric, *to which* parrhesia *is obviously akin. There is no "he" or /h/-phoneme in either word. Your assertion also belies the two end-of-line divisions of* parrhesia, *which, if one is to believe one of your statements, you must have been aware of. The division is borne out by the* par·rhe·sia *entry in the Third and phonemically substantiated by the [pə'rēzh(ē)ə] transcription.*

The "h" reflects the "rough breathing" of the Greek rho; *in two successive non-initial* rho's, *the first had a smooth and the second a rough breathing: hence the "rrh" in* myrrh, hemorrhage, *etc. The practice must have been abandoned at some time in Classical Greek, since both my Classical and Modern Greek dictionaries have the entry* parrēsía *(with stress on the* iota).

We do have a "he" or /h/ in parhelion, *but a look at the etymology in the Ninth shows that the Greeks had abandoned the rough breathing over the* eta *before passing the word on to the Romans and that we have etymologically restored it in both spelling and pronunciation.*

Parrhesia *seems to be a "hapax etymologicon," since I vainly looked for such other compounds as "eurhesia, cacorhesia, oligorhesia, and polyrhesia." The precise function of the* par(a) *prefix is also somewhat of a mystery. I am inclined to go with the Third's 3b: "perversion* < parabulia > < paracanthosis >*." The second exam-*

ple, incidentally, is missing as an entry! The unprefixed acanthosis *happens to be a disease of our "integument."*

Louis Marck
New York, New York

You wrote that someone "called this pattern" to your attention. Did he actually call the pattern? Or did he call your attention to the pattern?

Margaret E. Knowles
New York, New York

Front-Loading

Lane Kirkland, head of the A.F.L.-C.I.O., is probably the only major political figure who spent a good chunk of his time in a previous job writing speeches for his boss. (James Madison, a good writer, wrote the speeches for his secretary of state, but his main job was President.) As a certified, card-carrying wordsmith, Mr. Kirkland is alert to changes in the lexicon of labor and politics.

On a shuttle flight between New York and Washington, he plunked himself down in the seat next to me and said, "Front-loading."

I checked to see if the plane was overloaded in the front with passengers trying to escape from smokers; that was not his meaning. Frequently, friends speak to me in shorthand, expecting a word to signify an entire argument; just that day, in the airport, the man taking my ticket murmured, "Cockeyed," which was his reasoned analysis of my column that morning.

Since Mr. Kirkland was reading the Op-Op-Ed page of *The New York Times* (that's the page opposite the Op-Ed page), I turned to my own copy of the editorial, and there was the interesting term: "The 1984 campaign calendar could remedy that. It's 'front-loaded,' to let many other states register their choices for Presidential nominee at an early stage."

"That's a labor term," said labor's leader proudly, as politics has been getting more than expressions from labor this year. *Front-loading* a contract means placing most of its increases in its early portion; for example, if management offers a package of 9 percent wage increases over two years, labor seeks to *front-load* it with 6 percent of the increase payable in the first year, meaning the worker gets more dollars over the life of the contract. Labor skates recall the usage as far back as the early 1960's.

I have been staggering under my front load ever since. In finance, a *front-end load* is described by Merriam-Webster's *9,000 Words* as "the part of the total load [sales commission and expenses] taken out of early payments under a contract plan for the periodic purchase of investment-company shares." This contrasts with *no-load funds*, and both locutions were popularized in the early 1960's, when mutual funds made a big splash.

Both the labor and the financial uses may have been bottomed on a large piece of heavy construction equipment known as a *front-end loader*, so called because it has a shoveling or loading implement attached to the front of the vehicle.

At this point, a housewife will wonder what the etymological fuss is all about: Since 1960, a *front-loader* (and not a front-*end* loader) is a washing machine. Instead of throwing the clothes in the top, you stick them in the front. The same principle has more recently been used to describe tape decks and videotape recorders.

Then along came economics, raising its tattletale-gray head to make use of this term. "In the view of some economists," *The New York Times* reported on June 15, 1980, "the recession is 'front-loaded,' because the worst of the decline will be felt at the start, but to others it's 'double-barreled.'"

Finally, with the proliferation of primary elections held in March, politics took hold of the front end. On November 21, 1983, Phil Gailey of *The New York Times* wrote that national party rules "create a 'front-loaded' primary season that favors the campaign's front-runners . . . ," and a month later, candidate George McGovern was complaining that the bunching of primaries in March "really front-loads the thing."

I like *front-loading* because it vividly describes the way to get your dirty socks in the washer and/or your candidate out of the primaries. I do not like *front-end*, because the opposite of *front* is *back*, and the opposite of *end* is *beginning*. I realize, with Edna St. Vincent Millay, that the candle burns at both its ends, but too many of us say *front-end* or *back-end* when we mean merely *the front* or *the back*. Lighten the load.

Your memory falters. You most certainly can date front-loading washing machines earlier than 1960.

You (and I) were present at the great kitchen debate in 1959 when Richard Nixon explained, with sweeping demonstrative gestures, to Nikita Khrushchev that capitalism provided housewives with a choice of either top-loading or front-loading washing machines while communism provided no such selection.

> William J. Coughlin
> Wilmington, North Carolina

In your column on front-loading you discuss "front-end" and "back-end," which, you gently remind us, really mean the front and the back. Maybe; but in a bus the front and the back mean to me inside. *(Ask any black Southerner.) "Front-end" is the* outside, *where the window showing the destination is; and "back-end" is where the directional lights are and where small boys on roller-skates hang on for a free and dangerous ride.*

> Dorothea Mac Farland
> New York, New York

Hey—you must be about my age—remember when a girl with a full bosom was called "front-loaded"?

> Jack Gasnick
> New York, New York

I was interested in your paragraph about back-end. *In the part of Lancashire where I was brought up, and indeed in the whole of the North,* back-end *is often used, and always in the past—i.e., "last back-end"—to mean "last autumn or early winter." Concerning "back-end" and "front-end" of a vehicle, this usage, which is very common in Northern England, grew out of our use of tram cars, which you call trolley cars, I think. These tram cars were the same at the back and at the front. When they reached a terminus the tram car driver walked from one end of the car to the other whilst the conductor went down the car pushing the hinged seats so that they were now facing forward once again. The trams had identical sets of controls at the front and back. When he had finished changing the seats around the conductor got off the tram, took a long bamboo pole which was carried at the side of the tram and changed the hinged pole affixed to the top of the tram to face in the opposite direction. As there was no real front or back it was usual to say front-end or back-end. "She looks like the back-end of a tram," was often used derogatorily to describe an ugly woman. (I noticed on my last visit home that one of my sons, an Oxford graduate, used "She looked like the back-end of a bus," which I presume is an up-dated version of the same expression. I was quite shocked, I can tell you, you would have thought that after all that expensive education he would have said, "She looks as though she's fallen off a flitting" at the very least.*

Joe Cleary
Jacksonville, Florida

"At this point, a housewife will wonder what the etymological fuss is all about . . ."

Why ignore the need for "homemaker"? If it were a woman loading the laundry, she would not be married to a house. And, if you will position yourself in the 1980's, you will notice it isn't always a woman in front of a front-loader.

Mildred R. Murphy
East Patchogue, New York

Genie Out of Bottle

A dialectologist has to hang loose about pronunciation. Asked about the pronunciation of San Jose, a city in California, Professor F. G. Cassidy reports that the Spanish loan name is most regularly pronounced *San Ho-ZAY*, but often loses the *h* in *SAN-o-ZAY*, and is jocularly referred to occasionally as *San JO-sie*. Correctness is a function of context: If you're talking to the Chamber of Commerce, use the first; if you're singing "Do You Know the Way to San Jose?" an elision to *SAN-o-ZAY* is appropriate; and if you're kidding around, it's O.K. to kid around.

When the push of dialectology comes to the shove of etymology, however, great wordsmen stand their ground. They will make a persuasive pitch for pronunciation that preserves the root of a word, in the hope that they can affect the language for the better—that is, the more understandable.

"One word that seems to be making great headway in misbegotten form," Dr. Cassidy complains, "is *homogenous* with second-syllable stress."

"A homogeneous population is easier, less subject to stress because of few racial or ethnic conflicts" is a sentence that comes trippingly off the tongues of demographers, many of whom pronounce the word *ho-MOJ-en-us*. Wrong.

"The correct etymological form is *homogeneous* with the third-syllable stress," observes Dr. Cassidy, whose *Dictionary of American Regional English* is eagerly awaited by dialect freaks the world over [Volume I appeared in 1985] and who pronounces the word *homo-GENE-e-ous*. It comes from the Greek *homos*, meaning "same," plus *genes* (from *genos*), meaning "kind"—in other words, of the same kind, as in *homogenized milk*, which is not a mixture of milk fluid and butter fat that tends to separate but a mass that does not separate because it has been processed to make it all of the same kind.

That's what has been blowing away the old pronunciation of *homo-GENE-e-ous*. "The form *homogenous* is probably due to the influence of *homogenized*, widely familiar through its application to milk. If we quite correctly say *homogenize*, we analyze it as *homogen-* plus *-ize* and see no harm in using *-ous* rather than *-ize*. So we produce *homogen-ous*, and there goes that *e*."

You lose the *e*, you confuse the etymology; in a thousand years, who's going to know how the word came to be? These columns are not chiseled in granite, and even that breaks down, as Ozymandias discovered. Cassidy stands bestride the bridge: "However, to explain the process by which the new form comes about does not make the product acceptable. *Homogeneous*, five syllables, with stress on the third, is etymologically correct—and, though Greek, it rolls off the English-speaking tongue more naturally than *homogenous* does anyway."

If you need a mnemonic, geniuses say *homo-GENE-e-ous*, and only the shook-up say *ho-MOJ-en-us*.

Dear Bill,

"Cassidy stands bestride the bridge," say you. For shame! If the bridge were a horse, I might bestride it, verb-wise; or I might stand, preposition-wise, astride it, the bridge still serving as a horse; but as a lexicographer and, I trust, an honorable one, no one will ever catch me standing bestride anything.

And by the way, I hope your intent was not to liken the bridge to a fence—in other words, to charge me slyly with mugwumpery *(= fence-sitting, with one's mug on one side and one's wump on the other—charming word borrowed from our*

Natick brothers). I choose rather to believe that you had in mind the noble picture of Horatius at the bridge, and perhaps Noah Webster at my right hand, to hold the bridge with me.

> Fred [G. Cassidy]
> Director-Editor, DARE
> Madison, Wisconsin

I should point out that once you bestride something, you are astride it. Who except a giant can bestride a bridge? The bridge, not Doctor Cassidy, does the bestriding. How about athwart?

> Verne M. Marshall, M.D.
> Geneva, New York

Gin Up

On a flight to Paris, Secretary of State George Shultz was asked if the United States had stimulated requests from Caribbean nations to rescue Grenada. He replied, on the record: "We haven't been trying to gin up anything."

The verb *to gin up* has two meanings, each with a separate etymology.

In the first, or boozed-up meaning, *to gin up* means "to get drunk"—more specifically, to become inebriated on gin, an alcoholic beverage that gains its flavor and its name from juniper berries. Considered in context, this was probably not the secretary of state's meaning.

As a shortening of *to ginger up*, however, we have the definition put forward in Farmer and Henley's 1890–1904 dictionary of slang: "Gin up, *verb*. (American.)—To work hard; to make things lively or hum." Ginger is a spice, from the Greek *zingiberi* and from the Sanskrit word for "antler-shaped root," making it one of the few words whose root is a root. *To ginger up* means "to add spice to, to enliven," and its use has a diplomatic-journalistic pedigree: "Whether they were gingered up by the articles in the *Times* or not," wrote Benjamin Disraeli in 1849, "I can't say."

Perhaps you're on the wrong track with your discussion of gin up.

I remember Miss Mayefsky discussing this in a senior English class at Brooklyn Technical High School in 1955. She thought that to gin up *came from* "to gin," *to clear (cotton) of seeds with a cotton gin. The operative image is of running a raw material through a machine to get a final product.*

Thus, broadly, to gin up is to try to reach a final result or idea by some process of thought or action. So, if Secretary Shultz wasn't trying to "gin up anything," perhaps he simply wasn't trying to achieve a particular outcome.

By the way, where can a Brooklyn boy see a cotton gin?

Herbert Mann
Brooklyn, New York

No, my Yankee friend, gin up *is as American as pumpkin pie (which is more American than apple pie, a British immigrant) and comes from Deep South expressions connected with pulling seeds and husks from the fiber of a cotton ball, i.e., from a cotton gin, which every-schoolboy-knows was invented by Eli Whitney in the early 19th century. The original name Whitney used was "cotton engine," which was fine for his New England neighbors, but down South, where the device found its true home, the usual Southern aversion for unnecessary syllables took over and we have a "cotton gin" which today does not simply "hum," as I recall, but fairly "roars."*

At the height of cotton season (late July to early September in the part of Texas where I grew up) the gin was operated 24 hours a day in two 12-hour shifts which required a gin hand "to work hard" in order to "gin up" and bale all the cotton quickly to get it to the mills for the best price. Ginning is serious work and "gin up" should never be used frivolously. You might want to "gin up" some fun at a local "gin mill" but you do so at the risk of confusing apples and pumpkins.

To put it briefly, a good British executive might "ginger up his prospects," but his distant American cousin will "gin up some business" by working day and night with the pragmatic zeal his Limey brethren just can't cotton to.

Robert L. Jackson
New York, New York

My old Winston dictionary includes a definition of a gin as "a hoisting machine." In my work we used a "gin pole" in the form of a small pole attached perpendicularly to the base of a much larger pole with suitable cables to permit the easier raising of the larger pole. "Gin" seems to be derived from "engine." Nuf sed?

Edward W. Sanders
Geneva, New York

Your explanation of "gin up" was interesting, but may I offer another?

At the start of the Industrial Revolution, an engine lathe was known as a "turning

engine," just as a boring mill was a "boring engine." When users of steam engines
(on locomotives, steamships, factories, etc.) needed to replace a broken part, it was
not unusual for the operator to "engine-up" a new part. This quickly became
"gin-up," and has, in my experience, been used for at least 60 years; I have been
an engineer for that long, either active or interested from outside.

> Norman N. Rubin
> Silver Spring, Maryland

The term as usually used (at least in my experience) has the implication of manufac-
turing something, often a position paper or "scenario," either out-of-thin-air or by
taking pieces from a number of places. This would be consistent with the source
being jinn, alluding to making things appear as a genie would have done it. This
is a more satisfying etymology, at least to me, than that the term came from either
gin (alcohol) or ginger (spice). If this derivation is correct, then the term probably
should be written "to jinn up," which would not be inconsistent with the practice
of making a verb from a noun and ascribing to it the action that is performed by
the noun.

> Philip D. LaFleur
> Rochester, New York

Is it possible that "gin up" really is djinn up—"to conjure up by magical means"?

> Anne Feraru
> Fullerton, California

To "gin, ginger, or ginger up" is an old horse groomer's term. Gaited horses prance
into the ring with tail held (hopefully) high. For drooping tails, a piece of ginger
is inserted into said horse's fundament. I believe irritation rather than spiciness is
the essence of the origin.

> Peter J. Buxtun
> San Francisco, California

I wonder if Secretary Shultz was a horseman.

About sixty years ago a group of us, teen-agers, used to follow the small town
country fair circuit. We'd ride our horses to a fair each weekend and show them in
the saddle horse classes. Sometimes, after a fairly long trek to the fairgrounds, one's
mount would seem lethargic, disinterested in showing off. We'd pick the lad with
the longest finger and, while one of us held up the horse's tail, he would insert a

freshly chewed piece of ginger root in the appropriate aperture. The result would usually be a spirited performance, head and tail held high.

Gin up: enliven, excite, enthuse.

Perhaps some other phrases and gestures, regrettably still in use, could be traced to this practice. I hope it's been outlawed from the horsey scene, as has been the breaking and resetting of tail bones, and the poling of jumpers.

Edmund S. Smith
Waterbury, Connecticut

Gloomy Gus, Loser

Every generation needs an alliterative phrase to deride pessimists. The party in opposition, which is in business to view with alarm, must be derogated as a downbeat bunch of whining Gloomy Guses, running down their country at a time when everyone should know that we never had it so good.

In the presidential campaign of 1936, the Landon camp tried to point out that the Depression was still going strong and the country was in terrible shape; Roosevelt supporters hooted at them as *disciples of despair* floundering in a *fountain of fear*.

In the mid-1950's, with Eisenhower in office, Republican Clare Boothe Luce laced into the critics as *troubadours of trouble* and *crooners of catastrophe*. During this period, *prophets of gloom and doom* was popularized; it is attributed to Adlai Stevenson, but that does not fit into my theory, as it would be more likely to be directed at him than coined by him.

In the early 1970's, Vice President Spiro Agnew used the same alliterative technique to rout doomsayers with *nattering nabobs of negativism*, which was my own contribution to the political lexicon. (No, I am not to blame for *effete corps of impudent snobs* and cannot claim fellow speechwriter Pat Buchanan's *instant analysis*; but it seems that if you coin one phrase, you coin 'em all.)

Here in the 1980's, President Reagan's speechwriters have taken up the challenge. This time, they have reached into the *set* pejoration, as in Britain's prewar, appeasement-oriented *Cliveden set* or Washington's glitzy *Georgetown cocktail-party set*. Mr. Reagan, defending his economic recovery, went on the attack in the grand tradition, denouncing *"the sourpuss set* [who] cannot believe in our nation."

Will the *sourpuss set* make it as this year's derogation, as the *gloom-and-doom prophets* and the *nattering nabobs* once did? There is still time for late entries. Send your suggestions to Anthony Dolan, chief speechwriter, the White House, not to me. I'm out of that dodge.

Goodbye Sex, Hello Gender

At the Democratic convention of 1984, *sex* disappeared.

For some inexplicable reason, the word *sex*—probably from the Latin *secare*, "to cut, divide," and meaning the division into male and female—has been deemed too provocative to say out loud or to put into print. Not since Victorian prudes substituted *limbs* for *legs*—as in "piano limbs"—has euphemism held such sway.

Only a few years ago, the proponents of the equal rights amendment did not blush to strike down discrimination "on account of sex." Now, however, *sex* is taboo. The new word to characterize maleness and femaleness is *gender*.

This craven substitution has taken place despite stern warnings in this space. Two years ago, the word went forth to friend and foe alike that *gender* applied to grammar while *sex* applied to people. I issued the ukase: "If you have a friend of the female sex, you are a red-blooded American boy; if you have a friend of the feminine gender, you have an unnatural attachment to a word."

But everybody got off my ukase. It has become useless to argue any longer that *gender*, in most Indo-European languages, is a grouping without human groupies. In French, *le livre* is a book and *la livre* is a pound, but that does not mean books are for men and pounds are for women. It's just a way of classifying, that's all, divvying up the language to make it more understandable.

Such defenses based on logic are now useless. Grammarians watching the theft of *gender* from their special lingo feel like mathematicians watching *parameters* being ripped off to mean "limits." Our baby has been kidnapped by the Philistines, and nobody even remembers the kid's sex.

The rush of references, from the podium to the punditorium, to Geraldine Ferraro as "the first of her gender" to achieve nomination to the vice presidency has buried all organized resistance to the euphemism. Evidently the English language needs a word to be synonymous with *sex* and yet not seem *sexy* or *sexist*, and further resistance is pedantry.

What next? Since *gender* is more neutral than *sex*, what will *genderism* signify? Perhaps a raised consciousness of the need for equality; on that principle, *genderist* is the opposite of *sexist*, as we take the high road to glittering generalities.

Hallow Rings Hollow

Here is this month's red-flag pronunciation alert: "I am waiting for October 31 to roll around," writes Eleanor Blau of New York, "wondering whether that holiday will be mispronounced again this year. Is it sloppiness or ignorance which [sic] accounts for the mispronunciation of *Halloween* as *Holloween?*"

Neither; it's a newer way to pronounce it. *Halloween*, or *Hallowe'en*, is All Hallows Evening, with *hallow* meaning "sacred," or as a noun, a synonym for "saint." The first syllable is pronounced *hol* by some, but *hal* is still preferred in the United States. Although we pronounce *swallow* as if the first syllable had an *o*, we prefer not to do that with *hallow*, as everyone familiar with "hallow'd be Thy name" will attest.

In Merriam-Webster's Ninth Collegiate, this nice distinction is made: *Hallow-een* is pronounced *hal-uh-WEEN*, and a second pronunciation is listed with the *a* in the first syllable having two dots over it. That means the *a* is pronounced like the *o* in *cottage*.

I suspect that the pronunciation in this country is shifting, and the *hallow* is ringing *hollow*. When the kids come trick-or-treating at the end of the month, I'll ask them which holiday it is. Those that say *Halloween* will get an extra handful of candy corn, because I like to encourage traditionalism.

Did you really say "Those that say Halloween . . ."? *Whatever happened to "Those who"?*

> Gloria Maguire
> Indialantic, Florida

Hallowerror

"I was so surprised to see your definition of Halloween as 'All Hallows Evening,'" writes Virginia Owens of Belle Harbor, New York. "It therefore follows that Christmas Eve is the evening of Dec. 25. . . . Since you obviously don't read the *whole* definition when you look something up, I'm sending you the definition from the *Random House Dictionary*."

That publication has it accurately: "The evening of October 31; the eve of All Saints' Day; Allhallows Eve."

The point is that All Saints' Day is November 1, and Halloween is the night before. My error was in reaching back to the poetic use of *eve* and *even* to mean *evening*, as it does in *Beowulf*. Milton uses this sense in describing the fall of a god: "From morn/to noon he fell, from noon to dewy eve." But that's archaic; *eve* is no longer *evening*. It's "the night before." To all those kids who dutifully went out on the wrong night, I apologize.

Her Majesty Is Not Enthused

Bernard Levin, the brilliant British controversialist, has written a mind-enlarging book titled *Enthusiasms*. I became enthused while reading it, which caused me to wonder: Where do I stand on the verb *enthuse*?

The people at the *Oxford English Dictionary* put it in—they'll put anything in; they're reporters—but they didn't like it. Labeling *enthuse* "colloquial or humorous," they showed their distaste by condemning it as "an ignorant back-formation from 'enthusiasm.' " In the O.E.D. Supplement, however, Bob Burchfield and his gang added a few earlier examples without comment, suggesting this particular back-formation has a long history behind it that makes it hard to put down. The first use spotted was in 1827, by a young Scotsman in America, and by 1859 *The Congressional Globe* was reporting, "They are what they call in the country 'enthused'—run mad on the subject [of Cuba]."

But from 1870 on, language mavens have not been able to work up any enthusiasm for *enthuse*; experts and usage panels have been tut-tutting for a century, while more and more people have been using the word.

O.K., cut out that squabbling: *Enthuse* is in. Some purists will continue to say "to wax enthusiastic," but those are the sort of people who wax wroth, and Roth is beginning to get a waxy build-up.

While I'm at it, I judged a whole bunch of submissions in my "verbification" file, and these are the ones that made it: *to access, to curate, to intuit, to position.* These are the ones that flopped: *to concuss, to cheapshot, to funeralize, to liaise.* I do this on my own authority for my own use; you decide for yourself. I am still working on *to destitute:* "You are going to be very shortly destituted," said Representative John Dingell in debate on the floor of the House, "and you are going to destitute the rest of your fellow citizens."

Nope, I don't like it: try again next year. I'm sticking with *to impoverish*. Just can't get enthused over *to destitute*.

Dear Bill,

As (now) the world's living expert on enthusiasm, I have to tell you that I will never submit to "enthuse." But I will offer you another noun into verb, from the BBC. Executives there regularly go before a board, who review their work and decide whether they should be promoted. BBC people in that position can be heard saying "I am being boarded next week." Where will it end?

> Bernard [Levin]
> The Times
> London, England

If "to constitute" and "to restitute" and "to substitute" are well established in the language, why not "to destitute"? Is there really no place for neologisms based on long existing patterns until you place your stamp of approval on them?

> Herbert H. Paper
> Cincinnati, Ohio

Hide That Agenda

Thumbing through *The New Yorker* in 1984, Serena Rattazzi of Port Washington, New York, came across the phrase *a hidden agenda* in an article by John McPhee, followed by *a hidden agendum* later in the same piece.

"If I recall correctly, *agenda* means 'things to do,'" she writes. "It is a plural noun and, therefore, cannot be used with the singular article *a*."

Miss Rattazzi is so right she's wrong. Long ago, before committees took over the world, the word *agendum* meant "list of matters to be discussed." Good Latin students knew that *agenda* was the plural of *agendum*—only if you carried two lists into the meeting could you be said to be loaded with *agenda*.

Then along came *The Westmoreland Gazette*, published in England, which took to using the term *agenda-paper* in its coverage of a conference in 1887. By 1905, this breezy modernism was customary: "The Czar . . . and the Kaiser . . . are meeting today. . . . We are not given the agenda-paper of their conversation." Thus was *agenda* used to mean one list of items rather than more than one.

In the first volume of the *Supplement to the Oxford English Dictionary*, published in 1972, the lexicographers, taking note of the tendency to bastardize the Latin ending, defined the newest use of *agenda* in these words: "treated as a singular (a use now increasingly found but avoided by careful writers)."

Here we are in the 1980's, and if any executive were to begin a meeting with "What's on the agendum?" he would be consigned to corporate purgatory as some kind of neo-traditionalist weirdo. Committeemanship requires the diffusion of responsibility and the worship of the norm; any deviation from common usage brands the deviator as an individual not suited to task-force life. (Sorry, Charlie, language is language.)

Today's careful writers take care to avoid the appearance of pedantry. Although they still refuse to substitute *memorandums* for *memoranda*, they know it would make them look like Eustace Tilley, complete with top hat and monocle, to insist on *agendum* as the singular of *agenda*.

Miss Rattazzi's plaintive cry for a return to roots, though hopeless, is not useless: She has triggered a search for the evolution of a new derogation. Whence *hidden agenda*?

In the 1960's, *agenda* was taken from business and applied to political programs, mainly by academics: *The liberal agenda* was a common phrase and carried overtones of furrowed brows and compassionate lists. However, on April 19, 1976, *Newsweek* quoted an unidentified California politician as saying, "Those folks who have their own agenda for Hubert [Humphrey] underestimate Jerry Brown." A couple of months later, the newsmagazine quoted a Carter adviser, Dr. Peter Bourne, as saying that "everybody wants to win, and people are willing to subordinate their own agendas to do that."

One's *own agenda* is a list of personal desires or goals. This metaphoric extension of the list to be carried into a meeting suggests a mental list to be carried through life, with priorities neatly assigned, but—and here is the sense that gives the phrase piquancy—not to be publicly revealed.

Own agenda soon became *private agenda*. *Newsweek*, apparently with its own neologistic agenda, reported in 1980 that former Treasury Secretary William Simon worried Reagan staff aides "as a bit of a prima donna with a brilliant mind, an abrasive manner and a private agenda to pursue—an agenda some people now think includes the Presidency for himself." As this citation suggests, *private agenda* has a sinister connotation; the agenda-keeper seems to be accused of not sharing his goals with his colleagues. Columnist David S. Broder turned it into a compound adjective in 1980: "Crosscutting these visible contests are a great many private-agenda items, ranging from conventional to bizarre."

Evidently *private*, an adjective with a fairly good connotation, was not sufficiently sinister. (*Privacy* is good but *secrecy* is bad.) Hence, we have the appearance of *hidden agenda* as well as the archaic *hidden agendum* in *The New Yorker*, as well as the rising use of *secret agenda* in political parlance. *Secret agenda* brands the perpetrator as Machiavelli reborn.

I have had this subject on a list of possible future columns that I tucked away in my wallet, not to be seen by anyone, and I now know what to call the list.

Years ago, in the 60's, I was a communications minor at what was then San Jose State. The term hidden agenda *was in our textbooks and was discussed at length in group dynamics studies. It was to be negative or positive: If it was your plan to get a meeting to finish early, you could "facilitate" by recapping and reestablishing the thread of the agenda. Your "hidden agenda" was to make your date on time. If, however, someone purposefully led the meeting astray to keep a resolution from being adopted because they were secretly against it, that is using hidden agenda negatively. At least, that's a bit of what I recall. I've always been aware of it in meetings since then.*

Dene Bowen
Livermore, California

Nice try on the origin of hidden agenda, *but that term has been around longer than you surmise. It is psychology jargon to describe the plans of a manipulative person, and I have heard it used for at least eight years (since the psychiatry course in medical school).*

Lois L. Bready, M.D.
San Antonio, Texas

Agenda *is pure Latin from the verb* agere, *"to do," and it was taught to me as a perfect example of the gerundive form and means, "things which ought to be done," not a "list of matters to be discussed."* Agendum *would be for a meeting to do only one thing.*

(I learned that before I heard the word used for a meeting, before it was in common use in America. I remember, in the late 1930's, Mayor LaGuardia saying to a World Youth Congress rally on Randall's Island, referring to the things their conference would take up, "In your international parlance, you will call it an 'agenda.'")

Robert Schumacher
Transportation Engineer
Mount Vernon, New York

There's a joke about the singularization of a pluralized word like agenda, *especially when the word is Latin-rooted or Latin itself:*
  Scholarly-looking prof-type enters a bar. "Barkeep," he says, "a martinus please."
  "Martinus?" says the barkeep. "Oh, you mean a martini."
  The prof, sharply: "If I'd wanted more than one, I'd've said so!"

Gregory d'Alessio
New York, New York

Hotdogging It

"Sometimes there are hot dogs jumping around and saying things," said a glum Eric Dickerson of the defeated Los Angeles Rams, "but they [the Redskins] didn't rub it in."

A new meaning of *hot dog* has emerged: not a frankfurter, but a noun and verb taken from the expression of delight, usually pronounced "Hot Dawg!" In its new meaning, a *hot dog* is "one who unduly exults in the presence of the losers." This lack of grace in winning was criticized by Captain John Woodward Philip, who, in the 1898 battle of Santiago in the Spanish-American War, said, "Don't cheer, boys, those poor devils are dying."

The verb form is already in action: Cornerback Darrell Green, who raised his arm even before he had crossed the goal line in celebration of an interception leading to a touchdown, explained, "I wasn't trying to hotdog. I was just excited."

I believe that you overestimated the newness of hot dog. *It goes back nearly twenty years, at least in Philadelphia. There the "Big Five," Penn, St. Joseph's, Temple, La Salle and Villanova, play basketball with an intense rivalry. In the late sixties, when one player, known as a show-off, would be introduced at the start of a game, students from the opposing school would throw hot dogs from the stands.*

Bruce L. Libutti
Teaneck, New Jersey

One of the best sports uses of hot dog *was in a* New York Times *story some years ago—not sure how many—when Reggie Jackson first joined the Yankees, and Thurman Munson, then the Yankee captain, was quoted as saying: "There ain't enough mustard anywhere to cover that hot dog." In that instance, it just meant "show-off," it seems, and didn't include undue exultation in the presence of the loser.*

James A. Doyle
Merrick, New York

While the meaning you gave in your column is part of the whole, there are other usages, minus the element of win-lose. I really see it as a replacement of the older terms hotshot, showoff *or* daredevil. *A* hotdog *can be the guy in school who is a top make-out artist with the girls, or it can be someone addicted to flashy athletic feats (particularly, those feats carrying a large element of danger). Even objects can be* hot dogs; *e.g., a set of wheels with a "super" paint job and "jack rabbit" suspension. There is even a current film called* Hot Dog, the Movie *which regales us with the exploits, both sexual and athletic, of ski bums and bimbos.*

Robert O. Vaughn
West New York, New Jersey

Huggermugger

In a column criticizing the concessions made to the Syrians in Lebanese negotiations by then-envoy Robert McFarlane, later national security adviser, Joseph Kraft wrote: "For an American Presidential emissary to be deeply engaged in such huggermugger is at best undignified."

Huggermugger is not, as some modern urbanites might think, the name of an amorous thief. Nor is it slang. *Huggermugger* is a glorious Standard English word; as a noun, sometimes appearing as *huggermuggery*, it means "secrecy" or "confusion"; as an adjective, it sometimes means "jumbled," but usually means "secretive" with a connotation of "duplicitous." Here's how Shakespeare used it in *Hamlet:* As Claudius considers the problems surrounding him and the mistakes that have been made, he tells Gertrude of ". . . the people muddied, / Thick and unwholesome in [their] thoughts and whispers / For good Polonius' death; and we have done but greenly / In hugger-mugger to inter him. . . ."

This word was very big four centuries ago and deserves a revival. It comes from *hoker-moker*, a reduplication of the Middle English *mokeren*, "to conceal," and should not be confused with *higgledy-piggledy*, which is "scatterbrained," or with *skullduggery*, which is "trickery." Remember: If you use *skullduggery* when you mean *huggermugger*, you're all higgledy-piggledy.

Despite what most dictionaries say, never hyphenate *huggermugger*. When a word sneakily makes it through four centuries, it deserves to eject its hyphen. Consider another old word churned up by the conflict in Lebanon: *hardscrabble*.

Thomas L. Friedman of *The New York Times* wrote from Beirut of "an Israeli soldier standing watch on a hardscrabble hillside." This is an Americanism, first spotted in the report of the Lewis and Clark expedition in 1804: "Got on our way at hard Scrable Perarie." In that early usage, the words meant a barren place, where it was hard to make a livelihood. In *Moby Dick*, Herman Melville extended the use to mean "vigorous effort under great stress"; the author joined the words to make a compound adjective: "While taking that hard-scrabble scramble upon the dead whale's back. . . ." Later, the words were frequently applied to hillsides: "Many a farmer who had barely been able to eke a living from a hard-scrabble hillside . . . ," wrote Bellamy Partridge and Otto Bettman in 1946.

Now it is one word, which I use without a hyphen in veneration of its venerability, with a silent salute to Melville. The adjective today means "grudgingly yielding a living."

Inhumanism

Earlier in his tirade, Mr. Andropov laced into "hypocritical preaching about morals and humanism."

Humanism is a word that has been treated brutally. It began with a capital *H* to mean the rediscovery of Greek and Latin "humanities" literature that led to the Renaissance, as the Dark Ages' dependence on theological rigidities was replaced by a new reverence for the workings of the human mind. Then *humanism*, without a capital letter, took on a fuzzy meaning of the study of humanity in general or of fascination with human interests. Later it denoted a study of human nature, in contrast to the sciences, and, more recently, has been tossed about as a concern for the human condition.

William James, whose espousal of pragmatism made him the patron saint of White House chiefs of staff, offered this definition in 1904: " 'Humanism' is perhaps too 'wholehearted' for the use of philosophers, who are a bloodless breed; but, save for that objection, one might back it, for it expresses the essence of the new way of thought, which is, that it is impossible to strip the human element out from even our most abstract theorizing." A modernist school of thought held that humans were capable of ethical action and self-fulfillment without the aid of God.

I am developing an animus toward the word *humanism*. The schmoolike term has come to mean anything we choose it to mean. But it seems to have stung Yuri Andropov, who treated it as synonymous with or parallel to morality; perhaps he meant to denounce preaching about *humanitarianism*, which is the more specific promotion of welfare by alleviating pain and suffering, certainly a topic raised by those angry at the shooting down of the Korean airliner.

Mr. Reagan, not to be outdone by the Russians rhetorically, is a humanizer in his choice of words. Aware of the "gender gap" (strictly speaking, the "sex gap," but nobody in Washington will use that phrase for fear of appearing starved for affection), the President has banished the word *mankind* from his vocabulary. Along with the noun *cripple, mankind* has been tossed on the ash heap of history. Because Mr. Reagan is developing a decent respect for the opinions of you-know-what-kind, the operative White House word for all statements embracing the people of the planet has become *humankind*. The ash heap of history will record that it was during the Reagan administration that *mankind* was obliterated.

Humankind is rampant humanism in language. When I was growing up on Manhattan's West Side, I longed to be a "two-sewer hitter"—that is, capable of punching a rubber ball the distance between two humanhole covers. No longer can two-sewer hitters scorn the milk of *humankind*-ness.

Does humanism pay? The answer may be found in *Marshall Loeb's Money Guide*, a pocket-filling treasure of a book replete with definitions for such locutions as "rich-uncle mortgages." Mr. Loeb, managing editor of *Money* magazine, writes: "Are you looking for 'humanistic' mutual funds? There are several of these funds, which do not invest in companies that make weapons or pollute the environment. . . . The trouble is, idealism has its price. For the five years that ended Dec. 31, 1982, only one of these funds did better than the Lipper mutual-fund industry average gain of 121 percent." I shall not give that fund's name in this space because I am not a humanism tout.

Perhaps the single most distressing current use of humanistic *is as a replacement for "humane."*

This makes it all the easier for those who fear "humanism" in the name of their theology to disparage the "humanistic treatment" of criminals and other people considered to be outcasts of our present society.

Judith Childs
New York, New York

Internecine Incivility

In a political tirade, I wrote that the willingness of Speaker Tip O'Neill to dismiss the charges of Carter briefing-book pilferage by the 1980 Reagan operatives made me suspicious: Could Tip's unaccustomed nonpartisanship mean, I slyly innuendoed, that the "mole" in the Carter White House was a Kennedyite and that "internecine Democratic warfare may have kept on going through the 1980 campaign"?

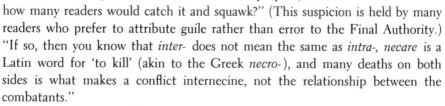

Back came this query from Andrew Norman of Palisades, New York: "Did you butcher *internecine* on purpose, to see how many readers would catch it and squawk?" (This suspicion is held by many readers who prefer to attribute guile rather than error to the Final Authority.) "If so, then you know that *inter-* does not mean the same as *intra-*, *necare* is a Latin word for 'to kill' (akin to the Greek *necro-*), and many deaths on both sides is what makes a conflict internecine, not the relationship between the combatants."

You have been misled, Mr. Norman, by the First Authority, lexicographer Samuel Johnson, who mistranslated the Latin in Butler's *Hudibras*. The words *internecinum bellum* meant "bloody war," "war of extermination," "all-out slaughter" (hence Mr. Norman's apt "Did you butcher *internecine* . . . ?"). When Big Sam looked at the word, he interpreted the *inter-* to mean "mutual," and defined the word in his dictionary as "endeavouring mutual destruction." From that moment on, that's what the word meant; in those days, lexicographers had clout.

For a few centuries, the adjective was used to describe civil wars, which caused great destruction on both sides; as Mr. Norman argues, the emphasis was on the slaughter, while the less important part of the meaning pointed to the two-sidedness of the bloodletting. In *Success with Words*, a lively and eminently usable new usage guide edited by David Rattray for *Reader's Digest*, that mainly bloody, also mutual, meaning is said to be "now the basic meaning of the word, with various further connotations or shades of meaning: 'pitting comrade against comrade, fratricidal' or 'causing regrettable fighting or quarreling among colleagues who ought to be working for a common cause,' or sometimes merely 'causing trouble within a group, internally disruptive.'"

I think the basic meaning of the word has shifted, and those later shades of meaning have taken over. Prescriptivists in the old Sam Johnson mistaken tradition may not be sanguine about it, but a lot of the blood has been wrung out of *internecine:* The *inter-*, or mutuality, has butchered the *necine*, or kill ratio. Today, *internecine conflict* does not mean "civil war" as much as uncivil pillow-throwing among members of the same organization.

Therefore, I stand uncorrected. "Internecine Democratic warfare" stresses the relationship of the combatants (*inter-*, the fact that Carterites and Kennedyites were all Democrats) and not the degree of slaughter (*necare*, what the mole did to Mr. Carter in the debate).

Do not pronounce *internecine* along the lines of *incarnadine*. The way to remember the pronunciation is to concentrate on the *ne*, as in *knee:* Interpersonal wars are started when somebody says, "Get your hand off my knee." (That's a mnemonic, pronounced *knee-MONIC*.)

Samuel Johnson wrote in the preface to his dictionary, "Every language has its improprieties and absurdities, which it is the duty of the lexicographer to correct or proscribe." (Quoted in the O.E.D. under impropriety.*) But he was, as you say, a prescriptivist.*

You flit freely back and forth between descriptivism and prescriptivism. Thus you will deny that internecine *means what it has meant for at least two centuries, since Johnson slightly altered its definition, and in the next breath command us to use* huggermugger *only as it was used four centuries ago. Sometimes you justify your policy in a particular case by appeal to authority, sometimes by claim of divine right, and sometimes by explicit or implicit reference to principles.*

This freedom of yours does not trouble me, except when I disagree in a particular case. But I would like to suggest a few principles that have some merit in judging whether to subscribe to or proscribe a usage that departs from past propriety:

1. *Does the shift extend or refine prior usage or does it in effect repeal it? Shifts of the latter type cause much confusion. Readers will unwittingly misunderstand texts written only a few years before. Does the shift produce benefits worth the price?*

2. *Does the shift fill a gap in the language or leave one? Wouldn't "warfare among Democrats" have served where you used "internecine Democratic warfare"? Conversely, if we let your usage stand uncorrected, what word have we to mean, literally or figuratively, "involving, or accompanied by, mutual slaughter"?*

3. *Is it pretentious? Is it being used because it sounds fruitily Latin or Greek or otherwise suggests the user's erudition—all the more so if most people aren't sure how to pronounce it? If so, its use should be held to a high standard of lexicographical orthodoxy.*

4. *Does the shift violate the word's etymology? If so, a dutiful lexicographer should correct or proscribe it, unless it fills a gap without leaving a bigger one. (Note that Dr. Johnson's definition of interne-cine erred in the opposite direction, toward good etymology; I cannot think of another word that uses inter- simply as an intensifier.)*

Andrew E. Norman
Palisades, New York

Incorrect. There is no such thing as a "mnemonic."
There is a "mnemonic device," there is "mnemonics" (sing.), but there is no noun labeled "mnemonic."
Ah, those feet of clay!

Mac Shoub
Montreal, Quebec

Ize Right?

Donald Rumsfeld, formerly our Middle East negotiator, was asked on the David Brinkley program about ways to retaliate against terrorist attacks. One of his suggestions was "to 'leprodize' the states that are engaged in state-sponsored terrorism; they can be isolated politically and economically."

Henry Hanson of *Chicago* magazine promptly called about *leprodize*. Was it a word? Should it be a word?

Leper, from the Greek word meaning "rough, scaly," is a description of a victim of what used to be called *leprosy* and has been euphemized to *Hansen's disease.* An adjective, *leprous,* predates the noun *leper* and was used by Shakespeare: the Ghost in *Hamlet* reported that the King "in the porches of my ears did pour the leprous distillment."

However, the only use of a similar verb form that I have been able to find was a 1592 usage of *leperize,* meaning "to smite with leprosy"; a figurative extension would mean "to treat as a leper is treated," which in olden times meant "to avoid, isolate, cast away." The old *leperize* seems more direct than Mr. Rumsfeld's coinage, *leprodize.*

Better than either, to my mind, is no verb at all. Just about any noun can be *-ized,* given a quick suffix turning it into a verb. But we should ask ourselves: Is this compression of a phrase necessary? We idolize verbifiers and finalize their coinages, but do they not contribute to stiltification? (That's a noun formed from *stilted* before your very eyes.)

Count me among those who make *-ize* constructions work hard before entering the language. I like "make a leper out of" or "treat as a leper," or, if you are sensitive to the afflicted, "treat as a pariah." (Not *pariah-tize*; that would cause confusion with *prioritize*.)

Dear Bill:

I stand corrected. From now on I am going to say "treat as a leper."

Thank you for correctizing me.

> *Donald [Rumsfeld]*
> *Skokie, Illinois*

Juggernaughty but Nice

Sanskrit has been doing very well in the early Democratic primaries.

After his victories over Walter Mondale in New Hampshire and Maine, Senator Gary Hart said he "may have brought a political juggernaut to its knees."

Juggernaut is from the Sanskrit word for "lord of the world" and was most often applied to the incarnation of Vishnu, one of the principal Hindu gods. His devotees were reported to have sometimes allowed themselves to be crushed beneath the wheels of the carriage on which his image was being drawn in a procession, which led to the current meaning of the noun in English: "an inexorable force that crushes whatever is in its path."

Meanwhile, *Time* magazine was writing that Mr. Hart "casts himself as the political avatar for younger Americans."

Avatar is from the Sanskrit word for "he comes down." In Hinduism, gods like Vishnu can come down to earth in bodily form; such incarnation led to the meaning of "embodiment" in English. *Time*'s usage meant that Senator Hart sought to portray himself as the embodiment of all that youth is or wants in American politics.

Scholars of Sanskrit are pleased with the sudden emergence of their field of study as the linguistic front-runner in the campaign, but must be troubled by the senator's metaphoric reach: A *juggernaut* may be stopped, slowed, derailed, side-tracked or forced over a cliff, but it may not be "brought to its knees." Even if dragged along by elephants, which I presume have the largest knees in the animal kingdom, the Juggernaut itself—which, by the way, should be capitalized—has no knees.

On the other hand, the notion of a Juggernaut with knees instead of wheels may be one of those "new ideas". . . .

Now we come to Juggernaut. *I notice you require a capital letter, which is apropos if it indeed refers to the Lord of the world. But if it is the Lord, and not his ten-wheeler, since man has made his God in his own image, Vishnu indeed has knees. Whether he can be brought to them is another matter.*

                                                                    Arthur J. Morgan
                                                                    New York, New York

Knowing Your Fiddlesticks

"Fiddlesticks! I'm going." So said one Soviet fighter pilot to another as he prepared to shoot down the civilian aircraft in Russian airspace. Or so the translation provided by the United States government goes; in fact, the Russian words used by the pilot to express his astonishment or irritation were *yolki palki*.

When pressed for an explanation of the literal meaning of *yolki palki*—a reduplication, such as *okey-dokey* or *higgledy-piggledy* in English—Michael Lysenko, a press officer in the Soviet Embassy in Washington, informs me that it "refers to Christmas trees."

Christmas trees? Under godless Communism? "If someone tells you something extraordinary that you don't believe, you might say, 'Oh, *yolki palki!* ' " reports the Soviet official. "Or if you're doing hard work and you have difficulties, you might use it. It's a mild exclamation."

Another Russian source defines the term as "twigs"; *Time* magazine, in exploring the etymology of the musty slang used by both United States and Soviet translators, offers "the sticks of a fir tree." These sticks—from a fir tree, which is often used as a Christmas tree—justify a translation to *fiddlesticks*.

Tragedies often churn up outmoded or colorful expressions that expose cross-cultural metaphors. Tass, the Soviet news and propaganda agency, translated a Soviet Army newspaper interview with one of the fighter pilots in which the pilot of the Korean Air Lines jumbo jet was described as a flyer who "knew his onions."

That expression was first spotted in English in 1922 and is defined by the *Oxford English Dictionary*'s supplement as "to be experienced or knowledgeable in the subject, etc., on hand." (I don't know what a "subject on hand" is; the English talk funny.)

Some slanguists have speculated that *to know your onions* is rooted in the work of Dr. Charles Talbut Onions, the last of the editors of the original *Oxford English Dictionary*, described by his successors as "for many years the doyen unquestioned of English lexicography." Like "to know your Shakespeare" and "to know your Cobbett," *to know your Onions* signified to some language students a familiarity with the work of the master. This is probably the folk etymology of some highly literate folk, since other common foods are used in similar expressions: to know your *oats* and *bananas*, as well as the more general *stuff*. (*Beans* are used only in the negative sense; though a smart person knows his *oats*, a dope doesn't know *beans*. This subject was treated exhaustively in a previous article, and a pile of mail came in with additional references; any reader who thinks I can give scatological examples in a family newspaper doesn't know his left elbow from third base.)

Just as the Russians are sometimes off-key in their use of American expressions, we sometimes misappropriate Soviet jargon. One such word is *adventurist*. Of late, American spokesmen have taken to denouncing Soviet actions around the world as *adventurist* when they mean *expansionist* or *aggressive*. To a Soviet official, when a policy is *expansionist*, that's not bad; but when a policy is *adventurist*, that's stupid. I am indebted to Under Secretary of Defense Fred Iklé for this selection from the works of Lenin, dated April 9, 1917: "The class-conscious workers stand for the undivided power of the Soviets . . . power made possible not by *adventurist* acts, but by clarifying proletarian minds."

To a Communist, *adventurism* is ill prepared and dangerously impulsive, while *expansionism* by Communist power is studiously prepared and necessary. (When practiced by others, it is *imperialism*.) American spokesmen who limit their meaning of *adventurist* to the shooting down of civilian planes, and do not extend it to subversion in Central America, know their onions.

On occasion, a slang term is chosen in English that can confuse not only the Russians but the Americans as well. When President Reagan told congressional leaders that he was placing additional marines near Lebanon, he was reported to have said that this action laid down "a marker for the Syrians."

What is a *marker*? To a gambler, it is an I.O.U.; to a bookworm, a bookmark; to an academic, a person who grades papers; to a military commander, a marker is a flag, buoy, stake or ship used to indicate the position of a unit.

Les Janka, the White House press assistant who is frequently called upon to translate from the Reaganese, offers this explanation: "The word could be *signal*; the word could be *warning*; the word could be *notice*." Such studied ambivalence is the essence of diplomacy, except to those who are of two minds about being ambivalent.

While yolki *are fir trees (more often New Year's trees than Christmas trees in the U.S.S.R.) and* palki *are sticks, the two words in combination form a euphemism for one of the strongest obscenities in Russian. (See, e.g., Meyer Galler and Harlan E. Marquess,* Soviet Prison Camp Speech: A Survivor's Glossary, *Madison: University of Wisconsin Press, 1972.) On the other hand, the euphemism is mild enough for the phrase to occur frequently in the speech of schoolchildren, as reflected in a recent novel for young people published in the Soviet Union.*

The construction is a kind of inverse acronym. Instead of forming a word out of the initial elements of a phrase, here we have a phrase made up of words whose initial segments combine to form part of the original obscenity. The only parallel I can offer comes from Yiddish, where the sequence of names Shmuel Mordkhe Kalmen *serves as a euphemism for a less acceptable name of the male sex organ, the spelling of which contains the first letters of the three names. (See Nahum Stutchkoff's Yiddish thesaurus,* Der oytser fun der yidisher shprakh, *New York: YIVO, 1950.)*

Robert A. Rothstein
Professor of Slavic Languages
University of Massachusetts
Amherst, Massachusetts

Your sources on Russian slang certainly don't know their onions. Yólki pálki *doesn't mean "fiddlesticks": it's closer to "Christ" or "damn," i.e., an expression of chagrin or surprise (as in the case of the Soviet fighter pilot's exclamation), not of doubt, disbelief, or derision.*

The expression has nothing to do with sticks of any sort, although yolka *does mean "fir tree" and* palka *"stick." Their juxtaposition is intentionally meaningless because it refers to an obscenity (an exceedingly common one) and reproduces the two stressed vowels of the latter, in which respect* yólki pálki *is akin to Cockney rhyming slang (for instance). A similar Russian euphemism is* yólki motálki *(motalka means "carding stick"), which reproduces not only the stressed vowels of the obscene phrase but the number of unstressed syllables between stresses as well.*

Michael Shapiro
New York, New York

Your literal translation of yolki palki *as "fir tree sticks" and, more idiomatically, as "fiddlesticks" to express astonishment or irritation is correct. You have certainly done your research well and have provided the reader with everything he ever wanted to know about* yolki palki *but was afraid to ask. However, I have an amusing addition that your Embassy sources failed to supply. It concerns nuances that may further account for the popularity of this expression. Namely, the first syllable* yo- *is the same as the first syllable of a stronger Russian exclamation, a "four-letter" word to be exact,* yob tvoyu mat'. *Compare the Anglo-Saxon equivalent "f—— you." During conversation, in order to enhance the ambiguity of his utterance, the speaker will often stretch out the first syllable to keep his listener guessing by beginning with "Yyyoooo . . ." and then ending it with* -lki palki, *or just* -lki. *An English approximation would be "fffuuuuu . . .r tree." Such ambivalent usage of the expression is particularly popular with adolescents trying to keep their parents or teachers on edge.*

I was impelled to bring this nuance to your attention for fear that such important gaps in semantic comprehension could lead to communication problems on the highest levels of East-West negotiations.

Philip P. Ketchian
Belmont, Massachusetts

Dear Bill,

Reading your column on "fiddlesticks" and yolki palki, *I imagined with glee the discomfort of Mikhail Lysenko when you called his embassy for an explanation. Yes,* yolki palki *does literally translate as "Christmas tree sticks," and it is a mild and common expletive in Russian.*

But the fact of the matter is that yolki palki *has no relation whatsoever to trees or sticks. The exclamation in fact derives from the premier Russian curse,* Yob tvoiu mat', *which means "Fuck your mother." It is a venerable and potent curse, and rare is the Lysenko who isn't aware of its relationship with the euphemistic Christmas sticks.*

The bond, of course, is the opening Yo, *as in "your." The traditional use of* Yob tvoiu mat' *requires strong emphasis on the* Yo. *The family version opens similarly, but then dribbles off into a safe and essentially inane direction. English equivalents might be expletives like "Jeez," "fudge," or "friggin'."*

Were I doing the translation, I might have been tempted to go the (expletive deleted) route, or to substitute a euphemism from my adolescence, like "Friggin-A, I'm going." "Fiddlesticks" seems unduly archaic and Victorian, and gives the impression of a roly-poly pilot with granny glasses and an A. A. Milne vocabulary.

Serge Schmemann
Moscow, U.S.S.R.

(1)   ("I don't know what a 'subject on hand' is . . .)." May I suggest that "on hand" refers to "now," as in the French maintenir *and the Latin* manu tenere, *translated as "to know for certain" and, literally, "to hold in the hand" (according to my Webster's), from which, of course, we get our words* maintain, maintenance, *etc.*

(2)   As for the reason for the misuse of adventurist—*perhaps there was a sound-confusion with* adventuress, *a term describing an "aggressive" woman who is "expansionist" in intent.*

(3)   To your list of "marker" meanings, may I add that, to a doodler, a marker is a doodling tool?

Jane Freeman
New York, New York

Every automobile license plate in Connecticut is called a marker *by the police.*

W. L. Ridenour
Madison, Connecticut

Leak of the Week

Since it became Reagan administration policy (in National Security Decision Directive 84) to make all future memoirs subject to a security check for as long as the Administration official lives, the torrent of leaks from the Reaganauts has become a burden for Washington newshawks and newsdoves alike. The leakers figure, if they can't save it for the memoirs, they might as well put out the inside stuff while it's hot.

Here is the latest murmured memo from the National Security Council, in "Suggested Talking Points for the President" on the subject of arms-control talks.

"In the Start negotiations," goes the secret memo to Mr. Reagan, presumably on which he was to base his position in meetings with reporters and diplomats, "we have established four basic conditions (reductions, equality, stability, verificability), but beyond that we are flexible."

Verificability? Not since Alonzo McDonald, the management consultant who unblocked the flow of paper in the Carter White House, called for ways "to improve our effectificity" has there been such an exciting new noun regurgitated by the bureaucracy.

That's what happens when you build on top of superstructures. The root word is the verb *verify*, from the Latin *verus*, "true." The noun that comes from that is *verification*, a nice mouth-filler of a word that denotes what we must insist we get from the Soviets, who are probably cheating down there in the missile holes. The adjective, in the mind of the N.S.C. bureaucrat, came from the noun, which led him to *verificable* and then to the noun *verificability*, two words that do not exist.

The trick is to go back to the verb, *verify*, for the adjective, *verifiable* and then for a noun, *verifiability*. If they can figure that out at the N.S.C., maybe we can get the Start talks started.

Lex Appeal

Do you know where to find the world's largest collection of English dictionaries published before the twentieth century? You could look it up, as Casey Stengel* is reputed to have said: Indiana State University, where 7,000 titles are available to students specializing in lexicography.

I know this because I have just joined the Dictionary Society of North America by sending $15 to Edward Gates, the society's secretary-treasurer, at the Office of Continuing Education, Indiana State University, Terre Haute, Indiana 47809.

* This is a misattribution, as former *New York Times* sportswriter John Radosta has pointed out. The line is the title of a 1941 short story by James Thurber.

This entitles me to copies of the latest learned papers on semantics, etymology, vernaculars and other heavy stuff that pop grammarians crave.

This shameless plug is placed here because the society has only 233 members—now 234—despite its round-heeled willingness to admit anybody with an interest in the field. I know, from having to fight off blizzards of mail whenever I refuse to defend the narrow mathematical meaning of *parameter*, that there are figuratively thousands of would-be lexicographers around. (Yes, I meant *literally*, and used *figuratively* in error, as a play on the word it modified; that's good for twenty letters right there.)

Now these people have a society all their own, which Lexicographic Irregulars consider a kind of linguistic Rapid Deployment Force. Perhaps the Dictionary Society, in future deliberations, will examine Justice Byron White's dissent in the landmark legislative veto case for his use of the adjectival form of *truism:* "I do not dispute the Court's truismatic exposition of these clauses." Marc Stern, a New York attorney, wonders: Did he err, meaning *truistic*? Was he coining a new adjective because *truistic* looks too much like *altruistic*, or because *truismatic* lends an automatic connotation to the noun *truism*? How should future dictionaries handle this? Do landmark decisions contain nonce words? Should a simple mistake be immortalized in a dictionary? I can hardly wait for the next meeting of my society.

I am afraid that Justice White cannot be accused of using a nonce word when he used truismatic. *The* Oxford English Dictionary *(1933 ed.) lists the word. And* Webster's New International Dictionary, Second Edition *has* "truismatic . . . Also truistic." *For unexplained reasons, however,* Webster's Third Edition *dropped the word and lists* truistic *and then amazingly comes up with a third variation by saying* "Also truistical." *In any event, it would appear that the problem is not how "future dictionaries" should handle this, as you indicate, since "past dictionaries" have already handled it. I am confident that, influenced by Justice White's usage,* Webster's *in its Fourth Edition will restore* truismatic *to its proper place in the lexicographic universe. In view of the above historical facts, such restoration cannot be characterized as "immortalizing a simple mistake."*

> Henry C. Lind
> *Reporter of Decisions*
> *Supreme Court of the United States*
> *Washington, D.C.*

Like, No

"On Tuesday, vote like our world is at stake. Mondale for President."

Would *like* become a conjunction in a Mondale administration? It is not as if this is an idle question: In 1968, the Nixon admen used the same mistaken construction in a conscious effort to sound colloquial and appear informal, and that was the beginning of the slide into Watergate.

Vote as if standards are at stake: Mondale if you like, but not with *like* substituted for *as* or *as if*. I liked Ike and wish all candidates could be like Ike, but I want them to govern *as* Ike did. The deliberate, forced use of *like* in advertising is an itsy-poo way of saying, "See how much a regular guy I am," and should be resisted. After going with the flow on *none*, I feel good about standing up against *like*, as a pop grammarian should.

"It is not as if this is an idle question." For shame! Try "it is not as if this were an idle question." Although I have not found it in any prescriptive grammar, people I know would use "as though" rather than "as if" after a negative: "It is not as though this were an idle question."

> Ray Lurie
> New Haven, Connecticut

Please be better than a "pop grammarian" and do not spurn the subjunctive!
"It is not as if this is an idle question. . . ."
"Vote as if standards are at stake. . . ."
How about "were"???

> Your non-pop grammarian,
> José de Vinck
> Allendale, New Jersey

In your column on the incorrect substitution of "like" for "as," you write: "It is not as if this is [sic] an idle question. . . . Vote as if standards are [sic] at stake." You twice make the same mistake with "as if," as if standards were not at stake. Why? It is not as if this were an idle question (or the first time you committed this error).

"As if" should invariably be followed by a past conditional and not by a present form. As Fowler puts it, *"The mistake of putting the verb in a present tense is especially common after* it looks *or* seems, *where there is the insufficient excuse that the clause gives a supposed actual fact."*

It would be most instructive were you to devote part of a column to *"as if"* agreement and also, perhaps, the use of *"as if"* versus *"as though."* It's not as if everyone already knew the difference.

> Rabbi Lyle Kamlet
> Mount Vernon, New York

Logue-Rolling

Think of the barrels of ink and reams of paper that could be saved by writing *dialogue* as *dialog* and *catalogue* as *catalog*.* Some people prefer their *logues* sawed off, and most dictionaries turn palms up and shrug.

I like to leave it the old way, because the *u* preserves the way the word was spelled in Latin, *dialogus* (taken from the Greek *dialogos*), and because a mania for neatness drains the blood from the grinning cheeks of language.

The linguistic swingers at the Library of Congress disagree. Brian Wilkie of Champaign, Illinois, points to a line on the copyright page of every new book published in the United States: "Library of Congress Cataloging in Publication Data." Before getting to the spelling problem, he denounces the "utter incomprehensibility" of that phrase; I bucked his letter over to Librarian of Congress Dan Boorstin (whose book *The Discoverers* is replete with etymological delights), who bucked it down to Henriette Avram, who writes what is surely known in the Library as "the hyphen letter":"Librarians use the three-word phrase 'cataloging in publication,'" explains Mrs. Avram, "to refer to the process by which cataloging information is prepared prior to the actual publication of a book and printed in the book itself."

Since the phrase is used to modify a noun, why is it not hyphenated? "The answer . . . is lost in administrative history. Were we to begin again, we certainly would hyphenate the phrase." So why not change it now? "When we inventory the forms, letterheads, administrative references, informational brochures, organizational charts and job titles which would have to be changed," Mrs. Avram replies

---

* Or *monologue* as *monolog*. See "A Monolog on Dialog," page 133.

wearily, "we conclude that the taxpayers' money would be better spent cataloging more books."

Not good enough, Library; stop the presses! The revelation that every publisher is being forced to commit a solecism in every single book published in America is repugnant to defenders of the First Amendment and of the hyphen. (Idle grammarians have been searching for a good crusade and this may be it.) Is the integrity of American literature not worth a few measly bucks? Should not the prestigious Center for the Book send an expedition into the mists of administrative history to find the culprits and hyphenate them unmercifully? Has the greatest repository of learning in the world sunk to the perpetuation of error in the name of cost-benefit ratios?

Back to the spelling of *cataloging*, as the Library of Congress prefers. What happened to the *u*? "This is simply American versus British preference in spelling," asserts Mrs. Avram, on firmer ground this time, adding a nice touch: "American librarians eschew the *u* with vigo(u)r, while British librarians favo(u)r it." The Library of Congress, in a spirit of Atlantic amity, sticks in a *u* when joining in a cooperative venture like "Anglo-American Cataloguing Rules," but "to the extent that an institution (or a professional group) can be said to have a preference, our preference, as American librarians, is to spell the word without the *u*."

I would hang on to the *u* because hoary orthography makes it easier to go on etymological digs, and for this reason, too: As an old philologue (who has seen philologists come and go), I am pleased by the way the *u* contributes to the correct pronunciation of the *g*: *Logue* is surely pronounced with a hard *g*, as in the word *log*; but in the participle form, the dropping of the *u* gives the reader no signal. For example, *cataloguing* is indisputably pronounced with a hard *g*, but *cataloging* could be pronounced *loge*, as in *loge seat*—there ain't no such place as a cataloging camp.

But the Library of Congress wants to be non-U; that's all right, even Noah Webster fell on his face trying to simplify spelling, and there's no need to be a theologue about long-recorded variants. On those missing hyphens, however, no cost-benefit excuses, please. Get it right. Hang the expense.

Perhaps you are not familiar with the work of Melville Dewey (Melvil Dui), the founder of decimal classification and patron saint of librarians, who was "deeply devoted to the cause of simplified spelling."* At Columbia's School of Library Service I was led to believe that librarians spell catalog *without the* ue *because Mr.*

Dewey wrote it that way—period. Luckily, we have been spared some of his other "sugjestions."

> Helen M. Allen
> Librarian
> New York, New York

* Dewey Decimal Classification and Relative Index, Edition 17. Forest Press, Inc. of Lake Placid Club Education Foundation. 1975. Vol. I, p. 57.

I enjoyed your column about the non-u spelling used by the Library of Congress Cataloging in Publication program [me]. Two comments:

Of course they've dropped the u: this is the me generation.

Second, the people at the National Geographic Book Service, who are not linguistic swingers but have been known to oscillate decorously on occasion, dodge the u/eschew problem neatly in their publications. They use a combination of words and the Cataloging in Publication logotype, thus:

> Library of Congress $\overline{CIP}$ Data.

I've only ever heard the logo pronounced "see eye pea," instead of "sip," which I suppose is also possible. What do the people at Elsie say? And do they ever, like Georgetown students in my day, call the Library of Congress > L.C. > "Elsie"?

> Robert Arndt
> Editor, Aramco World Magazine
> Dhahran, Saudi Arabia

I submit that your "a few measly bucks" should be "a measly few bucks." It's not the bucks that are measly, but the fewness.

> J. Bryan, III
> Richmond, Virginia

Loud Abjection

A politician isn't even safe with a cliché anymore.

In Governor Cuomo's keynote address to the Democratic convention, he spoke with all appropriate compassion: "In our family are [sic] gathered everyone from the abject poor of Essex County in New York to the enlightened affluent of the gold coasts of both ends of our nation."

The affluent did not object to "enlightened," but the poor raised the roof about *abject*. Gifford A. Cross, the Republican chairman of the Essex County Board of Supervisors (who is not poor, but feels for them), said that many county residents had gone straight to the dictionary to look up *abject* and discovered it meant "miserable, wretched, degraded and lacking in self-respect."

Abject, from the Latin, means "cast off"—the *ject* has the same root as *jet*—and that was its earliest meaning. It later came to mean "despicable": Shakespeare used it to describe "paltry, servile, abject drudges." John Milton used it to mean "wretched": "To lowest pitch of abject fortune thou art fall'n." Servility became the key: Thomas O'Connor, biographer of Disraeli, wrote, "Those who in adversity are the most abject, are in prosperity the most insolent."

In our time, the word has been married to *poverty*, in the cliché *abject poverty*; however, this phrase has taken on the connotation of "really deep poverty" more than poverty that reduces people to cringing servility. Undoubtedly, Governor Cuomo used *abject* as an intensifier for *poor* rather than as a description of the degraded condition of the fine people of Essex County.

The governor, and others, will now know better: *Abject* has a meaning all its own, and not as part of a cliché. It still means what George Washington had in mind while addressing the Continental Army before the Battle of Long Island (now Nassau and Suffolk counties): "Our cruel and unrelenting enemy leaves us only the choice of brave resistance, or the most abject submission."

You defend New York's compassionate and eloquent Governor by saying "abject" poverty describes "really deep poverty" more than the servile dimension of being poor. But it is important to remain sensitive to what the Talmudic sages early recognized: that being poor does limit one's freedom in very real and serious ways. That's why it is bad to be poor. When the writer of Deuteronomy said, "The poor shall always remain in the land" he was referring to poverty as a relative situation having to do with the amount of freedom one had compared to more fortunate neighbors, rather than to material possessions. Let us seek to alleviate limitations on the freedom many Americans lack because of their limited financial resources.

Jonathan H. Gerard
Dover, New Hampshire

A grammarian you is (except when you and The New York Times *insist on sticking apostrophes into the 1980s and other dates) but an historian you ain't!*

The Battle of Long Island (27 August 1776) was fought in Brooklyn (Kings County). How did you ever place the Continental Army and the battle in Nassau and Suffolk counties? Bloody abject, I'd say.

Frederick Van Voorhees Bronner
Cornwall, Connecticut

The Battle of Long Island took place primarily in Kings County, a.k.a. Brooklyn. Some local chauvinists even have the effrontery to call it the Battle of Brooklyn. These chauvinists are still active, since they have been recently successful in changing the name (and presumably the purposes) of the 121-year-old Long Island Historical Society to the Brooklyn Historical Society.

Rufus B. Langhans
Town Historian
Huntington, New York

I was disappointed to find a misplaced "even" in the first sentence: "A politician isn't even safe with a cliché anymore." In this position, "even," which is an adverb of degree or intensity, qualifies "safe," and it implies that one might be more than safe. Had you consulted your authority, Fowler, on the placing of "even," you would have written, "A politician isn't safe even with a cliché anymore."

George S. Hendry
Princeton, New Jersey

Men!

"In looking for a word that would describe an individual who hated men," writes Dr. Warren Guntheroth, professor of pediatrics at the University of Washington,

"I found none. Comparable words include *misogynist* for those who hate women and *misanthrope* for those who hate mankind." Dr. Guntheroth suggests a new word for what he believes to be an unlabeled idea: *misandronist*, using the Greek root for "man."

He's not the only one. At the City University of New York, Charlotte Alexander, teaching "Women in Literature," wrote *misogyny* on her blackboard for the hatred of women, and then—lo!—she put what she thought was a coinage for the opposite: *misandry, misandrous*, etc.

Good thinking, but no coinage cigar. *Misandry*, from the Greek *misandros* for "hating men," is in the 1961 Merriam-Webster New International Dictionary, and the Oxford Dictionary Supplement traces it to 1946.

The word is pronounced as "Ms. Andry," but I wonder why we need the Greek word for it. What's wrong with good, old-fashioned *man-hater*?

You know full well what is wrong with "good, old-fashioned man-hater." *It lacks etymological seriousness. It lacks those Greco-Latin roots that bestow the necessary PMLA patina.*

A misogynist can hold his head up. A man-hater is just a female crank.
> Maureen Mullarkey
> Brooklyn, New York

We have been taken by guile and surreption! When I read, at the end of your column, your simple suggestion for one who hates males, "man-hater," I automatically substituted "person-hater."
> Arthur J. Morgan
> New York, New York

Mindset in Concrete

Reporters at *Newsweek* magazine have their minds set on *mindset*.

Vogue-word watcher Albert J. Pucciarelli of Montvale, New Jersey, sends along two uses from a single issue: A Lockheed spokesman is quoted as saying: "We are not bound by a research-and-development mind-set," and Senator Howard Baker of Tennessee, who is keen on retirement from the Senate, says, "I need to shed the Congressional mind-set." To those citations, we can add this letter from Eugene V. Rostow to *The New York Times*, praising the reporter who "accurately portrays the mind-set of the officials who condescendingly dismiss President Reagan's statement that Israeli settlements in the West Bank are 'not illegal.' "

The word was presaged in a 1692 tract suggesting that a way existed to "give the Mind a noble sett" and in John Stuart Blackie's 1852 work about language learning: "In the . . . process by which the mother tongue is acquired, the mind acquires a habit and a set." Educational psychologists began using *mental set* in 1913, and *mindset* made its appearance in the mid-20's.

What does it mean? *Tendency, attitude* or *inclination* used to be the primary meaning, akin to *frame of mind*; now the primacy goes to *fixed state of mind* or *predetermined view*. Like a football lineman who goes into a three-point set, the person in a mindset is declared offside if he budges an inch. Those who grimly refuse to allow a compound noun to shed its hyphen have an antihyphen mindset.

Should you not have said, "Those who grimly refuse to allow a compound noun to shed its hyphen have a prohyphen *mindset"? Such persons, insisting on the use of the hyphen, can hardly be labeled* antihyphen.*"*

Stuart H. Steinbrink
New York, New York

Miss, Mrs., Ms.

Geraldine A. Ferraro—that is her maiden name—prefers the honorific *Ms*. However, many newspapers and magazines have stoutly resisted the adoption of *Ms*., some because it seems like propaganda for the women's movement, others because it conveys less information than *Miss* (used when the woman is single, or is using her maiden name) or *Mrs*. (used when the person is married or widowed).

To those publications resisting the privacy-protecting *Ms*., the Democratic vice-presidential candidate has asked that she be identified as "Mrs. Ferraro." Her reasoning is that *Miss* would indicate that she is single, which she is not, and *Mrs*. indicates that she is a married woman. Some newspapers, including *The New York Times*, have gone along with her request and refer to her as "Mrs. Ferraro."

But she is not Mrs. Ferraro. Her mother is Mrs. Ferraro. The Democratic candidate is the former Miss Ferraro, who is now Mrs. John Zaccaro, and who can also be described as Mrs. Geraldine Zaccaro or Mrs. Geraldine Ferraro Zaccaro. She has her choice of being known as Miss Ferraro or Mrs. Zaccaro, but not—to my way of thinking—as "Mrs." Ferraro, a person she is not.

You cannot simply decree, "Call me *Mrs.*, because I'm married, but use my maiden name, because I don't want to use my married name." On the contrary, no matter what politicians demand, writers of English should be consistent: The *Mrs.* goes with the married name; the *Miss* goes with the maiden name.

It's one thing to be deferential to feminists' wishes; it is another to twist the meaning of words to accommodate any political leader's desire to style herself any way she likes. If Mrs. Zaccaro or Miss Ferraro can be called "Mrs. Ferraro," why can't her opponent, Mr. Bush, ask to be called "Mr. Lincoln"? What if he asked to be called "Mrs. Bush"? Would newspapers refuse him the honorific he might prefer in this admittedly outrageous example just because he is not Mrs. Bush? Miss Ferraro is not Mrs. Ferraro, yet she gets the honorific she prefers.

That's not quite accurate: The honorific she prefers is *Ms.*, and the *Mrs.* is to her the lesser evil than to appear in a photo with her husband and three children with the caption identifying her as *Miss*, which does not quite fit in with traditional family values.

It breaks my heart to suggest this, but the time has come for *Ms.* We are no longer faced with a theory, but a condition. It is unacceptable for journalists to dictate to a candidate that she call herself *Miss* or else use her married name; it is equally unacceptable for a candidate to demand that newspapers print a blatant inaccuracy by applying a married honorific to a maiden name.

That leaves *Ms.* By using the title, as fuzzy as *Mr.* is to bachelors or married men, the person is saying, "This is the name I go by, and it may be mine or my husband's, and I may or may not be married." By accepting it, editors are saying, "This is what she styles herself, and you will have to find out elsewhere if she is married or if she started out in life with this name."

Ms. is deliberately *msterious*, but at least it is not deliberately *msleading*.

From the Editors of *The New York Times*:

Some days the Title Question appears to claim more time—and ignite more passion—than the East-West arms race.

We accept anyone's choice—in this case, Geraldine Ferraro's choice—of a professional name. But a title is not part of the name. Publications vary in tone, and the titles they affix to names will differ accordingly. The *Times* clings to traditional ones (*Mrs., Miss* and *Dr.*, for example). As for *Ms.*—that useful business-letter coinage—we reconsider it from time to time; to our ear, it still sounds too contrived for news writing.

Among traditional titles, why not heed the bearer's choice, assuming it isn't deceitful? Representative Ferraro's *Mrs.* seems no more a matter of "right" or "wrong" than the preferences of Beverly Greenough *(Miss Sills)*, Joan Dunne *(Miss Didion)*, Diana Silberstein *(Miss Ross)*, Meryl Gummer *(Miss Streep)* or Dr. Henry A. Kissinger (who favors *Mr.*).

As Mr. Safire might put it, they're all entitled.

I can't believe it finally happened. You are wrong and I am right. I've been waiting for this moment for years.

Mrs. *means "the wife of."*

I go along with you this far: Geraldine cannot be Mrs. Ferraro. Where we part company is with your assertion that she can be described as Mrs. Geraldine Zaccaro. No way. She can be Geraldine Zaccaro or Mrs. John Zaccaro (the wife of John Zaccaro). She cannot be "the wife of Geraldine Zaccaro."

As a truly tasteful woman I would never describe myself as Mrs. Edith Lank. In recent years I've become so liberated I don't even enjoy Mrs. Norman Lank. I call myself Edith Lank. Walter Mondale calls himself Walter Mondale. Why not call the lady Geraldine Ferraro?

I realize reporters have a problem when the person is mentioned a second time in a news story. Mondale is then called "Mondale." Ferraro should be called "Ferraro."

You're right, Mr. *is fuzzy. So is* Ms. *Honorifics are probably out of style. I addressed you as "William Safire" (whether you're married is irrelevant) and you are welcome, should you wish, to address me as*

> *Edith Lank*
> *Rochester, New York*

You wrote Ms. *(with the final period), after the models of* Mrs. *and* Mr. *The last two honorifics are contractions of* Mistress *and* Mister *and are therefore written with the final period in the manner of most abbreviations.* Ms, *however, is not an abbreviated word but an arbitrary symbol devised to parallel* Mr. *in avoiding reference to marital status. It should therefore be written without the period.*

Ernest Simon
Montvale, New Jersey

A Monolog on Dialog

"Gotcha!" I ejaculated (I've been rereading *Tom Swift and His Electric Rifle* and want to recapture that perfectly acceptable verb from the sex-advice crowd).

My glee was in catching Dan Rather with his grammatical anchor dragging. Introducing a debate among Walter Mondale, Jesse Jackson and Gary Hart, the CBS newsman called for "a dialogue among three men. . . ."

Had I been one of the debate participants, I would have turned to the moderator and said: "No, Mr. Rather. You can have a dialogue between two or a discussion among three, but you cannot have a dialogue among more than two people." This would have locked up the smart-aleck vote and attracted all those who enjoy seeing the media put down.

I would also have been egregiously wrong. My red-faced press secretary, the day after the debate, would have had to issue a "clarification" (nobody issues a correction anymore) along these lines: "Like most red-blooded, God-fearing, solecism-avoiding Americans, Mr. Safire, at age 54 or 53, has always thought that the *di-* in *dialogue* meant 'two,' as it does in *dichotomy* or *dichloride*. He realizes now he was in error and wishes to apologize to the legion of Greek-speaking Americans who have pointed out to him that the prefix *dia-* means 'across,' as in *diagonal* and *diameter*. He looks forward to having a dialogue with all of them and withdraws his diatribe against Mr. Rather."

That would have ruined my campaign in at least three states, throwing me off stride, enabling interlocutors to dwell on my minor problem and to ignore my message. To set the record straight: People have been confused about *dialogue* for nearly five centuries. The word *monologue*, meaning a "dramatic soliloquy" or speech by one person, was coined on the mistaken notion that if *dialogue* meant "two," then one person talking would be a *monologue*. Sir Thomas More took the mistake one step further in 1532: "As though it wer a dyalogue, or rather a tryalogue betwene himself, the messenger and me." Sir Thomas was beheaded by

Henry VIII and was canonized for his martyrdom; however, he is remembered by lexicographers as a saint who wrote *Utopia* in good Latin but didn't know his Greek prefixes.

The monologue-dialogue-trialogue misconception could be carried on to *megalogue*, a babble of a million rabble, or even *googologue*, the ultimate conversation, but it is still rooted in confusion. If you want to limit your meaning to two people, use *duologue* (which between Batman and Robin becomes a Dynamic Duologue).

When asked by Mr. Rather to list his weaknesses, candidate Jackson came up with a skillful riposte: "I spent so much time trying to maximize my few strengths, I don't have a lot of dialogue about my weaknesses." In this use, *dialogue* loses its specific meaning of "cross-talk" and becomes a general commodity, like the lumpish *conversation* in the Billy Joel song "Just the Way You Are" or the gossipy *chitchat*, the 1710 reduplication of *chat*, a conversational shortening of *chatter*.

Now that we have legitimized the noun as talk between two or among more, is it O.K. to use *dialogue* as a verb? Such a use has been recorded since 1597, and resistance to "I want to dialogue with you fine Greek folks" is misplaced.

If you think the noun has been overused—and no phrase is more worn to a frazzle than *meaningful dialogue*—try *colloquy*, which carries the connotation of "formal discussion" as if between two speakers on the Senate floor. More widely understood, if less chic, terms are *conversation* and *discussion*. Want to choose a direct phrase for what the with-it crowd likes to call *dialogue*? Let's talk it over.

You begin a sentence with "The word monologue, *meaning a 'dramatic soliloquy' or speech by one person. . . ." Actually, your appositive gloss of* monologue *is slightly inaccurate, at least in a dramatic sense (i.e., a dramatic monologue). A dramatic monologue is a speech by one person to a silent listener. A dramatic soliloquy is a speech by one person to no one. Both speeches by definition must be aloud, but in the former someone is listening while in the latter the character merely thinks out loud to a play's audience. Is the distinction worthwhile? Yes. When a character speaks his/her thoughts aloud to no one, that character tells the truth inasmuch as that character knows the truth. In a dramatic monologue, however, the speaker, knowing he/she has an audience present, may or may not tell the truth. Obviously a soliloquy makes it easier for the viewing audience to know what a character is really like, while with a monologue that audience must first determine the speaker's reliability before coming to terms with the truth or the falsehood of that speaker's speech.*

Thanks for giving a pair of professors a moment to sound off.

Hal Blythe
Charlie Sweet
Richmond, Kentucky

I think you're wrong about something, but it's not your fault. Dictionaries are to blame.

In "Monolog on Dialog" you define a monologue *as a "dramatic soliloquy." It ain't necessarily so—not in showbusiness, anyway.*

When Juliet does her "Thou knowst the mask of night is on my face," she's talking to Romeo and that's a monologue. When Hamlet spouts "To be or not to be," he's all alone, thinking out loud, and that's a soliloquy. The two words are not synonymous; the only thing they have in common is length.

If more proof is needed, just think about all those great monologists in vaudeville. Had Myron Cohen been billed a "soliloquist," he wouldn't have drawn flies. An aborted career and what a loss to the Ed Sullivan Show*!*

Back to dictionaries. Mercy me! they contradict themselves and each other. Now that you've been filled in, I do hope you'll straighten them out.

> *Judy Magee*
> *New York, New York*

Bravo to you for your attempt to reclaim some of our more expressive symbols from the Philistines—I used to enjoy throwing out an occasional "ejaculated" along with a few others which now bring embarrassed looks from my children. I will persist in referring to "verbs of being" as "copulative verbs" to my dying day.

The main purpose of this communication is to offer a correction to your discussion of the use of the prefix di- *and the two examples you used to illustrate its meaning of "two." You were correct with* dichloride *(di chlor̸ ide), but well off the mark with* dichotomy*. The letter elements* di *in that word are not separate elements, but are, instead, a part of a totality—*dicho*. Although the meaning carried is virtually the same as that carried by* di-*, they are of considerable difference structurally (dicho tom̸ y). The correct analysis of that word is as follows:*

> *dicho—indicating two parts or a division into two parts; also dichoga- mous (dicho gam̸ ous)*
>
> *tomy—indicating a cutting of a specified part or tissue; also craniot- omy (cranio tom̸ y) and lobotomy (lobo tom̸ y)*

> *Raymond E. Laurita*
> *Yorktown Heights, New York*

"Uneasy lies the head that wears a crown," whether of kingship or arbiter of language. Will the imperfections never end! In your would-be response to Mr. Rather's presumed error you have compounded the imperfections. I quote, ". . . but you cannot have a dialogue among more than two people." Therein lies your

error—you should have used "persons" not "people," since you implied a talk between two individuals. "People" refers to a community, a populace, human beings in abundance.* This error is so common that when a writer, lecturer, or journalist uses "persons" instead of "people" when referring to individuals it calls for a celebration. Radio and television commentators and journalists invariably follow a numerical statistic with "people," such as "fifteen people were hurt in a fire." Pure common sense refutes the logic of such a statement, yet hundreds of times daily this grammatical error assaults the airwaves and appears in print.

This usage is equally as common as the misuse of "like," which invites a comparison, but speakers and writers tack on a verb creating an awkward phrase and grammatically unacceptable usage. Weather reporters say, "It looks like it's going to rain." If they want to use that many words they should substitute "as if" for "like," or simply, "It looks like rain." It seems as if nary a media person exists who doesn't flout the English language as these erroneous forms of speech race out to reach, and teach, millions of listeners.

Mabel Garis
Amherst, Massachusetts

*See Random House Dictionary, *Webster's and* Wilson Follett.

Are you certain that it was Tom Swift who was guilty of that "perfectly acceptable verb" that you were trying to recapture from the sex-advice crowd? I recall that Sam, the youngest of the Rover Boys, was famous for his ejaculations but I always thought that Tom Swift was a cut above Sam, Tom and Dick Rover. Now that you have tarnished his image I can't help wondering about Frank Merriwell, Tom the Bootblack and all those other juvenile heroes of seventy years ago.

Guy Fry
West Grove, Pennsylvania

"Mousse Call"

Under the heading "Mousse is on the Loose," *Time* magazine reports that the latest fad in the $3 billion American hair-care industry is *mousse:* "Not a rich dessert, but a hair-styling foam."

To be candid, I was caught off guard and would have defined *mousse* as oil-industry jargon for the dark brown mixture of oil and water following an oil spill, posing a hazard to marine life and birds.

But foam is foam, and the frothy French word for it is *mousse*. The hot new word is probably rooted in the Latin *mel* for "honey," used to make *mulsa*, a mead or honey mixture that grabbed the Roman orgygoers. That delicious English word *mellifluous*, "flowing with honey," is related, as is the name of the character *Melibeus* ("a man that drynketh hony") in Chaucer's *The Canterbury Tales*. The French *mousse* may also be translated as "moss," that foamlike growth of very small plants.

About a century ago, *mousse* came to America as a description of a light spongy food, usually containing gelatin or egg whites. In the newest use, that food association is recalled and exploited: *Chocolate mousse* is a product for brunettes and *strawberry mousse* is for redheads.

"*Mousse* is a foam that stiffens hair into certain positions," says Lucien Sriqui of Lucien et Eivind, hair designers to the stars of Washington, in whose place of business more secrets are passed than in any Capitol cloakroom. (*Hair designer* seems to be replacing *hair stylist*; the old *hairdresser*, it appears, has blown dry.) "You can also mold hair with sculpturing lotions," confides Mr. Sriqui, "and *gels* do the same thing—each has a different selling point. *Mousse* is a popular way to treat hair these days, with the variety of styles: bobs, waves, windblown, boyish, cropped and the 'spike look' of the punks. *Mousse* is a way to control the hair, to shape it however you want."

Don't mess with *mousse:* What gets in your hair ultimately gets in your language.

You referred to ". . . mulsa, a . . . mixture . . ." If memory serves, mulsum is the correct spelling for the honey-wine mixture, a neuter singular noun.

> William A. Tisdale
> Burlington, Vermont

I liked your piece on the hair-styling "mousse." I have some in my bathroom and under the word "mousse" it calls itself "bodifying foam." I never heard of the verb "to bodify," did you? I laugh every time I see it. Maybe in the future a euphemism for death will be "debodification."

> Nina Lockwood
> Rochester, New York

My Dear Computer

Ahoy!

That was the word Alexander Graham Bell chose to be the salutation for his telephone calls. That nautical variant of *Hey*! did not catch on with landlubbers or phonelubbers; most telephonists experimenting with the new device preferred the more conversational *Hello*; thus, *Ahoy*! became A.T.&T.'s first divestiture.

Today we are searching for a salutation that befits a new form of communication. Old-fashioned "physical" mail—letters that fold into envelopes, postcards that have to be schlepped on human backs, even messages written on those pink "While you were out" pads—is obsolescent. While you were out, the world changed.

Oh, the Postal Service will linger on for a few generations, and absolutely-positively overnight delivery services will arrive breathlessly before noon in offices for years, but they know that the handkerchief fluttering on the horizon belongs to the computerized waver of the future.

The new (why "high"?) technology of transporting words and ideas has us in thrall; those who hang back, writing "Dear Whoozit" on paper, will soon be off the screens of the marketing geniuses who have fashioned the oxymoron "personal computer."

Because these machines are in the word-process of revolutionizing mail, language must adapt. We must remember who is in charge: Language comes first;

the method of communication comes second. With that firmly understood, we can cave in gracefully to the demands of electronic mail.

This department, ear tuned to the diode dialect, has advertised to Lexicographic Irregulars (Word-Process Corps) for an electronic etiquette. When reaching out across the ether through interminable terminals, how do we sign on to the human recipient? How do "hackers" bid each other an affectionate adieu? How do the rest of us affix the stamp of our human identity on our electronic messages?

"Most electronic mail systems automatically provide some sort of heading for you," explains Richard Wiggins, a systems analyst at Michigan State University's computer lab. "If I were to send a message to you over the mail system I wrote, it might begin like this: *7 Message from: Richard Wiggins (Date. Hour. Minute. Second.) Lines= 22 Seen. Re: Your column on electronic etiquette. Mr. Safire:*"

That's brisk and business-like, I suppose, but it makes me feel like a cipher, especially since the closing includes a "prompt" of *reply / ignore / delete / output* telling me to reply to the current message, skip it and feel guilty, delete it from my mailbox, or to out my put, whatever that means.

"Thus, the message is surrounded by a system-supplied header at the beginning," writes Mr. Wiggins, "and a system query at the end. Still, people often do choose to supply their own greetings and 'signatures.' In my example message above, I chose to include *Mr. Safire:* as a sort of salutation. The type of salutation varies from user to user. Some people begin messages with *Hi there*, and others may put in the word *Greetings*."

Not *Dear, My Dear* or *Dearest*, because electronic mail is—at least in its embryonic stage—less formal than a letter. It is more akin to an interoffice memo or a friendly telephone call, and you do not begin those with *Dear* unless you want to stimulate gossip at the water cooler.

(Date, hour: minute: second)/ From: Tom McSloy/To: William Safire/ TL 554-4062/ Z35TOM at IPODOS/ SAFIRE at NYTIMES/. Beneath that heading, duly printed out by a typist whom I take to be named Daisy Wheel, is this message: "Bill, this is what a piece of electronic mail sent to you might look like if you were on I.B.M.'s internal telecommunications network, VNET. All the gobbledygook at the top merely identifies sender and receiver, date and time. In my imagination, you are userid 'SAFIRE' at node 'NYTIMES.'"

We userids get all our mail at this node. "Since this is in memo format," continues Mr. McSloy at I.B.M. in Poughkeepsie, New York, "I don't use the *Dear* salutation; but I soften the opening line of most memos I write by using the receiver's first name. I use your first name, even though we have not met, because in I.B.M. everyone from the C.E.O. on down is called by his or her first name." (Presumably, if both boss and office boy are named "Bill," some process exists to differentiate them.)

Some correspondents see the mail of the future unadorned by any humanizing frivolity: *(Date, time) safire 5556666 NYT neibauer 70365,770 Saw EMAIL article. I don't see any problem. off (time).* The author of that chilling missive, Alan Neibauer of Philadelphia, envisions a marriage proposal similarly addressed and concluding *Happiest person in the world if you ***DATA CARRIER LOST ***ALL PORTS BUSY.*

Do computer manufacturers and software creators feel the need for social graces in messages? Evidently so; *user-friendliness* is the jargon for the way to take the hard, mechanical edge off communication between and among people and machines. "I tend to say *Hello*," writes Peter McWilliams, author of *The Word Processing Book.* Herbert Cooper of Queens Village, New York, goes further: "I feel electronic mail should be treated just like 'analogue mail,'" he writes, using a new retronym. "I always start my messages *Dear So-and-so* and end them *Love, Herb.* If my message is short (two sentences or less), I may write something like *So-and-So—The system is down.—Herb.* I feel there is no reason to develop special rules for electronic mail. Love, Herb."

Barry Fellman of Miami disagrees: "Since electronic mail is different from the stuff we've had before, I don't see why we should stick with the old rules of etiquette. Electronic mail should open with a *greetbyte* and close with a *goodbyte.*" That's only the beginning: "Since the computer uses one byte of memory to represent an alphameric character, the only logical choice for the opening greetbyte is *O.* The closing goodbyte should be *C.* Such brief openings and closings," argues Mr. Fellman, "will eliminate the needless typing of extraneous words and the inevitable headscratching that comes when you can't figure out how to address your boss or how to choose between *best regards* and *electronically yours.*"

All right, everybody, here's a chance to flame like mad was a message sent out over "usenet" by Ellen Walker at Carnegie-Mellon University in Pittsburgh, alerting users, or usenetters, to my search. *He didn't give an electronic address to send opinions to, so you'll have to use (yech) U.S. mail.*

Perusing all this old-fashioned mail about the newfangled mail, I can conclude:

(1) *Dear* will not make the transition from paper to screen. (Sorry, Herb.)
(2) *Ahoy*! is not a suitable substitute.
(3) Neglect of any personal salutation makes people feel uncomfortable, and a salutation will emerge.
(4) *Hi there*! will not do for a rising tycoon, though it may suffice for a kid breaking into our early-warning radar system.
(5) *Hello* is nice, especially if connected to a first name, but is probably too closely identified with telephone communication.
(6) The leading salutation at the moment is the use of a first name at the start of the body of the message, following the formal name

at the top of the address. Wise parents will stop naming children
Bill or Mary and will choose Ebenezer or Abigail, setting them
apart from all the other potential recipients of their mail.

How to conclude? *Thirty*, writes the old newshand. *Love*, writes Herb. *Off*,
snorts Neibaurer. Nothing, writes the man from I.B.M. My own preference:
REPLY / IGNORE / DESTROY.

My Little Chickadee

"Anyone who hates children and dogs," W. C. Fields was supposed to have said,
"can't be all bad."

In the current *Bartlett's Quotations*, credit is given to Leo Rosten, author of
The Joys of Yiddish, who used the line in a tribute to the great comedian in 1939.

Now comes word from John Duffie, columnist for *Monday* magazine, published
in Victoria, British Columbia, who found an article by Cedric Worth in the
November 1937 issue of *Harper's* magazine, in a piece titled "Dog Food for
Thought": "Mr. Buron Darnton relieved himself of a deathless truth: 'No man
who hates dogs and children,' he said, 'can be all bad.' "

Earlier citations will be welcomed; nobody who hates etymologists and antholo-
gists. . . .

I did not *say, of the incomparable W. C. Fields, "Anyone who hates children and
dogs can't be all bad." What I said, at that Masquers Club "roast," was: "Any man
who hates* babies *and dogs can't be all bad." (See the reports in* Time, *Feb. 27,
1939, p. 30, and the* L.A. Herald and Express, *Feb. 17, 1939.)*

*The peculiar events that preceded my entirely off-the-cuff remark (I was never
told I would be called upon to lead off the evening's tributes) are described in
detail in my darling book,* The Power of Positive Nonsense, *pp. 113–17. It has
amused me, down the years, to see the epigram attributed to Fields himself, which
is tantamount to having Washington credited with "First in war, first in peace,
first (etc. etc.)."*

Leo Rosten
New York, New York

I thought you might like to read H. Allen Smith's version of Leo Rosten's "dogs and little children" quotation. This is from Lost in the Horse Latitudes, *pp. 190–191, 1944:*

> *They gave a dinner not so long ago to honor W. C. Fields for having finished out forty years in show business. The speakers started speaking in the middle of the green beans and gooey sentiment was passed around in washtubs. Orators such as Eddie Cantor and George Jessel stood up and talked and let the tears flow down their cheeks until it was almost necessary to club them to the floor in order to stop them. Why they call those weepers comedians is one of the larger mysteries of life. There were other recitations, long and dull, and it was coming along toward two or three o'clock in the morning. The newspapermen were fidgeting and squirming and yawning and now and then gulping water to avoid heaving up their leg of lamb with mint sauce.*
>
> *At last the toastmaster struggled to his feet. Everyone uttered a quiet prayer, hopeful that this time he would dismiss the class. He didn't.*
>
> *"And now," he said, "just one more speaker and we'll call it a night. It is my pleasure, gentlemen, to present you with Dr. Leo C. Rosten, who has a few remarks."*
>
> *The newspapermen groaned. A doctor yet! Probably a professor ready to give a paper on "The Anatomy of the Belly Laugh." Dr. Rosten was not known to them at that time as the genius who, among other brilliant achievements, had given the world the incomparable H*Y*M*A*N* K*A*P*L*A*N.*
>
> *He stood up and said: "It is my opinion that any man who hates dogs and little children can't be* all *bad."*
>
> *Then he sat down, and the newspapermen emerged from their torpor and cheered him as if he had just announced the death of Hitler.*

Michael Jones
Bellevue, Iowa

My Name Ain't Mac, Buddy

Hey, you!

That is an unfriendly, condescending way to hail someone.

Sir?

That is the call of the wimp.

Say there, good buddy. . . .

Now we are into the complex field of interpersonal relationships expressed by salutations between people who do not know each other. The issue was raised in this space. . . . ("In this space" is long for "here" and the passive voice is an arch way of avoiding the first-person pronoun. Start again.) Not long ago, I wrote. . . . ("Not long ago" is wimplish, a language used by people who hail gas-station attendants with a timorous, milque-toasted *Sir?* The phrase *not long ago* not only fails to convey useful information, but is an anticommunicative device used by writers of wimplish to clear their throats. Start again again.)

In 1984, I posed a question that bothers everyone driving into a gas station and being greeted by the back of a gas-pump jockey: What is the most common way of attracting the attendant's attention? "In these parts," glumly responds Edmund DeWan of Urbana, Illinois, "the going solution is to dispense with the formalities and lean on the horn." That is unacceptable; horn-honking and engine-revving are for the tongue-tied, and this is a language column.

The response of Lexicographic Irregulars from Full-Serve Island reveals not only the diversity of our dialect in coming up with sounds attracting attention, but the richness of our vocabulary in giving names to strangers, as well as the nuance within each hailing that defines the status between hailer and hailee.

One sound used to gain attention is the loud greeting. Most popular is the interrogative *Hello?* similar in meaning to *Are you there?* Another is the determinedly cheerful *Good morning!* which should not be confused with the friendly greeting of the same name, but means: "I am here making this sound and I expect you to turn around."

Hey! by itself is rarely used, except in complaint; the call is almost always accompanied by some characterization of the person being called. More about the variety of hey-riders later. *Say* is less offensive than *hey*.

A barking locution that is on the rise is *Yo!* which requires no modifying appellation. *"Yo* is my favorite expression to use to get someone's attention," writes Charles Rausch of Manchester, Pennsylvania. "It is friendly and unassuming, unlike the antagonistic *Hey, you.*" The word was recorded in 1420 as a hunter's exclamation of excitement and, as *yeoh*, was heard in the West Indies in 1806 used by black sailors hauling in a rope. Its current popularity seems to have started in Philadelphia, as in *"Yo,* feel like a cheesteak sandwich on Sewth Street?" One meaning is "Hello" and "You there," with a cordial, informally polite connotation; a secondary meaning, when the syllable is given a more severe intonation, is "Watch yourself" or "Move out."

"I have nonprofessionally assumed a derivation from *here,*" responds J. L. Dillard, author of *Black English,* to a query about the origin of *yo,* "based on /hya/, a rather frequent Afro-Creole form. . . . The 'r-less' dialects, of which Black English is one, have final /-schwa/ in such words, and /schwa/ becomes /ow/ just as in *dynomite.*" As I get it, *here* is pronounced *HEE-yuh,* which changes to *HEE-yo,* to *HYO* and finally *YO.*

Professor Dillard's hunch is corroborated by Stephen Pickering, a night editor at *The New York Times,* who recalls, "I heard *Yo!* used in the Army as an acknowledgment, as a response by soldiers to their names being called out in roll call." The original response was *Present* or *Here,* and it is a fair assumption that *yo* came from *here.*

Back to *hey*'s helpers. Most hailings consist of an opening noise—*hey, say,* a whistle, or the more Neanderthal *um* or *uh*—followed by the hailname. These hailnames sometimes conceal codes of behavior or supposed taboos: "I yelled to a young man leaning over a car, *'Hey, pal,* do you serve gas here or what?' " writes Don Twomey of Jackson Heights, New York. "He yelled back, 'Don't call me *pal*—that's a Mafiosa word for *punk.*' Deciding immediately he was privy to information not at my disposal, I excused myself for my insensitivity and shot the hell out of there."

Hey, Mac and *hey, buddy* are terms most often heard in the Northeast, modifying the imperious *hey* with a friendly, neutral name. *Good buddy* is trucker's lingo used by CB'ers. My own preference has been *Hey, Mac*, perhaps reflecting my own regional background; Jesse Hackell of New City, New York, reports using it as in *"Hey, Mac*, how come you didn't come out to sell me gas when the whatchamacall-it went ding?"

A study of hailings done by the *Dictionary of American Regional English* lexicographers at the University of Wisconsin shows that sex, age and social class affect the way people address other people.

If the gas-station attendant is considerably younger than you are and is male, by far the most frequent name you call out is *son* or *sonny*. If you are formal or want to sound stern or authoritative, you will say, *young man*. *Buddy*, with its diminutive *bud* and variant *bub*, trails behind, with the Southern *boy* less frequently used now because it is considered an ethnic slur. *Man*, as in *Hey, man*, is favored by many blacks, as are *dude* and *bubba*. *Fella* is heard, as is *kid, lad, sport* and *buster*. Recently, I have heard *guy* gain frequency.

If the male attendant is older than you, a note of greater respect is expected: Choices include *brother, neighbor* and *friend*, and in the West, *pardner*. According to *DARE*, the most frequent name is *mister*, closely followed by *sir*, then the more occasional *buddy, fella, Mac, Jack, Joe, pal* and *you*. Most elders do not mind being called *cap'n*, but there are those geezers who get riled up by *gramps*, and many old men dislike *stranger*, when it is you who are the stranger. To Richard DeLia of New York I am indebted for *ace*, which has a 1930's sound, *champ* and *chief*. Hal Goodtree of Montclair, New Jersey, once a gas jerk himself, recalls being called *Slick*. The British form, *mate*, is sometimes heard here, as are the rare *old chap* and *my man*.

Female attendants get called *miss* overwhelmingly, with no connection to age or marital status, followed by *ma'am* by those who are more respectful or want to call attention to the age of the hailee. In recent years, *lady* has lost some of its harsh sound, and *Hey, lady!* is accepted with fewer complaints. However, *sweetie, hon, cutie, good-lookin', doll, peaches* and *honeybunch* may invite the twisting of a gas line around the neck. Not even *beautiful*, reverently whispered, is considered acceptable. Nobody says *toots* anymore.

When women hail young men, the names range from the formal *young man*, to the neutral *hello*, to the come-on *tiger* and *handsome*. Women hailing other women usually choose *miss*, but have been heard to blossom with *dearie* or *dear* and to tallulah with *dahling*. With the demise of the television series *The Goldbergs, Yoo-hoo!* went out.

What hailname is used at androgynous service stations, when the age and sex of the gas-station attendant cannot be determined? At that point, hailers are afflicted with immediate politeness, because they cannot say "Hey, sir or madam," which is the equivalent of saying "Hey, you of indeterminate age and sex."

At that point, the practice of Coral Samuel of West Tisted in Britain is to be recommended. "I would say, '*Excuse me*, my engine seems to be burnt out.'"

"Yo" is a naval term. It is my response of preference when answering the roll call in the Democratic Caucus. ("Here" seems a little too much like fifth grade, and could give the Minority Leader ideas.) Those West Indian sailors in 1806 were hauling in a line, not a rope. There are five ropes on a ship. One is the wheel rope. I forget the other four.

Daniel P. Moynihan
New York, New York

Your column on the various meanings of "yo" was interesting, but did not, I feel, go far enough. An underground "gossip tabloid" known as "The Daily Dish" ran the following:

"YO" ENTERS THE DICTIONARY

After years of debate, The American Standard Dictionary *has decided that the word "Yo" has entered common English usage and has listed it in their forthcoming edition. It is defined as follows: yo / yo' / Amer. interj. (you or your) 1. Hey! 2. Hey, you! 3. Hey, you guys! 4. Hey, what's goin' on? 5. Hey, what's happ'nin'? 6. Hey, man, what's kickin' down? 7. Give me one of those. 8. Want one of these? 9. How much is that? 10. What time is it? 11. Hold that train door! 12. Gotta match? 13. Gotta light? 14. I got this. 15. You got that? 16. Look out! 17. Gimme some. 18. Watch out! 19. Get back! 20. Watch yourself! 21. Catch! 22. Here! 23. There! 24. You! 25. You, there! 26. Did you see that? 27. Uh-huh. 28. Okay. 29. Right. 30. I got it. 31. Check it out! 32. Look at that! 33. Look at this. 34. Right on! 35. Tell it like it is. 36. Go for it! 37. Get down! 38. Do it!*

The author is one Jim Mullen.

Nina Garfinkel
New York, New York

In reading "My Name Ain't Mac, Buddy," I was struck by the fact that throughout your discussion of yo you failed to mention its German connotation. I grew up in southern Manitoba, an area much settled by Mennonite Germans. (In fact, there are more Mennonites concentrated there than in any other place in the world.) These fine people speak Platt Deutsch, or *Low German, a language they have carried with them from Holland, to Switzerland, to the Vistula delta, to Russia's steppes, to China, to Canada and the United States—and then from North America to South America.*

The Mennonites use the word yo *rather than* ja *for the affirmative. They use* nay *rather than* nein *for the negative.*

Kathleen Teillet
Alberta, Canada

You cited the use of "yo" in 1806 by black West Indian sailors in hauling a rope. I can easily visualize a gang of seamen in the sweltering heat of the West Indies pulling in unison and at each pull shouting "Yo!" Unfortunately, they would not have been hauling a rope—nope—they would have been hauling a "line."

According to Chapman Piloting, Seamanship & Small Boat Handling, *56th edition, by Elbert S. Maloney, page 24:*

"Rope" may be bought ashore at the store, but when it comes aboard a vessel and is put to use it becomes a line.

So, unless those West Indian sailors were hauling the item from the store where it was just purchased, they were hauling a line.

Steven P. Kraft
Washington, D.C.

While on business in Taipei, I read your article on the expression "yo." Perhaps you have already learned that this is pure Chinese Mandarin—exactly the word Chinese use to answer roll call.

The word itself means "to have" and is used much as the French use "if y' a." It is normally pronounced with the 3d tone (falling, then rising), but for roll call a more curt pronunciation is desired. Therefore, either the 2d (sounds like "who" as in "Who?") or 4th (sounds like "no," as in "for the last time, no!") tone is used. I can recall American sailors in the late '40's answering with perfect imitations of these tones they'd heard in Tsingtao or Shanghai.

You probably know of the extensive contacts Americans have had with Chinese in this century. It should be no surprise that they took to such a neat, sharp little word as "yo." Black English indeed!

Gerald C. Thomas, Jr.
The Plains, Virginia

Dear Bill:

Your roundup of terms for greeting strangers or summoning attention was one of your best. Will you add that in shouting "Mac," one is unwittingly saying "Son"?

> Jacques [Barzun]
> Charles Scribner's Sons,
> Publishers
> New York, New York

A stewardess on Eastern Airlines has solved the problem. Her name tag reads what she is so frequently called: "O Miss."

> James G. Sampas
> Chevy Chase, Maryland

Your feeling that the ace *in "Hey, Ace" comes from the thirties is almost surely wrong. A pre–World War II dictionary* indicates that the word refers to a flier who has shot down at least five enemies. The expression was retained in the second war, and in Korea and Vietnam. In a later-fifties boot camp (Air Force) the expression was used pejoratively, and its etymology was obvious to all of us. The expression "Hey, Ace" was used by the Air Force enlisted men of my time in exactly the fashion you mention. I would be surprised to hear anyone of other than Air Force background use it.*

> Douglas McGarrett
> Jamaica, New York

* Webster's Collegiate Dictionary, *Fifth Edition, 1936, says the term is of WWI vintage.*

With reference to the "Hey, Mac" dilemma, the best technique I have seen for attracting attention, which works especially well in restaurants, was demonstrated by a colleague of mine. He would turn in the general direction of the waiter or waitress and intone in medium voice, "Say, uh . . . ," with a slight pause between the say *and the* uh. *Scores of heads would turn, and one of them is certain to be the one sought. This also works in busy newsrooms, on airplanes, at baseball games, etc.*

> Jeffrey Kutler
> New York, New York

Re: My Name Ain't Mac, Buddy
  You forgot "Beau"!

Your friend from Brazil,
Hanns John Maier

Dear Bill:
   The word "Chief" had always seemed to me to be the best way of getting the other guy's attention. In 1962, Kathy and I moved from Jersey City to the Philadelphia suburbs. While we were living there we once took a trip to Washington with another couple (he was originally from suburban Connecticut; she was an Army "brat" who had lived all over the country). We needed directions, so I rolled down the car window and yelled to a man on the corner, "Hey, Chief . . ."
   The other couple found this hilarious and even a bit vulgar. Until then I had innocently assumed that every normal person yelled "Hey, Chief" as a way of catching the attention of a stranger. I soon dropped the salutation from my vocabulary since explaining New York-isms to strangers never works. What I rely on now is "Excuse me?" (with the question mark) which is, I admit, pretty bad.
   About a year after that incident, I read Thomas Wolfe's great short story (yes, he could write short pieces) "Only the Dead Know Brooklyn," in which one of the characters, trying to describe the way to get to Brooklyn by subway, calls the other one "Chief." The story was written in the late 1930's, so "Chief" goes back at least that far. What is its origin? Is it the American version of the British "Governor"? It is, to me, the quintessence of New York street corner democracy because it hails a stranger in a way that brings him into the conversation you want to start and does so in a way that doesn't look as if you are dragging him in since you have greeted him with a term of honor.
   My kids tease me a bit when I revert to my Jersey-City-isms and they find "Chief" pretty funny. But it seems to me to be the best word I know of for the intended purpose. It isn't wimpish and it isn't threatening. But it is so hopelessly New-Yorkish that I don't think it can gain universal acceptance.

Bill [Gavin]
McLean, Virginia

It is apparent that you haven't used your CB radio for some time, since the term good buddy *has for several years been used as a derogatory synonym for the more pejorative terms applied to homosexuals. Far more acceptable these days in CB etiquette are* driver *or simply* mister—*except for women, of course. Better yet, ask the other person what* handle *he or she prefers.*

Doug Matyka
Stone Mountain, Georgia

Yo, Mr. Safire:

In regard to your column entitled "My Name Ain't Mac, Buddy" I wish to furnish some minor corrections to the portion that dealt with Philadelphia and the uses of "Yo."

Item 1. Cheesteak (sic) Sandwiches

One never, never orders/eats a cheesteak sandwich. This would be a social faux pas as gross as ordering a hoagie with mayonnaise instead of oil. Cheesteaks are stand-alone delicacies; they require no explanatory tags. Remember always: A cheesteak is a cheesteak is a cheesteak. If you were to attempt to purchase a "cheesteak sandwich" in Philadelphia, you would be immediately exposed as a visitor, or laughed right off the corner of Ninth and Passyunk (pronounced "pas'shunk").

Item 2. "Sewth" Street

The above-captioned is, I believe, your phonetic spelling of South Street. "Sewth" actually sounds a trifle Canadian. I am not a native of Philadelphia, but I have worked here long enough to know that the correct phonetic spelling is "Saaoowth."

Item 3. Proper Use in Sentences

The example you gave lacked the critical element in any Philadelphia question. Beginning a question with "Yo" is fine; however, one must also end the address correctly. I submit that a more accurate phrasing of the example you gave is:

"Yo, feel like going down Saaoowth Street for a cheesteak, or what?"

If you ever need details on cheesteak etiquette, I will be happy to explain the meanings of "Cheesteak, with" and "Cheesteak."

> Kathryn Reid
> Huntingdon Valley, Pennsylvania

Contrary to your assertion, there are those who still use the word "toots." My wife frequently calls me by that endearing term, and I often respond in kind. And lest you think that we are relics of a bygone era, our ages are 35 and 32.

Yours, in defense of "Toots's" everywhere,

> Mark M. Lowenthal
> Reston, Virginia

One day (many years ago) when I was on my way to school, a driver stopped and asked me, "Hey, Mac, which way to the post office?" I said, "How'd you know my name was Mac?" He said, "I just guessed." I said, "Then guess which way to the post office."

Mac E. Barrick
Shippensburg, Pennsylvania

P.S. "Hey buddy," is most common around here. I use, "Say, can you tell me . . ."

My Nomen Is Klatura

Certain foreign words, taken whole into the outer circle of the English language, rotate quietly within the band assigned them by whatever elite did the importation, bothering nobody else. Then, suddenly, a satellite word slips through the frequency barrier and comes closer to Mother Tongue; it is not yet absorbed and is rarely used by most native speakers, but it is tried out by jargonauts, neologists and avant-gardians often enough to rate a close look by swinging linguists and sexy lexies.

Such a word a generation ago was *apparatchik*, the Russian word for "member of the Communist Party, or *apparat*," which spent its first decade bandied about by Sovietologists in United States think tanks and by spooks at Langley, then made its way into scholarly journals, then to spy novels, and finally into the real world of English words as a snappy synonym for "bureaucrat," with an added pejoration of "slavish."

Today the Russian word working its way in is *nomenklatura*. In his book *How Democracies Perish* the French political philosopher Jean-François Revel writes: "Communism . . . necessarily looks outward because it presides over a failed society and is incapable of engendering a viable one. The *nomenklatura*, the body of bureaucrat-dictators who govern the system, has no choice, therefore, but to direct its abilities toward expansion abroad."

My hard-line buddy puts the word in italics and defines it, a signal to the cognoscenti that they might not know this term yet, but a quiz will soon follow. In the same way, when *New York Times* columnist Flora Lewis used the term in 1981, she followed the word with this parenthetical definition: "(the secret list of people eligible for responsible jobs)." In 1975, *The Economist* did a similar thing: "the *nomenklatura* or name list of top officeholders is classified as well."

Before that, in the 1971 *Area Handbook of the Soviet Union* from the United States Government Printing Office, the word was translated into English: "The appointment of key personnel in the government, industry, the military and other important institutions is done through a system called nomenclature *(nomenklatura)*, which is a listing of positions and personnel. . . . The purpose of the *nomenklatura* system is the rational selection of personnel. . . . In practice, however, the political considerations often outweigh the professional in making the appointments."

I like Flora Lewis's definition best. *Nomenclature* is an English word coined in 1610, from the Latin *nomen*, "name," and *calare*, "to call," and means "a system of naming." That's a far cry from this secret Russian list that you have to get on to get anywhere. As Professor John Bailey of Georgetown University puts it: "The list is like a computer printout that gives the names of people in various positions with descriptions of their jobs. Making this *nomenklatura* is necessary for being on track for career advancement."

Although the term is not yet tested enough to be in the general dictionaries (O.K., citators, scramble!), its Latin antecedent can be found in Eric Partridge's *Origins: "nomenclatura*, a calling of names, hence a system of naming," which is from *"nomenclator*, a slave whose office it is, in a court of law, to call the names of the clients." (Prior to this was the Greek herald Stentor, whose loud voice in the Trojan War gave birth to the adjective *stentorian*.)

What an apt etymology: from the name of a job for a slave to a secret list of jobs held by the elite in a slave society. *Nomenklatura: The Soviet Ruling Class*, a book by Michael Voslensky, defines the word as a vast system of political patronage. Lexical apparatchiks, get those citation files working—this word is going to make it.

In traditional French diplomatic practice (i.e., international) from at least 1400 to the mid-nineteenth century, a "nomenclator" was a codelike list of names, words and syllables with accompanying cryptotext versions, often in numbers. The list of names usually was short, and various secondary permutations might be carried out before enciphering in order to make a cipher-breaking lucky "guess" less likely. Within the field of such a cryptosystem, the list of names for which codes are assigned defines the list of significant friends—and enemies. See David Kahn's The Codebreakers *(New York: Macmillan, 1967; New American Library paperback, 1973).*

> *H. Duncan Wall*
> *Librarian*
> *Philadelphia, Pennsylvania*

*You cannot say, "*Nomenclature *is an English word coined in 1610, from the Latin* nomen, *"name, "and* calare, *"to call. "It was taken full-blown from Latin, and 1610 is merely the earliest "citation. "*

Lest your juxtaposition of calare *and "to call" be viewed by some as an "exception" to Grimm's law (just as erroneously as* habere *"to have, " "have" being cognate with* capere *and* habere *with "give"), let it be stated that the root of* calare *is reflected in "to low, " "to hale, " and "to haul. " "To call, " on the other hand, comes to us from Old Norse and the only other possible reflections of its apparently "expressive" root are to be found in "clatter, " the gallinaceous Gallic cock, and "Glagolitic, " the last two being obviously exempt from Grimm's law.*

> *Louis Marck*
> *New York, New York*

Dear Bill,

Thank you for mentioning my modest contribution to the circulation of the neologism nomenklatura. *Of course, you are entirely right: a "nomenclature" is, technically, a list of names, usually even a systematic and scientific list. Originally "the people on the list" was the true meaning of* nomenklatura *in Russian, or rather, in Sovieto-Russian. But today, as is the way of all words frequently used, to say that somebody belongs to the* nomenklatura *just means that he belongs to the ruling class. The "list" implication has disappeared in this context only, of course.*

Look at sycophant, *which you used in another of your columns, about Reagan's entourage. First, in Greek, it meant an "informer, " then it took the meaning of "hypocrite" in general (it is the French meaning), and then (in contemporary English) of a "servile flatterer. "*

> *Jean-François Revel*
> *Paris, France*

The word nomenclature *and its usage is very familiar to me and thousands of other former U.S. Marines. Frankly, up to now, I thought the word to be familiar to most Americans. To quote from my good ole' trusty* Guidebook for Marines, *1955 edition (part of my "initial issue," mind you): "Before taking the rifle apart, you should know the nomenclature (that is, the names) of all visible parts." Each chapter on weapons has an opening section, "Nomenclature and Stripping."*

During boot camp the word was drilled into our heads thousands of times when a drill instructor would thrust a part of a rifle, pistol, machine gun or even parts of combat gear into our faces and scream "Nomenclature, nomenclature!" We would respond "Sir, operating rod catch assembly, U.S. Rifle Caliber .30 M1, Sir," and we damn sure got it right. After boot camp, nomenclature was commonly used to describe ordnance and other supply items.

Nomenclature was also (and maybe still is) a jargon word used in the questioning on the background of another Marine. For example: "What's this guys nomenclature?" It was also applied to the ladies we met: "Man, that girl's nomenclature won't quit!" (there's a "sometimes" secret list for you); and to more serious inquiries: "What's their (enemy) nomenclature?" meaning size, ordnance, deployment—in other words, a complete listing or breakdown. Such usage, proper and jargon, lists people and things in a way similar to the Russian nomenklatura, *although I am sure that the Russians did not get the idea from the United States Marine Corps!*

Richard Cronin
Mechanicsville, Virginia

Never Call Retreat

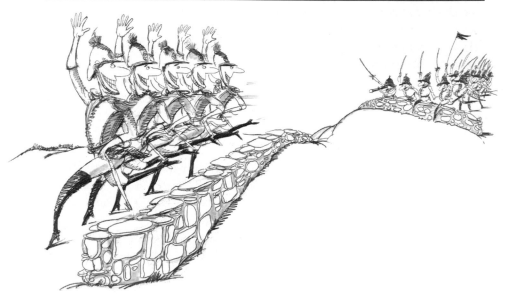

When President Reagan made his decision to remove the United States Marines from their hooches at the Beirut airport in 1984, he then faced another decision: what to call the action removing the marines from the action.

Not even the most cockeyed optimist or euphoric euphemist would call the planned operation an *advance*, but it would be unfair, or perhaps too painfully pejorative, to call the disengagement a *retreat*. What were the President's choices?

The difficulty of finding nondiscouraging words for the end of a military affair is not new: When General George McClellan thought it the better part of wisdom not to assault the Confederate defenses at Richmond in June of 1862, he conducted what he called a "change of base." This official description of the movement away from the enemy's capital received a skeptical reception in the Northern press.

The neutral term for turning troops away from the enemy and moving them rearward is *withdrawal*, a word that preceded *retreat* by more than a century and was first recorded in a military context in 1475: "None suche were never sene withdrawers or fleers frome batailes." Over the centuries, *withdraw* has gained in dignity, separating itself further from the craven *flee*. But *withdrawal* is a word for neutral observers to use and may not be *le mot juste* for participants who want to put a good face on the move backward.

That's where *redeployment* comes in. *Deploy*, from the Latin *desplicare*, "to scatter," means "to position forces on a wider front"; *redeploy* originally meant to do that again when a new general wanted to scatter his forces to his own design. Although British use spreads the action over labor and material management, American use is mainly military: The term was first sighted in a February 12, 1945, issue of *Time* magazine: "The new blueprint for U.S. redeployment calls for an army of 6,500,000 men to defeat Japan."

However, *redeployment* has gained a new connotation of "reassembling in a new position farther from the front." The Israelis used that euphemism in 1983 to describe their movement of troops from close to the Beirut airport to a position behind the Awali River. Accordingly, President Reagan chose that noun for his decision: "I have asked Secretary of Defense Weinberger to present to me a plan for redeployment of the marines from Beirut airport to their ships offshore."

Since repetition weakens euphemisms, Mr. Reagan needed a synonym for *redeployment* in his statement. In a phrase submitted to him by national security adviser Robert McFarlane, a military man, he said: "Even before the latest outbreak of violence, we had been considering ways of reconcentrating our forces. . . ."

Reconcentrate does not mean "I have to think hard about this again." It is a verb that has been in business for more than three centuries, meaning "to bring together," and for the past century has almost exclusively been applied to military affairs: "He abandoned further attempts on Kintang," wrote Archibald Forbes in 1884 about General Charles George (Chinese) Gordon, "and on the 24th had reconcentrated at Liyang." By choosing *reconcentrate*, Mr. Reagan sought to give the impression that the force was just as effective but in a different place, out of harm's way.

This attempt made sense, especially in light of the President's dismissal as "surrender" of House Speaker Tip O'Neill's suggestion of a few days before that the marines be moved to ships offshore. He could also have chosen *retrograde movement*; when I called General Maxwell Taylor for suggestions about advances to the rear, he said, "Off the top of my head, the best I can think of is *retrograde*, but that's no good." He's right: As a verb, *retrograde* is intransitive, often used to describe the receding action of a glacier, and reaches too far for a suitable euphemism.

In *The New York Times*, headline writers accepted *redeploy* as a suitable description of the move of Americans, but preferred *pulled out*, a more neutral term, to describe the removal of the British troops. The *Washington Post*, searching for an accurate and neutral phrase to describe the withdrawal, aptly headlined U.S. MARINES TO LEAVE LEBANESE SOIL—the land, not the area.

Pull out, the verb meaning "extricate," has been in colloquial use for a century. Jack London's 1907 use first attached the term to the military: "While there, we met McAvoy, Fish, Scotty and Davy, who had also pulled out from the Army." The noun *pullout* is more exclusively military than the verb. *Pullout* was later softened by *New York Times* headline writers to *pullback*, a word used for *setback* as early as 1591, but more recently used for *military withdrawal:* The Baltimore *News-Post* commented in 1951 that "those who think the Red pullback is leading up to something don't put so much stock in the Reds' abandonment of prepared defenses." A less well-known term, *exfiltrate*, the opposite of *infiltrate*, is used by commanders who want to pull out of an area in a very quiet way.

Angry hawks blazed away at the President with dysphemisms to counter his *redeployment* and *reconcentration. Cut and run* was a favorite, especially since Mr. Reagan had shown himself fond of the phrase in attacking critics the week before the decision to withdraw. The *American Dictionary of Slang*'s citation for this is from Will Henry's 1954 *Death of a Legend:* "We dassn't stick here and we dassn't cut and run." According to Farmer's and Henley's *Slang and Its Analogues, cut and run* was "originally nautical—to *cut* the cable *and run* before the wind."

Equally harsh was the denunciation of the move as a "bug-out." That word started as a verb in the 1950's, probably among hot-rodders, and became associated with retreat during the Korean War. In 1951, M. R. Johnson wrote in the New York *Herald Tribune:* "Commanding officers hated the word because of the psychological overtones of defeatism. Men talked of 'bug-out gas' and 'bug-out jeeps' and 'bug-out routes.' They anticipated retreat and they prepared for it."

Let me not back off, in this discussion, from the word *retreat*. It is rooted in the Latin *retrahere*, "to draw back," which makes it close etymological kin to *withdraw*, although that verb has come to connote less of a defeat. But why do we say *beat a retreat?*

That comes from the drumbeat at sunset that used to call the roll and end the day, which was similar to the beat used to march troops to the rear. Later, a French cavalry bugle call, said to date back to the Crusades, was added to the beating of retreat.

"The ceremony of 'retreat,' " explains Whitney Smith, secretary general of the International Federation of Vexillological Associations, "is associated with the custom of lowering the flag at the end of the day. Traditionally and historically," he says, aware that those two adverbs do not mean the same, "flags were flown only during daylight by our military, although it has changed since World War II." (Presumably the flag that waved through the night in Francis Scott Key's poem should have been lowered at dusk.) The linguistic link between the ceremony and the battlefield *retreat* is in the sense of *retirement*—originally, retire from the field of battle, and now retire (fall out and disband) from the day's activities.

This exhaustive treatment of the argot of absquatulation will draw mail from irate G.I.'s who will point out that the operative term for retreat is *how able* (from the old phonetic-alphabet signification of hauling one's person), and from vexed logicians demanding to know about Dr. Smith's federation. A vexillologician is one who studies flags, white and otherwise.

Dear Bill:

I enjoyed your military lexicon of (concealed) defeat. If you reprint it in a collection, as I hope you do, you will want to correct desplic- to displic-, and perhaps add that its original meaning is "unfold." Plico is to double or fold (implicit, implicate, explicate, etc.).

Displico led to French déployer and déplier, from which our deploy and display. The reason the Latin dictionaries give the meaning "scatter" is that the locus classicus is in Varro, an agricultural writer who used the verb for his special purpose. But Korting gives displico = unfold.

> *Jacques [Barzun]*
> *New York, New York*

Your connotationally unfortunate glossing of displicare (not desplicare) as "to scatter" seems to be due to either WIII or AHD. The verb does not seem to be Classical Latin to begin with; in any event, the etymological meaning is "to unfold." The immediate source of our "to deploy" is the French déployer, first attested in the 12th century. Déploiement is dated 1538, the Spanish desplegar 1438. The 1983 Petit Larousse defines déployer des troupes as "les faire passer d'une formation de marche ou de transport à une formation de combat." But déployer has wider metaphorical applications: You can deploy courage or efforts, locutions that, aided and abetted by the German non-military entfalten, I may have been guilty of in English. (What I should have said is "display," which has nothing to do with "play" but is of the same origin as "deploy" and has been in English four centuries longer.) In German military parlance, there is no single equivalent, but only discrete expressions such as swarming out or marching to battle, whose application to the present situation could only be by way of utter sarcasm.

As for retrograde, it would be no euphemism at all, since its non-technical meaning is "to decline from a better to a worse condition" (WIII).

I loved your vexillological! Vexillary, vexillate, vexillation, and vexillum are all entries in WIII, which may spare you the irate mail of logicians anent Dr. Smith, whom I would call a vexillologist, as does 6,000 Words, where these "new words" are found s.v. vexillology. The 1983 Larousse also has vexillologie as an entry not found in previous editions, probably on the strength of Smith's "international" federation.

> *Louis Marck*
> *New York, New York*

As a military historian, I think Reagan missed a good bet when trying to euphemize the Marine withdrawal. He should have used the verb recoil, *in the sense that it means to shrink back from a blow, but also to recoil in the serpentine manner of preparing to strike again, or reculer pour mieux sauter. Reculer also means to "fall back," another term the White House could have used, since it implies a tactical withdrawal without necessarily suggesting pulling out of the area altogether. But then, unless the Marines can walk on water, it's difficult to envision a shore-to-ship evacuation as "falling back."*

> Stanley L. Falk
> former Chief Historian of the Air Force
> Alexandria, Virginia

With respect to the Marine movement, how about good, plain old "reposition"? It sounds positive, it looks positive, and it is noncommittal.

> J. B. Skelton, M.D.
> Glen Ridge, New Jersey

I read with glee your letter from America and was immediately reminded of the BBC. Whenever Rommel had just beaten us again the BBC always said we had retreated from Tripoli, "according to plan"—it's wise to have a retreat plan, retreats are sometimes necessary, vide Corunna and Dunkirk.

> Robert Becker
> Associate Director
> International Herald Tribune
> London, England

When it seemed that the British would be forced to bug out of Egypt during World War II, Winston Churchill received this message from the battle zone: "Our forces are now engaging in a fluid action."

> Jay B. Rosensweig
> Lexington, Kentucky

Noble Savage

"How about a rundown on the use of *savage* as a verb?" writes John Moran of Larchmont, New York. "It strikes me as barbaric."

Frank Millikan of Arlington, Virginia, waxed even more wroth. In a letter to the *Washington Post*, he pointed to an editorialist's characterization of a statement by George McGovern as urging "his colleagues not to savage the front-runner"; the editorial writer added a tut-tut at voters who "laugh as comedians savage" politicians.

"Journalists' lurid fascination with power," complains Mr. Millikan (probably using *lurid*'s original "pale yellow" meaning in derogation of journalism), ". . . radically distorts our world perspective. Let's assume it is accurate to say that Druse militia *savage* Christian Phalangists. Walid Jumblat may even verbally *savage* Amin Gemayel. But can't we think of a better word to describe what Democratic contenders—some of them pacifists and comedians—do or refrain from doing to Walter Mondale?"

I noticed the outbreak of the verb form of *savage*, too—in my own writing and in this infinitive-worshiping use in *Time* magazine: "As the campaign warms up, it becomes easier for the press evenhandedly to let Republican and Democratic candidates savage one another."

Are we treating the language brutally with this frequent use of *savage* as a verb? First off (why first *off*? I mean *first*, comma, and not *firstly* either), let us admit to ancient usage as a transitive verb: John Speed, the seventeenth-century historian, used the phrase "if they had not been sauaged with a too carelesse rudenesse." In the 1796 novel *Marchmont*, Charlotte Smith wrote, "She used to savage me so . . . that I shall never go near them anymore," a form roughly similar to that used by candidates today in reference to ungrateful feminist leaders.

Certainly we are using the verb frequently. Nexis, the computerized library, does not yet enable us to search for a word used as a verb rather than as a noun, but a back-door way of looking—at *savaged* and *savaging*—churns up some 2,500 uses of these other tenses. We have undoubtedly sunk our teeth into this verb.

I'm all for it. Yes, it is becoming a vogue verb, and deft writers will avoid its overuse, but it solves the *brutalize* problem. You did not know we had a problem with brutalization? Here it is, cold turkey, with the bark on, right in the kisser: *Brutalize* means both "to make brutal" and "to treat brutally." That is confusing; doves often said, "Our bombing brutalized the Cambodians," and hawks did not know whether they were being accused of turning Cambodians into brutes or treating them harshly. Who knew, from the ambiguous *brutalize*, if policy makers were being accused of bestializing or victimizing?

The verb *savage* solves the problem of fuzzy brutality. Although some instances can be found of *savage* meaning "to make savage," almost all the citations point to a clear "to attack brutally, to strike viciously."

That means we are moving toward a happy separation of verbs that assigns precise meanings to each. Thus, we can use *brutalize* when we mean "infusing some otherwise innocent fellow with a lust to murder" and use *savage* to denote "to indulge in cruel or barbarous deeds."

Nor should we balk at metaphoric use: The way some of those pacifists savage pacifists in debate is enough to brutalize any gentle television viewer.

The verb to savage *is one of long use among Kentucky politicians and hardboots (one word).*

When a ridden horse turns its head and tries to bite its rider, it is trying to savage. More usually, when, in a race, a horse turns its head and tries to bite a horse ahead or coming from behind, that horse is said to have savaged its opponent. Not a new verbal use at all: it goes back, to my knowledge, to the turn of the century.

Kentucky politicians have been known to try to savage their opponents in close races.

Check with any good Thoroughbred periodical or with a Kentucky hardboot. The capital T in Thoroughbred is used advisedly.

> Martin J. Welch
> Louisville, Kentucky

Not Knowing from Beans

How do you characterize stupidity? When a shortstop comes up with a really bonehead play or an economist with a crackbrained scheme, what is it that you say he does not know?

Beans. According to Professor Frederic G. Cassidy, the world's foremost dialexicographer (whose eagerly awaited *Dictionary of American Regional English* began publication in 1985), when his interviewers ask "To show stupidity, you say, 'He doesn't know ⸺,' " the word most often given to fill in the blank by Americans of every region was *beans.*

Some variations on this emphatic use of the bean employ the preposition *from,* as in "He doesn't know split beans from coffee." These unable-to-differentiate derisions include the alliterative *beans from barley, beans from baloney, beans from buttons, beans from bats, beans from apple butter* and *beans from bullfrogs.* In the North, he doesn't know *beans when the bag's open,* while Southerners are more inclined to say *beans with the sack open.*

DARE's interviewers seek not just regional differentiation but variety, to show the richness of the American dialect. *He doesn't know from nothing* occurs once for every five references to beans, followed in frequency by *He doesn't know straight up, A from B, if he's coming or going*, and a locution I had never heard, *He doesn't know sic 'em*, possibly a derogation of a dog that could not understand a command to bite a prowler.

Those are the big ones; inventive native speakers also express their disdain for the dopes for not knowing *the time of day, night from day, A from izzard, enough to come in out of the rain, enough to shut the gate, enough to pour sand in a rathole, his right from his left* and the ever-popular *which way is up*. You can also detect an occupational reference in *whether he's bored or punched* and a Western word picture in *how to pour* (any liquid) *out of a boot* and *He doesn't know cow chips from kumquats*.

So much for stupidity; in perusing another *DARE* frequency list—on words for a lump that comes up on your head when you get a sharp blow or knock—I noticed a curious phenomenon. (No, not all phenomena are curious.) Most people surveyed said *knot, bump* or *goose egg*, but 4 percent said *hickey.*

Hickey? People who call knots on their noggins *hickeys* don't know the way to the mill. I looked up hickey in several dictionaries and discovered, to my horror, that this word (probably derived from *doohickey*, a doodad or gizmo) is still most frequently defined as "a pimple." That's last generation's lingo; a pimple has for the last twenty years been called a *zit*, and a person with a proliferation of *zits* is called by his kind playmates a *crater-face* or *pizza-face*. Anybody who calls a *zit* a *hickey* doesn't know how to write his name and certainly doesn't have both oars in the water.

A *hickey's* primary meaning today is that telltale red mark left on your neck when that wild and nutty partner of yours decides to embarrass you with a too-visible souvenir of passion. It is a greater source of scarf sales to teen-age girls than any winter wind.

So if you're one of that bopped-on-the-noodle 4 percent who goes around calling a *konk* or *pump knot* on your head a *hickey*, get with it, or people will say you don't know *big wood from brush*.

Back in the 60's, Mr. Safire, I overheard, "He doesn't know shit from shinola," for the first and only time in my life.

Later in the decade I coined the euphemism "He doesn't know grits from Granola," to be said by a Southerner in a novel I was writing.

Charles F. Dery
San Francisco, California

Always thought you were a couple of apples short of a full bushel. Ought to know that everybody says, "He don't know sic 'em from c'mere."

> Robert A. Ruhloff
> Ashfield, Massachusetts

Here's one I've heard more and more lately. Instead of saying, "Let's turn on the stereo" or "Let's listen to the radio," it's now, "Let's crank some tunes." I'm sure that comes from the hand crank on old phonographs (Victrolas? How's that for an old-fashioned word!), though radios certainly never had cranks on them.

> Dan Woog
> Westport, Connecticut

"[H]ow to pour (any liquid) out of a boot" is never the way I've heard it. In the first place, the only fluid I've ever heard referred to is piss, which, I admit, has no more business in a boot than any other fluid. And in the second place, you left off the best part of the phrase, the ending: "with the instructions written on the heel."

> Irene Schneider
> Brooklyn, New York

Dear Bill,
It would appear to me that you do not know from borscht.

> Fred [R. Brown]
> Washington, D.C.

The 4 percent interviewed who called a "knot on the noggin" a hickey *may represent a small percentage of Americans. They represent a large percentage of New Orleanians.*

New Orleans has its own dialect. Hickey *is a term for a knot on the head. Some other New Orleans words and expressions come from French, as* making groceries *for shopping,* making ménage *for cleaning house. Some words such as* cayoodle *for a little dog are found in other parts of the country. (Cayoodle turned up in New England.) Other expressions, such as* neutral ground *for traffic island, are local.*

New Orleans words and expressions, like other regionalisms, are disappearing. Few people still call a thirsty hangover hot coppers. *Other words, such as* pyrooting *for "rummaging in a closet" or "searching through a drawer," are still understood but not often used.*

> Carolyn Kolb
> New Orleans, Louisiana

As an addendum to your discussion of hickey *I have enclosed a dermatologic discussion of this word by Morris Leider, M.D., which you might find interesting and amusing:*

> *Of dermatologic interest is application of the word to a pimple (papulopustule) and to the erythematous and later ecchymotic mark (passion purpura) of a playful bite or pinch, usually on the cheeks (of the face or buttocks), the neck or breasts, inflicted or incurred in hanky-panky.*

Dr. Leider, a friend and colleague, is Professor Emeritus of Dermatology at this institution and is a practicing dermatologist in New York City. In this item, which appears in his book, A Dictionary of Dermatologic Words, Terms, and Phrases, *he shows his usual distain for the pomposity of most medical writing.*

Stanley A. Rosenthal, Ph.D.
New York, New York

Nowhearthis Inc.

A clever and pernicious trick is being played by image makers, and the print media are being duped. The trick is the use of typography to make a name stand out and sell in editorial copy.

A company named TelePrompTer may have started the business of implanting a capital letter in the midst of a name. This was followed by BankAmericard (now Visa), which compressed the name of Bank of America's credit card into a single word but tried to preserve the capitalization of the first letter of America. Then the bathroom-cleaner people came up with VANiSH, with only the *i* in lowercase, the middle of the word looking as if it were vanishing. This was followed by NutraSweet, an artificial sweetener that would not hyphenate but was unwilling to forgo the capital letter in the middle, and most recently by PEOPLExpress, an airline that calls itself "People Express" but styles itself half-capital, half-lowercase.

It is all a stunt, designed to gain the reader's attention by playing with capitalization. And too many editors have been gullibly grazing on this stuff, intimidated by lawyers who claim the funny-looking printing is the "real" name of the company, not to be tampered with or straightened out in any way.

Where will it all end? What will editors do when faced with a need to write about a company named "Leverbuyout WOWEE!!! Incorporated"? Come to think of it, the title of my next book will be *SAfIRe's NeXt bOOk*, and if any reviewer tries to put that in simple English type, I will sic my copyright lawyer on him.

No. Let us draw the line here and now. A logo is not a name; a logo is a graphic representation of a name that newspapers are not required to copy in identifying the product. When we write "Coca-Cola," do we put it in the old script type that is the company's trademark? Of course not; why, then, do we do nip-ups with the language when the graphic artists fiddle with their logo? They can change it to "CocaCola," but the rest of us do not have to follow.

The people at G. D. Searle can call their sweetener anything they want and emblazon it on cans of Coke in intermittent capitals, but I will write it "Nutra-Sweet," sometimes "Nutrasweet." (To launch a counterattack on VANiSH, however, I will write it "vanIsh.") Keep Madison Avenue out of the copy, copy editors!

With that diatribe out of my system, I will take the next month off to work on *SAfIRe's NeXt bOOk*, which is a pretty catchy-looking title.

TelePrompTer may or may not have been the first to implant a capital letter in the midst of their name. I do not know offhand when they began such usage (or exactly when their prompting device was introduced in the early '50s) but my earliest recollection of such usage dates from September 1953 when 20th Century-Fox introduced the wide-screen format which they called CinemaScope.

Fred von Bernewitz
New York, New York

Oh, the Pain

In my other incarnation, as political haranguer, I took an incorrect swipe at Vice President Bush in 1984.

He wrote me: "I have been tempted to call you in reaction to items in your column which have had me incorrectly positioned on foreign-policy issues. I have resisted that temptation. . . . "

In reply, and in the hope that his bonds of confidentiality would be loosened, I wrote: "Oh, would that George, with that permanently painful expression on his face, succumb to temptation!"

A *New York Times* editor, David Binder, gently took me to task: *"Painful* or *pained?"*

Those related adjectives are not exact synonyms. While both can mean "feeling pain," *painful* means "giving pain" and *pained* means "receiving pain." When the dentist jabs you with that Novocain needle, the shot is *painful* and your expression is *pained*.

According to Fred Mish, editorial director of Merriam-Webster, there are four meanings to the suffix *-ful:* "First, it means 'full of,' as in an *eventful* day. It can also mean 'characterized by,' as in your example of *painful*. The suffix can also denote 'resembling or having the qualities of,' as in *masterful*. A fourth meaning would be 'tending to or given to,' as in *mournful* for one who is given to mourn."

Usually, though not always, the giver is *ful* and the receiver is *ed*, as in *forceful* and *forced;* however, *bashful* is not the giver for the recipient *abashed*. Careful writers do well to remember this usual pattern, to avoid using *awed* when they mean *awful*.

Obviously, the correct adjective to describe the expression on Mr. Bush's face is *pained*, not *painful*. (Mr. Mondale's expression is *mournful*, however, not *mourned*.)

Is splitting hairs like this worthwhile? You bet it is. Only when a reader knows the writer is on guard can the reader relax and enjoy the prose. Alexander Pope, two and a half centuries ago, used the word describing the infliction of pain in a couplet to illustrate the labors of the precise writer:

> *While pensive poets painful vigils keep*
> *Sleepless themselves to give their readers sleep.*

Onomatopoeia

The word *onomatopoeia* was used above, and it had better be spelled right or one usage dictator and six copy editors will get zapped. That word is based on the Greek for "word making"—the *poe* is the same as in *poetry*, "something made"—and is synonymous with *imitative* and *echoic*, denoting words that are made by people making sounds like the action to be described.* (The *poe* in *onomatopoeia* has its own rule for pronunciation. Whenever a vowel follows *poe*, the *oe* combination is pronounced as a long *e: onomato-PEE-ia*. Whenever a consonant follows, as in *poetry* and *onomatopoetic*, pronounce the long *o* of Edgar Allan's name.)

---

* See "Zapmanship," page 323.

Henry Peacham, in his 1577 book on grammar and rhetoric called *The Garden of Eloquence*, first used *onomatopoeia* and defined it as "when we invent, devise, fayne, and make a name intimating the sound of that it signifieth, as *hurlyburly*, for an uprore and tumultuous stirre." He also gave *flibergib* to "a gossip," from which we derive *flibbertigibbet*, and the long-lost *clapperclaw* and *kickle-kackle*.

Since Willard Espy borrowed the title of Peacham's work for his rhetorical bestiary in 1983, the author went beyond the usual examples of *buzz, hiss, bobwhite* and *babble*. He pointed out that one speculation about the origin of language was the *bow-wow theory*, holding that words originated in imitation of natural sounds of animals and thunder. (Proponents of the *pooh-pooh theory* argued that interjections like *ow!* and *oof!* started us all yakking toward language. Other theories—*argh!*—abound.)

Reaching for an alliterative onomatope, the poet Milton chose "melodious *murmurs*"; Edgar Allan Poe one-upped him with "the *tintinnabulation* of the bells." When carried too far, an obsession with words is called *onomatomania*; in the crunch (a word imitating the sound of an icebreaker breaking through ice) Gertrude Stein turned into an onomatomaniac.

What makes a word like *zap* of particular interest is that it imitates an imaginary noise—the sound of a paralyzing ray gun. Thus we can see another way that the human mind creates new words: imitating what can be heard only in the mind's ear. The coinage filled a need for an unheard sound and—*pow!*—slammed the vocabulary right in the kisser. Steadily, surely, under the watchful eye of great lexicographers and with the encouragement of columnists and writers who ache for color in verbs, the creation of Buck Rogers's creator has blasted its way into the dictionaries. The verb will live long after superpowers agree to ban ray guns; no sound thunders or crackles like an imaginary sound turned into a new word.

Took me a while to get to the point today, but that is because I did not know what the point was when I started.

"I now zap all the commercials," says the merry Ellen Goodman. "I zap to the memory of white tornadoes past. I zap headaches, arthritis, bad breath and laundry detergent. I zap diet-drink maidens and hand-lotion mavens. . . . Wiping out commercials could entirely and joyfully upend the TV industry. Take the word of The Boston Zapper."

The rule as stated in your comments upon the word "onomatopoeia" has one exception of which I am aware, to wit: "subpoena." "Subpoena" is pronounced as a long e: sub-PEE-na.

If I am mistaken and "subpoena" should be pronounced sub-POH-na, *I shall*

ZAP those attorneys whose mispronunciation would be an embarrassment to the legal profession and quote "The Raven" "Nevermore!"

> *Judge Howard E. Levitt*
> *Supreme Court of the State of New York*
> *Mineola, New York*

When coining words for sounds like this: /Boom, bang, crackle, buzz or hiss/ Onomatopoeia/Is a good idea.

> *Edmund Conti*
> *Summit, New Jersey*

A former English teacher, I have been an avid reader of your "On Language" for years. I was particularly taken with your recent article on onomatopoeia, for it recalled a long ago ninth grade class discussion of Huckleberry Finn. *I was reading aloud Huck's description of a storm, rich in imagery and sound effects:*

> *It was one of these regular storms. It would get so dark that it looked all blue-black outside, and lovely; and the rain would thrash along by so thick that the trees off a little ways looked dim and spider-webby . . . and then a perfect ripper of a gust would follow along and set the branches to tossing their arms . . . and next, when it was just about the bluest and blackest—fst! it was bright as glory . . . and now you'd hear the thunder let go with an awful crash, and then go rumbling, grumbling, tumbling down the sky towards the under side of the world. . . .*

Pale Lilac Speaks

Every morning, I start out the day with *oatmeal*.

Not the cereal, the color: I set out for work in a cap that is described on the label as "7¼, Oatmeal." I used to think of *oatmeal* as lumpily *gray*; this cap is *ivory*, with touches of brown, like the scratchy little things that fleck my scruffy oatmeal soap. In my pocket is a torn-out ad from Lord & Taylor, seducing me with "a shirt of red, royal or white silk and pleated linen trousers in white, oatmeal or black."

Everybody knows that *oatmeal* linen trousers are somewhere between *ivory* and *brown*, but what color is *royal* silk? It must be *blue*, a shortening of *royal blue*, which is lighter and more brilliant than *navy blue*, taken from the British naval uniform, which is a darkly purplish blue, not quite as black as *midnight blue*.

Used to be, colors were named after things in nature, like foods and flowers. *Rose* was a color—pinkish red—until roses began blooming in a variety of colors. Then different shades of roses began getting names, like the *Windsor rose*, after a noted British family, and a marketer of fingernail polish in the 1930's called one of its shades *Windsor*, snipping off the *rose*. (That's what just happened to the *blue* in *royal blue*.)

Those were the simple days of color naming, with *lemon* yellow, *forest* or *emerald* green, *periwinkle* or *robin's-egg* blue, and *tomato* red.

How unimaginative. Today, when flowers are used as a referent, the color can be *amaranth*, a genus of plants that includes pigweed, tumbleweed, and the sadists' favorite, love-lies-bleeding; the color described is supposed to be a purplish red. Similarly, Saks Fifth Avenue is advertising an oversized safari jacket, "for summer moves and all-out pizzazz," in *colored-up sagebrush*. Sagebrush is a forage plant common in dry, alkaline areas of the western United States and has a cowboy connotation; the color probably comes from *sage*, of the mint family, usually dark green. (According to a study for Avon cosmetics, flowers sell better than food.)

When *earth tones* became the fashion rage, the plants and creatures of the forest and sea became the base of color naming. Diet-conscious decorators and copywriters, coming back to the office after a seafood salad, came up with *oyster*, similar to the old *pearl gray; salmon*, which is slightly pinker than lox; and *shrimp*, not yet listed in the dictionaries as a color but which strikes me as pinkish beige, tilting toward pink, very close to *sand-dune pink* and *warm coral*.

Bisque is an offshoot of *shrimp*; it is a creamy soup made from shrimp, lobster or rabbit and looks ivory with a hint of pink. Both *shrimp* and *bisque* are more *pink* than *beige*.

These "natural," or muted, colors—what you see when you look at the Grand Canyon—include *taupe*, a favorite of outdoorsy catalogues like those of L. L. Bean, a brownish gray, the color of moleskin. (It is also the color of the field rat, but rats and reptiles are rarely used in color naming.) Another earthy color is *ruddy*, defined in dictionaries as "healthy red" but in fashion a dull red; in British slang, it is the euphemism for *bloody*, and the current notion of this color is close to that of drying blood.

"Earth tones are now dead," declares Ken Charbonneau, chief color man for Benjamin Moore Paints, "and pastels have become very important. Right now, we are dealing in *Garden Pastels & Romantic Whites*, which are pretty, pale, soft colors. Our soft yellow is *jasmin*, a pale feminine blue is *first frost*, an off-white green is *sweetwater*, and our pale lilac is *white sapphire*."

White sapphire? Isn't that gem known for its blueness? "Naming is a form of seduction," explains the paint man. "*Ivory*, about the oldest color, was in 20th place in our sales several years ago. We changed the name to *Oriental silk* in 1973, and in two years it rose to sixth. That name sounds fragile, of course, so it would never do for an exterior paint; outside, you want *Tudor brown* or *Richmond bisque*. Durable-sounding. *Bisque* sounds better than *beige*, which is overused."

Beige, French for the natural color of wool, is rooted in *bambax*, Latin for "cotton." From the cotton base has risen the word *bombast*, meaning "padded oratory." Columnist Mary McGrory asked a health-food-store manager in San Antonio about the possibility of Texas Senator Lloyd Bentsen as a running mate for Walter Mondale: "Bentsen's beige," was the reply. "So is Mondale, and you don't need two of them."

Not everyone thinks that "earth tones" are dead (though most would agree that an all-beige ticket would not excite the electorate). The Coach Store, a leather emporium in several cities, advertises *mocha*, a chocolate brown named after an Arabian coffee; *tabac*, with an 1894 origin as "tobacco-colored," and *putty*, named after the mixture of chalk and linseed oil used to fill cracks, which is a more appealing name than, say, *concrete gray*.

The earth tone showing most signs of life is *khaki*, the Hindi word for "dust-colored," which means "dull, yellowish brown." (*Dirt* is rarely used in colors because it has been pre-empted by *dirt-cheap*.) Soldiers are often infuriated when fashion designers confuse *khaki* with *olive drab*, which is greenish brown and especially suitable for camouflage.

What comes after earth tones? Black and white, say some, with black known from *pitch* to *jet* to *ebony*. Pastels, say others, with a remembrance of earthiness: "What was *pastel peach* is now *snow peach*," says Janet Eackloff of the National Paint & Coatings Association, who thinks that gray is being mixed in many pastels. (She spells it American *gray*, not British *grey*.) In olden times, *pearl gray* was popular; a darker shade was *charcoal gray*; now, for men's underwear, there is a medium tone called *locker-room gray*, similar to what used to be derogated as *tattletale gray*.

Makeup people like the mythical Roy G. Biv (who changed *rouge* to *blush*) think that this turn toward pastels will include more white, which is why *snow* is modifying *peach*. However, department-store executives like Geraldine Stutz of Henri Bendel suggest we keep our eyes squinting for *neon colors*, also known as *acid colors*, a trend from England that features *taxi yellow*, for people who like to hail their colors.

Is there any rhyme or reason to the nomenclature of color? The National Bureau of Standards tried to collect the names being bandied about for colors a generation ago, in order to show where each stood on a spectrum. The last time *Color—Universal Language and Dictionary of Names* was reprinted was in 1976, and I think the bureau has given up hope of trying to help consumers make out the difference between *shocking pink, pizzicata pink* and *hot pink*.

Many professional enamelists have found a way to standardize the description of colors by avoiding language. The Munsell Color Notation System assigns a letter and number indicating hue and position on a color wheel, a number denoting color value, or degree of lightness, and another number indicating chroma, or brightness. Thus, when I asked Sylvia Hamers, an artist who teaches enameling at the Smithsonian Institution, for the designation of a blue sky on a sunny day, she replied, "10B 8/6. Very pretty."

Should consumers demand a similar standardization of color nomenclature when shopping for stuff to slop on their eyelids? Ought we to write prescriptions for a designated amount of pink, and no more, in *shrimp*? Shall we stipulate that a *slate gray* is henceforth darker than, say, a *Dorian Gray*?

I think not. That would interfere with freedom of poetic speech. I asked a good-humored old friend, Dan Moriarty, now vice president of Revlon, which of the 269 shades of lipstick had the sexiest name. He replied: *"Afterglow* is a strong pink, almost an ecstasy." (Is dat you, Dan?) That word, originally meaning "the light after sunset," is now defined by Merriam-Webster as "a reflection of past splendor, success, or emotion" but of late has gained an almost exclusively sexual connotation.

The language of color has departed from the constraints of description and entered the realm of poetry. Suggestiveness is all. That's this week's word from *Pale Lilac*.

You register surprise at the color name "white sapphire" and imply that this is a misnomer. This is not one of your gems, Mr. Safire. Rubies, blue sapphires, and white sapphires are all forms of the mineral corundum (which is aluminum oxide). Sapphire is also the collective term for gem-quality corundum, whatever the color. The color is due to the presence of impurities. Rubies contain traces of chromium, blue sapphires have traces of iron and titanium, and white sapphires have no significant impurities (a very pale color indeed). Although the Greek word [for sapphire] originally meant "a blue stone," both white sapphire and sapphires in the collective sense are mentioned in my 1950-vintage Oxford English Dictionary, *so those meanings have also been around for some time, albeit not quite as long.*

> Michael T. Hahn
> Quakertown, Pennsylvania

How can salmon be slightly pinker than lox which is Yiddish for Lachs *which is German for salmon?*

Although sapphire is the most glorious blue this side of the cerulean sky, it is white as well and often used as the crystal on watches.

> Joseph J. O'Donohue IV
> San Francisco, California

I take my OYSTER pen in hand to write you. (Notice WINDSOR stationery).

I loved your column, especially after reading a Bloomingdale's ad not five minutes previously that advertised T-shirts in BLACKBERRY, JET BLUE and SAGE GREY.

Just one question, though—when something is described as "EGGPLANT," does one look for the PURPLY BLACK on the outside or the GREENISH-YELLOW on the inside?

I must go put on my GUNMETAL and GRAPE pullover and drive my KHAKI car to the office!

> Mrs. Alan Miller
> Matawan, New Jersey

Paths of Glory

This department is dedicated to ripping out the weeds of mixed metaphors before they take root in the language, especially on well-trodden paths.

David Gergen, the White House director of communications, has announced his intention to depart; he will no longer be Superflack, in charge of the care, feeding, leakage and intimidation of the White House press corps, nor will he present such an inviting target for congressmen searching for the villain in the Briefingate investigation.*

Informed of Gergen's impending departure, Robert McFarland, NBC's bureau chief in Washington, recalled the time Mr. Gergen tricked the newsies by interrupting a live news conference with the warmhearted presentation by Mrs. Reagan of a birthday cake to the President. The NBC executive, who otherwise lauded the White House aide for providing "accessibility," added, "That was the only time he led us down the primrose path."

The *primrose path* is one of ease and sensuality, a metaphor coined by Shakespeare in *Hamlet:* "Do not, as some ungracious pastors do," says Ophelia to Laertes, "Show me the steep and thorny way to heaven, Whiles, like a puffed and reckless libertine, Himself the primrose path of dalliance treads."

That *path of dalliance* is that of the philanderer, dallying along the way where the lovely primrose—a light yellow flower of the genus *Primula*—grows. For more than three centuries, that phrase has served as a poetic reference to hanky-panky, specifically the fooling around between hypocrite and maiden.

In the twentieth century, a second, somewhat parallel but distinctly different, path opened up: the *garden path*. Its first partial use in print was found by the gnomes of Oxford in a 1925 novel: "They're cheats, that's wot women are! Lead you up the garden and then go snivellin' around. . . ." Two years later, G. D. H. Cole, the biographer of pioneer media giant and vituperator William Cobbett, wrote in a novel: "to lead Flint up the garden-path and relieve him of his cash."

Thus, *to lead up the garden path* is a colloquial phrase meaning "to entice,

---

* See "Play Down the Alibi," below.

deceive, mislead, humbug"; slanguist Eric Partridge speculated it comes from "gently suasive courtship."

The *garden path* is the road of the deceiver, leading to disillusion; the *primrose path* is the road of the libertine, leading to a barren life of fun and games. Some will say the two roads lead to the same end, but that, as they say in publishing, recks not a good rede; synonymists see a chasm between the two metaphors.

Mr. Gergen, we may say, did not lead us often up the *garden path*; only the most thoroughly seduced newsies would claim he led them down the *primrose path*.

Play Down the Alibi

In a political piece about Briefingate (or Debategate, or The Purloined Papers— the slugline did not instantly crystallize), I suggested "it may offer a we-wuz-robbed alibi to a dismal Carter campaign."

"*Excuse* and *alibi* are quite different words," responded William Clayton of the English Department of Garden City Senior High in New York, "the former meaning 'I did it and here's why'; the latter meaning, 'I could not have done it because . . .'"

That's the way it used to be in the days of Sherlock Holmes. An *alibi*, from the Latin for "elsewhere" (and usually modified by *ironclad*), was a defense in law: "I am demonstrably innocent because I was in the bosom of my family when the murder took place." That meaning of being innocently elsewhere still exists: "You can't pin that rap on me—I could not have purloined those papers because I was traveling on *Air Force One* when they came in over the transom at headquarters."

However, the noun *alibi* has taken on a second meaning of *excuse*. (That is pronounced with an *s*, while the verb form of *excuse* is pronounced with a *z*—no wonder foreigners have trouble with English.) Why? An alibi was a specific kind of excuse, and its meaning spread into a general synonym. Ordinarily, I would resist this kind of fuzzification, but *alibi* in this second, more general meaning serves a purpose. An *excuse* is neutral: You can have a good or a bad excuse, although no *excuse* is as strong as a *reason*. A *pretext*, usually married to *flimsy*, is a phony excuse, a false reason that conceals the real motive. An *alibi* is an excuse put forward in a whining or self-righteous manner; the word is a derogation of an excuse, and it is nice to have an *alibi* around with which to zap sneaky people who try to get off the hook.

Later in the same piece, I pronounced media judgment on Briefingate with "but nobody is going to downplay this now." Marvin Stone, editor of *U.S. News & World Report,* circled *downplay,* wrote across the clip, "what happened to standards?" and attached a little note: "Bill—you are undoing all my good work with my young staffers who think you are smarter than I am."

Downplay is telegraphese, like *downhold.* (U.P.I. editors used to end messages to foreign correspondents with the not-so-cheery "Downhold expenses," leading to the formation of the press association's "Downhold Club.") The word is elbowing its way into dictionaries, but the inversion of two words into a single-word substitute is offputting.

Play down is a clear compound verb, offering a contrast to *play up;* the verb and noun *play* is from *display,* the attention given to a story in a newspaper. To *play down* is to de-emphasize, minimize, and break a press agent's heart. We don't say *upplay,* why say *downplay?* Why not leave well enough alone and play down the controversy?

Downplay is inelegant, trendy, and puts me off. I promise henceforth to play down stories (but not to hold down expenses) and never to use *downplay* again. Yes, Marvin, there are still standards for all your young staffers to cling to. Ignorance of the law is no excuse, and for sloppiness in prose, I offer no alibi.

"To play down" now comes into the picture and Mr. Edward B. Marks, my music publisher employer when I was 16 years old, offers this one in his memoirs They All Sang. *Herman's, an 8th Avenue and 25th Street cabaret, had a wine room and girls. Every time a girl was bought a drink, it went into the bartender's ledger for a commission, but the girls had their limit by daybreak and would drink tea instead. The bartender would prepare "play-downs." He would rub a few drops of liquor around the rim of the glass to give it a convincing smell and the good customer would pay for liquor!*

Jack Gasnick
New York, New York

You write, "To play down *is to de-emphasize, minimize, and break a press agent's heart."*

Are you sure about minimize?

Here's Theodore Bernstein, p. 278 of The Careful Writer: Minimize *does not mean to belittle, depreciate, diminish, make light of, pooh-pooh,* play down *[emphasis added], or shrug off. It means to reduce to the least possible, that is, to a* minimum. . . . *The word* minify *means to diminish, to lessen, to view or to depict something as less or smaller than it really is."*

I don't want to make a big thing of this, or maxify it.

Steve Zousmer
New York, New York

You identified downhold *to be telegraphese. From my bygone newspaper days, I recall another staple of telegraph vocabulary—*wrapup, *used as both a verb and a noun. One telegraph word that, thank heaven, did not find its way to general usage was the acronym for "soon as possible," i.e.,* sap. *The superlative of* sap *was, as you might imagine* sapiest, *as in the following message:*

WHY IN CHRIST CUM U SEND NO STATS? UPDATE STATS FOR WEEKEND WRAPUP. SAPIEST.

Hugh Ellis
Jersey City, New Jersey

Dear Bill:

Downhold *originally applied principally to holding down the volume of news agency copy when correspondents were writing too much, telegraph costs were getting out of hand or there was a large volume of news generated by some major event such as war, and other types of news had to be accordingly restricted. As you know, telegraph charges were based on the number of words transmitted. If you could consolidate two words, such as* hold *and* down, *into one word,* downhold, *you would save the cost of a word. Words could cost as much as $1 apiece if sent from remote parts of the world or at urgent rates.*

Clifton [Daniel]
New York, New York

P.S. My favorite cablese, which I would not dictate to my very proper secretary, is "upstick asswards." Saves three words.

Your amusing item about telegraphese coinages as downplay *and* downhold *recalls the wartime years when, in editing the Overseas News Agency file, we used to have fun creating combos that would get by the Western Union billing department. You understand, of course, although you didn't say it, that the motivation behind the telegraphese (or cablese) was to* downcut *the cost of cables which were reckoned by the word. The trick was to create a combo that would get by the WU billing department, which almost invariably refused to accept as single words such combinations as* downplay *and* downhold *and charge us for two separate words. WU also barred any of dozens of doubleups using the Latin* un, *such as* unreport, unpublish, unfile. *We never really lost at this game since, for every time the WU hawks spotted one of our illegal combos, they would miss one or two of the less obvious ones.*

H. R. Wishengrad
New York, New York

Colleague Bill Safire (Thus avoiding "Dear . . ." and "Memo to . . ." and other inappropriate forms):

Not to burden you, but as for alibi, *you needed to go no farther than* Webster's International Unabridged 2nd Edition: *1. Law. The plea of having been, at the alleged time of the commission of an act, elsewhere. . . . 2. A plausible excuse; also, any excuse. colloq."*

But note well the colloquial.

What bothers many of us are the rules, perhaps obsolete in the permissive 1980's, laid down by our mentors and bosses in our apprentice days. You may have commented on decimate, *a word much used as a substitute for "nearly wipe out" or "almost destroy." Webster's 2nd gives its first definition as "To take the tenth part of," but its third as "To destroy a considerable part of."*

I have resisted using decimate *in the third sense since I was a young reporter in the Washington Bureau of the* Wall Street Journal *(1941–44) and Barney Kilgore, then managing editor, handed down a ruling! Don't use* decimate *unless you mean it! To reduce by one-tenth, etc.*

Alibi *was similarly forbidden when I moved to the* Times' *Washington Bureau, where Arthur Krock and Bureau manager Luther Huston insisted that* alibi *meant being elsewhere, legal definition or no legal definition.*

And another such taboo was unique, *Turner Catledge, then managing editor— weary of reading that actions by Congress or the Treasury Department or the White House or whatever were "unique"—told us, "nothing that man does is unique." Perhaps debatable, but I've been wary of "unique" ever since.*

Walt [Waggoner]
New York, New York

Your article re: alibi *scratched a mental itch I've had since the mid-sixties when I heard that old Four Seasons' classic "Big Girls Don't Cry." On the off chance that you haven't heard it, the falsetto refrain "Big Girls Don't Cry" cleverly parallels a story of teen-age heartbreak, challenging us to come to the conclusion (the awesome denouement of the song) that in fact "Big Girls Do Cry."*

*This ironic sleight of hand is seemingly explained in the line "that's just an alibi."
Wrong!*

*Since the phrase "Big Girls Don't Cry" is used to hide from an insensitive world
the shameful fact that they do, what Frankie Valli really meant was "that's just a
patently false statement which does not correspond to the brute facts of reality."
Ahhhhhhhhhhh!*

Chip Benjamin
New York, New York

I am sure you can find earlier citations for alibi *as "excuse" but it was certainly the
point of Ring Lardner's story, "Alibi Ike," which was published in the '20's.*

Ruth Schwarz
Bellport, New York

Pogey-Bait

In a piece drawn from the dinner-table talk at the home of John and Annie Glenn,
I reported that the senator had used the word *pogue* to describe "a rascally
politician"; Lexicographic Irregulars were invited to suggest derivations.

We have a launch. "The last time I heard the word *pogue*," writes James
Stevenson of *The New Yorker*, "was in the summer of 1951 at Parris Island, South
Carolina, where, as part of the term *pogey-bait*, it was frequently snarled or shouted
by my platoon's drill instructor. He, and other Marine Corps regulars, used it to
refer contemptuously to candy, chewing gum, soda pop, ice cream and similar
treats favored by civilians." Mr. Stevenson adds ruefully: "It did not occur to me
at the time to interrupt the sergeant and ask him the derivation of the word. I'm
sorry now."

"Candy, cookies, cake and ice cream were known as *pogey-bait*," agrees Don
Moran of Brooklyn, "the fare of young boots. Saltier marines drank beer."

If *pogey-bait* was candy, then logic suggests a *pogue* or *pogey* was someone
attracted by the bait. "A *pogey-bait marine*, or *pogue*," writes Marine Corps
Captain J. F. Collins, now stationed at Camp Lejeune, North Carolina, "is someone who does not share in the hard life of the *grunts*—clerical or supply personnel,
for example." This definition is supported by Joe Golden of East Berne, New
York—"a clerk or any person that works in an office"—and by John Howley of
Rockaway Park, New York: "The company clerk in a rifle company was called an

office pogue, and everybody in a rifle company called everybody in headquarters *company pogues*." In the 1978 Vietnam War novel *Fields of Fire*, by James Webb, a glossary entry deadpans: *"Pogue:* a marine assigned to rear-area duties."

"No matter how close to the front lines you were," writes former infantry officer James Kirk of Rocky River, Ohio, "unless you were the point man, there was always someone else who considered you a *pogue*. As a platoon commander, I considered the company commander and his headquarters personnel to be pogues and was in turn considered a pogue by my squad leaders who, in turn, were considered pogues by their subordinates."

Although the term probably has a homosexual origin, that meaning seems to be fading. A former naval person who was at the Glenn dinner party that night recalls that *"pogey-, pogie-,* or even *pogy*-bait was universally used to describe candy, as in Hershey bars or Mars bars or Milky Ways. The candy was the bait, and *pogey* (spelled however) referred to young persons of the opposite sex, whose resistance presumably could be worn down by offers of candy."

Jeremiah O'Leary, a reporter for the *Washington Times*—and, like Senator Glenn, a former marine—offers this analysis: "In the strictest sense, the word refers to pederasty and seems to derive from the era of the China Marines stationed in Shanghai in the years before World War II. But *pogue*—I'll use your spelling because I doubt if anyone really knows how to spell a word that is almost never written—can be either a deadly insult or a term of amiable affection, depending entirely on who uses the word, the tone of voice and to whom it is being applied. . . .

"A marine might say, 'Jones is a good old pogue,' of someone held in very high regard. A more subtle meaning might be *fuddy-duddy*, which is how I deduced Glenn was referring to the *old pogue* he used to know in Ohio. In short, the word has a reverse meaning from the original simply because it was so commonplace an expression."

Mr. O'Leary, like many other marine veterans who responded to the query, does not believe the current meaning of the term is intended to cast aspersions on a candy-loving recruit as a sissy or wimp: "Marines of Glenn's generation and mine use the word only as a term of affection or about someone who is mildly incompetent.

"For etymologic derivation, if I cared enough," concludes Mr. O'Leary, "I'd look in a Cantonese or Mandarin dictionary, because the origin is clearly of Chinese roots."

That etymology does not come readily to hand, but many Irish Lex Irregs have pointed out that *pogue* is a Gaelic word for "kiss": "There is an Irish play called *Arrah-na-Pogue*," writes T. J. Moorehead of Norwich, New York, "by Dion Boucicault, set in County Wicklow in 1798. The heroine is known as Arrah-na-Pogue (Arrah of the Kiss) because of the ingenious way by which she smuggled escape plans to a rebel held in Wicklow jail." That is a charming story, far better than the scatological Gaelic rhyming epithet put forward by other correspondents, and contains the overtones of political chicanery alluded to by Senator Glenn.

Before leaving the etymology of *pogue*, let us admit to the possibility of being totally off base. James Anderson of the *VFW Magazine* tossed in this disconcerting afterthought: "I think it should be noted that the pogy is a common fish on the Atlantic seaboard and dictionary references link it with menhaden. No doubt *pogey-bait*, hence *pogue*, arose from the worthlessness of the fish except as a source of oil or fertilizer. Combine this with the large number of Marine Corps bases on either coast and you have its probable origin."

Until I saw your reference to pogues I thought an acquaintance of ours had made up the word. George Clifford, M.D., was doing research among alcoholics at the Detroit Receiving Hospital in the early 1950's. When asked what he was doing, he would say "I'm a pogue doctor (to rhyme with rogue); I deal with poor old guys—or you can spell it with a "u," that's for poor old unhappy guys."

I don't believe that George is a native Middle Westerner. It looks as if the poorhouse connection with the Receiving Hospital brought about the use of the term there.

> Charlotte Gault
> Marysville, Ohio

You say that "if pogey-bait *was candy, then logic suggests a* pogue *or* pogey *was someone attracted by the bait." Logic may suggest a lot of derivations, but a* pogey *is not a* pogue, *nor a* poge, *nor a* pogie, *nor a* pogy.

A pogey, *or* pogie, *is a hospital—usually a prison hospital or a hospital for drug addicts, or a workhouse.*

A pogue *is a male homosexual, and that's all it is.*

A poge *is a purse.*

A pogy *is a bait fish.*

Pogy-bait (sometimes misspelled pogey- *or* pogie-bait) *is bait made from the pogy fish, a menhaden, a fish used as bait to catch other fish. It is usually cut up to make chum—which is a bait used for chumming.*

Candy, cookies, cake, ice cream and such stuff are considered, by macho Marines (and their ilk), as no better than fish bait—sweet kid stuff unfit for the stomachs of "a few good men."

> Frank N. Potter
> Newport News, Virginia

As for pogey, *see Spears'* Slang and Euphemism *dictionary, which has four entries of interest. Oddly, Bruce Rodgers'* The Queens' Vernacular *has none, which suggests the term has lost its original "sodomy" meaning in American English—rather like* bugger *in this respect. I was surprised, by the way, that you didn't give us any indication of the pronunciation of the word as John Glenn used it: Spears seems to be suggesting that it begins like the word* Roger—*unlike the fish* pogy *(rhymes with* fogy*).*

Ronald R. Butters
Editor, American Speech
Durham, North Carolina

This letter refers to your discussion of the word pogue. *I would like to bring to your attention a quotation from* From Here to Eternity. *In a conversation about picking up queers Prewitt says: "If the guy turns out to be a jocker and you get pogued, go see the Chaplain."*

James Jones's use of language in that book is uninhibited and excruciatingly accurate, so it looks as though Jeremiah O'Leary has it right. The word refers to pederasty. Let's hope that the Marines have not deteriorated as much as the meaning of that word apparently has.

Julian S. Herz
Tinton Falls, New Jersey

The enclosed Chinese dictionary references show these possible links to the pogey-bait *reference in your column:*

- *A 1958 Pinyin dictionary published in Peking shows* poge. *Only common usages appeared in that short handbook, which formed part of a campaign to simplify the official language.*
- *A large English-Chinese dictionary published in Hongkong in 1957 defines the adjectival form as "licentious."*
- *The venerable* Matthews *Dictionary defines [it] as "to break through the rule." More interesting, it defines* Pogua jih nien—*literally, "the year of breaking the melon"—as meaning "sixteen-year-old girl." Pogua would sound very like* pogey *to Marine ears. Matthews' listing for* deflower *is* poshen—*literally, "to break the body." That phrase has the same verb, but quite a different sound.*

From these references, I infer that Marine garrisons may have encountered pogey *as a local phrase for "virgins," and that the phrase* pogey-bait *may have come into use with the meaning "candy to attract virgins." Either Chinese or Western pederasts could have extended that meaning to boys.*

But this is merely dictionary speculation. For authority you would need to find somebody who will admit to a close familiarity with Chinese street slang eighty-odd years ago.

Hugh Stokely
Vienna, Virginia

To follow up on my pogey-bait *note,* Tzuhai, *a Chinese etymological dictionary published on Taiwan, states, in my rough translation: "In vulgar use, 'age 16' is* pogua." *It's interesting that* Tzuhai's *relatively modern analysis does not limit gender.*

Tzuhai *then quotes an earlier reference: "In vulgar use, a woman deflowered is* pogua." *That literally means "break melon." I surmise that Chinese street slang extended this to refer to a girl available for deflowering—and then later to a young boy.*

As alternative etymology, Tzuhai *goes on to present the scholarly pun referred to in the Matthews dictionary—i.e., since the character* gua *resembles the character for 8,* ba *written twice, it is used to refer both to the age two times eight, or 16, and the age eight times eight, or 64. I surmise that the "break melon" usage came first, and that a later scholar found the visual pun to "age 64" amusing, in the classical Chinese tradition of drunken literature.*

The theory that Marines encountered pogua *as a phrase for "virgin" fits your Collins/Golden/Howley references to rear echelon types. In my naval days, I've heard "candy-ass" used that way by combat troops—a phrase with impressive cultural similarities to* pogey-bait.

Again, this is all dictionary guesswork. If a Chinese has ever used the phrase pogua *in my hearing, then I failed to catch what was being offered.*

Hugh Stokely
Vienna, Virginia

The word po *is common in Shanghai and refers to an old lady, whether in the literal sense, as in an older female relative, or in the slang use (the same we have) of one's wife as one's "old lady." It broadens in meaning to convey girlfriend and then prostitute, which now is more commonly referred to as "little old lady"—xiao lao po. The Marines on the shore must have had occasion to hear and use this word in that context, and it is natural to assume that* pogey-bait *meaning "candy" and the usages of* pogue *to indicate "amiable affection" and also "mild incompetence" would derive from this derivation.*

H. Christopher Luce
New York, New York

Although an infantry officer for most of my Korean tour, I was for a time assigned as an Air Observer with the 6147th TAC Group ("Mosquito"), then stationed in Ch'unch'ŏn, a small village about 15 miles south of the 38th Parallel. Our Korean mess personnel were augmented by a number of teenaged schoolgirls who, appropriately attired in plain blue dresses, waited on tables. Ranging in age from 13 to 18 these musame *(Japanese, I believe, for a young maiden) were shy, innocent and good-natured.*

At lunch one day I greeted our young waitress Rose with the opening lines of that old standby "Rosie, you are my posie . . ." At the last word her hands flew to her face and she ran off in a fit of embarrassment. A short time later the head waitress (all of 19 years I recall) came over and remonstrated with me as to what I had said to Rose. When I repeated the lines she stormed at me with uncharacteristic vigor: "You bad, you No. 10 Lieutenant!"—this last remark flung over her shoulder for all the world to hear.

Putting on a brave face I left the mess to seek out our Korean house boy. When I told him what I had said and the reaction it got, he explained by word and gesture that the word posie *was probably mistaken for* pogey, *which he implied was a slang expression for the female pudenda. With difficulty he explained that it also referred to someone's "shack job" or steady bed partner. In effect then, Rosie assumed that I was proclaiming that she was my steady "piece." Things remained tense between waitress and writer until I was able to find a flower catalogue to illustrate what a "posie" really was.*

We know that the Korean language has many loan words stemming from repeated martial-cultural invasions by the Chinese and Japanese. One example is the term musame *referred to above. Intended to apply to young maidens it was quickly corrupted by GI's to* moose *and universally applied to all Korean women. One fluent in Korean could undoubtedly give you dozens of similar Japanese or Sino loan words. Thus, as Mr. O'Leary points out, it is entirely probable that* pogey *crept into Marine usage during the China Station days to assume a Yankee semantic of its own. Further, your writer sayeth not!*

James M. Catterson, Jr.
Port Jefferson, New York

Dear Bill:

I don't mean to intrude on your pogie bait *contest, but* pogy/pogey/pogie *originally meant a workhouse or poorhouse in 1891, and sometimes an old people's home. (It seems to be from the word* poke, *to confine, and it is related to* pokey, *the 1919 word for jail.)*

Bait once meant feed for horses and then came to mean a light meal or snack,

*as with travelers while on a journey, for which the OED has citations from 1570
to 1883, labeling this use as* dial.

Thus, by the 1890's pogie bait *meant a box of edible goodies, as one might send
to a friend in a poorhouse, hospital, school, or in the army. Though all of our cites
date from 1918 (World War I), and your correspondents mentioned having heard
it in various branches of the armed forces, it was in some wide student use, especially
in private schools, in the 1890's and early 1900's.*

Stuart [B. Flexner]
Editor in Chief
Reference Department
Random House
New York, New York

*In 1971, during the Viet Nam conflict, I worked with several chief petty officers who
waxed eloquently about the distinction between* Gidunk *(pronounced, gee' dunk,
g as in get) and* pogey bait. *Gidunk is ice cream while pogey bait is candy. Gidunk
can also refer to the area adjacent to most military bases' exchange or messing facility
that houses vending machines or a snack bar. "I'm going over to the gidunk to buy
me some pogey bait, . . . you want something?" usually meant that the person was
headed to the snack bar to get a candy bar and had offered to fetch something for
his friend.*

Bruce Pickard
Lieutenant Commander
U.S. Coast Guard
Washington, D.C.

*In the mid-1950's I was an officer in the Marine Corps. While stationed at the
Marine Corps Air Station at Cherry Point, North Carolina, I made the acquaintance
of three elderly Commissioned Warrant Officers. They boasted that they were
numbers 1, 6, and 7 on the list of active Marines, all of them having enlisted in
1914, just in time to be sent to Veracruz, Mexico.*

*As a "college Marine" with a degree in English and philosophy, I was interested
in the derivation of* pogue *and* pogey-bait *and asked the three gentlemen what they
knew of the phrase. The three, all of whom had served on the Yangtze River Patrol
in Peking and in Shanghai, stated that they first heard the word* pogue *in Shanghai
applied to young Chinese boys who were prostituted by their parents to "round-eyed"
soldiers with peculiar tastes in sex.* Pogey-bait *was given to street children to entice
them to engage in sexual acts. Their recollection was clear that the words were not*

used in Northern China and that the words were brought "state-side" by old China Marines.

Leonard H. Rubin
Scarsdale, New York

Your piece on "pogue/pogey" reminded me of a Buffalo-area expression. When a kid grabs on to the back of a car's bumper and slides on the snow, that's "pogeying." "Let's go try and pogey on that car," e.g.

   What do other areas of the country use to describe this poor-kid's form of skiing? In Rochester, it's called "skitching": ski plus hitching.

Gary Muldoon
Rochester, New York

As adolescents (circa 1962) in Amherst, New York, a suburb of Buffalo, friends of mine and I used to pogey. *This winter "sport" was conducted as follows: After an adequate snowfall, say a foot or so of fluffy stuff, we would gather at a street we knew was smooth underneath, attired as usual for a Niagara Frontier winter, with special precautions of heavy-duty gloves and non-nubbly boots. Then we would conceal ourselves along the roadside and await the lumbering advance of one of the giant cars of those days. When it reached our position, we would dart out, as well as possible, and in one graceful motion grasp onto the rear bumper and assume a crouching position. The result was an exhilarating glide —as long as our hands held out, our stance remained flawless, and the driver didn't dead-brake!*

   I was forced into semi-retirement the night my dad happened to glance into his rear-view mirror (in a '59 Merc—a great ride) during one of our sessions. He arrived home to find my gloves still stuck on the chrome, and when I showed up later, my pogeying *career was (excuse me) on the skids.*

Mark H. Dunkelman
Providence, Rhode Island

I don't know whether this has any relation to the U.S. Marines' use of the word, but in Canada pogey *is widely used to mean relief, welfare or, by extension, unemployment insurance. Thus a Canadian might speak of someone who is out of work as being "on pogey."*

Kevin Branigan
Rochester, New York

Although in the United States the pogy is considered a trash fish, because it is not edible, it is widely used in the manufacture of margarine in Europe. The U.S. Food and Drug Administration bars such use in the United States because of a lack of proper refrigeration on most pogy boats. The pogy is itself used as bait, as well as for fertilizer.

The lowly pogy has achieved fame and its own place in primary school fable, having been generally identified as the fish munnawhattiaug, which the legendary Squanto of the Massachusetts tribe taught the Pilgrims to place in each hill of Indian corn. When crops along the East Coast failed in the early 19th century, experiments by one Ezra L'Hommedieu, based on the then already legendary Squanto story, led to the early development of the largest commercial fishery in North America—The Menhaden Fishery.

Neal D. Hobson
New Orleans, Louisiana

My own philological studies indicate that most of the slang words in English can be traced to perfectly respectable sources in the Indo-European linguistic stock. In my opinion pogue *is related to the Indian word* poque *or* poak *or* poke, *meaning a timid person who stays behind, a person who does not come forward due to timorousness, or by extension of meaning, a coward. In several modern Indian languages this word survives in varying forms. The interchangeability of* g *and* k *is a well-known phenomenon in the morphology of Indo-European languages—e.g.,* gow *in Sanskrit and* cow *in English,* gavi *in Sanskrit and* cave *in English. There are many slang words in English which are cognate to perfectly respectable words in Sanskrit. Similarly, there are several slang words in modern Indian languages which are cognate to scientific words in Latin or words found in Chaucer's English.*

B. Deva Rao
Sofia, Bulgaria

Principle Versus Value

"Words are the tokens current and accepted for conceits," wrote Francis Bacon almost four centuries ago, "as moneys are for values."

Since Bacon's time, two of those words have added to their meanings. *Conceit*, in the singular, now is most often taken to mean "unwarranted pride" rather than "idea." And the word *values*, in the plural, is no longer limited to material worth. The word *values* has become the all-embracing vogue term for "God and country," the work ethic, respect for family, coming to the dinner table with your hair slicked down and your mouth watering for apple pie with a slab of very American cheese.

Only a few years ago, *principles* were the big thing in politics; lately, that word has been shunted aside for *values*, usually modified as *family values*. The phrase *traditional values* is also used, by people who probably mean *historical values*. What happened in American life that replaced *principles* with *values*? What's the difference between the two words?

At the beginning was the *principle:* The Latin *principium* meant "source, origin, beginning." That came to mean a primary truth that formed the basis for other beliefs and then to mean a rule for ethical conduct. The word, as well as the kind of conduct it signified, was put forward by theologians.

Not so with *values*. Rooted in the Latin word for "strength," the plural meant what Bacon used it to mean: material worth. It gradually came to acquire a meaning of intrinsic worth. And then, about fifty years ago, psychologists and sociologists glommed on to the word and made it their own, until politicians came along recently to adopt their meaning.

In this sociopolitical meaning, *values* are neither standards of intrinsic worth nor eternal verities. They are relative, not universal: Sociologists used the term to describe the behavior that is accepted by consensus. These values are emphasized within the society and become central to each member's social acceptance: For *Titanic* passengers, "women and children first" was a value, while among some aborigines, "kill only what you need to eat" is a value.

Values can change but *principles* do not. David Guralnik, editor of *Webster's New World Dictionary*, explains: "*Principles*, being theological in origin, are fixed, invariable, absolute, eternal. *Values*, being in a sense scientific, are nontheological and therefore subject to change and alteration as the demands and needs of a society change."

A woman's place is in the home: That was once a value, but times and that value have come a long way, baby. (*Titanic* passengers, both in recognition of cultural developments and the Democratic candidate for Vice President, would now think of editing their value to "children first.")

"If you work hard and play by the rules," said Geraldine Ferraro in her acceptance speech at the Democratic convention, "you can earn your share of America's blessings. . . . Those are the values I taught my students."

The value system of one society puts a high worth on work; another society may think of work as an unfortunate necessity and put a higher worth on the contemplative life or chasing around.

Principles are what you stand for in life; *values* are what you stand around in among your friends. *Principles* are stern and unyielding; *values* are warm and supportive. I try to keep my fuddy-duddy political views out of these language pieces, but the fact that *principles* are out and *values* are in says a lot about politics in both parties today.

How is it possible to claim that you try to keep your fuddy-duddy views out of the language pieces? Earlier in the column you state that "The word values . . ." *and you go on to list the clichés of fuddy-duddyism.*

To have balanced the piece, you might have included justice for all, economic opportunity, care of our elderly, or any other list of values that reflect concern for those who cannot get near that mythical piece of American pie. You must know of the folk song that promises "pie in the sky, when you die."

Pauline Lurie
Morristown, New Jersey

Probab-lee

"I have heard the word *probably* pronounced with the accent on the last syllable with alarming frequency lately," writes Gary Kosloski of North Royalton, Ohio. "Is this new, or perhaps regional? Is it giving a new emphasis to the indefinite?"

At the University of Wisconsin headquarters of the *Dictionary of American Regional English*, Dr. Fred Cassidy replies that the only one of his experts who has heard that last-syllable pronunciation is from New York City.

"If it is a new trend," says the man from *DARE*, "it may be limited to the New York City area, may be a foreign pronunciation, and must be quite recent. I would expect it to occur only when the word is in a stressed position—such as when it starts a sentence or is tacked on the end—but not as a modifier."

I have heard this *probab-LEE* down here in Washington and have always assumed it to be a Southern genuflection toward Robert E. Lee. If an Ohio correspondent has caught it as well, there may indeed be a new emphasis on the indefinite.

While I'm at it, let me correct a recent reference to Dr. Cassidy as a man who stands "bestride the bridge." He points out that *bestride* is a transitive verb and *astride* was the preposition I wanted. One *bestrides* a horse, but one sits *astride* it. I appreciate that leg up, because I was asleep when I wrote the sentence, probab-lee.

Probab-lee *falls quite familiarly on my ear. I have heard it a lot in British Guiana (Guyana), Barbados and Trinidad. It may derive from Welsh English pronunciation which sings through so much Caribbean speech.*

> Robert MacNeil
> Executive Editor
> The MacNeil/Lehrer Newshour
> *New York, New York*

Until I read your column I hadn't noticed that there are Americans who never pronounce probably *as* probabLEE. *When I was growing up in southwestern Virginia this pronunciation was just as frequent as the correct one, which is, of course,* prob'ly. *It is more accurate to describe* probabLEE *as having its last syllable drawn out in a rising inflection, rather than as being accented. I always had the impression that* probabLEE *was interchangeable in both sound and meaning with "That could be" or "Could be." In the South this phrase is also spoken with the same rising inflection, rather than with a stress on* could.

There were no formal rules on when to use each pronunciation, but now that I think of it probabLEE *was often an off-handed way of answering or dismissing a question without committing ourselves. If it was evident that the questioner was seeking confirmation of his own opinion, it would have been rude to answer "I don't know, and I don't care," or even "I don't think so."* ProbabLEE *was a way of not agreeing while remaining agreeable. It hardly ever meant* probably. Prob'ly *meant "probably," and sometimes "undoubtedly."*

"Do you think this dress will be all right, dear?" "ProbabLEE."

"Do you think the South will rise again?" "Prob'ly."

If probabLEE *is indeed spreading north it will be interesting to see whether its contribution to genteel speech survives the journey.*

C. Leon Harris
Plattsburgh, New York

Just a short note on the misplaced accent in "probably," which gives it the sound of "probab-lee'-ee."

You cite an opinion that this is recent and eastern, and you counter with your own experience with this pronunciation in Washington, calling it "southern." In my experience the usage is strictly southern-midwestern-southwestern, rural, and in addition has a gently sarcastic tinge. I've heard it in the Missouri Ozarks from 1972 onward (when I moved there) and also in Oklahoma, Arkansas, Texas, and southern (rural) Illinois. Probab-lee' has a meaning distinct from prob'-ably in these areas. It is most often limited to one-word replies to over-evident questions, hence my terming it "gently sarcastic."

Example: In 1974 my husband and I were helping a Missouri farmer haul hay. He, his two sons, wife, neighbors, and the pair of us had sweated the whole day in 100° heat, bucking 50 lb. bales onto flatbed trucks, then driving them to the barn, tossing them down, and finally stacking them in the barn, where the temperature was 120° under the tin roof.

As we were leaving, all sweaty, hay-covered, and exhausted, I wanted to make one last pleasantry to these people, so I turned to our boss, Virgil Esrich, and asked, "Think it'll be as hot again tomorrow?"

"Probab-lee'-ee," was his answer, delivered with a wry face.

Or, again, this example: Our car wouldn't start one afternoon in a small town in Oklahoma where we had stopped for lunch on a cross-country trip. A man who'd been in the diner where we were saw this and came over. I opened the hood and saw that the battery connector gizmo wasn't on right. The man noticed this too, got a tool, reconnected the battery, and told my husband to try it now. Just before he did, I (again in a desire to be pleasantly folksy) asked the man if he thought that'd fix the trouble.

"Probab-lee'-ee." This was accompanied by raising his eyebrows, nodding, and looking at my husband, not me, as if to dismiss me for my foolishness.

Hope this info helps solve the question. I do not think this accenting of "proba-bly" is a mistake or any kind of degeneration, manifestation of ignorance or lack of education, or such. It seems to be deliberate, to carry a particular subtext, and to connote something subtly different from "prob'-ably," a pronunciation these same people use when the word comes up in the middle of a sentence or in serious reply to a question.

Catherine Yronwode
Editor in Chief
Eclipse Comics
Forestville, California

*It seems to me that in New York you are more likely to hear "probly" and even (believe it or not) "prolly" than probab*lee.

E. S. Heller
New York, New York

Pro-Macassar

You want to know why most Americans who have visited Peking think the Chinese leaders are stiff-necked? Because they hold meetings in huge, overstuffed chairs that are lined up next to each other, and participants talk to each other over their shoulders. If your meeting lasts longer than an hour, as they always do, you wind up with a stiff neck.

Next time you see a film clip of a visiting American talking to some counterpart in the Great Hall of the People, notice the way he squirms around in the big armchair, sits on one buttock, and trys to address the Chinese diplomat next to him without having to rest a chin on a shoulder.

Another thing you'll see, probably when President Reagan makes it over the Great Wall, is an *antimacassar*. Antimacassars, which have also vanished from the United States like rubber sink stoppers on chains, are fixtures on Chinese chairs.

When you see these lacy ornaments on the arms and backs of the chairs, remember that they originally performed an important function: protecting the fabric from macassar oil, from the Macassar district on the island of Celebes, an oil used to slick down hair.

Today the word is used as an evocation of the musty drawing rooms of the Victorian era: "Eros and Antimacassars" was the title of a review in the *Washington Post* of Peter Gay's *The Bourgeois Experience: Victoria to Freud*. Today's antimacassar goes by the brand name Scotchguard, a spray to protect fabrics from hairsprays. *Plus ça change.* . . .

If "Beltway bandits" is spelled with a capital on the first letter of the first word, because the Beltway is a real road, then I think we should spell antimacassar *"anti-Macassar," because Macassar is a real place (and a real strait, where we beat the Japanese in a naval battle).*

> Art Morgan
> New York, New York

There is no "u" in Scotchgard. I know, 'cause my wife keeps a can in every room lest I sneak out wearing an untreated necktie and shower myself with gravy at lunch.

> Al Siegal
> New York, New York

Puffing Up Deflation

Inflation, as we have been told a thousand times, is the cruelest tax of all. Inflation, goes the political-economic cliché, steals your savings and hits hardest at the poor. Inflation is a word to be said with a frown; the only time a smile is permitted is when inflation is down.

Comes now *deflation*. How are we to react to this word?

AFTER YEARS OF ABSENCE, DEFLATION CAUSES WORRIES, said *The New York Times* in a front-page headline, followed the next week by an editorial-page headline, DEFLATION CAN ALSO HURT.

"The market appears to be getting more concerned about deflation than it was about inflation," said economist Gary Ciminero. "Recent indications of deflation include dividend cuts, salary freezes and OPEC's oil-price freeze, the dollar reaching new highs daily and sinking precious-metals prices."

"Members of the Fed talk of inflation when every market signal is warning of deflation," said Representative Jack Kemp, who wants the Federal Reserve Board to loosen money and thereby reduce interest rates, an action that some people fear would reignite inflation and abort the recovery. (*Abort* is as close to *recovery* as *awash* is to *oil*.)

The linguistic question is not how to define deflation, which is the contraction of the supply of money or credit that is followed by a decline in the prices of goods and services. The question is: Does deflation have a pejorative connotation? Is it something to be wished for or worried about?

Where you stand depends on where you sit. If you're a farmer or you own commodities like beans or you have been collecting gold bricks, deflation is a bummer. If you are a consumer and you have been watching the prices of the things you want to buy rocket up out of reach, then deflation is your big chance: The money you have is worth more. You should smile at the prospect of some deflation, provided the drop in real prices does not slow down the economy to the point that you lose your job.

The adjective used to make *inflation* fearsome is *runaway*; the adjective to wipe the smiles off the faces of consumers watching prices come down at long last has not been chosen yet, but the modifier for *deflation* is likely to be something like *headlong*, meaning "headfirst" or "reckless"; academic types may prefer *precipitate*, meaning "sudden," or *precipitous*, if the image desired is "steep."

Politicians who want to appeal to both farmers and consumers will safely deplore both runaway inflation and headlong deflation. But what of those who like to be in favor of something? *A little inflation* or *moderate deflation* is unexciting; *flation* falls flat; and *nonflation* has not yet been coined.

Try *price stability*. People stopped talking about that years ago; maybe it's due for a comeback.

I often ask the students in my Money and Banking class to give me a good definition of deflation. *Many a student has bristled upon receiving no credit for the definition you gave. This definition is incorrect because it includes one possible cause. A decline in the money supply or credit may cause deflation but so may other events, including an increase in output or a decrease in aggregate demand. I doubt whether even the most ardent monetarist would insist that price declines are solely a monetary phenomenon. The definition I expect from my students is that deflation is a fall in the price level.*

> Eugene N. White
> Assistant Professor of Economics
> Rutgers University
> New Brunswick, New Jersey

I don't think your "headlong deflation" has much of a future. This is because speedy deflation is virtually unknown. A few percent a year price decline is about the maximum. (Prices and wages are far more resistant to decline than rise, the economists say.)

Even in the Great Depression prices fell only 22 to 23 percent, 1929–33 although output fell 30 percent in the same span. This may explain why hyperinflation is a known word and hyperdeflation does not seem to be in the language.

> Corbet Hanchett
> San Francisco, California

Punch-Line English

When a reader inquired into the origin of the expression *don't make waves*, I pointed out in this space that the widely used catch phrase was the punch line of an old joke on the theme of not causing a bad situation to worsen.

Lexicographic Irregulars were then asked to survey the language for other examples of punch-line English. I now have a file bulging with the wheeziest chestnuts in any comic's routine, but some of the submissions provide a needed etymology of well-worn lines that make points to insiders. Foreign students of the language, as well as native speakers who never heard the jokes, hear phrases that seem idiomatic. The phrases are not idioms; rather, they are dangling punch lines to forgotten stories, remaining in the language like the smile of the Cheshire cat.

Don't make waves, for example, has its derivation explained by John Bailey Lloyd of Beach Haven, New Jersey: "The soul of a debauchee arrives in hell. The Devil offers him the choice of one of three doors to enter and stay for eternity. From behind the first door comes the sound of drinking and revelry; from the second, the sound of merriment; from the third, a chorus crying, 'Don't make waves.' Curious, he chooses the third. The Devil opens the door to a Dantesque scene in which thousands of souls are standing up to their chins in foul muck and mire, wailing to each new arrival, 'Don't make waves!' "

That's the classic background to that catch phrase, recounted in as inoffensive a way as possible. Refinements exist: Whenever a specific religious group is to be derogated, the Devil is said to add, "Wait till the [name of group] come by in their speedboats." However, I estimate that fewer than half the users of the phrase know the original old joke.

Sometimes a cartoon caption makes it into the language. When told, "It's broccoli, dear," a with-it moppet of the 1920's told her mother, "I say it's spinach, and I say the hell with it." Carl Rose of *The New Yorker* drew the cartoon, and E. B. White supplied the caption, which is a phrase still used to signify: "Don't confuse me with the facts when I want to indulge my prejudices."

Another *New Yorker* cartoonist, Peter Arno, drew a cartoon of a mangled wreckage of an airplane, frantic rescue squads at the scene, with the aircraft designer, plans under one arm, saying, "Well, back to the old drawing board." This 1941 caption, often accompanied by a profound sigh, is now used for any brave or resigned reaction to situations in which the best-laid plans gang aft a-gley.

Most dangling punch lines, however, have left long stories behind. "Ready when you are, C.B.!"—indicating enthusiastic ineptitude—is used by moviegoers who have never heard of mogul Cecil B. De Mille. When that phrase was cited in my original query—incorrectly, as "Whenever you're ready, C.B."—an anonymous supporter in *The New York Times*'s systems support (is this a system?) sent this etymology: "C. B. De Mille was filming an extravagant scene which called for the entire town set to be destroyed.

"He set up three cameras. The scene was played, the town destroyed. Picking up his megaphone, the great director asked: 'Camera One—how was it?' The reply: 'A real work of art, C. B., but the film broke.' De Mille, undaunted, called out: 'Camera Two—how'd it go?' 'Brilliant, C. B., but I left the lens cap on.' Desperate now, De Mille called: 'Camera Three—come in, Camera Three!' And the punch-line: 'Ready when you are, C. B.!' "

Native speakers who react to this etymology with know-it-all sneers are invited to a higher level of difficulty. "An expression from my youth has itched me mightily for the past year," writes Franklin Gracer of Yorktown Heights, New York. "I presume it is the punch line of a long-lost joke. The line is: 'No soap, radio.' It is a purely verbal memory, but includes the pause indicated by the comma. Do you have any idea of the provenance or meaning?"

Several readers asked the same question. Here is the joke: A lion and a lioness were taking a bath together. The lion said, "Please pass the soap," and the lioness replied, "No soap, radio."

That's a joke? You don't get it? That's the point: It is a test, not a joke. "This unfunny two-liner grew out of a lunchtime discussion in the basement of Slocum Hall at Syracuse University," writes Jan Rubin of Oakland, New Jersey, "of the fact that some people find it difficult to admit their ignorance." Her group made up a nonjoke—with a meaningless punch line—to see how people would react when told the story. If they joined in the general laughter, they were fearful of admitting they did not see the point; if they confessed, "I don't get it," they were honest. Evidently, to this day, *No soap, radio* is floating around, disembodied, meaning: "If you laugh, you're a phony."

"What's this 'we' jazz, paleface?" is an expression that has come to mean "I do not associate myself with your remarks." The provenance is recounted by Dr. Daniel Hely of Carlisle, Pennsylvania: "Surrounded by hostile Indians, the Lone Ranger turned to his faithful companion and said, 'Looks like we're done for, Tonto,' to which the red man replied as cited above." Dr. Hely traces this ridicule of the presumptuous use of the first-person-plural pronoun to a story told about a supposed May 1927 radio communication: "What do you mean, 'We,' Lindbergh?"

Yiddish is a superb source of punch lines: "But who's counting?" and "So I lied" have already been explained in this space. "But what have you done for me lately?" and "Who's minding the store?" are self-evident. "Don't make trouble" is the whispered advice from one man facing a firing squad to the man next to him demanding a blindfold, and "That's half the battle" is a matchmaker's expression of relief after having gained a proud mother's permission to arrange a marriage between her pipsqueak son and Princess Anne. Edward Bleier of Warner Brothers Television supplies the story behind "I once had a car like that," an expression of mock sympathy: "A Texas rancher asks to see the largest ranch in Israel and is shown a spread of only six acres. He describes his own ranch by saying he can start driving at sunup on the longest day of the year and finally, at sundown, he would still be driving on his own property. To which the Israeli replies, 'I once had a car like that.' "

We come now to the punch line that has forced its way into reference works despite its scatological origin and, as reflected in the mail, is the most famous example of punch-line English. In *Webster's Ninth New Collegiate Dictionary*, under the verb *hit*, is the phrase *hit the fan*. Considerations of good taste preclude my explaining to visiting Martians the lead up to this punch line, but E. W. Gilman of Merriam-Webster comments: "Even though the story was based on highly improbable assumptions (for one, that the fan was working in reverse), the image evoked was vivid enough to have won itself a small place in the language."

The lexicographer adds: "I think that the popular phrase of a year or two back, 'That's all she wrote,' is also probably a punch line, but I have never heard the story."

He has touched on one of the great mysteries of punch-line English. In World War II, a *Dear John letter* was a communication from the girl back home that she had decided to sit under the apple tree with another; in that connection, *That's all she wrote* became current. It was probably attached to a joke, but the joke has been lost to civilization's collective memory, same as the meaning behind the ancient *dead as a doornail*. That is why today's research on punch-line English is so vital; centuries from now, some distraught human being will look up from the depths of despair and whisper, "There must be a pony in here somewhere." Lexicographers will know, thanks to these lines preserved on some diamond-hard disk, that he is punch-lining President Reagan's story of the optimistic kid who was shown to a roomful of manure.

There are more, but not tonight, Josephine. No more, Mr. Nice Guy. There's nobody in here but us chickens.

Your comment referring to "dead as a doornail" indicates that the meaning behind the phrase has been lost.

In this connection, you may want to examine its very early use:

"He bar him to the erthe, As dead as dornayl to deme the sothe."
—William of Palerne (E.E.T.S.)

Charles F. Gill
Mathews, Virginia

Thank you very much for printing both my punchline and the joke.

It's still a cheap way to assemble a joke book.

Now, here's a real linguistic enigma: if the officially incorporated name of this company is "Warner Bros." (emphasis added), why does The Neue Yorke Thymes insist on spelling it "Warner Brothers" (emphasis added)?

By what right does the Times change people's names?

Edward Bleier
New York, New York

In the 14th century William Langland wrote "as dead as a doornail" in The Vision of Piers Plowman, line 182 in Part 2. In Henry IV, Shakespeare had Pistol reply to *Falstaff's* query, *"What! Is the old king dead?"* with *"as nail in door."* And of course, there's *Dickens'* *"Old Marley was dead as a doornail."*

Helen Hahn Smith
New York, New York

No! The damned souls who dreaded waves neither wailed nor cried. The only sound from behind their door was a low murmur. The (bleep) was over their chins; and they had to stand on tiptoe, stretch their necks, and keep a stiff lower lip. To wail or cry out could cause a ripple, and a mere ripple would mean disaster.

David R. Ebbitt
Newport, Rhode Island

As a young person in Bridgeport, Connecticut, I had friends who belonged to Black Baptist churches. Riveted in my memory is the encounter of one boy and two girls with whom I was talking, all of whom had been baptized at the same time. The girls' comments were that the boy "made waves" in the baptismal tank! Don't make waves might apply to that, if not derive from it.

The other memory is of childhood baths—in a tub—where we would be admonished not to get the water sloshing around—and over the edge—of the tub!

Rev. Clifford H. Field, Jr.
Shelton, Connecticut

It is not President Reagan's story. Myrna Loy acted in a play in the 60's called There Must Be a Pony, *based on a book of the same title. (It took a whole book to get to that punchline.)*

Sonya Trachtenberg Breidbart
Scarsdale, New York

I think you are justified in not explaining to your visiting Martians—out of considerations of good taste—the scatalogical implications of the punchline "hit the fan." Yet it would seem quite in order to point out that this phrase actually has become, to us earthlings, a part of folklore, to wit:

Once upon a time there lived a wise and generous Emperor named Shan, greatly beloved by all his subjects. It was his custom to invite them, on his birthday, to the great courtyard of his palace, there to listen to their problems and give them, so to speak, their day in court.

And so, the populace thronged to the palace and acclaimed their beloved Em-

peror. But one thing disturbed them: they had heard sinister rumors that their Emperor was subject to fits. *At any given moment, so the soothsayers warned, he would fly into an ungovernable rage, scream imprecations, and threaten his court with unspeakable tortures.*

But the populace, loyal to their sovereign, crowded close to hear his birthday message. He talked to them as a father talks to his children.

But in the middle of his discourse, his fit seized him. Pandemonium erupted. Like a fearsome contagion, the Emperor's frenzy infected his subjects. Panic-stricken, the howling mob trampled over each other to escape. The palace was left in a shambles.

After many years, the events of that horrifying day gradually submerged into legend. And yet, among the survivors there were those who would ask each other: "Where were you when the fit hit the Shan?"

Karl Kohrs
Port Chester, New York

Your article made me think of a punch line which you will not publish for two reasons, one of them being that it is in Dutch and therefore used in Holland only, and the other reason? Well, judge for yourself . . .

"Wie spreekt van betalen?!" . . . Who says I'll pay for it?! It is supposed to express your surprise if you believe something is a gift and it ain't but you've got to pay for it. Here's the story:

Amsterdam . . . a little guy follows a nice-looking girl who tries to get rid of him. She turns corners from one street to another, faster and faster. Nothing doing; our little friend doesn't give up. Finally she turns and shouts furiously, "I am no prostitute," whereupon—and you have to give it the right Amsterdam intonation which one can easily find in New York—his somewhat angry reply: "Who the hell speaks of paying!!"

Walter L. Odenheimer
Brussels, Belgium

With regard to "That's all she wrote . . . ," I believe I may be able to shed some light.

Your reference to a "Dear John letter" is aimed in the right direction, but off the mark. I'm pretty sure the original letter referred to is a song performed by Ferlin Husky and Jean Shepard back in the forties sometime called "The Dear John Letter." This was a country song, and would naturally be unfamiliar to a New Yorker such as yourself. And the Jean Shepard who sang on the record is a lady, not the all-night radio star of old WOR. Now as to being off the mark. . . .

In the late forties or early fifties, another country song, written by folks named Ritter and Gass (the former might possibly have been Tex Ritter, I don't know), was

*performed by one of the most popular country singers of all time, Hank Williams.
It was called "Dear John," and had nothing to do with war. The first verse related
the story of a man who wakes up in the morning to find a very short note from his
wife or girlfriend, "Don't make me no coffee, babe." Then Hank goes on to sing
"That's all she wrote, 'Dear John, I've sent your saddle home.' "*

*So, if this is the origin of the expression, and I wouldn't be at all surprised, there's
no joke and no punchline, although there is, of course, the scatalogical "saddle,"
which was undoubtedly intended by the writer. (Cf., a relatively recent country song,
"I've got the Horse and You've got the Saddle.")*

Douglas McGarrett
Jamaica, New York

*I'm quite sure the phrase "That's all she wrote" is from a song popular in the first
decade of this century, which, however, has suffered a change of gender, as well as
a slight change in the wording. The meaning is there, though.*

*Here it goes, as I remember it from fifty or sixty years ago, when my mother used
to sing it to me:*

> *There was I
> Waiting at the church,
> Waiting at the church,
> Waiting at the church,
> Wond'ring if
> He'd left me in the lurch,
> O how it did upset me (-set me);*
>
> *When all at once
> They brought me round a note,
> Here's the very note,
> And this is what he wrote:
> "I can't get away
> To marry you today,
> My wife—
> Won't let me."*

*I believe those are the correct words, but I seem to recall that sometimes mother
would sing, "And this is all he wrote," making more of a point of the horrible news.
They were different days.*

Arthur J. Morgan
New York, New York

The reference to a "Dear John letter" had become so popular a few years ago that it was a fairly common practice among girls short on compassion to terminate an affair by sending to their no-longer-wanted friends a letter consisting of the single line "Dear John" and their signature.

The missing joke may now be easily retrieved from oblivion: Bill tells his friend Tom: "I don't understand this; I have just received a letter from Jane in which she addresses me as 'Dear John.'" Tom asks "What does she say in the letter?" and Bill replies with the punch line: "That's all she wrote."

Ferdinand P. Beer
Coopersburg, Pennsylvania

"Dear John" and "That's all she wrote" came together in another country music song popular during the Korean War. As I remember:

I got up this morning, a note upon my door,
"Don't make me no coffee, babe; I won't be back no more."
That's all she wrote, "Dear John, I sent your saddle home."

Stanley H. Roe
Hamilton, New York

You say the meaning of "I say it's spinach, and I say the hell with it" has to do with unwillingness to abandon a prejudice. I use the line occasionally in another sense, it being: "I detect an egregious falsehood which I am unwilling to overlook for the sake of politeness." (This assumes that the kid was right and Mom was conning him.)

Bill Stavdal
Victoria, British Columbia

I believe your "Punch-Line English" interpretation of the broccoli-spinach cartoon and punch line is off the mark.

Your explanation, "Don't confuse me with the facts when I want to indulge my prejudices," implies that the mother who served the green stuff was telling the truth. In fact, the mother was trying to pawn off the spinach, as mothers of that era were inclined to do, by giving it a more palatable and exotic identity. I think Popeye was propagandizing for spinach about that time, also. Hence, the only interpretation of "I say it's spinach, and I say the hell with it," is "You may be older and wiser, but don't take me for a fool!"

Naomi C. Matusow
Armonk, New York

On punchlines: I challenge Jan Rubin's claim to the origins of "No soap, radio."
When I was growing up in Brooklyn in the 1950s we used the same gag for the same
reason. We often had a second one in reserve as well: Two sailors are stuck on an
ice floe in the North Atlantic. One asks: "How are we gonna get outta here?" The
other replies: "Don't worry. My father owns a toothpick factory."

"Ready when you are, C.B.!" actually happened. According to both C.B. and
Henry Wilcoxson, his assistant director (and Mark Antony to Claudette Colbert's
Cleopatra), the incident occurred during the filming of the scene where Moses
begins the Exodus from Egypt. De Mille set all of his thousands of Hebrews in
motion, only to have it go just as you reported it. This incident was recounted on
a PBS special about De Mille.

Mark M. Lowenthal
Reston, Virginia

"No soap, radio" was a part of my growing up in the East Bronx. We used the "joke"
about two elephants in a bathtub even less kindly than your New Jersey informant
did, to make fools out of those who didn't understand the no soap no-joke. Simple
malice was the game. (Tough times in the East Bronx, even then.) I think it was
current around Bruckner Boulevard circa 1952—is that an early sighting???

Joel Latner
Rochester, New York

Aw, c'mon now, Safire—"No soap, radio" a test, not a joke? Balderdash! Anyone
who worked in radio during that transition period when radio drama was giving way
to TV drama but both forms still existed, knows both the tagline and the story. The
explanation: On TV the scene described would require a real bar of soap, but on
radio a reference to a bar of castile did not require that the actor actually show or
produce the item. Thus, "No soap, radio"—a cop-out for something not at hand
when needed.

Joe Gottesman
Beverly Hills, California

It is 1947, I am 18, a graduate in the top 10 of my high school class, the four-year
Latin Prize Certificate ensconced at home, a reputation for high humor, and a
freshman in college. I am on my first date with an "older man" (22), a returned
serviceman attending a neighboring college. He brags incessantly about how well
he has done "socially" while stationed in Japan, and part of the pitch is the fact

that he brought home dozens of gorgeous silk scarves that any woman would do anything to have. I call him an egoist. With great gusto he informs me that there is no such word, and that I mean "egotist." A wager is made, and my booty would be a silk scarf.

Second date: We are in his car, he is driving north on Madison Avenue, approaching the red light at Smith Street. He stops the car, reaches into his coat pocket, takes out a tightly folded silk scarf, and, with thinly veiled annoyance, hands it to me. No words are spoken.

The light changes, the car moves. His voice takes on a cheerful note, and he tells me the latest joke he heard at his fraternity house. It was about the lion and the lioness taking the bath together. I didn't laugh; he triumphed.

Dear, dear William, for 37 years have I searched for someone who could explain the significance of "No soap, radio" to me. Bless you. What a relief. Bless you. Thank you.

> Marilyn Roth
> Whitestone, New York

In your article on joke punch lines which have come to be used as catch phrases, you overlooked a very popular one: "You can't get there from here."

Supposedly a tourist gets lost and asks a farmer how to get to Horsechester. The farmer thinks, starts to suggest going 4 miles east and turning left at the old schoolhouse; then thinks again, says maybe you head south to the second gas station and then west 20 rods . . . finally, he resignedly avows, "You can't get there from here."

> Lynn Welch
> Denver, Colorado

Your final paragraph contains an error, perhaps deliberate. The expression as I know it is "No more Mr. Nice Guy," meaning "I'm not going to be a nice fellow any longer." Your inclusion of a comma after "more" changes the meaning to "That's all there is there ain't no more."

Also, perhaps due to misconception when I first heard it some fifty years ago, I cannot agree with E. W. Gilman's feeling that the fan had to be running backward; the visual impact is of the fan blowing forward and outward (onto the assemblage) when "it" hit the fan.

> A. Thomas Veltre
> West Caldwell, New Jersey

You misquoted Robert Burns. In his poem "To a Mouse," Burns wrote "The best-laid schemes (not plans*) . . . gang aft a-gley."*

Edward S. Dermon
Roslyn Heights, New York

Another punch-line idiom—actually a caption—comes from a cartoon in The Reporter *dating back some 25 years. Two men are manacled to the wall spread-eagle fashion, five feet off the ground in what is obviously a dungeon. Some dozen feet above them there is a metal grille in the ceiling, apparently the only entry. The two, in rags, unkempt and thin, are in conversation. The one on the right is saying to the other: "Now, here's my plan." I don't know how widespread this caption is, but I saw the cartoon reproduced on ashtrays, aprons, cocktail napkins and I've heard and used the line.*

Louis T. Milic
Cleveland, Ohio

An added starter for your collection of punch lines which have evolved into popular sayings: "I may be crazy, but I'm not stupid."

I'm sure you recall the gag behind that adage. A motorist gets a flat tire in front of a mental hospital. He removes the lug nuts and places them in the hubcap, but a passing car strikes the hubcap and sends the nuts flying. A patient, watching the scene from behind the hospital fence, then suggests that he remove one nut from each remaining wheel in order to mount the spare tire. The driver says, "That's brilliant. And you're in this hospital?" And the patient responds with the punch line.

Philip Weinberg
Jamaica, New York

I liked the paragraph on "What's this 'we' jazz, paleface?" about the Lone Ranger and his faithful Indian Tonto.

Do you know what Tonto means? In Spanish it means stupid. I wonder how many faithful followers of the Lone Ranger know that.

Charles A. Bertrand, M.D.
White Plains, New York

Even more interesting to the humor pro is a joke where both straight line and punch line are in the common vernacular. I call this a "Punch Line Sundae":

"What's a nice girl like you doing in a place like this?"

"Just lucky, I guess."
I'll try to keep my eyes open for good examples of these categories. But never on a Sundae.

Art Yaspan
Jamaica, New York

You may well not have this one. I have never met anyone else who knew it. I heard it many, many years ago at the old B&O Railroad.

There had been a terrible train wreck. Two expresses had collided full tilt. Hundreds were killed. The only witness was the gateman at the crossing. He was put on the stand at the investigation.

Q. Where were you at 2:30 p.m. on March 17?

A. I was sitting in my shack and I heard trains whistling for the crossing.

Q. What did you do then?

A. I got up and went outside and looked up the track and there came No. 91 headed south about eighty miles an hour.

Q. Then what did you do?

A. I looked down the track and there came No. 92 headed north about eighty miles an hour.

Q. What did you do then?

A. I went back inside my shack and I sat down and I said to myself, that's a hell of a way to run a railroad.

Thaddeus Holt
New York, New York

P.S. There used to be an Andrew Sisters song—or maybe it was Betty Hutton—of which the tag line was "the pencil broke, and that's all she wrote." But maybe the song followed upon the phrase.

"It only hurts when I laugh."
  "That's a hell of a way to run a railroad."

"Who's minding the store?"
"Waiting for the other shoe to drop."
"Bimbam, thank you ma'am."
"But what have you done for me lately?"
"But it's the only game in town."
Well, that's the way it is. Goodnight Bill. Th-th-th-th-that's all folks.

Edward B. Swain, M.D.
West Hartford, Connecticut

Respectfully Disagree

When you disagree with your superior, or your friend, or someone you respect, how do you put him in his place? Answer: by putting him in a figurative place or state.

The Reverend Paul A. Wickens, a priest in the Archdiocese of Newark, is in a feud with his archbishop, at least in part because of the prelate's support for a nuclear freeze. After Father Wickens suggested that churchgoers withhold their Sunday contributions, the archbishop decided to suspend him and to evict him from the rectory.

The rambunctious priest announced coolly: "I believe my archbishop is in schism."

Where is *schism*, anyway? That word—originally pronounced "sizzem" but now more often pronounced "skizem"—is a noun meaning "split." In theological circles, however, Splitsville is a most specific state of being. I consulted Father William Hill of the Catholic University's School of Theology for a definition.

"In schism refers to a division in canonical terms," he replied. "That division may be disciplinary as opposed to doctrinal. Doctrinal issues would involve ideas like the belief in the divinity of Jesus, while disciplinary matters have to do with the exercise of authority—for example, one bishop intruding upon another bishop's area. It is possible to be *in schism* in disciplinary issues without being divided in doctrinal areas."

I ran across a similar state a generation ago, researching the origin of Franklin Delano Roosevelt's use of "new deal." Judge Samuel I. Rosenman told me that he had drafted the peroration to Mr. Roosevelt's acceptance speech to the 1932 Democratic National Convention: "I pledge you, I pledge myself, to a new deal for the American people."

Raymond Moley, another Brain Truster and later a columnist for *Newsweek*, took sharp exception to this when I called about it. He pointed to evidence in a book of his, *After Seven Years*, that showed the phrase was suggested by him. How did Professor Moley react when it was pointed out that his old colleague remembered history somewhat differently?

He did not direct his ire at the man personally; Raymond the Mole did not say that Sammy the Rose had a lousy memory or was mistaken or wrong. Instead, he chose a delicate but unbudging usage: "When Rosenman says that he wrote it," Moley said, "he is in error."

Disputants who use civil phrases like that are in a graceful state. Where do you hear an argument these days that goes "You're in schism" or "You're in error"? I'm in awe.

R.S.V.I.P.

"The Honorable Ronald Wilson Reagan," begins the formal-looking invitation mailed to a few million potential contributors, ". . . extends his personal invitation to you to play a major role in the 1984 election by becoming a sustaining member of the Republican National Committee."

So far, so phony; it's not a real invitation; it's a solicitation using the President's name. But direct-mail solicitors have a certain responsibility to observe the formalities when they presume to go formal. The G.O.P. fund-raisers start with a gaffe on the envelope: "R.S.V.P. Requested." Inside, on the "invitation," the gaffe is compounded: "Please RSVP."

R.S.V.P., which should have the periods after each letter, stands for the French *Répondez s'il vous plaît*—literally, "Reply, if it pleases you," or more colloquially, "Please reply."

Although an "R.S.V.P." is a noun for an invitation with *R.S.V.P.* on it, the letters do not lend themselves to redundancy. ("SALT talks" or "START talks" are in error, too, since the *T* stands for *talks*, but not everybody is expected to know arms-controlese. Every writer of formal invitations is expected to know how to write a formal invitation.) "R.S.V.P. Requested" is gauche, and "Please RSVP" ridiculously redundant.

If English is to be used at the corner of an invitation, to the dismay of etiquetters, the correct phrase would be "Please reply." What they mean in this case, of course, is: "Don't come—send money."

There are two other redundancies that I have repeatedly encountered in my twenty-one years as a magazine editor: "A-C current" and "RAM memory." One guess as to what the "C" and "M" stand for in these abbreviations.

I have finally adapted to computerists' widespread use of "RAM memory" (which really should be read as "random-access memory memory"), but I have never gotten used to "A-C" or to "alternating current."

Paul M. Eckstein
Bayside, New York

Saying a Mouthful

A delicious affectation is being served at many posh American restaurants. The waiter appears with a menu, which only clods are expected to look at; the cognoscenti await a recitation of the unlisted specials of the day. This obviates the need for little cards paper-clipped to the menu and conceals the price of the items to be ordered.

The waiter's performance is delivered in the present progressive, the preferred tense of restaurantese. "George in the kitchen is making a calf's liver, lightly sautéed in polyunsaturated oil," he reports. "He's doing fresh fish, too, which we're serving with a sprig of wilted dill." This tense indicates action in the present as well as in the future: At this very moment, George is sloshing on the corn oil and will continue the sloshing throughout the lunch hour. Never does the waiter say, "We have" or "The special is"; that is the simple present tense, which is now used only in lowfalutin fast-food establishments.

Centre Court, a steak house in Manhattan, advertises "interesting *verbal specials.*" Presumably these are articulated in the present progressive rather than listed in print (although *verbal* covers both *oral* and *written*).

"What do they mean by 'interesting *verbal specials*'?" demands Alexander McKeveny of East Islip, New York. "Is salty language used to describe the soupe du jour? Perhaps a multilingual staff serves bons mots for dessert?"

My own favorite verbal special is *omelette aux fines verbes*, with a side of *grammar gratinée*. But never try to put down a waiter during his recitation. Asked what the soupe du jour was, one waiter replied with appropriate condescension: "It's the soup of the day."

Say It Right

People are worried about pronunciation—other people's, usually. Karen Rosenberg, who describes herself as a physical anthropologist, writes from the University of Michigan about the frequent mispronunciation of *dissect*. "Most people pronounce it with a long *i*," to rhyme with *bisect*, she points out. Both share the same Latin root, *secare*, meaning "to cut," but while *bi-sect* means "to cut in two," *dis-sect* means "to cut apart." Confusion over the meanings may have led to confusion over the pronunciation: *Dissect* is pronounced with a short *i*.

I have been mispronouncing that word ever since we dissected those poor frogs in the bio lab of the Bronx High School of Science. So why not go on mispronouncing it—won't common usage cover me? The answer is no: In that case, *dissect* loses all meaning when it rhymes with *bisect*. (Mail will come in from dissenters, however they pronounce themselves.)

Meanwhile, J. M. Cuthbertson of Chatsworth, California, has been watching convention television and objects to announcers who pronounce *machination* as *mashination* instead of the correct *makination, ek cetera* instead of *et cetera*, *barbituates* instead of *barbiturates*, and *sherbert* instead of *sherbet*. (Supporters of Senator Gary Hart and other eaters of kiwi fruit never make that last mistake; for yumpies, it is *sorbet*, pronounced *SOR-bay*.)

Announcers can avoid error by turning to the *NBC Handbook of Pronunciation*, by Eugene Ehrlich and Raymond Hand Jr., now in its fourth edition, with an introduction by Edwin Newman. (*Announcers* do not call themselves that anymore; Newman writes that *broadcasters* and announcers of various types now call themselves *newscasters, anchors* and, on the commercial side, *spokespersons*; detractors call nonwriting newsies *rip-'n-readers*. Many old fogies in the audience persist in using *announcer*, however, in fond remembrance of crystal sets and "Mr. Keen, Tracer of Lost Persons." The word has not been aggressively banished, as *stewardess*—now *flight attendant*—has been, because *announcer* is not sexist; however, most of today's broadcasters limit its use to a description of Norman Brokenshire.)

The handbook supplements dictionaries because it helps out on the pronunciation of celebrated people's names. The last name of Konstantin Chernenko, the Soviet leader, is pronounced *Cher-NEN-koh*, according to NBC, though some Russian experts would stick a *y* in that middle syllable, to sound like *NYEN*; those people called Brezhnev *BREZH-nyev*. Standing in the wings is Mikhail Gorbachev, pronounced *Mee-high-EEL Gor-bah-CHAWF*. (Remember that name: Moscow party boss Viktor Grishin certainly will.)

Harper & Row, which sent me the book, adds in a covering note: "Please indicate, after your comments, your correct title." Here goes: *LANG-widge MAY-ven*.

Maybe, just maybe, if I dissected those poor frogs with the geniuses at Bronx High School of Science, instead of the common delinquents at DeWitt Clinton, I would not have to read the Times *to learn how to become a real maven. I might also know how to pronounce* research *instead of alternating pronunciations so that I will be right at least half the time. Do you learn to rĕ·sûrch' or rē'sûrch or is there a special and appropriate Safirism to cover the situation? At Clinton we had more mundane things to worry about, like blocking left hooks and keeping one's teeth in place.*

M. Reich
Rockville, Maryland

You gave our pronunciation of Konstantin Chernenko's last name as cher-NEN-koh, *and that is indeed the way you read it in the uncorrected bound galleys. Before the book went to press, a press officer at the Soviet consulate in New York City told us with Soviet sternness that the correct pronunciation is* chər-NYEN-kə.

Russian names are difficult to pronounce, even for trained interpreters at the United Nations, who gave us the pronunciation you printed. The sad fact for lexicographers is that regional variations are at least as common in Russian as in British and American English. Fortunately, the NBC Handbook *got this one right.*

Rest assured that chər-NYEN-kə, *replete with two schwas, is the correct pronunciation of the gentleman's name.*

If you decide to so inform your readers, you might also wish to point out our pronunciation of Menachem Begin's last name. The common mispronunciation can be traced back to Time, *which slyly wrote that Begin rhymes with Fagin. A check with an Israeli press officer at the consulate in New York City enabled us to pronounce the name correctly as* BE-geen, *with the BE as in bet. I think it might be good for your readers to know this, even though the mispronunciation is deeply rooted by now.*

Eugene Ehrlich
Pleasantville, New York

The value of your column must be considered greatly deflated by your having overlooked among the notable failures to "Say It Right" of broadcasters and newscasters.

Iran and Iranians, frequently mispronounced Eye-RAN *and* Eye-RAN-ians *(suggestive of Cockney British servicemen in* WWII *with* Eye-TAL-ians*).*

E. H. Leoni
New York, New York

I wish you had said something about the consistent and annoying habit of mispronouncing the word "processes." It almost drives me mad to hear it pronounced "process-eez" by people who should know better. Please, in some future column, tell them to stop it.

Philomene DiGiacomo
Staten Island, New York

I would imagine that the NBC Handbook of Pronunciation *deals effectively with the pronunciation of individual words, taken out of the context of phrases and sentences. What is needed, however, is a book that will show newscasters how to articulate the final and initial phonic values of adjacent words. Careless articulation of these values causes overlapping, which changes the sound, and sometimes the meaning, that was originally intended.*

Such overlapping frequently occurs on morning news/talk shows, when referring to segments of time: "the yower"; "thĭ sour"; "fûr stower"; "secon dower"; "sekə nower"; "thĭ să fower"; "fûr stă fower"; "neck stă fower."

In order to be articulate, initial vowel sounds should be glottal. When the sounds of adjacent vowels overlap, the intermediate phonic value of [y] or [w] will occur: "a beautiful day in the yeast"; "the lesser of two weevils."

When a final consonant overlaps an initial vowel, it becomes the initial phonic value of that word: "The Yimeral Dial"; "our roperators are standing by"; "The Soviet Chunion"; "a Britĕe shot"; "The Boston Collie Jiggles"; "attack psych."

The final sound of [s] or [st], overlapping an initial voiced consonant, forms a blend or "cluster." The vocal cords remain at the open posture, changing the voiced value to an unvoiced value: "Pap Spear" (Pabst Beer); "fûr skrade"; "sixty bates" (six debates); "the hiyə spidder"; "the Giant skoal line"; "a Spanĕ shkaleon"; "Bo Derrick Spolero"; "thi Spuds for you"; "the crew ĭ spuckle dup"; "Edward Zair Four Space."

When the final, unvoiced sound of [s] follows a vowel, or a voiced consonant, it is, supposedly, changed to the voiced sound of [z], but . . . "Dinver Smile High Stadium"; "President Reagan skrandfather"; "America Steam"; "In the worts of Lincoln"; "The Cup spattle The Mets"; "Iran Skhar Gisland"; "The women stubble sfinals"; "The Yarm Stalks Brokawgh."

The call letters and names, used to identify networks and programs, produce some interesting phonetic varieties: "Thĭ sĭ Scable News Network"; "Sē Yĭ Nĭn Stay-break"; "Sē Bē Yĕ Snüz"; "The Yea Bē Sē Swide World of Sports"; "New Swatch Weather"; "Eye Witnə Snüz"; "The Yĭn Bē Sē Sport Swirled."

It is a bewildering paradox that anyone would ponder the addition of [y] to Chernenko, or the omission of [r] from sherbe(r)t, and tolerate the inaccurate diction that results from overlapping adjacent phonic values. And since, in so far as I know, there has been no objection to, or comment about, such linguistic inexpertise, I wonder . . . could it be that no one cares enough, or that no one knows enough, to demand anything better.

I believe that the attitude of abject apathy toward such overlapping, is indicative of a pervasive lack of phonetic literacy in our society, brought about, and perpetuated by the completely un-scientific approach for teaching, and learning, the phonic values that are inherent to the words of our language.

Have an iced Ā,
Leonard T. Wagner
Vidalia, Georgia

Scoreless on the Year

The perfect Christmas gift for a sportscaster, as all fans of sports clichés know, is a scoreless tie. The Squad Squad frowns on that locution, insisting that all scoreless games are tied, but those less finicky about redundancy argue that not all ties are scoreless: After the gift of a scoreless tie, what ensues is the eagerly sought "sudden death."

That observation places us in good field position for a discussion of the battering the language is taking from monster-man announcers who come to play. "He's two for four on the day or thirty-five out of fifty on the year." *On* the day, *on* the year? "The wide range of meanings of *on*," writes Leslie Oster of New York, "does not include a meaning for which one visualizes the athlete standing on top of the year's statistics."

"Idioms is idioms," retorts the legion of laid-back commentators, who see no need to defense the complaints of grammarians keying on them. Indeed, some of their new verbs have earned a place in the denotation of meaning—*defense* as a verb, for example, does not mean "defend"; it means "play defense against," which is slightly different—but others merely repeat another formulation and are coined merely to save space. "SOX NO-HIT BY ROOKIE," a recent headline in the *Chicago Tribune*, used *no-hit* as a verb to mean "were pitched a no-hitter"; it is useful to space-hungry headline writers, but I would vandermeer it in ordinary speech.

In the same way, I would go along with the objection made by the pundit of Scottish extraction down the hall that the sportscaster who said, "Theismann audibleized the play," was playing the language too much by ear.

Sportscasters who make the game more vivid with colorful language deserve our kudos (careful—there is no such thing as a single "kudo"), and theirs is a very physical, not to say opportunistic, vocabulary. But too often, a dreary bureaucratese slips into their talk: Instead of "He's warming up in the bull pen," we hear, "There is bull-pen activity," or instead of "It's third and one," we hear the pompous "We're in a third-and-short situation." Sports is an activity that should admit no "situations"; former coaches who presume to inflict us with this deliberate language-grounding should suffer a long hang time. (And while we're at it, there are no "former Heisman Trophy winners" and will not be until somebody wins a former Heisman Trophy.)

The greatest contribution to grammar made by today's sportscasters is the development of the *historical future* tense. The doddering reader will recall the use of the *historical present* by Damon Runyon, a writer who was once a sportswriter, as in "When I hear Bugs Lonigan say this, I wish I am never born." Listening to the score of *Guys and Dolls*, based on Runyon's stories, one is hard-pressed to hear a single past tense. (The uniforms of nose tackles are deliberatedly hard-pressed.)

"Sports broadcasters are the only reporters I know of," writes Burnett Anderson of Washington, "who describe past events in the future tense." He notes the following examples:

"That will [*future tense*] bring up a third-down situation" is used to describe a play that has already taken place and has created the third down.

"He swings and he misses—that'll [*future tense*] be strike two" reports a strike that has already been taken. Similarly, "The kick is good; that'll [*future tense*] make it 21–10" refers to points that have already been scored.

"A friend who considers himself an authority in these matters," writes Mr. Anderson, "says the use of the historical future is proper because the event does not fall into the past until legitimized by the umpires, referees and official scorers. I concede grudgingly that there may be some validity to this theory, but it doesn't hold water when you see a mighty whiff at the plate and hear, 'That will be strike two.'"

If this accepted usage in sports spills over into the general language, we will hear how "something has happened next week," which, as grammar fan Anderson notes, "will bring up a devastation situation."

Let us all, then, beware of playing catch-up in the way we appropriate language from sportscasters and metaphors from sports. (Is Senator Glenn keying on Mondale?) In a piece disparaging the use of *human* when *man* as short for *mankind* is meant, I wrote of the time when "I longed to be a 'two-sewer hitter'—that is, capable of punching a rubber ball the distance between two humanhole covers." (In Chicago, that would be headlined as SOX TWO-SEWERED BY ROOKIE.)

The correction lobbed in the other day was: "You mean it is the distance between *three*, not two, humanhole covers." "You forgot," writes (wrote? brings up a letter from?) Jerry Eskenazi of *The New York Times* Sports section, "that you're standing on one sewer (the manhole cover that serves as home plate). Thus, you hit it two sewers down.

"I know," insists Mr. Eskenazi, "I did it. Once. I was fifteen and it was spring. . . ."

You seconded the contention of a reader that "Sports broadcasters are the only reporters I know of who describe past events in the future tense."

Both of them have short memories or are too young to remember Waite Hoyt, a Hall of Fame pitcher who after his retirement as a player in 1938 was a two-decade sportscaster for the Cincinnati Reds. He described plays in the past *tense.*

I was not born till two years after Mr. Hoyt left the mound for the last time, and have never been to Cincinnati. But I have corresponded with him often over the years, and three years ago asked him over the phone why he would say, during a play, "X hit the ball a-a-and Y caught it for the third out." His explanation: "I was describing action that had already occurred, so I used the past tense."

Such usage would sound strange today; but Mr. Hoyt is a fellow native Brooklynite, so he must know whereof he spoke.

George J. Friedman
New York, New York

Allow me to supplement your discussion of colorful sports grammar by noting the increasing use by baseball players and managers of what I will call the "subjunctive present past tense" in post-game interviews.

In recalling a pivotal moment in the contest, the manager is frequently quoted as saying something like: "If he lays down the bunt, we lose the game." Invariably, the usage refers to an event that didn't occur, but if it had, would have produced a negative effect on the user's team. As far as I can tell, the construction is limited to baseball and has yet to find its way into the broadcasting booth.

However, if Safire writes about it, we can't defense it.

Daniel B. Payne
Boston, Massachusetts

No *to Mr. Cosell's use of "intercept" as a noun. For fifty years of pro football (and since 1906, when the forward pass was introduced in the college game) "interception" was a perfectly decent, hard-working noun.*

But yes to "on the game," "on the season," and "on the year." I will explain. First, to deal with Leslie Oster ("of New York") and Leslie's clever comment. Of course " 'the wide range of meanings of on does not include a meaning for which one visualizes the athlete standing on top of the year's statistics.' " You notice, however, that Leslie cites only one of that "wide range of meanings." My dictionary lists twenty-four different definitions for "on," and only one of those, the first, has anything to do with anything being "on top of" anything.

So let us then examine the many definitions ignored by Leslie (and yourself) in your sweeping disavowal of "on the game," etc. What about "9) with respect to"? Certainly with respect to the player's performance in the game, he went three-for-four. Not good enough for you? Then take your pick of the following: "in a condition or process of," "forward, onward, or along," and/or "with continuous activity." If you can do something "on" a particular occasion (I went to bed on Sunday afternoon because I was exhausted after the boring sermon), then George Brett can certainly make three hits out of four at-bats on a particular game. Wait, you shout, that takes in none of the above definitions. Agreed, but those were merely for reinforcement (statistics as an ongoing process, a continuing entity). I would argue that "on the game," "on the season," and "on the year" are all proper because of "13) used to indicate time or occasion." You would not, I hope, argue that a baseball game is not an occasion, and seasons, years, and careers are simply multiples of those brief, but defined (three outs, nine innings) occasions.

On Tuesday I will resume teaching 6th and 8th grade English. On the night I have written five letters. I have never done much on any game, because I can't hit the curve. On the game Carl Yastrzemski went one for three, but he popped up in his last at-bat. On the season (read: on several games) he hit as well at age 43 as he did as a rookie. On his career (read: several seasons) he hit over 400 home runs. On that note . . .

Richard E. "Nick" Noble
Southborough, Massachusetts

You stated that there are no former Heisman Trophy winners. I disagree.

Picture me standing next to Roger Staubach and Earl Campbell. The former Heisman Trophy winner is telling me about the thrill of winning a Super Bowl, and the latter Heisman Trophy winner is looking on with envy.

How's that?

Bill Weiss
Rego Park, New York

Our local ABC television station has been interrupting Monday Night Football *each week with this plea: "Stay tuned for the* Late Night News, *upcoming right after the football game."*

Whatever happened to "following" the football game or "right after" the football game? I called the broadcaster to protest his usage and he replied: "I had to fill ten seconds." After a long discussion, he agreed the usage was poor, and he has since avoided upcoming *even during his news broadcast. That's how I spell RELIEF.*

Warren Witherell
East Burke, Vermont

As a history teacher in a Brooklyn junior high school, I have always been fascinated by athletes named after well-known historical figures. A number of quarterbacks, mostly from Southern colleges, have been named after Jefferson Davis; in recent years, the New York Jets drafted a defensive back by the name of Admiral Dewey Larry. (He was, to my chagrin, cut. Did the Turk bring his pink slip in a manila envelope?)

Your mention of the phrase "hang time" brought the following thought to mind. What would announcers and related media-types do if a punter ever emerged with the name Nathan Hale? Would Howard Cosell really be blathering about Nathan Hale's "hang time"—or am I being overly optimistic? Please advise.

James R. O'Mahoney
Brooklyn, New York

Secret Plan

A delicious, sinister phrase has been an early centerpiece of the Democratic campaign against Ronald Reagan: The President is charged with harboring a *secret plan* to raise taxes after the election.

Walter Mondale has already frankly asserted that he would raise taxes to lower the deficit, while laying the secret-plan bait in two punchy sentences in his acceptance speech: "He won't tell you. I just did."

The President promptly stepped into the trap, by insisting he had "no plans" to raise taxes. In Spokesmanspeak, the signal-ridden language of pressrooms, the phrase *no plans* is a term of art meaning "not ready for announcement yet." (A calibration further, *no present intention*, means "We will announce it Monday.")

The no-plans response enabled the Democrats to blaze away with the charge that the President had a *secret plan* to raise taxes. In retreat, Mr. Reagan finally had to say he could "never say never" (and the originator of that great presidential axiom remains unknown), but he would raise taxes only as "a last resort."

The *secret-plan* ploy had worked again. Cartoonist Wayne Stayskal of the *Tampa Tribune* showed a pollster at a doorway being told by a housewife: "I'm a registered Democrat . . . but I've got a secret plan to vote Republican!"

Mr. Mondale was ready with his secret secret-plan plan, because he had been on the receiving end of the charge this spring. Senator John Glenn, slamming his primary opponent's undue caution, said, "To be so cautious that your platform consists of secret plans to be revealed after the elections—to be that cautious is not leadership, it's politics." *The New York Times* headline over the story zeroed in on the catch phrase: GLENN SAYS RIVAL HAS "SECRET PLANS."

These happy hand-me-downs made me smile, because I was writing speeches for Richard Nixon in the spring of 1968 when the phrase was first used as a political charge.

In a speech about Vietnam, the candidate for the Republican nomination pledged to "end the war and win the peace in the Pacific." Supporters of George Romney, who was the Rockefeller stalking-horse in the New Hampshire primary, promptly elevated that vague Nixon promise to a "plan" and demanded more details. In the Nixon camp, we knew there was no plan; some specific ideas for negotiation were scheduled for delivery in a speech on March 31, 1968, but that speech was scrubbed when President Johnson announced his retirement that night.

Governor Romney kept hammering away, "Where is your secret plan?" Within a week, a false quotation had been manufactured: Nixon was widely quoted as having said, "I have a secret plan to end the war." Such a statement would have been, on its face, nonsense for any political figure to say, but many newspapers ran it as gospel. Nixon never said it.

Years later, in the White House, the Nixon speechwriters would see the false quotation surface in some column; we took delight in writing the columnist: "We're trying to find the origin of that remark. Do you happen to have the clip?" This straight-faced query led to red-faced embarrassment, which satisfied some of our mediaphobia.

Today, the secret-plan charge has become part of many artful campaigns. It is a means of attacking a generality-peddling politician for not being specific enough; if and when the opposition promiser is suckered into revealing a plan, the attacker then says, "See? We smoked him out," and blazes away at the specifics of the newly revealed (and usually newly created) plan.

Credit belongs to George Romney, who was laid low by his use of *brainwashed*. Who remembers the firestorm over *brainwashed* anymore? Nobody; yet *secret plan*, little remarked at the time, has found its place in the art of invidious inveighing.

Dear Bill:

I read your "secret plan" piece with particular interest, because I was one of the reporters covering Nixon the day the whole thing started.

You give George Romney too much credit. Milt Benjamin did it. Benjamin then was a UPI staffer in Boston, and now is with the Washington Post.

Nixon was campaigning in one of those old mill towns, and gave a speech in which he said that if elected he would—as you recounted—end the war and win the peace in the Pacific. He was asked how, and said he would not discuss specifics because—and this is rough paraphrase—it would undercut LBJ.

I wrote a lead that used the end the war/win the peace quote, followed immediately by Nixon's refusal to say how he'd do it.

Milt wrote a UPI lead saying that Nixon said he had a secret plan to end the war in Vietnam. No quotes around secret plan.

This accomplished two things. It beat hell out of my story and got him all the play, and it created the secret plan issue.

I recounted this in The News Business, *the widely unread book John Chancellor and I wrote in 1983. Stan Karnow heard about it and used it in his book on Vietnam. Stan told me that the producer of the Vietnam TV history on which he'd worked earlier had spent vast amounts of time and money searching the 1968 campaign files for tape of RN saying he had "a secret plan." Since he never said it they never found it, but the producer apparently wouldn't take his staff's no for an answer and insisted that they keep hunting.*

Now even the pusillanimous pussyfooters of history know that he didn't say it. Maybe we should offer this to the Trivial Pursuit people. The question of who didn't have a secret plan to end the war would be a stumper for all but the 817 people who read our book and the untold millions who read your words columns.

> Walter [Mears]
> Vice President and Executive Editor
> Associated Press
> New York, New York

You are WRONG. Mr. Nixon did say, "I know a way to end the war" and he said it in the Strafford Room of the Memorial Union Building of the University of New Hampshire at Durham.

A student asked, "How do you plan to end the war?" and Nixon said, "I'm not telling yet."

I will never forget this as I was filled with fury that while my friends were being killed this man said he had a way, but would not tell.

Like it or not, you are very mistaken.

> Polly Webster
> Durham, New Hampshire

Shambling Along

"America's Mideast policy is in shambles," declared former national security adviser Zbigniew Brzezinski. In a wholly different context, Judith Miller of *The New York Times* wrote from Beirut: "The Lebanese economy is in shambles."

A variety of correspondents have wondered: Why has *shambles* lost its article? Why isn't our policy, or their economy, in *a* shambles? *To make a shambles of* comes easily to the tongue, but you never hear *to make shambles of*. Which, then, is correct: shambles with or without an *a*?

First to the etymology, which will give us a clue. The Latin *scamnum* is a bench; that was later applied to a bench offering meat for sale and later to a meat market or slaughterhouse; in time, *shambles* became a plural noun taking a singular verb for "place of great carnage." In this century, the bloodiness has drained from the word, and it now denotes a place of disorder, like a teen-ager's room. ("You call this a place to live? You've turned it into a shambles!")

The place of disorder—exemplified by the messy apartments in the cartoons of

George Booth, with mangy cats hanging from dangling lampshades—is often used as a metaphor for a system. Here is where we can find the place for the mysterious article: If you refer to a single scene of confusion, call it *a* shambles. (One teen-ager's room is a shambles.) If you want to excoriate more than one such scene, refer to *shambles* without an *a*: Teen-agers generally make shambles out of their rooms.

Where does that leave us with metaphoric usage? In discussing policy or an economy, we are speaking of a series of messes, not just one neat little mess: Hence, Mr. Brzezinski and Miss Miller were correct—grammatically, at least—in comparing the Middle East policy or the Lebanese economy to more than one scene of shambles and therefore leaving out the singularizing *a*.

Some irate reader is going to limp in with a query about the verb *to shamble*, recalling the poem about Lincoln's "length of shambling limb." Go back to the beginning: That shuffling walk comes from the Latin bench, which often had poorly made legs, and people with such limbs had an awkward or clumsy gait.

Shambolic

Once in a great while, language shamans get to taste the delicious flavor of mint: Instead of merely reporting on new words, they coin one themselves. Fourteen years ago, while joining in the gleeful derogation of "welfare" in the White House, I came up with a label for the sort of welfare program that contained a work requirement: *workfare*. The coinage was no big deal, as the word has a specialized rather than a household use, but *workfare* keeps popping up without any plugging from me.

Shambles is a word that has been explored in this space. Accompanied by an article—*a* shambles—the word denotes a specific place of disorder. Without the article—just plain *shambles*—the word's meaning widens to embrace messed-up plans or areas of the world. In sum, our Lebanese policy is in shambles; Beirut is in *a* shambles.

Of late, our British cousins have taken to using an adjective: *shambolic*. Frances Julius of London sends me clippings, which she calls "cuttings," of these uses: "The Government's handling of the ban on unions . . . has been little short of shambolic," editorialized *The Daily Telegraph*. Ian Wrigglesworth, a member of Parliament, called on the foreign secretary to resign because the decision to ban trade-union membership at the Cheltenham communications center was handled "in a shambolic way." (Why don't we have American politicians with names like Wrigglesworth? Perfect moniker for an embarrassed press spokesman.)

None of the current general dictionaries have (yes, "none have") the adjective *shambolic* yet, but *The Barnhart Dictionary of New English* defines the word as "disorderly; in a shambles." Its only citation is from a June 18, 1970, article in *The Times* of London, describing the tidy newspaper office of a Japanese correspondent: "a standing reproach to the standard image of shambolic newspaper offices strewn with waste paper and inflated egos."

The author of that article was Philip Howard, the resident language maven at *The Times*, whose pieces are currently available in the United States in a book, *A Word in Your Ear*.

Perhaps Mr. Howard did not coin *shambolic*; I'm afraid to ask. At least he is the first cited user, and that distinction is significant to those of us in this fraternity. Since the use of *shambles*, with and without the article, is growing in America, it is likely that *shambolic* will make the transatlantic leap, unless it sounds too much like *symbolic* spoken after too many drinks.

Your column suggests Philip Howard, "resident language maven" at the London Times, *may have coined the word "shambolic."*

No way.

The word has been a favored utterance of British army drill instructors for at least three decades. I entered that service in 1953 and our squad, of routine incompetence, was regularly excoriated for being "the most shambolic 'orrible shower of over-heducated nig-nogs (i.e., officer candidates) ever to disgrace 'Er Majesty's uniform."

The dazzling fluency of such tirades, generally administered at an eyeball-to-eyeball range of six inches, strongly suggests that they have been evolved and polished through several centuries of parade ground bombast.

Even thirty years later, none of the language shamans at Quadrant Research is likely to slur the differences between "shambolic" and "symbolic"—until the sixth or seventh stiff scotch.

J.T.W. Hubbard
Syracuse, New York

The word "shambolic" sounds like a good invention. But you make no mention of the use of the word "shambles" meaning a slaughterhouse. I came across this recently in Vexed and Troubled Englishmen 1590–1642 *by Carl Bridenbaugh. I was unfamiliar with the word as it relates to a building. It is so noted in the dictionaries I have. I had to look it up to know what the author was referring to. The transition from a slaughterhouse to a place of disorder is understandable.*

E. F. Hiscock
North Chatham, Massachusetts

Sharp Elbows

"No man lives without jostling and being jostled," wrote Thomas Carlyle in 1838. "In all ways he has to elbow himself through the world, giving and receiving offense."

In the world of politics, elbows have become the single most important possession of a candidate. "This campaign shows that Mondale, far from being a patsy," wrote Michael Barone in the *Washington Post*, "is a politician with elbows."

The metaphor of a person using his elbows to make room for himself is international: In 1980, a Bonn politician was censured for charging that candidate Franz Josef Strauss was a man allied "with usurers and wheelerdealers and is a man with razor blades on his elbows."

The not-so-funny bone has a revered place in slang: *To bend the elbow* is to take a drink, and an *elbow* is a cop, the name taken from the way some policemen elbow their way through a crowd for their prey. An *elbow shaker* was defined in Grose's *Dictionary of the Vulgar Tongue* in 1785 as "a gamester, one who rattles Sir Hugh's bones—i.e., the dice." That early slang compendium also defined *elbow room* as "sufficient space to act in"; *out at elbows* as "in declining circumstances," and *elbow grease* as "labor. Elbow grease will make an oak table shine."

A change of connotation is taking place in the political use of the word. Not long ago, *to have sharp elbows* was not considered a compliment, as was apparent in the calumniation of Mr. Strauss. Today, a politician without elbows is as lost as a politician without principles. The display of elbows is evidence of necessary *macho*.

On occasion, the elbows still go a bit too far. In *Caveat*, the memoirs of nuance-ridden Alexander Haig, he captions a picture of himself with hands on hips, elbows prominent: "The 'take-charge' image had taken hold. . . . My photograph (jaw jutting, arms akimbo) had been on the cover of *Time* magazine."

Much too *macho*. *Akimbo* comes from the Old Norse *kengboginn*, the shape of a bow when it has been bent back, and it is a position that bespeaks pride or hostility. In sum, a political figure today must have elbows, but they must not be too sharp, and he must not display them to photographers.

An arrest by a policeperson is called an elbow *not because he or she elbows through the crowd but because a suspect is quickly pacified by being grabbed from behind with an elbow under his or her chin, the rest of the "collar" made up by the remainder of the policeperson's arm.*

Chris Cowap
New York, New York

The word macho, *which means "male" or "manly," is* not a noun; *it is an* adjective *(or predicate adjective.)*

Examples:

1) Mi esposa tuvo un hijo macho—*My wife had a male child.*
   Hijo *means* either *child or son.*

2) Mi hermano es muy macho—*My brother is very manly.*

The noun you are looking for is machismo, *"maleness." Machismo is pronounced* ma-CHEES'-moh.

Ross Aguirre
Arcadia, California

Shoo-In

Citing the lowering of the "misery index"—that addition of the unemployment rate to the inflation rate—Leonard Silk, economics columnist of *The New York Times*, wrote: "Mr. Reagan could have some reason to regard himself as a shoe-in."

Judy Westerman of New York assumes that *shoe-in* is a typographical error for *shoo-in*, and wonders if writers will not turn to other up-to-date phrases of finality like *carved in stone* or *made in the shade*. But when queried, Mr. Silk does not take refuge in the old typo excuse (which has grown difficult since word-processing terminals have made us our own typesetters).

"I used *shoo-in* to mean 'a walkaway, an easy win,'" says my colleague, who is known to lexicographers as the coiner of *double digit*. "I don't know why I spelled it *shoe-in*. I just bought some shoes." It could be that this misspelling, a frequent one, is influenced by *shoehorn*, a verb meaning "to insert into a difficult space" or "to fit in with difficulty."

Slang metaphors change their meanings as they are applied in different fields. Mr. Silk's political meaning, "easy win," is accurate; in racing, however, where the term originated, the term retains a more sinister meaning. *To shoo* is a centuries-old colloquialism for "to urge a person or animal to move in a desired direction." Back in the bad old days, corrupt jockeys would form a "ring" and bet on a single horse, holding back their own mounts while they "shooed in" the winner. In a horseracing *shoo-in*, the winner is the only horse trying to win; that corrupt connotation does not apply in politics.

In a related development from the world of in-and-out, this letter from Judge Theodore Trautwein of the Superior Court of New Jersey: "The other day my law clerk told me that she had really *lucked out* on the purchase of her new car. I asked her if she was happy with the deal. She was indeed!"

The appellate jurist poses the slanguistic issue: "When things go bad, one is 'out of luck' and vice versa. Hence, I would have employed the expression *lucked in* under her circumstance." He requests my ruling.

The judge is going by the book: in the *Dictionary of American Slang, lucked out* is defined as "to have met with ill fortune." But that was back in the 1940's, and lots of things have been turned on their heads since then. In 1954, *American Speech* magazine was citing campus usages of *to luck out*, meaning "to achieve success by good luck," with the example of not being assigned Saturday classes. Today, *ba-a-ad* means "good," reports of economic growth can prompt stockmarket downturns, and *to luck out* is *to luck in*.

I'm speculating because the lack of research on this point has been unfortunate, but I think this has to do with the way *out* is used to form new verbs. In standard English, we have such compounds as *break out, sit out* and *fall out*, so the device is not new; but in slang, we have witnessed an Out Explosion, as coinages have ranged from *drop out, cop out* and *sack out* to the more recent *veg out, pig out* and *spazz out*.

Out is in and *in* is out. Along the way, *luck* ran out—that is, *to luck in*, or fall into luck, became *to luck out*. The other form still exists, but the *in* is almost always *into:* One may *luck into* something, but the usage is not nearly as common as *to luck out*.

That's the breaks, judge. Appeal denied. Listen to your clerk, get with it, and you will have it made in the shade.

Just a note to suggest that perhaps Leonard Silk was putting two and two together subconsciously when he referred, intentionally, to Mr. Reagan as a "shoe-in."

Two immediate horse racing references strike me. The first is the nickname of the great jockey Willie Shoemaker, The Shoe. The second, which completes the equation, is the wonderful Damon Runyon poem about the jockey Earl Sande entitled "Sande Booting Them Home."

Thus, perhaps, we can see that Mr. Silk's "shoe" fits pretty well and is quite wearable as a slanguage metaphor.

Robert M. Isaacs
Bridgeport, Connecticut

Short Quick In

"We are not going to get drawn into some kind of a long-drawn conflict," President Reagan was quoted as saying about the presence of the United States Marines in Lebanon.

Long-drawn? I had always used those words as part of *long, drawn-out,* an exercise in verbal lengthening that was more evocative of interminability than *prolonged* or *protracted.* Synonymists say that *extended* connotes an increase in range, *elongated* denotes a lengthening in space, *prolonged* means going beyond the normal limits, and *protracted* carries the impression of needless extension into boredom. *Long-winded* is limited to oratory; when Senator Hubert Humphrey was told he was running on too long, he liked to reply: "I am reminded of the little girl who said she knew how to spell *banana,* but never knew when to stop." This has been a *long-drawn-out* paragraph.

That phrase, without any punctuation, is from John Milton's 1632 poem "L'Allegro": "In notes, with many a winding bout/Of lincked sweetnes long drawn out." The phrase was turned into an adjective in 1904, modifying a noun as in "long-drawn-out story."

Was the President correct in joining and hyphenating the *long-drawn* part and dropping the *out?*

Yes. *Long-drawn,* without the *out,* is the first use listed in the *O.E.D.* after Milton and stands by itself in many dictionaries along with *long-drawn-out* as an alternative. When the three words are used together, lexicographers agree that two hyphens and no comma are the accepted form.

Credit the President with the proper use of two of Milton's three words. But the question nags: Why, in using a phrase to describe a never-ending rigmarole, do some people cut it short?

A quibble here, if you please. A hyphen is not, in my definition, a mark of punctuation. Here it is a mechanical device to indicate that the words "long drawn out" are joined into a compound phrase used as an adjective preceding a noun.

Milton uses the phrase after *the noun, and no hyphens are needed.*

Benjamin W. Griffith
Co-author, Essentials of English
Carrollton, Georgia

The Skinny on Skinny

In a piece explaining why a *czar* is not a *tsar*, I referred to a leak from the Justice Department as "a puddle of hot, inside skinny."

Seeing those words in print, I experienced the emotion that Frank Mankiewicz has named a *klong*, the sudden rush of minor horror that seizes your heart when you realize you have forgotten your own dinner party and everyone has probably showed up two hours ago, pounded on your door, and left in fury. Writers feel klongs when they see in cold print a mistake that escaped all previous readings in warm type.

The reason for my klong in this case is the meaning of *skinny*. It means "inside information, the real lowdown, the hot poop." As it appeared in this space—"inside skinny"—it was hopelessly redundant or, as some members of the Squad Squad have pointed out, redundundant. All *skinny* is, ipso facto, "inside," and *inside skinny* is as unnecessarily repetitive as Tom Brokaw's description of China as "exotically foreign" or the decision by the town fathers of St. Petersburg, Florida, to name a square "Plaza Place," thereby squaring the square.

(Squad Squad members who have sent in the statement by President Reagan that "I have reiterated more than once to our Cabinet . . . ," with demands that the redundancy be skewered, are in error; Mr. Reagan was on safe ground because it is possible to iterate, then reiterate, and then reiterate again and again and again, to use an F.D.R. expression. [There is only one *instant replay*, however.])

"Was your reference to 'a puddle of hot, inside skinny' intended to titillate," asks Joan Ross of New York City, "or have I missed a leak somewhere? I don't even know what *cold*, inside skinny is."

Because that word appeared in this space previously—"I demanded the skinny on 'expeed' "—and received no challenges or queries, I assumed it was a slang term widely understood. For example, it appeared in John Carmody's television column in the *Washington Post* in 1983: "We'll give you the full skinny tomorrow." Its meaning is clear; as the patron saint of research, Casey Stengel, used to say, you could look it up.*

Unfortunately, you could not and cannot look it up. A search of all the slang authorities, from Hotten and Farmer of the nineteenth century to Partridge and Flexner of the twentieth, with a side chase into all my dictionaries of Americanisms and all the current general dictionaries at hand, turns up no such meaning for *skinny* as "the latest scoop from Group."

We are not concerned with the meaning of *skinny* as an adjective, which used to be "excessively thin" and is now "attractively slender." We are on the track of *skinny* as a noun. In that part of speech, *skinny* has been reported as denoting a class in chemistry at Annapolis; a similar noun, *skin-a-guts*, is a very thin person, and a *skinner* was a member of a marauding gang professing allegiance to the American cause during the Revolution. Obviously, none of these previous noun usages offer a clue to the term's current meaning.

Stuart Berg Flexner, placed on the spot for not having this meaning in the latest *Dictionary of American Slang*, proceeded to knock himself out in researching and speculating about its origin:

"*Skinny*, as a noun, comes from an earlier adjectival use meaning 'of, like, or exposing a lot of skin.' This use was prevalent from the 16th to the early 20th century: In modern days we say something is *skin-colored*, but in olden days the term was *skinny-colored*. In other words, *skinny* refers to skin itself, and our modern use of this word to mean 'thin' is quite recent.

"By 1835," says Flexner, "*to skin*, which had previously been used only to refer to skinning animals, took on the slang meaning of 'to cheat or plagiarize, as on a school test,' the image being that one skinned the information from another's brains or paper, and soon thereafter *skinny* was used by students as a noun to mean 'cheating, especially by plagiarizing or copying another's work.' For example, *The Dictionary of Americanisms* shows that there was an 1854 Yale University student song which included the line 'I skinned and fizzled through' in order to graduate. This use of *skin* and *skinny* has continued ever since the 1830's, and by the 1950's

_____
* See my note on page 121.

students were using *skinny* to mean the information or inside authoritative facts which one copied or plagiarized."

The slanguist is ready to pounce. "It seems to be this student use that was picked up in a description of security leaks as 'hot, inside skinny.' Thus *skinny*, originally meaning the material or facts copied by a student cheating on an exam (which, I guess, is a type of leak), is applied to other information or facts which are obtained surreptitiously or unethically.

"Although the original use of *skinny* in this cheating and taking of information goes back to the image of skinning an animal, this original image has been lost and I believe that those who use the term now probably relate *skinny* to 'the bare facts' being exposed as naked, or perhaps even as playing it close to the bone."

And that's how they talk in Fat City.

Bill,
I'm happy you watched.
And do you suppose Mr. Wick, in the broadest sense, is part of the Administration's exotic policy?

Tom [Brokaw]
New York, New York

From as far back as the Second World War, within the United States Naval establishment, the phrase used is the straight skinny *or* skinny *as in "Give me the straight skinny" or "What is the straight skinny?"*

According to Naval Correspondence *system regulations, at least one carbon copy is typed with each letter distributed, i.e., sent out locally or otherwise. This carbon copy is typed on either light green colored, or white very thin tissue called manifold sheets. These tissues came to be called skinnies, and are filed at the issuing activity.*

The question "What is the straight skinny?" was usually directed to someone in one of the clerical ratings, who had access to the filing cabinets or who had either typed up an outgoing message or had filed an incoming message, and had early access to information. Radio communications ratings also wrote their incoming and outgoing communications on manifold copy (skinny).

Subsequently, "What is the straight skinny?" was asked of anyone thought to have inside or latest information.

DTGI D. E. Copper USNR
Montgomery, New York

Dear Bill:

Duty demands that I confide to you an indelicate application of the word skinner.

When I was a boffin working with the Navy during WWII, I spent some time at a Loran station in Newfoundland that was manned by Coast Guard personnel. On a couple of occasions, when I was walking to the settlement of Bonavista with these young men, we—or I hope, they—were treated to rude shouts from local boys, addressing them with the word noted above.

It was a word often used by the more vulgar denizens of the island to denote a man inordinately zealous in pursuit of the female.

The word did not much surprise me, for a few years before in some Franco-American conversations with a New Hampshire man from near the Canadian border I had learned the phrase to chercher le peau *with the same meaning.*

Alexander [McKenzie]
Eaton Center, New Hampshire

I was amazed by your dissertation on skinny—*the noun. I kept wondering when you were going to arrive at the meaning that I was somewhat familiar with when growing up in the U.K.*

Surely a "skinny" originally referred to the wax "skin" or master used by the old cyclostyle duplication machines, some of which were built by the Gestetner Company—resulting in the not infrequently used verb "gestetner something."

"Give me the skinny," or "Let me have the skinny" was the request of the author, editor, or manager who wanted to check the original, or master, of a flier, or newssheet, pamphlet, or whatever before it was irrevocably run off for release to the public. Thus the person who saw the skinny had the first information!

I'm pretty confident this is the origin of the expression, although it is quite a long time since I was slightly associated with activities which occasionally generated skinnies.

Keith M. Gardiner
Flushing, New York

None Are Is Correct

Sue me: I construe *none* as plural. "Obviously, none of these previous noun usages offer a clue to the term's current meaning," I wrote a few months back, matching the subject *none* with the verb *offer*, not *offers*. This drew a note from Patricia

Dale in San Rafael, California, at the Society for the Advancement of Good English: "Oh dear, I hope you are not committed to considering that the word 'none' is plural!"

That stung me into doing it again, and this time I added the parenthetical "yes, 'none have' " after the horrid deed, as a mail-puller. Sure enough, this missive from Peter Kihss of Jamaica, New York, who is now retired and remembered as the reporters' reporter and the last man permitted to use an old-fashioned typewriter in the city room of *The New York Times*.

"None used to be singular, taking a singular verb, in my starting newspaper days," writes Pete, recalling the John Peter Zenger era, "even in my 1952 return to *The New York Times*. Eventually style changes made it plural, as now. This always left me uneasy, as presumably it has done to others of your readers."

That uneasy feeling extends to many newspapermen who follow *The Associated Press Stylebook*, which clings to the old construal of *none:* "It usually means no single one. When used in this sense, it always takes singular verbs and pronouns: *None of the seats was in its right place."* The old fogies at the A.P. add: "Use a plural verb only if the sense is no two or no amount: *None of the consultants agree on the same approach. None of the taxes have been paid."*

Here's the problem: Most people think that *none* means "not one" or "no one." Centuries ago, it did. Then it came to mean something broader: "not any," or literally, "not ones." With that newer meaning, most people who said *none* were referring to several, or a group, or a bunch—more than one—which is another way of saying they construed *none* as plural. And when you think of more than one in your subject, you are inclined to match that plural subject with a plural verb: *none have*, rather than *none has*. (Sure, a collective noun like *group* is construed as singular and takes a singular verb: *The group says*. Sorry, but the language is not consistent; not my fault.)

The old poets had a good idea: They matched their predicates to *none* depending on how they construed their subjects. For example, when Dryden wrote that "None but the brave deserves the fair," he had in mind "not one single person." (I wasn't there—Pete Kihss covered Dryden—but that's what I think he had in mind, and that was why he chose the singular *deserves*.) On the other hand, Andrew Marvell in "To His Coy Mistress" had in mind a few corpses when he urged his damsel to immediate action with "The grave's a fine and private place/ But none, I think, do there embrace."

Here's the solution: When you think of a few people or things as your subject —in other words, when you construe *none* as plural—go ahead and use the plural verb: *none are, none go, none have*. But when you think of one person or thing— when you construe *none* as "not a single one," as singular—then it is O.K. to use the singular verb: *none is, none goes, none has*.

But what do you do when you're not sure? Most of us, when we say *none*, mean "not one, or him either, or the three of them, or come to think of it, the whole lot of them or the bunch of it." On these occasions, we tend to think of quantity or amount, and the safest bet is to construe *none* as plural: *none are*.

To all of you who insist that *none* should mean "not one," let me urge you to make life easy for yourself and clear for your listeners or readers by saying *no one* or *nobody* or *not a single particle*. Nobody can misconstrue that as anything but singular, and it happily joins the singular verb: *not one is*.

Only a generation ago, *New York Times* usagist Theodore Bernstein was writing, "String along with *none* as a singular . . . ," with exceptions. Today, *The New York Times Manual of Style and Usage* says: "*None*. Construe as a plural unless it is desired to emphasize the idea of *not one* or *no one*—and then it is often better to use *not one* or *no one* instead of *none*."

I'll buy that: Not one but the brave deserves the fair.

Dear Bill,
Since none *plays the role of* no + *understood noun, this is the same problem that arises in choosing between* no + *singular noun and* no + *plural noun. My impression is that singular or plural is chosen on the basis of one's expectations as to whether there would be more than one if there were any. For example, during the interval between the death of one pope and the election of his successor, one could say,* No pope is currently reigning, *but not* No popes are currently reigning. *Similarly, with reference to a musical competition in which the judges decided not to award a first prize, one would say* No contestant was awarded first prize. *But not,* No contestants were awarded first prize. *(It works the same way with* None of the contestants: was, *not* were.*)*

Jim [James D. McCawley]
Department of Linguistics
The University of Chicago
Chicago, Illinois

A great example of rationalization. I especially liked the way you torpeoded all us old-timers with that cheap shot about being from the John Peter Zenger era.

And The New York Times Manual of Style and Usage. *The Bible of the trade or, as some people say:* The Bible is to Religion as The New York Times Manual of Style and Usage *is to proper usage of the English language. It's infallible. So what that K mart spent millions of dollars establishing a logo with a lower case* m *in mart?* The New York Times *finds this unacceptable and says K mart is wrong and should change its name to K Mart with an upper case M in Mart.*

Anyhow, no matter how you rationalize it, none is still short for no one and no one is singular.

Stanley H. Slom
A Singular Person
New York, New York

Some years ago I had a dispute with the editors of a scientific journal over my use of a plural verb after the word "none," or after a collective noun, when the sense was plural. Citing Fowler (who quaintly calls these "nouns of multitude") was not persuasive. However, I won my case after submitting the following sample sentence, which was constructed entirely in accord with the principles that seemed to be guiding the editors: "A number of us believes that none of those who are living in glass houses is in a position to throw stones."

Bernard D. Davis
Boston, Massachusetts

I enjoyed "None Are Is Correct" until you tried to prove your thesis about "none" with the quote from Andrew Marvell. I hope you included the quote to trigger reader response. "But none, I think, do there embrace" is a fine example of the subjunctive, not the present plural.

I think "none" means "no one" or "not one" still and takes a singular verb. I like your trying to prove otherwise with quotes from poets. Try again. I bet you can't do it. At least, you haven't done it yet.

Margaret De Vane
Hamden, Connecticut

Construal?

Not in Random House, *nor as far as I can find in the* Compact Oxford—*the latter gives* construe *as a substantive as well as a verb.*

F. H. Nicoll
Princeton, New Jersey

The Sleaze Factor

"More than a dozen members of your Administration have left under some sort of a cloud," said a reporter to President Reagan in a press conference, "and this is what the Democrats are calling *the sleaze factor*."

"I reject the use of the word *sleaze*," retorted the President, and when the C.E.O. of the Free World rejects the use of a word, that usage and the rejection thereof merit attention in this space.

Sleaze, a slang noun that Merriam-Webster dates back to 1954, is a back-formation from the adjective *sleazy*. Before that, the operative noun was *sleaziness*. (On that analogy, "There's a queasiness in my stomach" will soon give way to "I've got a case of the *quease*.")

Etymologists at *Webster's New World Dictionary* speculate that *sleazy*, the adjective, came from an area of Eastern Europe, now part of Poland and Czechoslovakia, called Silesia. A delicate cloth woven there was called Sleasie-holland, which was easily torn and quickly came to look shoddy, or "sleazy."

The corruption-oozing noun was popularized in American politics in 1980 by a mean-spirited right-wing columnist for *The New York Times*, who seized upon it to derogate a farrago of ethical corner-cuttings by friends and relatives of President Jimmy Carter. His column about the mishmash of muck was titled "The Politics of Sleaze" (to which Bert Lance retorted: "There's more muck*rakin'* than there is muck*makin'*").

Turnabout is always fair political play, and Democrats in the House of Representatives began characterizing the pattern of Reagan administration miniscandals as *the sleaze factor* in March 1984. The earliest use of the phrase that I have been able to find was in *The Christian Science Monitor* on March 21: "Asked about the 'sleaze factor' in the campaign, Senator George McGovern told reporters Tuesday [March 20] that he expected to see more mention of it." He was prescient: The next day, at a planeside news conference on March 21, Walter Mondale said that the "main unifying factor" among Democrats in the 1984 election "will be the 'sleaze factor' in this Administration," since almost every week "another rotten apple falls from the tree."

No sooner had this phrase begun to put down roots than a counterphrase appeared: "This is *the Teflon factor*," wrote Tim Carrington in the *Wall Street Journal* in April, "which refers to the President's apparent political immunity to most of his aides' mistakes or misdeeds. . . . Ronald Reagan's ability to deflect embarrassment seems nothing short of uncanny." *Teflon*, from polyte tra-*fl*uorethylene, is Du Pont's trade name for a coating bonded to metal to keep food from sticking to the pan. (The substance is also used on medical instruments and has been misused by cocaine snorters; the use in political metaphor recalls another commercial item appropriated for campaigning, "Mr. Clean.")

Will *the sleaze factor* stick to Mr. Reagan, or will *the Teflon factor* ward it off? This is the first direct clash of political phrases in 1984, and we will have to observe closely to see which triumphs.

Sleaze vs. Teflon

In a piece on political coinages, *the sleaze factor*, a charge against the Reagan administration, was pitted against *the Teflon factor*, an inability of Democrats to make sleaze stick to Mr. Reagan personally.

Sleaze-slingers will be pleased to learn that the phrase was probably coined by Laurence Barrett of *Time* magazine, as a chapter title in his 1983 book, *Gambling with History*. Although it is more difficult to get the originator of *the Teflon factor* to stick to the pan, it was Representative Patricia Schroeder (Democrat of Colorado) who first referred to "the Teflon-coated presidency." Under the influence of *the sleaze factor*, some factotum changed that to *the Teflon factor*. (Teflon, a trade name, is capitalized; sleaze, a back-formation, is not.)

I believe you have scrambled a metaphor by defining the Teflon factor *as "the inability of Democrats to make sleaze stick to Mr. Reagan personally." The Teflon, sir, is in the pan, not the egg. Therefore, the* Teflon factor *refers not to an inability of the Democrats but to an ability of the President: his ability to shed the spatters of what goes on close about him. The presence of a Teflon pan in the kitchen does not change the characteristics of the eggs. It only provides one slick surface to which they will not stick.*

Stephan L. Cohen
Brooklyn, New York

Spell Your Dreams Away

You think a concern for correct spelling is for sissies? You think haranguing pundits and fearsome lawyers overlook the niceties of orthography?

Several years ago, when United Press International reported that Frank Sinatra had stated that "William Safire is a goddamn liar," I took occasion to remonstrate with the reporter on his spelling of the adjectival epithet. Although most newspaper stylebooks prefer an *n* at the end of the unhyphenated compound word, I objected. My argument was that, since the *god* portion of the word is properly not capitalized (referring to a small god, as in *godfather*), the *damn* at the end is not a curse; in effect, the new word means not "accursed by God" but merely "very much"—a *goddam liar* is "very much a liar." With the damnation removed, the *n* should be removed also; it is not pronounced, anyway.

Comes now Mr. Sinatra's press agent, Lee Solters, with a blast at Kitty Kelley, the author of several unauthorized biographies of celebrities. Writes Mr. Solters: "Modern mud-slinging's miniscule mistress of malice, Kitty Kelley, has announced she will pen an unauthorized biography of Frank Sinatra."

In that sentence, *pen* is a cutesy verb for "write" (I am penning this on a word processor) but is permissible in a showbiz context, where web chiefs jet coastward; however, *mudslinging* has long since lost its hyphen, and *minuscule*—with a *u* near the middle, not an *i*—is the only correct spelling of the word meaning "small, minor." The word's spelling has been confused by *miniskirt*, but the error remains an error.

The majuscule crooner's flack was using alliteration, of course, perhaps in parody of *nattering nabobs of negativism*, a phrase made famous by Mr. Sinatra's close friend Spiro Agnew. (The then-Vice President used it along with *hopeless, hysterical hypochondriacs of history*, which I thought was a nice updating of Adlai Stevenson's blast at pessimists as *prophets of gloom and doom*, and Clare Boothe Luce's rap at *troubadours of trouble*. Had I known the alliterating would degenerate to *modern mudslinging's misspelled minuscule mistress of malice*, I would have stood in bed.)

As I was clipping the misspelling of *minuscule* to put in my zap file, a telephone call came from an attorney who is Mr. Sinatra's equal in the not-to-be-messed-around-with set. It seems that, in a piece embracing the word *hugger-mugger*, meaning "secrecy," I cautioned readers not to confuse its meaning with *skullduggery*, meaning "trickery."

"You do not spell *skulduggery* with two *l*'s," said Roy M. Cohn, menacingly. "It is a word with which I am very familiar. One *l*."

Tough guys care about spelling. Remember that, kids, and none of your goddam minuscule skulduggery.

Over the years I have often found myself in disagreement with Roy M. Cohn's political positions. Now, it seems, my disagreements extend into the spelling arena. Tell tough guy Cohn that skullduggery *can correctly be spelled with one* l *or with two* l*'s.*

I congratulate you on your vigilance in pointing out the correct spelling of minuscule. *Perhaps you could devote future columns to words that I constantly see misspelled:* accommodate, benefited, harass, sherbet, supersede.

I must question a word that you used. Your sentence began, "As I was clipping the misspelling of minuscule *to put in my zap file." Shouldn't the word be* into, *since* into *suggests movement?*

Edward S. Dermon
Roslyn Heights, New York

Your column states (perhaps I should say you *state in your column) unequivocally that "minuscule—with a* u *near the middle, not an* i—*is the only correct spelling of the word meaning 'small, minor.' "*

You are in good company (Davies in Success with Words *and Bernstein). But* Webster's Third New International Dictionary *introduces a wrinkle to your smooth prescription, to wit: "miniscule: var of* MINUSCULE."

This would seem to indicate that popular acceptance of the i *spelling is on its way. Something tells me that you, Bernstein and Davies are fighting a losing battle, at least on this word.*

Mark K. Solheim
Washington, D.C.

May I disagree with you on the spelling of goddam?

Your explanation of the meaning as "very much" should have indicated that it is derivative or implied from the original sense which is patently, "god damn." The word is usually an explicative form, but has been used as an adjective and a verb. The spelling has been corrupted to goldarn, goldurn, goddam, *and other forms. Nevertheless, your informed speaker or writer knows that the preferred spelling is* goddamn. *The* damn *is from Latin,* damnare, *to condemn. If you choose to drop the* n, *as you do, you may do so, but I don't think you can really justify it as preferable to* goddamn.

> David Shulman
> New York, New York

Would have stood in bed, indeed. I could hear the groans all the way from Ebbets Field. Whadda put-down! As if moving the Dodgers to L.A. wasn't enough. Like I said as I toined my autographed photo of Dazzy Vance to the wall, "He should *of stood in bed." Not* should have, *but* should of.

> Arnold H. Weiss
> Lawrence, Kansas

The Spirit Is Mean

"There is not a more mean, stupid, dastardly, pitiful, selfish, spiteful, envious, ungrateful animal than the Public," wrote essayist William Hazlitt in 1821, castigating a group that is rarely reviled. With prescience (considering the brouhaha about exit-polling that burst forth over a century later) he added: "It is the greatest of cowards, for it is afraid of itself."

If Hazlitt had been writing today, he would have used one adjective that now does the work of those eight: *mean-spirited*. The rise of this word—paralleling either an increase of mean-spiritedness or an escalation of the attack on mean-spiritedness—is a perfect example of the way an old and occasionally-used term, straggling along behind the march of language, can be rejuvenated and rushed to the vanguard when the moment arrives for its special meaning. Only a word can fill a void.

This parasynthetic compound had a religious upbringing: "Away with that mean-spirited religion," adjured Francis Bragge in 1694, discoursing on the parables. Five years later, Matthew Henry used the word in his *Meekness of Spirit:* "Meekness is commonly despised as a piece of cowardice and mean-spiritedness." The word was then competing with *mean-souled*; both meant a lack of generosity, compassion, charity or love.

Mean, the adjective, signified "common, vulgar," not far from "middle" (a meaning that is preserved in its noun form in mathematics), with a connotation of "narrow, stingy, sickly, stunted." Later, *mean* came to denote "cruel," and people were accused of being "old meanies" (in today's slang, *mean* conjures "expert," as in "He throws a mean curveball"). But mean-*spirited* retained the "stingy, narrow" definition of *mean*, indicating a smallness of soul. (This paragraph has been written without using *mean* as a verb, which would have led to *"mean means,"* a cause of confusion.)

Then, for a couple of centuries, mean-spirited lay low. Few found it useful: Poet James Russell Lowell decried "what is essentially vulgar and meanspirited in politics," dropping the hyphen, which led a lexicographer working on Merriam-Webster's *Third New International Dictionary* into listing the word without the hyphen. (Today, Fred Mish, editorial director of Merriam-Webster, admits that the preponderance of his citations uses the hyphen, and he promises to reinsert the hyphen in future printings. You have to watch these guys all the time.)

For generations, people got along with *ignoble, abject* and *sordid*, but *ignoble* became bookish, *abject* became too closely associated with poverty, and *sordid* slid over to moral corruption. The linguistic gap opened and quickly widened. How were we to characterize those who did not have a greatness of spirit—indeed, who showed a marked lack of compassion in their outlook?

In the mid-1970's, *mean-spirited* began to take off. Daniel P. Moynihan, then the outgoing ambassador to India and always a writer sensitive to words popular in academies before they become outright vogue terms, wrote in *U.S. News &*

World Report in 1975 to condemn the United States Congress for "so many mean-spirited and inane restrictions in its aid legislation." *Newsweek* that year glommed onto the word, first quoting Senator Edmund Muskie calling on President Ford "to put a stop to such mean-spirited demagoguery" and then quoting a diplomat in Vietnam as saying he believed that the Vietcong had become "too mean-spirited to ease Saigon's discomfort."

By the 1980's, the adjective was in full flight, as my computer count shows. Americans like *mean-spiritedness* as the new noun; the British prefer *meanness of spirit*. *The Times* of London zapped Prime Minister Thatcher for "the *meanness of spirit* displayed to Caribbean leaders and the American administration over Grenada."

The mystery is: How come we cannot find the word in any of our best-selling dictionaries? *Webster's New World*, the Merriam-Webster *Ninth New Collegiate*, American Heritage, Random House—zilch. (At least they all have *zilch*.) Do you suppose they're all waiting for the others to go first? (In truth, each wants to be first out with a new word that is not merely a nonce word; to suggest otherwise illustrates mean-spiritedness.)

"The term really doesn't have an exact synonym," says Dr. Mish, pointing to two sets of words that come close: *small-minded* and *narrow-minded* in one group and *ungenerous, petty, picayune* in the other. In his personal judgment, and not committing the organization yet, he thinks the precise antonym is *magnanimous*.

Now we have it: The rise of *mean-spirited* is bottomed on the lack of another word for "not magnanimous." That's how the language fills in its holes. A word of caution: If you mean *lowly, ill-tempered, corrupt, dastardly, spiteful* or any of Hazlitt's choices, use those words and give *mean-spirited* a rest.

The thing I have to contribute to your exploration of mean-spirited *is the classic antonym to* magnanimous: pusillanimous, *for which* OED *gives the etymological meaning* "small, petty spirited," *and my old-reliable* The Century Dictionary of the English Language, *Copyright 1889, plainly gives the definition:*

> *Lacking strength and firmness of mind: wanting in courage and fortitude; being of weak courage; faint-hearted; mean-spirited; cowardly.*

> *Robert N. Yetter*
> *Houtzdale, Pennsylvania*

Your mention of Dr. Mish's thinking that magnanimous *is the precise antonym of* mean-spirited *immediately set my Latin word-hoard astir. And sure enough:* WIII *does have an entry* parvanimity—*"opposed to* magnanimity." *But the adjective* parvanimous *is regrettably absent.*

Louis Marck
New York, New York

There is no connection whatsoever between the adjective mean *"common, vulgar" and the noun* mean *used in mathematics. The adjective is a native English word derived from Old Eng.* gemaēne *and cognate with Ger.* gemein; *if you trace it back further, you will find that it is akin to Lat.* communis, *"common." The noun, on the other hand, is derived from Old French* meien *and ultimately from Lat.* medianus, *"middle" (from which we also get the word* median). *Lest you fall into a similar trap in a forthcoming column, I should like to point out that the verb* mean *is a completely separate word (of native English vintage and related to Ger.* meinen). *In other words, the three lexical items written* mean *are etymologically unrelated homonyms, precisely like the three words* sound, *i.e.* sound *(of music), (Long Island)* Sound, *and (safe and)* sound.*

The next time you get the urge to engage in some off-the-cuff etymologizing, dear Mr. Safire, please reach for the dictionary instead—or, better yet, get Mr. Guralnik on the hot line. You owe that much to your legions of faithful readers, who innocently imagine that everything you tell them is the last word in linguistic erudition.

Louis Jay Herman
New York, New York

In discussing "mean-spirited"—and its hyphenation or lack thereof—you hyphenated "occasionally-used." There is no need to hyphenate compounds composed of "ly" adverbs and participles or adjectives; in fact, to do so is wrong.

Freda Brackley
Northampton, Massachusetts

You wrote, "the preponderance of his citations uses."

I felt uncomfortable. You forced on me the old question of the number of the verb with a collective noun. You could ease the discomfort and write, "most citations use" or "more citations use," according to the numbers of them you found.

Richard M. Gummere, Jr.
Tarrytown, New York

Squad Squad Hat Trick

"When I make a mistake," said New York's Mayor Fiorello La Guardia with pride, "it's a beaut." When the *Washington Post*'s clean-writing editorialists sink into solecism, they do so with a splash.

"Personal ethical probity is surely the minimum we require of an attorney general," opined the newspaper in medium dudgeon. Members of the Squad Squad quickly rounded up the unusual subject: a double redundancy, or reredundancy, or redundandundancy.

Probity means "uprightness"; other synonyms are "honor" and "integrity," but *probity* carries the connotation of "proven honesty." Perhaps that is because the word comes from the Latin *probus*, "proper," which led to *probare*, "to prove, test." That is the purpose of a Senate *probe*—to test the bona fides of a nominee, to prove him proper—as if by sticking a sharp instrument, which has come to be known as a probe, into the subject.

If you have probity, you have passed the sometimes painful test of honesty and can be said to possess ethical strength. If you have *ethical probity*, you have a problem with English because you are engaging in tautology, which is saying the same thing over again and weakening your words by repetition. (In that sentence, *again* is redundant; when you say the same things over, you are saying them again.)

Ordinarily, I would let America's Princess Meg cop a pleonasm, but her "ethical probity" was preceded by *personal*. Sometimes probity can be corporate, but in the context of this editorial, individual honesty was the subject, and *personal* is wholly unnecessary. (In that sentence, *wholly* is unnecessary too, but performs a function of emphasis; as you see, I am battening down the hatches for a counterattack. And do I need *down* with *battening*?)

Probity, not ethical probity, and definitely not personal ethical probity, is what is needed at the Department of Justice, house of probes. Its possessor pays only a psychic income tax, for as Decimus Junius Juvenal wrote in the second century A.D., *Probitas laudatur et alget:* "Probity is praised and starves."

Sorry. Probitas laudatur et alget (Juvenal) does not mean "Probity is praised and starves." Praised, yes, but merely neglected. Algeo, algere means "be cold"—by transference, "neglected" (Cassell's Latin Dictionary, Macmillan, 1977).

Franklyn Alexander
Evanston, Illinois

Why, pray tell, is tautology a language crime?

Why is "saying the same thing over" necessarily weakening one's words? What is virtuous about bare bones sentences?

Repetition may not be the soul of brevity but it sure does a lot for emphasis.

Ina Bradley
Westport, Connecticut

Squad Squad Strikes Yet Again

"Global investing makes a new debut," announces a poster in the window of Dean Witter Reynolds, the stockbrokers. Jeff McQuain, a researcher who has just joined the Squad Squad to ferret out redundancies, suggests that the brokers must have sold short on the old debuts.

A *debut* is a first appearance; Brenda Frazier, the debutante, came out once, and that was it. Any subsequent appearance is a reappearance. Global investing may be having a renascence or may be making a comeback, but it cannot be making a second first appearance.

The word comes from the French *jouer de but*, "to play for the mark"; a *butt*, or end, is what the player seeks to win. Shakespeare's Othello announces, "Here is my journey's end, here is my butt"; in gaining that first end, we introduce our play or begin our life in society. We have only one bite at that apple.

The Squad Squad does not limit its scrutiny to the investment community; its vigilance extends to the White House itself. Helio Fred Garcia, who styles himself an "Irregular Lexicographic Irregular," points to a copy of President Reagan's letter to the Federal Election Commission announcing his intention to seek the Republican nomination for—in the President's words—"the office of the Presidency of the United States."

Asks Mr. Garcia: "Did he get the title wrong? My gut feeling is that Mr. Reagan is seeking his party's nomination for the *office of President of the United States* and that the Presidency of the United States refers, at least in part, to that office. Is there such an office as 'Presidency of the United States'?"

There is not. One *is* President; one *occupies* the presidency, which is an office. One cannot occupy the office of the office of the President; that's redundant. Although this will stimulate controversy—*Harper's Dictionary of Contemporary Usage* writes that *"Presidential refers to the office of the Presidency"*—I hold that the President has already made the first mistake of his second term (if he is really running, and if he wins).

Dear Bill:

Your gloss on debut *is not quite satisfactory. First,* jouer de but *is no longer current; no French person would understand it. Second, according to Littré, it means playing from, not toward the goal, and he says that in bowling the first shot was made from the goal—why, he does not explain. Third, four other modern dictionaries (including the large* Robert*) say that the word denotes the first play in several games, without specifying which games.*

It seems agreed, then, that the common use (with de *changed to* dé*) is derived from some games and that the goal* (but) *is involved, but what the true original meaning is remains obscure.*

> *Jacques [Barzun]*
> *Charles Scribner's Sons, Publishers*
> *New York, New York*

The words end *and* but *are both archery terms.* Jouer de but *could very well be, too, although I don't know this.*

An end *in archery is "a flight of arrows or a portion of any specific round" (*Encyclopedia of Archery, *by Paul C. Hougham [A. S. Barnes & Co., N.Y.], 1958). A better definition comes from* Archery, *by Keith Schuler (Barnes, 1970). It says, "The number of arrows shot by one person before scoring and removing them from the target." The phrase* he kept up his end *is derived directly from this use in archery.*

A butt *always has meant an archery target—in olden times it was a mound of earth but nowadays it may be a bale of hay or something similar. The term is used in Henry VIII's accounts—he usually lost money shooting at the butts. (Incidentally, the center of the target on the butt was called, in that Henry's time, the "prick.")*

What I am trying to say is that Shakespeare undoubtedly knew these uses and when Othello made his announcement, he meant that "this is the last target at which I will loose my arrows"—and, really, in the proper definition of end *we have more than one bite at the apple. You always leave an arrow in the quiver in case you happen to stumble across a gorilla or a lion or a dragon or whatever.*

As you suspect, I'm an archer and, at age 69, I shoot in national archery contests. The point is, a butt *and an* end *are not the same—the* end *is the chance and the* butt *is the target.*

> *W. R. Higginbotham*
> *New York, New York*

Couldn't Brenda Frazier make a new debut as a movie actress after a first appearance as a debutante?

> *Frederick Mosteller*
> *Cambridge, Massachusetts*

Stine or Steen?

White House spokesman Larry Speakes had a bad day. He had been ordered to slap down the chairman of the Council of Economic Advisers, Martin Feldstein, who had been differing a little publicly with the Reagan party line on budget deficits. (As the antideficit wags say, Ronald Reagan is destined to be the only President with his picture on a postage-due stamp.) But instead of merely castigating Professor Feldstein for wandering off the reservation, Mr. Speakes appeared to make fun of the pronunciation of his name.

A reporter first mispronounced the Feldstein name in his question, saying *"FELD-steen"* instead of the way the economist prefers, *"FELD-stine."* Mr. Speakes then misspoke, picking up the error, and corrected himself with a muttered "Could never get his name straight." That was promptly interpreted as unseemly ridicule or, even worse, an ethnic slur, and another White House aide then was forced to put out word from anonymous ambush that the President was "furious" at his spokesman.

Mr. Speakes was indignant at what he considered a bum rap: "I would also look very carefully," he cautioned the press corps, "at who mispronounced Feldstein's name." Let him who is without sin cast the first Special Envoy to Central America.

That throws into stark relief (no, Abe Stark was not a relief pitcher for the Brooklyn Dodgers) the issue of the pronunciation of names in America today. Which is "correct"—the way you pronounce your name or the way most others pronounce yours and other, similar names?

Your house may not be your castle, but your moniker is your property to pronounce the way you like and to correct others about. Tony Dorsett of the Dallas Cowboys prefers *"Dor-SETT,"* and pronunciations rhyming with "corset" are incorrect as applied to him. In the same way, quarterbacks named Taliaferro may want their names Anglicized to "Tolliver," which is stretching it, but if Cholmondeley is pronounced *"CHUM-ley,"* it's Tolliver in the pocket. We cannot go overboard—I cannot demand that everyone pronounce my name "Robert Redford"—but within bounds of common sense, it's our call.

Sometimes people with hard-to-pronounce names simplify life for others by making the spelling easier; at other times, people who insist on pronouncing names their way change the spelling to fit the pronunciation. In my family, the name is usually spelled Safir (from the Hebrew word *sofer*, "scribe"); according to Aunt Toots (Mrs. Dorothy Goodman), my father and all my uncles and aunts pronounced the name like "sapphire." In the Army, I tired of correcting the sergeants, who called me everything from "safer" to "zephyr," and added an *e*. Nobody in the family followed; I am now the only one correctly pronounced by strangers and am a black sheep at a bar mitzvah. I think Morley Safer is a relation.

What about *steen* and *stine*? Is there any rhyme or reason to the chosen pronunciation? Everyone named Stein, and Stein alone, pronounces the name *stine*. Stein is a stein is a stein, as Gertrude used to say. Yet Andrew Stein, borough president of Manhattan, has an industrialist father named Jerry Finkelstein, who pronounces the last syllable *steen*. When son Andrew shortened the name, the pronunciation automatically shifted.

Here are a few *stines:* John Steinbeck, Albert Einstein, Gloria Steinem, Mayor Dianne Feinstein; the "eye" pronunciation of the *ei* can also be heard in the names of Dwight Eisenhower, Carl Reiner, Caspar Weinberger and Barbra (only two *a*'s) Streisand.

Now here are a few *steens:* Leonard Bernstein, Carl Bernstein, Robert Brustein. Gambler Nicky Arnstein married Fanny Brice, played by Barbra Streisand, in a confusing ee-eye-o.

A pattern is seen by John Algeo, professor of English at the University of Georgia. "The German names are usually pronounced with an *eye* sound. Most of the Jewish names have had the American influence of the *ee* sound, as in the words *weird* or *receive*, particularly that *ei* after the letter *c*." Professor Algeo notes that, in Yiddish, a sound change occurred, with the *ei* pronounced as a long *a*, as in *stain*, but changed in American-influenced Yiddish to *ee*. "The ending of *stein*, pronounced *steen*," he concludes, "reflects an American influence."

From this, we can formulate Stein's Rule: Although names ending in *stein* can be pronounced either *stein* or *steen*, names consisting exclusively of *Stein* are pronounced *stine*. (In the rare case of a person named Stein refusing to go along with the crowd, this is changed to "Steen's Rule.")

Leonard BernSTEEN indeed! Maybe his mama pronounced it that way, but I've never heard Lenny's last name said any other way but BernSTINE—except by the uninitiated!

Felice Itzkoff
Forest Hills, New York

You, sir, are in error. We Bernsteins of Boston are committed, even committable, "stines."

However, I have been known to answer to either ("eether")/either ("eyether") pronunciation.

Burton Bernstein
New York, New York

Dear Bill:

I've always assumed that social position determined the "stine/steen" controversy.

For example, I'm certain that Albert Einstein's mother called him "Al Einsteen" who would grow famous and become "Albert Einstine."

It was predominately "Leonard Bernsteen" pre West Side Story *and predominately "Bernstine" thereafter.*

My father always says "steen," my mother, a bit more class conscious, occasionally says "stine."

One would expect a gambler to be looked upon as a "steen" (Nicky Arnsteen). I can also understand a Washington Post *reporter remaining a "steen" (Carl Bernstein).*

"Martin Feldstine" obviously thinks he's made it, which clearly explains his annoyance with the one syllable Speakes.

As to "Jerry Finkelsteen" he drove his son to abandon the family name to become the non-controversial "stine." Andrew knew his father (a man of prominence) had earned his "stine" and Andrew didn't wish to be denied his real birthright.

For me it is a dilemma. Have I made it or haven't I? I say "steen" in person, but "stine" over the phone.

Clearly, I haven't come to grips with myself.

Arthur [J. Finkelstein]
Irvington, New York

You cite Professor John Algeo's contention that the Yiddish pronunciation of ei *as in STAIN was Americanized to STEEN. This is only partially correct. The* ei *as STAIN pronunciation is common for Yiddish of Russian or particularly Lithuanian origin. Polish, Hungarian and characteristically Galician Yiddish renders the* ei *as STEIN (STINE).*

Samuel Dershowitz
Jerusalem, Israel

Dear Bill:

In your speculations on the origins of "steen" and "stine" in the pronunciation of names ending in "stein," you fail to mention one possible ethnic-linguistic factor: The ending of German Jewish names is invariably pronounced "stine," while the ending of Russian Jewish names is pronounced "steen" in America.

The Russian language does not easily formulate the sound "stine," and the Russian tongue resists it. Names that end in "stein" in German are pronounced "shtain" in Russian.

Clifton [Daniel]
New York, New York

Herewith a footnote to the "Steen-Stine" matter. The film mogul Joseph E. Levine reportedly favored "veen," but the Metropolitan Opera's James Levine prefers "vine" according to those at Channel 13. That his choice is not preferred by all musicians is indicated by the duo-pianists of yesteryear. They inserted an h after the first letter and also varied the ending, the result being "Lhevinne" about which little pronunciation controversy existed during their long and illustrious careers.

Thomas G. Morgansen
Jackson Heights, New York

Why did you capitalize "anglicized" in the Stein piece? I'm sure you know there are no proper verbs.

Charles Granade
Princeton, New Jersey

If I remember aright—and the neurons are decaying—Mike Taliaferro was a quarterback for the Jets, perhaps in the pre-Namath era, perhaps later, perhaps as a back-up. I think he went on to the Patriots. To the best of my knowledge, he did call himself "Tolliver," as you suggest, and that's the way the broadcasters played it.

Now, as you can see from the enclosed clipping (from The Stanford Observer*), there's a wide receiver playing for Stanford who goes all the way. No anglicized pronunciation for him, and no Italianate, highfalutin (where did that word come from? Does anyone use it now?) spelling, either.*

The first Taliaferro in this country came to Virginia around the middle of the 17th century, from England. I suspect his grandfather, or great-grandfather, had come to England as a member of Henry VIII's Venetian Guard—but I can't prove it. For the last three centuries, or more, all the Taliaferro's have pronounced their name "Tolliver," as I do. If that be "Anglicizing," make the most of it, as Patrick Henry said in another context.

By the way, "Taliaferro" was the middle name of both Sam Rayburn and Booker T. Washington.

Taliaferro Boatwright
Stonington, Connecticut

Please! You should not complain that ex-quarterback Taliaferro pronounces (Anglicizes, you said!) his name "Tolliver" just as his father, grandfather, and forebears down the centuries have pronounced that fine old English name; a name brought over—as the story goes—by a Tuscan smith or ironworker (Tagliaferro) in the contingent of William the Conqueror. Nor, to those who deal with the English language, should the relation between pronunciation and spelling seem so perverse. We can presume that the original hard g *was aspirated and then dropped in pronunciation (as the Tuscans of Florence are doing with the hard* c *today) and in spelling. Then if we drop the last vowel, as in present southern Italian dialects, and voice the fricative* f, lo—*Anglicized these 900 years, Tagliaferro becomes Tolliver.*

> R. K. Adair
> New Haven, Connecticut

Your article reminded me of the differing pronunciations of the name "Shapiro." Coming from Philadelphia, I always heard this name pronounced with a long i. *When I moved to Connecticut I was told to look up a relative of a relative with that name. As soon as I said "Sha-PIE-ro" he knew I was from Philadelphia, as everywhere else the name is pronounced as "appear" with* sh *and* o *added, he said. Was he right?*

> Marlene Wenograd
> West Hartford, Connecticut

Aunt Toots is undoubtedly reliable as to the pronunciation of your name; your etymology, however, is flawed.

The only authoritative work on the transmission (and transliteration) of Hebrew family names was published by E. S. Rabinowitz in two issues of the Hebrew quarterly Reshumot, *a journal for ethnography and folklore, edited by Droyanov, Bialik and Raunitsky, and issued in Tel Aviv from 1925 to 1930.*

Rabinowitz lists SAPHIR (in Hebrew) and transcribes it as both Sapir *and* Safir. *(It means "sapphire.") SAPPIR is mentioned in Exodus 28:18 as one of the stones in the priestly "breastplate of decision." So you have a very distinguished name.*

SOFER (scribe) has a variety of pronunciations, depending on the speaker's country of origin. A Lithuanian Jew would pronounce it safer *(like in Morley), a Polish Jew* soifer, *an American Jew* sofer. *Nobody, but nobody would sound it like* safir, safire *or* sapphire.

My own interest in names stems partly from the trouble I have with my very simple name—Feffer. How can it be mispronounced? Yet I am called Fifer, Fiffer, Peffer, and Pepper. When I spell it on the telephone, I always add "F as in Frank"; without this formula my mail is sent to Sesser. Sometimes I say "S as in Srank"; then the envelope is addressed correctly.

> Solomon Feffer
> Retired Chairman, Department of Hebraic Studies
> Rutgers University
> Newark, New Jersey

I knew an English family who lived in Fairfield until recently. Their name was spelled the way you spell your name, "Safire," but they pronounced it "Sayfree." Another possibility!

> *Jeanne Varaljay Reed*
> *Fairfield, Connecticut*

Erratum

Music lovers the world over have joined in an orchestrated chorus of denunciation about a false assertion in a piece about the pronunciation of *stine* versus *steen*. Leonard Bernstein, the conductor, is a *stine*, and I had better believe it.

Morley Safer, I wrote in the same piece, may be a *relation*, because his name and mine are similar. Carl Taylor of Morgantown, West Virginia, disputes the locution: "I doubt that Morley would appreciate being designated a *relation*—even if by chance he should happen to be a distant *relative*."

Both nouns mean "kin"; *relative* has been around only three years longer than *relation* (1657 versus 1660), and they are interchangeable. If I had it to write over, I'd choose *relative*, because *relationship* is slopping over everything these days: At least a *meaningful relative* is not a cliché.

Straightening "Straits"

"We will use whatever means is required," said President Jimmy Carter in 1980, "to keep the Straits of Hormuz open."

Nearly four years later, candidate Gary Hart was asked what he would do if the Iran-Iraq war led to an attempt to close the thirty-mile-wide sea lane at Hormuz, where the oil tankers of the Persian Gulf pass through to the Gulf of Oman and on to the oil-thirsty world. He called for "an international force to keep the Strait open."

The difference between the Carter commitment and the Hart policy is that Mr. Carter wanted to keep the *Straits* open, while Mr. Hart wants to keep the *Strait* open.

Who is correct? In a political harangue written in my other incarnation, I entitled an essay "In Desperate Straits" and railed at the easy acquiescence of hawks and doves to a knee-jerk defense of the *Straits*. In the final edition of *The New York Times*, my *Straits* was changed by a straitlaced copy editor to *Strait*.

"The headline poses no problem," writes Richard Borden of the United States Information Agency in Washington, who is willing to accept a time-honored phrase and who cannot fault my verbatim quotation of President Carter (although he thinks I should have put a [*sic*] after "means is"). "But when a columnist in his own name perpetuates the error at the chokepoint of the Persian Gulf, one must ask himself, 'Whither wends this weary world? Where's my polestar?' "

Here's the latest twinkle from Polestar: A struggle is underway between geographers and lexicographers over the clipping of the final *s* from *straits*. *The Associated Press Stylebook* takes the clipping for granted, as if the debate were over: "Strait: Capitalize as part of a proper name: *Bering Strait, Strait of Gibraltar.*" *The New York Times Manual of Style and Usage* recognizes the problem: "Strait (passage) is almost always singular: Bering Strait, Strait of Gibraltar, Strait of Malacca. An exception is the Straits of Florida, although some authorities, but not the *Times*, make that singular, too."

Hold on, now. *Bering Strait* sounds right to me, but my ear likes *Straits of Gibraltar*. And the stormy passage between mainland South America and Tierra del Fuego is, to my recollection, the *Straits of Magellan*. Is some language-neatener trying to seduce Norma Loquendi?

The geographers play it *strait*. "The proper name of one passageway uses the singular *strait*," says Caren Bashore at the National Geographic Society. "We go by what's on our maps, and in the case of Hormuz, the proper reference would be the *Strait of Hormuz*, singular."

Never *straits*? "The only exception I've found is the *Straits of Mackinac* between Lake Michigan and Lake Huron, which is divided by an island into more than one strait."

Lexicographer Sol Steinmetz isn't having any of that: "The common usage is *straits*," he says, and points to the *Oxford English Dictionary* for early support. "The word is usually plural with a singular sense," reported that superauthority, "e.g., the *Straits of Dover, of Gibraltar* . . . A few writers, chiefly of gazetteers, use the singular consistently throughout.

"Geography-conscious people still insist on *strait*," adds Steinmetz, "but with most people, there is a tendency to use the plural with geographical terms. *Narrows*, which is the narrow part of a river or valley, and *barrens*, barren land, are thought of as a collective thing with many parts."

The battle is joined: gazetteerists prescribing no final *s*, supported by most newspaper stylebooks, lexicographers at Merriam-Webster and Webster's New World going along, while other lexicographers bridle at the gazetteers' domineering.

The word itself comes from the Latin for "strict": A straitjacket is not what the well-dressed traveler dons for a cruise through the Dardanelles, but is the name of a tightly binding garment. "It matters not how strait the gate," wrote William Ernest Henley, "How charged with punishments the scroll, I am the master of my fate; I am the captain of my soul." The poet, who was one of the leading slang lexicographers of his day, saw the gates of heaven as strait—tight, narrow, difficult to get through.

My advice: Go with the familiar; follow your ear. If you're happy with the Straits of Gibraltar or Magellan, use the final *s*; if the place name is new to you, let the gazetteer crowd have its way. Hormuz is unfamiliar to most Americans, and the *Strait of Hormuz* is therefore the name I would use, going along with Gary Hart and the stylebooks. But retain the singular sense: "The Straits of Gibraltar is a passage." "The Strait of Hormuz is the next Quemoy and Matsu."

If you are a columnist, this will be straightened out to lockstep conformity in the last edition, with the final *s* neatly clipped off all *straits*. That is because the stylebook is the master of your fate, but you remain the captain of your soul.

I'm for keeping the Straits of Hormuz and all Straits whatsoever. The geographer, looking at his flat drawing, may see and think a single strait. *But, as an old Navy man, I know that the navigator thinks of* straits *every inch of the way, knowing he'll be in desperate straits if he doesn't. Similarly,* barrens *are continuous barren patches as you plod along. Same for* narrows *and* rapids *(no one would think of just one spurt of white water by one rock). I'm for the physically active actuality that named* straits straits *in the first place.*

> Sheridan Baker
> Ann Arbor, Michigan

My father worked in Singapore, which was then in the Straits Settlements. I asked him the same question. He told me the Straits were not the passage itself but the two sides that narrowed the waterway, the strictures—as in Scylla and *Charybdis, which formed what we now call the Straits of Messina.*

> Hugh M. Pease
> Alexandria, Virginia

You told us a struggle is underway *between geographers and lexicographers. That's O.K. with me, but my dictionary has it as two words,* under way. *Anyway, weigh to go!*

> Moe Kregstein
> Oradell, New Jersey

Street-Smart

How to Raise a Street-Smart Child is a book by Grace Hechinger, which is published by Facts on File and subtitled *The Complete Parent's Guide to Safety on the Street and at Home*. (That possessive is troubling; apostrophe-smart grammarians prefer either *a parent's guide* or *the parents' guide*.) At the same time, Bantam Books offers Mark McCormack's *What They Don't Teach You at Harvard Business School*, subtitled *Notes From a Street-Smart Executive*.

The origin of *street-smart* is shrouded in the mists of urban slang. To speculate: A colloquial variant of *to be smart* is *to have the smarts*; I recall using *street smarts* as a noun applied to big-city politicians in the 1950's. (In 1973, *The Village Voice* wrote that Mario Cuomo "had the ability to listen and is more intelligent" but that Mario Biaggi "had street smarts.") I suspect the hyphenated compound adjective was formed from that noun. A related noun, used in business, is *street sense*.

The term that is in the *Webster's New World Dictionary*, the Merriam-Webster Ninth Collegiate and the *American Heritage Dictionary* is *streetwise*. This is defined along the lines of "able to cope with life in crime-ridden urban neighborhoods," but the only people who say *streetwise* these days are office-bound lexicographers; out in the back alley, where the books are shipped and the ripoffs and instant-remaindering take place, *street-smart* is used.

The term has an air of sassiness and an anti-intellectual overtone. To have the *street smarts* is to be possessed of asphalt-jungle cunning, the knack of punching a ball the length of two sewers, and the ability to get along by going along with a tough and sometimes violent environment. Rarely pejorative, when used in politics the adjective carries a connotation of praise. Writing about Walter Mondale's selection of Geraldine Ferraro over Mayor Dianne Feinstein, Jane Perlez of *The New York Times* used the word this way: "Mr. Mondale had been impressed by Mrs. Feinstein's intellect, but he chose a woman schooled in the *street-smart* ways of Queens politics."

Grace Hechinger catches the built-in class defiance in the word when she defines it this way: "A *street-smart* person, large or small, may not know which fork to use, but will know whether to stay and fight or run away."

You seem to construe "The Complete Parent's Guide (etc.)" as equivalent to "The Parents' Complete Guide."

However, the construction exactly parallels The Compleat Angler *and "apostrophe-s" seems better than "s-apostrophe" here.*

> Grant Sharman
> Hollywood, California

I must admit you had me going for a while with that "apostrophe-smart grammarians" observation regarding Ms. Hechinger's treatment of urban savvy. I knew there was something wrong, but I couldn't bring it into focus, at first. I've got it now!

You fell into a simple, and somewhat surprising trap. In the author's subtitle, the word "The" doesn't refer to the "Parent's," or "Parents'," but to the "Guide" itself. The interjection of the adjective "Complete" (not "Compleat," as you might have imagined), which clearly modifies "Guide," not the immediate forebears whatever their grammatical niceties, changes the rules. All that being so, it doesn't matter whether she wrote "The" or "A," either is acceptable, and neither has the influence you suggest.

> David W. Nicholas
> Princeton, New Jersey

In the twenties, when I was of junior-high-school age, living in Williamsburg, Brooklyn, we used to play "association" or "touch football" on the street. The main requirement of skill was to be able to throw a football in a tight spiral. The measurement of distance was indeed the "sewer."

The standard usage of "sewer" involved a double solecism. (I know that "solecism" is not the best word here, but it is the best I can do on short notice and without specialized dictionaries.) First, what we called a "sewer" is actually a "manhole cover." Secondly, a "sewer" was not a manhole cover, but the distance between consecutive manhole covers.

Here is a chain of distortion that starts with a subterranean drainage channel and ends up with a number.

> Joseph Lehner
> Jamesburg, New Jersey

While some of us could hit three *sewers with a good stick and a live "spaldeen" (of blessed memory) none of the guys could PUNCH much more than a sewer—or even tried. While, in my suburban retreat, I can't go out to measure more than cesspools, "a sewer" has to be 30-40 yards. Not even Marvin Hagler can punch a spaldeen 60 yards. You ain't street-smart!*

> Melvin J. Breite, M.D.
> Great Neck Estates, New York

Sure Thing

Mario Cuomo, governor and diarist, was described by Martin Nolan in *Washington Journalism Review* as being a language purist: "In a conversation late one night at a West Side trattoria, he insisted on the correct antecedent with a plural verb and wondered how language had become corrupted. He was instructed by that eminent grammarian Jimmy Breslin, who said with Breslinesque certitude, 'Listen, Mario, *media* is the plural of *mediocre!*' "

Certitude was the correct word there; *certainty* would have been wrong. Oliver Wendell Holmes wrote in 1918: "Certitude is not the test of certainty. We have been cocksure of many things that were not so."

Although both words are rooted in the Latin *certus*, for "settled, determined," a useful differentiation has developed that is worth trying to preserve. *Certitude* is subjective, based on faith; *certainty* is objective, based on facts. *Certainty* is when you know it in your head; *certitude* is when you feel it in your bones. (I'm pretty sure of this.)

"Certainty is when . . ."? "Certitude is when . . ."?

How sure are you of the above constructions? Whether you feel it in your head or in your bones, it's still a bonehead construction (either one). See, for example, Harbrace Handbook of English, p. 267:

> *WRONG: A sonnet is when a poem has fourteen lines*
> *RIGHT: A sonnet is a poem of fourteen lines*

Samuel Beckoff
Sunnyside, New York

Sweet Talk

A euphemism (from the Greek for "to speak with words of good omen") is a pretty word for an ugly thing. "I have just been invited by the radio," writes Marshall Gorridge of Wilmette, Illinois, "to call in if I have a dependent with a chemical problem. Now, I don't know if any of my dependents have chemical problems; since none of them are research chemists, I suspect not. What is more, none of them are drug addicts, which is what the radio was really getting at." In a similar vein, Nancy Wu of Springfield, Illinois, sends along a letter from the Republic Bank of Dallas which goes to a new length in avoiding the dread word, *loss:* The Sun Production Company merely had a "net profits revenue deficiency."

A second category of euphemism is the pretentious renaming of a familiar activity. These are not strictly euphemisms, because they do not prettify the ugly; the word being upscaled (what's wrong with "improved"?) is merely familiar. The latest of these is the new phrase for *doorman*, which William Arnstein of New York informs me is *access controller*.

When striptease artist Georgia Sothern asked H. L. Mencken for a new word to dignify *stripper*, he came up with *ecdysiast*, which—according to *Kind Words*, a thesaurus of euphemisms by Judith Neaman and Carole Silver—comes from *ecdysis*, the shedding of an outer layer, as in the molting of birds. (Miss Sothern had a feather act.)

A new word is needed for this second category; until a good one comes in, the working title will be *pompotitles*. These are not only applied to jobs, but to objects: Bill Finlay of Dorchester, Massachusetts, wrote to *The New York Times* objecting to the use of the word *tugboat* in a headline: "May I suggest the term *towboat* be used to replace the word *tugboat*. Here's why: (a) The companies are towboat, not tugboat, companies; check their yellow-pages listings. (b) The boats *tow* barges, ships, scows, etc. They do not *tug* them. (c) Similarly, when your car is disabled, do you phone for a tugtruck? (d) The word *tugboat* should be laid to rest along with *choo-choo trains* and *flying horses*."

His suggestion is a drag: Both *tug* and *tow* are rooted in the Indo-European base *deuk*, "to draw or pull," which turned out in Latin to be *ducere*. For the captains of these vessels to insist on a pompotitle gives me a tow on the heartstrings.

A third type of euphemism is a cover-up word for parts of the human body too delicate for mention: A century ago, *limbs* were substituted for *legs*, and before that, *bosom* was the word for people who could not bring themselves to speak aloud of breasts. This cover-up was further veiled with *bazoom* and the most recent "we full-figured gals." These words are euphemized not because they are ugly but because they deal with matters unmentionable in polite society, mixed company or tearooms. (Whatever happened to tearooms? Whatever became of polite society?)

A political example of that type-three euphemism, for which a word is urgently needed, occurred at the Madrid Conference to monitor the operations of the Helsinki Final Act. (Strange name for a treaty; will Helsinki ever reopen?) A beautiful idea needed description in terms not too titillating. The Soviet Union did not want to mention "freedom of the press" in agreeing to reduce some restrictions on press freedom; accordingly, the phrase chosen was "the freer and wider dissemination of printed matter."

Reading William Safire's example of euphemism as a pretentious renaming of a familiar activity (access controller *for* doorman), *I was reminded of a familiar signboard at our town's baker long ago which read, "T. ROZARIO, formerly* Professor *of* Culinary Science *at the Governor's Cuisine" (the governor he referred to was more of a glutton than an epicure). Our town also boasted then of a shop of tailors who advertised on their signboard as "SARTORIAL ADVISERS to the former Maharaja," though the Maharaj was known to wear only* dhoti *(like the toga of ancient Romans).*

But the pièce de résistance *was a parody of such euphemisms strung together in a sentence by a native wit in our local English language daily some 40 years ago. It read: "As* His Sacerdotal Eminence, *in his resplendent robes specially created by a team of his own* Sartorial Specialists, *took his exalted place among the Village aristocracy, there were telltale signs on his half-bald pate and visage that the* tonsorial artist, *who is also reported to substitute occasionally as a* Culinary expert *in the Bishop's Palace, had done a bad job of it." (The bishop, needless to say, didn't take kindly to the Victorian humour and effusion.)*

Winston Churchill had a built-in weakness not only for hyperbolic language but also for wordy euphemisms. Who doesn't know that he relished lies *only when served as* terminological inexactitudes?

Unfortunately (for most readers) euphemism of the above type is esoteric. In order to be effective and witty, it has to be rid of bombast and circumlocution. "Brevity", after all, "is the soul of wit!"

K. N. Ninan
Bombay, India

Anyone who knows beans (or peas for that matter) about contemporary euphemisms is aware that a tearoom is a public pissoir frequented by cruising homosexuals.

Alfred Stern
New York, New York

What ever happened to what ever, pray tell?

Andrew E. Beresky
New York, New York

Mr. Finlay's suggestion that the word "towboat" be substituted for the word "tug-boat" is more than a drag. It is historically inaccurate.

The word "tugboat" is derived from the name given to the first coastal steamer utilized to tow boats: the S.S. Tug, built in England about 1817, probably by John Wood. Tugboats do indeed tow barges and ships, but that does not alter the fact that for over one hundred and fifty years they have been called tugboats.

Imagine reading "Scuffy the Towboat" to the next generation of children!

Kenneth Gordon
White Plains, New York

You quote Bill Finlay re tugboats vs. towboats. He says that they tow barges, ships, etc.

However, tugboats-towboats also push. On our big rivers—the Mississippi, Ohio, etc.—this is the common mode of moving the barges. Yet these powerful boats are called tug boats and tow boats.

Is there a better word? Pushboats?!!

Louis A. Otto, Jr.
Aurora, Colorado

Taint So

As Democratic convention time approaches, the accusatory words most on the lips of the Hart forces are the verb *to taint* and its putrefying participle, *tainted*.

Delegates pledged to Walter Mondale who were elected with the help of what Senator Hart says are illegal campaign funds are *tainted delegates*; they were elected with *tainted money* and may lead to a *tainted convention*. There has not been such an explosion of the word's use for a decade, since the profusion of descriptions of innocent or sanitized Republicans *untainted by Watergate*.

The Watergate era was surely *taint's* heyday. After the June 1972 break-in, G. Gordon Liddy admitted that he realized all his memorandums could be tainted; when press reports linked H. R. Haldeman to a cash fund supposedly used to finance "dirty tricks," the re-election committee chairman worried that it brought the "taint of wrongdoing" only a step from the President himself. In 1975, *Newsweek* wrote, *"New York Times* columnist William Safire escaped any possible taint of Watergate by leaving his post as a White House Special Assistant before the spring of 1973." In those days, to be *tainted* was one step beyond being *linked*.

The verb is probably a blend of the Middle English word for "touch," *taynten*, and the Anglo-French verb for "color," *teinter*. *Tainted* was originally applied to spoiled corn and was first used about a person in the 1619 play *The Knight of Malta*, in which a character is condemned: "Treason and tainted thoughts are all the gods thou worship'dst." The word's sense began as "spoiled, stained with contamination" and was extended to mean "foully influenced, morally corrupted." Edmund Burke, in 1775, hailed Americans as students of the law who "snuff the approach of tyranny in every tainted breeze."

When *taint* makes a comeback, that means corruption is the issue. Even as the tainted delegates made their way west, the Democratic National Committee produced a television commercial depicting "more scandal-tainted officials than we've seen since Richard Nixon and Watergate. . . ."

In an appositive development, *simon-pure* is getting some publicity. At the State Department, Ambassador Robert Morris conceded that the United States had taken some steps toward economic protectionism, but insisted, "If we are not simon-pure, we remain fairly credible."

The phrase means "untainted." Delegates to conventions who are unencumbered by charges of being the creatures of ill-gotten funds are *simon-pure* delegates.

Who is this *simon* and why is he so *pure*? More important, why is he uncapitalized and hyphenated?

The term comes from *A Bold Stroke for a Wife*, a 1717 play by Susanna Centlivre, in which a character named Simon Pure is impersonated by another character; one point of the plot is to discover the "real" Simon Pure. Like the character of Mrs. Malaprop in Sheridan's play *The Rivals*, the name soon became a noun for a quality in a person.

That quality, in Simon's case, was authenticity. In its adjective form, the compound gained a hyphen and lost its capitals: In 1894, William Dean Howells wrote glowingly of "American individuality, the real, simon-pure article."

In eponymy, names turn into words and lose their capital letters, as Captain Boycott and Amelia Bloomer will attest. As a noun, *Simon Pure* is two words; as an adjective, it is lowercase and holds the hyphen. That keeps the adjectival form untainted.

May I suggest that the word "tainted" had its innings before Watergate. In 1913 when the Rockefeller Foundation was established, critics of the arrangement sniffed haughtily that the Rockefeller fortune was "tainted money." Almost immediately a well-known vaudeville performer included in his routine a wisecrack that was soon circulating widely: "Sure it's tainted: 'taint yours and 'taint mine!"

Henry F. Graff
New York, New York

You could have carried "taint" back a little further. Shakespeare, who died in 1616 and thus predates anything written in 1619, had the ghost in Hamlet *saying, "Taint not thy mind against thy mother aught, Leave her to heaven," etc., etc.*

Which always made me think, "If 'tain't not my mind, then what the hell is it?"

Lewis S. Haber
South Bend, Indiana

Talmudistic

Shimon Peres, the Prime Minister of Israel, on a recent visit to Washington, met a group of heavyweight media thumbsuckers and used an adjective that none of us had heard before.

Before going into a lengthy explanation of the complex West Bank settlement policy of his government, he said, "I'm sorry if this sounds Talmudistic."

Talmudic is the word some diplomats have used to describe arcane and sometimes highly creative reasoning; in the 1970's, it was a Henry Kissinger favorite. The Talmud (the Hebrew word means "instruction") is a collection of Hebrew books of civil and canonical law interpreting the Old Testament and extending its reach. *Talmudic* means only "of or pertaining to the Talmud"; a *Talmudic scholar*, one who studies those books, is called a *Talmudist*.

The meaning intended by diplomats is not "pertaining to the Talmud"; therefore, *Talmudic* is incorrect. Their intended meaning is "similar to the work done by an imaginative Talmudist, who can find practical solutions to today's living by reinterpreting the old texts in a creative way."

That word is *Talmudistic*, and it is almost four centuries old. In 1593, Thomas Nashe wrote about "Th'almudisticall dreames." Fifty years later, Ralph Cudworth used the word to describe a group of believers and noted, "Besides these Talmudisticke Jewes, there is another Sect . . . that reject all Talmudicall Traditions."

In choosing *Talmudistic*, Mr. Peres has revived a useful English adjective. We can hope that his diplomacy will be as resourceful as his linguistics.

Shimon Peres' use of Talmudistic *is obviously correct by analogy to* legalistic. Legalistic *is to* legal *what* Talmudistic *is to* Talmudic. *Both* legalistic *and* Talmudistic *are pejorative terms.*

Frank I. Finnel
Great Neck, New York

Tapetalk

Secretly recording telephone conversations may be ethically wrong, but the tapes are linguistically revealing. Here, on the relentlessly faithful magnetic tape, is the language unadorned, denuded of literary pretension and stripped of the requirements of public presentation. Tapetalk is the way people actually speak, and the willingness every decade or so of some officials—who have little concern for their callers' privacy—to push a button that preserves that speech gives the world a chance to eavesdrop on the lingo as she is spoke.

When Charles Wick, director of the United States Information Agency, recorded a conversation with White House Chief of Staff James Baker, this colloquy occurred:

WICK: I got Axel Springer's right-hand man to fly in from Germany.

BAKER: Right.

WICK: Clem Stone can't make it because he is going to be in Germany, but said, "Put me down for whatever you think is necessary."

BAKER: Right.

WICK: I got Dwayne Andreas, Henry Salvatori.

BAKER: Bottom line. What happened?

The brisk, no-nonsense chief of staff used the expression *bottom line* with a slight variation in the widely accepted meaning. *Bottom line* originally referred to earnings figures and then rooted itself in business jargon as a compound adjective, in *bottom-line responsibility*. Its widest general use today is "What's the bottom line?"—meaning "What is the essence of the problem?" or "What are the consequences?" To some extent, that was the meaning Mr. Baker expressed, but in context, his meaning was "Get to the point."

Thus, thanks to Mr. Wick, lexicographers now have a citation for a second meaning of *bottom line:* If spoken peremptorily, following two crisp "Right's," it means "Stop wasting my time."

In a subsequent taped conversation with his aide, Mark Everson, Mr. Wick complains of some group that "it is too narrow."

EVERSON: That is why we can't . . .

WICK: A perspective. Yeah.

EVERSON: . . . we can't craft a program.

Craft is an old verb, meaning "create with the strength and skill of the hands," which has had a recent voguish revival. No longer is *craft* limited to handwork; now brainwork can be done by hand. This practice offends Joseph Alsop, the retired columnist, who deplores the repeated use of *faux* (a ritzy term for *fake*) in *The New Yorker* magazine. One article used *faux-papier-mâché, faux-rock porcelain* and *faux-brown-paper-bag*. Mr. Alsop observed that "the responsible writer spared me the pain of a claim that these objects had been 'beautifully crafted.' "

Crafting a program is like *fashioning a plan*—a good metaphor when originally used, but false elegance now that it has become hackneyed.

In another tape recording by Mr. Wick—this time a dictated diary entry, not a secretly taped recording of somebody else—the U.S.I.A. director recounts a meeting with President Reagan during a motorcade in February 1982.

"As we first got into the car with the President, he said, 'Say hello Charlie, I am having a lot of problems with the right wing and what is this talk about Phil Nicolaides.' I told him that I have put Nicolaides into the Voice of America and had taken him out. That he was a loose cannon."

Loose cannon has been careening around the deck of language with great frequency of late (some would say *careering* around, but I prefer *careening*—*careering* is what bureaucrats do). In the "Among the New Words" section of *American Speech*, the phrase was described in 1983 as "someone or something that has become uncontrollable." Its earliest citation is a Public Broadcasting Service panel show, *Washington Week in Review*, on February 6, 1981: "Is [he] a loose cannon?" Citations from the 1970's or earlier are invited from Lexicographic Irregulars.

Don Hauptman of New York City submits this description of the literal effect of a loose cannon, taken from Victor Hugo's 1874 novel *Ninety-Three:* "A frightful thing had just happened. One of the carronades of the battery, a 24-pounder, had broken loose. This is perhaps the most frightful of all accidents at sea. Nothing more terrible can happen to a warship on the open seas and under full sail."

Since Mr. Wick has made these contributions to the study of current bureaucratic jargon, he deserves an answer to his own query in his "Daily Notes" dated November 22, 1982: "Give me the definition of 'irrendentism' (in Argentina)."

The misspelling is not his fault, since it was a transcript of his taped dictation. *Irredentism* is from the Italian *irredenta*, "unredeemed": In the nineteenth century, Italian irredentists sought the return to Italy of lands lost by the mother country. Since then, the *-ism* has been applied to any advocacy of taking back "lost" land; in Argentina today, there is still talk of regaining the Malvinas Islands (called the Falklands by the British), which is why Mr. Wick was inquiring about the meaning of the term and why Argentine children are encouraged to see their irredentist twice a year.

Andrew Friedland of Philadelphia clipped a column I wrote about Mr. Wick and circled this line: "In an interview in his home, *New York Times* reporter Jane Perlez and I. . . ." The astute reader inquires: "Is Jane Perlez a man? If not, I think you might have made a mistake in your sentence construction. What do you say?"

I say what Charles Wick should have said when first confronted with questions about secret taping: Nobody's perfect.

You said you would prefer careening to careering. As an avid reader of Forester's Hornblower saga, I can assure you they are not at all the same. To careen a ship is to drag it up on a beach and tilt it to one side, in order to repair shot holes or scrape off barnacles. Any sailor who suggested that a loose cannon careened would probably have a rope tied around his middle, be thrown over the bow, dragged along the barnacle-sharp keel, and hauled back up over the stern. Careening may mean tilting, or falling over, but not careering.

Douglas J. Stahl
New York, New York

I hope the next time you careen a warship to get rid of the barnacles on your bottom, there isn't a loose cannon careering about on deck.

Arthur Morgan
New York, New York

If "Wanton Prebendary" sounds too stuffy, how about "Loose Canon"?

P. C. Starrett
San Francisco, California

Among the Yiddish phrases I managed to pick up from assorted aunts and cousins of the generation preceding me, one of the most useful has been de oontersta shuora—*literally, "the bottom line"*—oontersta *being the Yiddish usage of the German* unterste, *or "lowest," and* shoora, *the Hebrew word for "line." It was often used to interrupt or reply to a long-winded recital with the question: What is the* untersta shoora? *What point are you trying to make? Or: what actually happened?*

It seems to me that this meaning long preceded the referral to earning figures and that the phrase probably entered into the business jargon by way of Yiddish.

Miriam L. Varon
Brookline, Massachusetts

I see "Right" twice, but "Right's," not even once. I believe the comma belongs outside of the quotation marks, not being part of the quotation. Further, I wonder if the " 's" belongs outside the quotation marks as well ("Right" 's), although this seems awkward. Do I remember that the apostrophe can be used in plurals such as "The Jacobs' are coming," not indicating possessive?

Herbert N. Jacobs, M.D.
San Francisco, California

Bully Coinage

In a piece about "tapetalk," the etymology of *loose cannon*, meaning "one who blunders about and causes trouble for his own side," was explored.

Thanks to Henry Graff, professor of history at Columbia University, we now have one of those rarities, a firsthand account of a conversation held nearly a century ago that uses the phrase and may have led to its popularization. It comes from *The Autobiography of William Allen White*, published in 1946.

"It was after dinner on September 18, 1901, in Washington," writes Professor Graff. "On the day previous, the state funeral for President McKinley had been held in the Capitol. On the morrow, Theodore Roosevelt, the new Chief Executive, would take over the White House. Now he sat in the parlor of his sister Bamie's house, excitedly regaling with his views and plans his friends William Allen White, the editor and publisher of *The Emporia Gazette*, and Nicholas Murray Butler, the Columbia educator. But the energetic young President had a nagging concern: How would he occupy his time and mind when he had completed McKinley's term, had had one in his own right, and was still only 50 years old?

He declared: 'I don't want to be the old cannon loose on the deck in the storm.' "

Theodore Roosevelt was a big contributor to the American lexicon. Not only *bully pulpit* and *hat in the ring*, but *big stick, pussyfooting, malefactors of great wealth, weasel words, mollycoddle, muckraker, parlor pink* and *lunatic fringe* were either minted or popularized by him. To this reverberating list we can now add the currently voguish *loose cannon*, and in his memory we can all give an extra squeeze to our teddy bears tonight (from a song about him, "Teddy, You're a Bear"). Among the presidential phrasemakers, he stands tall. (O.K., Graff: *standing tall.*)

First off, I must confess I was not in on the beginnings of the "loose cannon" imbroglio, and know nothing of how it originated, and some of its other nuances.

In fact, I'm not sure if any mention was made early on of the Joseph Conrad short story . . . the one of the heroic sailor who sacrificed his body and personal safety in pursuing and eventually tying down a loose cannon on his ship's deck, and was ceremonially summoned to the bridge to be saluted and cheered by the crew, given a medal by the captain for his heroics . . . and summarily removed to the yardarm where he was hung for letting the cannon get loose in the first place!

                                                              Pete McGovern
                                                              Westport, Connecticut

The Teeny-Weeny Master Spy

As everyone who gathers intelligence knows, sometimes the smallest bit of information is significant when juxtaposed with a huge mass of data. How is this minuscule (not *miniscule*) bit of data best described? Computer operators speak of *bytes*, which are the equivalent of characters on a typewriter: "Character" is a word made up of nine bytes, or characters. Other disciplines have other words, such as *peewee, pint-size* and *infinitesimal.*

At the C.I.A. in this modern era, the preferred term of art was used by Director of Central Intelligence William J. Casey. In a letter to Senator Carl Levin, before agreeing to put his financial holdings into a blind trust, Mr. Casey disputed Senator Levin's argument that the C.I.A. chief had unique access to information: "That really doesn't hold water," Mr. Casey wrote. "It takes only a teeny-weeny bit of information to exploit, if one has that purpose. . . ."

Tiny, the *Oxford English Dictionary* tells us, had a nursery form of *teeny* in the early nineteenth century, which then became *teeny-tiny* and ultimately developed, in the 1890's, to *teeny-weeny* and *teentsy-weentsy.* The phrase has traveled well into the twentieth century; dissatisfied travelers on T.W.A. have derogated the transworld carrier as "Teeny-Weeny Airlines."

Director Casey is to be commended for his use of such a vivid, if childlike, reduplication in his characterization to the Senate of the diminutiveness of data. He has also vigorously denied any knowledge of passing along purloined Carter documents in what has been dubbed "Debategate," but which will be remembered as "Molehill," if the scandal turns out to be itsy-bitsy.

"How is this minuscule (not miniscule*) bit of data best described?"*

Datum—*something given or admitted as a fact; something actual or assumed as a basis of reckoning.* Data—*plural of datum.*

Now then: "bit of data"? Please, Mr. Safire.

> *Ted Dow*
> *Arlington, Virginia*

That Says It All

The ultimate shorthand is upon us. A single phrase is rampant in the American language, a phrase that seems to encapsulate long arguments and reduce complex explanations to a single line.

When asked on television why he did not specifically apologize for Watergate, Richard Nixon had this to say: "There is no way you could apologize that is more eloquent, more decisive, more finite, or to say that you are sorry, which would exceed resigning the Presidency of the United States. That said it all."

The earliest citation for the expression *That says it all* in the *Barnhart Dictionary* files is from the letters section of *The Atlantic* magazine in 1963. "He has said it all," wrote Florence Hascall, adding, "And said it with more bite than we teachers say it every day in our lounge."

That says it all, often accompanied by a cutting motion of a flattened hand, began its move in the mid-1970's. In a review of the career of Alfred Hitchcock,

Newsweek's Paul Zimmerman wrote in 1975: "His apostrophized name above the title says it all—'Alfred Hitchcock's "Deceit." ' " (That's the quotation hat trick: a quote within a quote within a quote.) The following year, Malcolm Forbes wrote in his magazine about *A Chorus Line* and suggested that seeing the show added little to the experience of buying the recording: "The platter says it all." And that year, a trade publication, *Coal Outlook*, reporting about mine safety in the Carter administration, wrote, " 'Defend the brave men who work for us in our deep mines.' That quote from the Carter camp says it all."

What is this *it all* that everybody is saying? The expression goes beyond the mere "everything" to encompass "all that is possible." For example, "the man who has everything" is an impoverished oaf compared with "the man who has it all." Helen Gurley Brown, the *Cosmopolitan* editor who discovered *Sex and the Single Girl*, entitled her memoirs *Having It All*—that is, living life to the *ne plus ultra*—and "it all" meant a combination of love, success, health, money, good looks, fame and contentment sometimes summarized in fast-food restaurants as "the works."

Although the phrase *to do it all again* appears in the language as far back as 1200, the extended meaning of *it all*—"to the fullest potential, and then some"—took hold in the past generation. A household detergent named All advertised proudly: "All does it all"; an easily duped mark is said "to buy it all"; a libertine is one who has "tried it all."

Curiously, *that says it all* crops up often in comments by or about Richard Nixon, who adopted the phrase early and used it often. Stephen Rosenfeld of the *Washington Post*, reviewing a book by Nixon, asked, "Why are we reading a book by Richard Nixon? . . . Doesn't Henry Kissinger's not-so-Delphic blurb—'could not be more timely'—say it all?"

To say it all means "to reveal the essence" or "to signal the bottom line," as if what small amount has been said or shown is a synecdoche for all that could possibly exist on the subject. (O.K., forty letters will come in protesting that I meant *metonymy*—the name of one thing for another associated with it, as in "Oval Office" for "the presidency"—and not *synecdoche*, which is the use of the part to stand for the whole, as in "head" for "cattle." You know what that says about this column's readers?)

In "That Says It All," you refer to a triple-play-on-words as a "quote within a quote within a quote." For Lexicographic Irregulars and Language Snobs, shouldn't that be a "quotation within a quotation within a quotation"?

Gary Muldoon
Rochester, New York

Finite and Dandy

In a piece on the growing use of "that says it all," I quoted Richard Nixon explaining why he did not apologize for the sins of Watergate. His resignation from the presidency, he said, said it all: "There is no way you could apologize that is more eloquent, more decisive, more finite. . . ."

José de Vinck of Allendale, New Jersey, takes exception to the former President's use of that last word: "What he means is not *finite*, but *final*."

Right. *Finite* is enjoying a vogue in a meaning that is stealing the finality from *final*. Many speakers are using *finite* when they mean "specific" or "tangible"; they should stop that. Centuries ago, *finite* had a meaning of "fixed, determined," but that sense of the word atrophied. Today, *finite* means "with limits, bounded"; it is the opposite of *infinite*, which means "endless, extended beyond measure." (So how come *finite* rhymes with "twilight" while *infinite* sounds like "in a bit"? Because pronunciation is perverse, unlike synonymy.)

Finite evokes limits. In grammar, a *finite verb* is limited in tense, person or number, as in "I *apologize*" or "He *apologizes*." A nonfinite verb is one in which the action never starts or stops and always needs help from another verb, as in a gerund (*"Smoking* is dangerous to your health") or a participle ("That *smoking* gun is mine").

Which returns us to Mr. Nixon. He did not intend to say that his action in resigning was a limited apology; he meant the opposite, that his resignation "said it all," that his act was emphatically apologetic. Therefore, he should not have said *finite*, narrowing his act's significance, but should have said *final*, adding emphasis.

Look at it this way: In language usage, do I cravenly limit my presumption by claiming merely to be the Finite Authority?

Thinking Big

Jack Nicholson, the actor, does not consider himself a mere star. Nor is *superstar* world-classy enough. He calls himself a *megasuperstar*.

John Naisbitt, the futurist, wrote a book about what he called in his introduction "10 major transformations taking place right now in our society." To put pizazz in the title, he called these *megatrends* and produced not only a *megaseller* but a marketing catchword: A salesman for Cabbage Patch dolls was quoted at Christmas as saying, "This craving for tactile sensations is a *megatrend*."

As a prefix, *mega-* is very big these days. Stars get Big Bucks, but superstars and their *mega-* superiors get *megabucks*, a term coined in 1946 by American scientists to describe the amounts of money needed to finance atomic research.

Scientists were long familiar with the prefix, having used it in such medical terms as *megadont*, "having large teeth." (Today, *megadon't* means, "Don't even *think* about doing it.")

The swelling of *mega-* has caused the diminishment of most of the other great prefixes. What's become of *arch-*? Remember Professor Moriarty, the *archcriminal* who was Sherlock Holmes's *archenemy*? Remember when right-wingers and other political troglodytes were called *archconservatives*? All gone.

Falling along with the *arch-* is *hyper-*, but for a different reason: The prefix of *hypersensitive* and *hypertension* has now become the noun *hyper*, with an assist from the metaphor of the hypodermic needle. Nitpickers are still called *hypercriti-cal*, but they are more often called nitpickers. (I am thinking of Clay Conley of New York City, who has stared at the slogan of *The New York Times* so long he was impelled to write: "Shouldn't 'All the News That's Fit to Print' be 'All the News That's Fit to Be Printed'?" He has earned his way into the Nitpicker's League, the hyperspinoff of the Nitpickers League.)

Super-, now often pronounced as an arch, exaggerated *soop-a*, has a 1940's feel. *Superman*, George Bernard Shaw's translation of the Nietzschean *Übermensch* and a name popularized by the comic-strip hero created by Jerry Siegel and Joe Shuster, is now a nostalgia item: The movies about him today gently mock the innocent days when a Man of Steel could be a big shot. Who goes to a tiny, mom-and-pop *supermarket* anymore, when *discount food chains* sprawl across *shopping malls*? Giant Foods now has *food-pharmacy combos*, and other low-overhead operations call themselves *warehouse stores*. A spread with more than 100,000 square feet takes its name from the French *hypermarché*, as *hyper-* makes its inroad into *super-*'s domain. (They've just opened Esplanade Mall across the street from my office; the Squad Squad may picket, because an *esplanade* is a mall.) Congressmen may probe *superfunds*, Chinese diplomats may roundly denounce all *superpowers*, and those of us in Washington will not soon forget the *Super Bowl*, but the current meaning of the prefix *super-* is "big in the old days."

Ultra- never made it big. Ultraman was a knockoff of Superman, and as an avid comic-strip reader, I was sure Ultraman could be easily drowned by Submariner. *Ultra-* is a literary prefix, used occasionally in terms like *ultrafashionable* or *ultralib-eral*, and is now used to coin technical or fashion terms like *ultrafiche* or *Ul-trasuede*.

Now we get to the Four M's: *meta-*, *mega-*, *macro-* and *maxi-*. (*Magni-* is insignificant.) For this information, of great interest to marketers of olives, I turn to Sol Steinmetz, who has put the language of size under his microscope at Clarence Barnhart Books.

"*Meta-* shares with *super-* the sense of 'surpassing, transcending,' " says Mr. Steinmetz, "as in *metaculture*, *metahistory* and, in recent years, *metacriticism*, *metasystem*. Frankly, I foresee no exciting future for this rather prim professorial prefix."

Mega- has had a popular run of about a generation and, I have a hunch, may be peaking. "Both the latest prefix of bigness," says Sol, "and perhaps the one that will ultimately attain the widest use, is *maxi-*, created in the 1960's from *maximum* to contrast with the successful *mini-*. *Maxi-* has been steadily gaining ground since its humble emergence as a prefix for a garment length in *maxicoat*, *maxidress*, etc. Recent examples of its use include *maxicassette*, *maxibudget*, *maxisecret*, *maxitaxi* and *maxisingle* (phonograph record)."

My money is on *macro-*, ever since I went shopping for a lens for close-up photography. *Macrocosm* goes back to the 1600's and has beaten out *megacosm* to mean "universal" or "the great world." We now have *macroeconomics* for those seers who like the Big Picture, and with the onset of *micro-* as a preferred prefix for little things, the contrasting *macro-* offers growth opportunity with minimum downside risk.

"*Mega-* is a MEGO," aphorizes commentator Daniel Schorr. *MEGO* is an acronym for "My eyes glaze over" and is an appropriate note on which to end this item.

I was somewhat put out by your assigning an ancillary role to the hypodermic in connection with the evolvement of your somewhat nebulous noun "hyper." As I put it in one of my "General Linguistics" exams at Adelphi University: "I've got you under my skin," sang the nurse as she wielded the ———."* To put it another way: If you fall into the Potomac at this time of year, you may die from hypothermia; a sunstroke in the Sahara may bring about the same result from hyperthermia.

The unfortunate near-identity of hyper- and hypo- (with the present "hype" administering the coup de grâce) goes back all the way to Indo-European roots: In the AHD Appendix, we find: "uper. Over." and "upo. Under, up from under, over." And our "uprising" is a "soulèvement" in French.

Your Ubermensch is sadly bereft of his umlaut, as was "Deutschland Uber Alles" in various recent instances in the Times. That, as I pointed out in an unpublished letter, could have been cured by using the correct German lower-case über alles.

Louis Marck
New York, New York

* *I have therefore always maintained that, etymologically at least, you can't mainline with a hypodermic!*

Your column on superlatives cast more shadows than it shed light. Nearly every one of the terms you cite—meta-, macro-, and so on—refers to different aspects of bigness. Meta-, for example, refers to a more comprehensive level which subsumes others. In family therapy theory, for example, a meta-message tells you the context in which another communication is to be understood. ("I don't know what you mean" conveys "I understand perfectly" when accompanied by a sly smile and a tone of mock exasperation. The latter is a meta-communication, a communication about the communication.) None of your correspondents' examples contradict this.

Only super- and mega- compete directly. Ultra- suggests "the end, the ultimate," a different shade of meaning than super-, "the most." And hyper- suggests an intensification of the quality, as hyperactive *and* hyperspace *(the "Star Wars" invention), which are nothing like* mega- *or* super-. Megaspace *might be that immense part of outer space which we think of as infinite, and perhaps a modern-day creative talent with the work habits of Thomas Edison would be called* megaactive *(though not by me).*

By the way, I have heard hyper *by itself for several years now—as, I'm feeling hyper today." It means "racey" (pronounced like racy) or speedy, or buzzy, full of energy or excitement. But it is the kind of excitation which is felt to be too much, as though one has had too many cups of coffee, or uppers. It is as though the speaker has had a huge mental laxative—a metaphysic—things go through the mind a mile a minute.*

Joel Latner
Rochester, New York

I think you may find it amusing that megadosing *is defined as "taking at least ten times the RDA (National Academy of Sciences' Recommended Dietary Allowance)."*[*]

Newton D. Bowdan, M.D.
Holyoke, Massachusetts

[*] *"Implications of Vitamin Use,"* FDA Drug Bulletin, *vol. 13, n. 3, November 1983, p. 27.*

The most convenient unit, in discussing the federal budget, is probably the gigabuck *(one billion dollars).* Giga-, *I believe, comes from* gigantic. *The federal deficit has now soared beyond one* terabuck *(tera- denotes something monstrous, as in tera-toma; this seems appropriate). If inflation really ever gets out of hand, we may have to think about the* exabuck, *which is a million terabucks. I am not sure of the meaning of* exa-, *but I have a feeling that it means "out of this world."*

John T. Edsall
Cambridge, Massachusetts

Shouldn't that be "Nitpickers' League"? Or am I only qualifying myself to be the sole member of the Hypernitpicker's League?

James G. Christenson
North Caldwell, New Jersey

Your column caused me to consider the question of what the eventual meeting of the respective champions of the NFL and USFL will be called. I would like to suggest "Mega Bowl."

Richard Hockman
New York, New York

Times Marches On

Those of us who consider the substitution of *humankind* for *mankind* to be unmanly (there's a word on the feminist hit list, along with "unwomanly") can compensate with our approval of a recent decision by the editors of *The New York Times* to allow women to wed.

A year ago, Chinta Gaston, of Washington, wrote: "I perceive a new rule of grammar lurking on the pages of the Sunday *Times*. 'Laura Ladd Wed to Luke Bierman,' *but* 'Frank Hoffecker 3d Weds Leslie West.' The rule? 'The verb *to marry* and its synonyms take the passive voice when the subject is female, the active voice when the subject is male.' "

Nothing could have been more sexist than such discrimination in wedding announcements. Sure enough, there used to be a rule of etiquette, not of grammar, that "the man must wed the woman." A group of editors went to the news editor and said that the rule was an anachronism. He promptly agreed. Now it's "Linda Murawski Marries Thomas Varela" and "Laurie Abrams to Wed Dr. Steven Wexner," as well as the other way around. I'll subscribe to that. (Somebody play "Here Comes the Groom.")

Times *marches on, you write, applauding the recent decision by* The New York Times *editors to allow women to wed, rather than to be wed; use of the passive voice when the subject was female, the active voice when the subject was male was sexist and an anachronism.*

Yet Times' *policy regarding women's first names remains sexist and anachronistic, and is inconsistent and uninformative to boot. If you publish this letter, I will be identified as Lucille G. Natkins, but when my daughter's wedding was announced in your pages I was Mrs. Mortimer J. Natkins. And a woman's identity is just a tad obscured in news stories that refer to "Mrs. Tommy Manville" or "the Tommy Manvilles."*

Sexist language-wise, the Times *doesn't exactly march on; it kind of schleps.*
                                                    Lucille G. Natkins
                                                    Great Neck, New York

"Times Marches On" certainly didn't deal with this wedding announcement:

                    "Dr. Mona M. Shangold to Wed Nov. 24"

Will she keep her own name or be just plain Dr. 24?
                                                    Francis W. Rodgers
                                                    Rensselaer, New York

Today's Especial

Some of my special correspondents get especially incensed at the way some voguish copywriters, especially for specialty stores, are substituting *specially* for *especially*.

"Very specially priced" is the way Gucci speaks of merchandise on sale. "At a specially selected theater near you!" advertises a movie-maker. "Specially sweetened," says Manischewitz Wines of its Concord grape blend. Which of these is correct?

Especially is an adverb that means "markedly, outstandingly, emphatically, unusually." To be *especially* incensed is to be moved to write a language maven.

Specially is not the same. That adverb means "for a special purpose." I have been *specially trained* to detect obfuscation in political speeches; my readers are *specially prepared* to find mistakes in my work. (They are especially happy to do so—unsuitably gleeful, in fact—but the *especially* before "happy" means "to a marked degree," while the *specially* before "prepared" means "for the particular purpose of finding grammatical nits to pick.")

Therefore, when Gucci's salesman heaves a loafer at me with his "very specially priced," I may duck with a smirk at his unwillingness to use a word so crass as *sale*, but I understand that he means that his merchandise is priced for the purpose of quick sale. In that case, *specially* is correct; *especially priced* would be festooned with price tags.

Same with the Concord grape wine: It is *specially sweetened*, because the manufacturer wants to sweeten it for the purpose of appealing to palates that pucker at the thought of dry wine. As a result, the wine is *especially sweet*—that is, sweeter than the roses in May—and I have put an *e* at the beginning of the adverb because I have changed the meaning from "for a particular purpose" to "to a large degree."

What about "a specially selected theater"? If the advertiser is saying, "I have selected this theater because it has a reputation for showing this kind of avant-garde stuff," *specially* is correct; if he wanted to say, "Boy, was this theater selected!" he would choose *especially selected*.

Got it? If so, you're a very special person, especially these days.

To the Manner Hoisted

At a secret meeting in the Treasury Department—only inside stuff today—a staff aide told the secretary, Don Regan, that another Administration staffer was likely to be "hoist on his own petard."

The secretary, who was an English major at Harvard and sometimes refers to himself as "the English major" in interoffice memorandums, instantly sourced the quotation from Act 3 in *Hamlet:* "Let it work; For tis the sport to have the engineer/Hoist with his own petar." He went on to say that the word *petard* was derived from the French word for "dagger."

When challenged on that derivation by an unusually forthright aide, the secretary muttered, "Where is Safire when I need him?" Unfortunately, I was inundated at the time with Department of Justice leaks, and Mr. Regan had to do his own research. His follow-up memo to senior staff at Treasury:

"The English major was wrong on the definition of 'petard,' and thus the origin of the phrase 'hoisted on his own petard,' but right on the source of the quote:

" 'Let it work; for 'tis the sport to have the enginer

" 'Hoist with his own petar.'

"Shakespeare clearly had in mind the dictionary version of *petard*, 'a small bell-shaped bomb used to breach a gate or wall,' and thus intended the phrase to mean to be injured by one's own ingenuity. It is possible, also, that Shakespeare was punning, since it's very likely he was aware of the French root from which *petard* was derived (see dictionary for further study).

"The English major was, in fact, thinking of the word 'poniard,' which does mean 'dagger,' and indeed was used in olden days in close hand-to-hand combat."

Secretary Regan's delicacy in referring to Shakespearean scatology shows he is to the manner born. (*Manner*, not *manor*; that's the way it appears in the First Folio at the Folger Library. No, it isn't in Shakespeare's handwriting, but *manner* is the first reporting of the word, and I go with earliest citations.)

The English major (or the Times?) *was wrong in arranging the* Hamlet *quote like a rhyming curtain couplet that would seem to call for a varsity-varmint pronunciation of "enginer." The quote extends from the end of line 205 to the middle of line 207.* The curtain couplet of that last scene IV of Act III come in 11. 214–15, but is followed by "Come, sir [i.e., the dead Polonius], to draw toward an end with you./Good night, mother."*

> Louis Marck
> New York, New York

* *The virgule and capitalization are correct in the first memo.*

Mr. Regan (aka the English major) was brilliant in his research on the word "pétard." However, he made a second gaffe when explaining to the senior staff at Treasury that he was "thinking of the word 'poniard,' which does mean 'dagger'. . ." Sacré bleu! *The French use a "poignard" when stabbing people! (a poniard would be difficult to pronounce).*

> Mary-Kay P. Byron
> (aka the French major)
> Tuxedo Park, New York

Up the Downtime

"To shore up the candidate's energy," wrote Bernard Weinraub of *The New York Times*, "Mr. Mondale's staff members inevitably provide 'downtime' for Mr. Mondale. This consists of two hours in a hotel, where he checks into a suite to phone Washington, take a shower and change his clothes, to rest."

Like *drop-by*—a lightning-like appearance at a cocktail party that is neither attendance nor rejection of an invitation—the noun *downtime* has become fixed in political-campaign terminology.

Although the word is usually assumed to be computer lingo, a computer check of the word's use shows a general commercial-industrial origin: A *New York Times* story of March 27, 1971, quotes William Innes, an executive of the Ford Motor Company, saying that Ford plants would have "virtually no *downtime*" between production of 1971 and 1972 models. In January 1975 *Aviation Week* magazine reported on Air Siam's "six-day-a-week schedule with relatively little *downtime*." A month later, *Forbes* wrote about oil-drilling gear that "offered protection against expensive *downtime.*"

The New American Computer Dictionary explains that "data-processing centers set aside some periods for scheduled *downtime*, during which preventive maintenance is performed, but downtime in general is considered bad. . . ."

You can say that again. When Earl Smith, the wire-room chief at the Washington bureau of the *Times*, cheerfully strolls down the hall and sings out, "The system's crashing!" I hit my "save" button and immediately lie down. If the system gets downtime, so do I. And whether it is time to tie together the synapses of a system or figure the synopsis of a campaign, *downtime* is one word, no hyphen.

Of course, Euro-optimists are on *uptime*.

Regarding your discussion of "downtime": Even though you say your research shows "a general commercial-industrial origin," I think the relationship to the computer age is clear, if only in pervasive computer-age perceptions and attitudes that it reflects.

When a computer is down, it is as if it, and the information contained therein, does not exist. If a candidate is not "candidating," he or she does not exist (as a candidate) and hence is experiencing "downtime." The same perception/attitude is in each of the commercial-industrial examples you gave. If a factory is not producing, it does not exist (as a factory). "Downtime" thus becomes a sort of oblivion. That is why The New American Computer Dictionary, *which you cited, can consider downtime bad.*

There is, of course, something very existential in this perception/attitude, but it is no more existential than digital clocks, which flash moments of time (not in time) in isolation, totally unconnected to anything before or after, as opposed to analog clocks, which show moments in time, in continuous relationship to what went before and what comes after.

The term "turnaround time," which perhaps dates from the days of trolleys and trains that needed to be literally turned around at the end of the line, has a similar, if not the same, meaning as "downtime"—the time needed to get a person, machine, factory, etc., ready to go again—but its connotation is far more benign. A person, machine or factory in turnaround does not cease to exist. Its elemental nature, its relationship to the world, continues, even if it is not, at that moment, performing its task. Turnaround time is transitional, a period of resting that can include repair and rejuvenation and that results in a reaiming. Thus it can have very positive connotations. An economy in turnaround is more likely pictured to be heading for an upswing than heading downward, whereas an economy in downtime has ceased to be; it is at best totally stagnant.

I'd opt for the use of turnaround time over downtime. I think the former more closely reflects reality than the either-you-are-or-you-aren't connotation of the latter. Turnaround time suggests a worthwhile respite, whereas downtime has the feel of a cold, bleak, empty place, a place to be avoided, which is maybe why industry adopted it, believing, wrongly, that any such time is a waste.

Barbara Novack
Laurelton, New York

Downtime in the commercial printing industry predates the electronic age by many decades. Downtime for press maintenance is a sometime necessary evil, but downtime because of lack of business is what ages plant managers and printing salesmen rapidly.

Irene M. Dobbins
San Francisco, California

"Down time" is a term used in the maritime industries for probably more than a century, as the case reports in both England and the United States show.

It generally refers to the non-use of a vessel on behalf of the charterers so that they do not pay for those days, i.e., while laid up for repairs, or by reason of deviation caused by the owner.

The term is also used for loss of use of the vessel to repair damages caused by a collision, or the fault of another vessel, such as a tug is grounding the tow. The time out of service for repairs is also called "down time."

If memory serves me, I recall an opinion by Mr. Justice Joseph Story using that term, and you know when he sat on the Supreme Court.

Arthur Roth
Miami, Florida

I have worked in steel mills and can witness that the expression "downtime" was current at the Kaiser plant in Fontana, California, at least as early as 1955. I cannot say at this distance whether it was one word or two.

I believe the Fontana plant was built during World War II; certainly many

workers there in the 1950's were veterans of older plants in the East. Chances are
the expression goes way, way back in industries so capital-intensive they like to run
around the clock.

Tom Ferrell
New York, New York

Waldenslim

The Thrill That Comes Once in a Lifetime, Unexpected Etymon Division: "I was
reading Henry David Thoreau's 'Walden,' " writes Erik La Prade of New York
City, citing page 248 of the Modern Library edition. In writing about the partridge, Thoreau says in an 1854 pastoral essay: "It is Nature's own bird which lives
on buds and diet-drink."

Sorry, Erik, no low-cal cigar: That seemingly modern phrase, *diet-drink*, is rooted
in a 1600 work, *The Letting of Humours Blood in the Head-Vaine*, by Samuel
Rowlands: "We gaue the Brewers Diet-drinke a wipe." Many such decoctions in
the nineteenth century contained sarsaparilla; the irony is that today you can't find
a deli to serve a diet sass.

Walls Have Ears

"As soon as there is a whiff," said Felix Rohatyn, the financial savior of New
York City, "a whiff of anything remotely relating to money, everybody goes off
the wall."

The financier was talking about the reaction to the happy news that New York's
Municipal Assistance Corporation, which he heads, may have as much as a billion-
dollar surplus. The unhappy news is that Mr. Rohatyn has misused the expression
off the wall.

From the context of his statement, it can be seen that he meant everybody "goes
crazy" or "blows his cool" or "loses his perspective." The slang expression he
reached for, but did not quite grasp, was *up the wall*.

To be driven *up the wall* is to be driven mad; the term is taken from the action
of a drug addict, deprived of his drug, literally trying to climb the walls of a cell

to vent his frustration and panic. This should not be confused with *over the wall*, a prison term for "escape," or *to the wall*, a business term for "bankrupt." British slanguist Eric Partridge tracked *up the wall* to 1944, labeling it "American service- man use," and it probably began its climb in the United States before World War II.

Off the wall, however, denotes craziness of a less frenetic sort and is a child of the 1970's. It means "zany, unconventional, unusual, off-beat, far-out"; the conno- tation is of extreme originality, and the expression is most often spoken in worried wonderment or amazed admiration. The first citation in Wentworth and Flexner's *Dictionary of American Slang* is from a 1970 article by Jon Landau in *Rolling Stone*: "his off-the-wall sense of humor."

Comparing dictionaries, one finds that *American Heritage* and Merriam-Web- ster's Ninth both have *up the wall* ("into a state of extreme frustration or distress," "into a state of intense agitation, annoyance, or frustration") while *Webster's New World* has that and, in addition, *off the wall*, defined as "1. unsound of mind; crazy; 2. very eccentric or unconventional."

The latest up- or off-the-wall front is the compound adjective *wall-to-wall*, which began in the 1940's as a description of carpeting: covering a floor from wall to wall, without a border of floor showing, which our British cousins call "edge-to-edge" or "fitted carpeting."

In the 1960's, this flat description was applied metaphorically to other objects to give an encompassing or jammed-together connotation: *Time* described a car with "a wall-to-wall front grille that conceals the headlights"; *The New Yorker* reviewed Bobby Hackett's "series of wall-to-wall mood-music recordings with Jackie Gleason"; in *The Atlantic* in 1970, Paul Warnke wrote of a sea filled with "enough ships that there wouldn't be room for theirs—wall-to-wall ships," and *Women's Wear Daily* reported sighting a disco "crammed with wall-to-wall bod- ies." Merriam-Webster is on the ball here with a definition that goes beyond floor covering to "ubiquitous."

M.A.C. chairman Rohatyn is a man accustomed to wall-to-wall critics; he will have one fewer if he stops driving us up the wall with his misused *off the wall*.

Dear Bill:

On behalf of the City of New York, where everyone speaks real good English, I am delighted to extend a speechwriterly hand to all etymologists south of Wall Street.

Off the wall does indeed mean "crazy" or "unpredictable," but you don't give the origin of this term. It comes from pool halls, where amateur players usually select their cue stick from among the warped and wavy collection in the wall racks. A pool hall pro carries his own custom-made cue, and would never play with an "off the wall" stick.

Other than that you discussed walls with great clarity, disproving the idea that walls do not a prism make.

Clark Whelton
Assistant to the Mayor
New York, New York

I think that I can offer some additional insight on the expression "off the wall." I first heard this expression used around automobile racing tracks in the late 1950's and early 60's. It referred originally to erratic racing car drivers who were constantly hitting and bouncing "off the (retaining) wall." At some point it expanded to mean a driver who was a little crazy, one whose brains were slightly addled from repeated contact with the wall.

Dr. David F. Ward
Curator, Watkins Glen Racing Museum
Watkins Glen, New York

As an artist, I know that when a painting hangs on the wall with one or two corners jutting into the room, it is "off the wall"—i.e., warped.

Marilyn Ashbrook
Media, Pennsylvania

I had always simply assumed that "off the wall" was an extension of "flakey." I noticed that people progressed from referring to someone as "flakey" to "a flake" or "strictly off the wall."

Kay Arthur
Rowayton, Connecticut

Your comments about "off the wall" and "up the wall" missed something else askew in Mr. Rohatyn's statement.

One gets sent up the wall, or, as you say, driven there. Similarly, someone or something is off the wall, or acts off the wall or eventually gets off the wall. But "goes off the wall" makes me go crazy (even as it supports your conclusion that he meant "up the wall").

Joel Latner
Rochester, New York

After reading your column on connotations of the phrase "to the wall," I would like to offer a couple that were prevalent in Harlem during my youth.

Whenever the term "to the wall" was used it was modified by "rushed" in that an individual was "rushed to the wall" (hands on the wall with the legs spread) by a police officer to be searched and/or arrested.

Another meaning of the phrase "rushed to the wall" pertained to an unfortunate individual involved in an impromptu execution by firing squad which usually took place in a motion picture.

Leroy Richardson
Jamaica, New York

I have been one of your British cousins for the past 36 years (the last seven in the USA, the previous 29 in Britain). Although I have conversed with all echelons of British society, I have never come across the term edge-to-edge as meaning "wall-to-wall." I have only heard wall-to-wall and fitted. The former is clearly used both by the Britains and their American cousins. The latter does not necessarily mean wall-to-wall; just that the carpeting is fixed down and—unlike loose rugs—cannot be moved (unless the tacks are removed). Clearly a carpet can be fitted while leaving one or more borders of uncarpeted floor between the edge of the carpet and the wall.

The term edge-to-edge seems to me—when related to carpeting (it could clearly relate to any items that have edges that can be adjacent)—to concern the fitting of carpets in a room which is too large to permit the use of a single piece cut from a roll. In that case, the edges of the pieces of carpeting are fastened together to form a seam. Wall-to-wall carpeting can clearly be done without such edge-to-edginess —if the room has one dimension of its floor that is no wider than the width of the carpeting roll. Carpeting can be fitted, without its touching the walls. Indeed carpeting could be fitted edge-to-edge without its touching the walls.

I hope you don't feel I've put you on the carpet over this.

Jan R. Harrington
New York, New York

Welcome to Splitsville

When teen-age infinitives get ants in their pants, they will say to each other: "Let's split." Their stodgier parents, suddenly afflicted with a splitting Jordache, ask themselves: "Why do so many infinitives split these days?" In another sense: What can be done, perhaps through counseling or required cooling-off periods, to stem the stampede to Splitsville?

For centuries, writers have been warned to avoid splitting infinitives. *To split gleefully* is preferred; *to gleefully split* is frowned upon. For some reason, the insertion of an adverb between the *to* and the rest of the verb in its infinitive form causes most arbiters of newspaper style to say sternly: "It is to laugh heartily," and never: "It is to heartily laugh."

For example, when Charles M. Lichenstein, the deputy chief of the United States Mission to the United Nations, felt provoked by Soviet slurs on American hospitality, he said: "The United States strongly encourages member states seriously to consider removing themselves and this organization from the soil of the United States." He went on to say: "We will be at dockside bidding you a farewell as you set off into the sunset."

An alert *Wall Street Journal* editorialist quickly pointed out the metaphoric "difficulty of sailing into the sunset from New York harbor." The United Nations' location on the East Coast permits sailing into sunrises only. The cliché is from old film travelogues.

However, a transcript of the United Nations tape shows Mr. Lichenstein to have hewed strictly to the grammarian's delight in the use of the infinitive: "Seriously to consider" shows that the statement was composed with great care. Most people would have said "to seriously consider." Would they have been wrong? Was Mr. Lichenstein, so right in his reading of popular opinion, incorrect in his ultracorrectness?

Wire-service stylebooks frown on most infinsplit. "In general," generalizes the Associated Press, "avoid awkward constructions that split infinitive forms of a verb. . . . Awkward: *She was ordered to immediately leave on an assignment.* Preferred: *She was ordered to leave immediately on an assignment.*" The United Press International agrees: "The splitting of compound verb forms, including infinitives, is not necessarily an error, but often is awkward. . . . Awkward: She was ordered *to* immediately *leave* on an assignment. Better: She was ordered *to leave* immediately on an assignment."

These two unfortunate young women, torn from their warm terminals by identically sexist assignment editors and peremptorily sent out into the street to compete with each other, are used as examples of the awkwardness of the split infinitive. But that's not the problem at all: Most of the time, the split infinitive looks natural and the unsplit form looks pedantic. *To strenuously object* is certainly as natural to the tongue and eye as *to object strenuously*, and both are less awkward than *strenuously to object*.

The real problem is this: If neither way is awkward, is it right and proper to split the infinitive? Who has attached a stigma to the placement of the modifier in the middle?

Not the great grammarians. George O. Curme, the superstar of grammar two generations ago, wrote: "Since the 14th century . . . the split infinitive, by virtue of its decided advantages, which are unconsciously widely felt, has been gradually gaining ground. . . . Although this new drift has long been regarded by many who do not understand it as plebeian or vulgar, there have never been any real grounds for such an attitude, for it has never been characteristic of popular speech." He cites Abraham Lincoln's plea to border states for compensated emancipation: "How much better *to thus save* the money which else we sink forever in the war?" That is more graceful than *thus to save or to save thusly*.

Henry Fowler agreed. "A real s.i., though not desirable in itself, is preferable to . . . real ambiguity and to patent artificiality." He chose the infinitive-splitting *to better equip*, rejecting *to equip better* as "ambiguous (*better* an adjective?)" and *better to equip* as "a shouted reminder of the tyranny" of artificiality in the pedant.

Jacques Barzun, in *Modern American Usage*, came up with a good reason for the curious reluctance of the Miss Thistlebottoms of the world to split infinitives in writing: "The temptation to split an infinitive is extremely rare in spoken English, because the voice supplies the stress needed by the unsplit form. . . . It is in written work that splitting is called for, and desk sets should include small hatchets of silver or gold for the purpose."

If you want to emphasize a point, splitting an infinitive is a good way to do it. *The A.P. Stylebook and Libel Manual* finds it acceptable when necessary to convey the meaning. The example used is: *"He wanted to really help his mother."* The U.P.I. agrees; its example is: "He wanted *to* really *help* his mother." (What collusion is going on here? Not only do the A.P. and U.P.I. join in kicking their women reporters out on the streets, but they also speak in unison to make men look like the heroes on Mother's Day. Why this conspiracy-in-restraint-of-usage controversy? Replies Christopher French, editor of the A.P. stylebook: "A.P. and U.P.I. collaborate on building a stylebook. It's a gentleman's agreement to keep things the same as nearly as possible. We do have differences, but roughly two-thirds of the book is the same.")

In light of all this, I recommend that infinitive splitters of the world unite: We have nothing to lose but our hangups. If we want *to touch lightly* on a topic, we should preserve the integrity of the infinitive form; if we want *to viciously savage* it, we are free to split the infinitive to smithereens. No stigma attaches to the splitting, nor did it ever in the minds of many of the most prestigious usagarians. Let us put the modifier in the place—before the *to*, just after it, or after the verb—where it works best for our purpose of stress or grace.

If you are not satisfied with the Voice of Final Authority booming in this space, listen to George Bernard Shaw, creator of 'Enry 'Iggins: "Every good literary craftsman splits his infinitives when the sense demands it." He called for the immediate dismissal of the pedant hired to chase split infinitives and concluded: "It is of no consequence whether he decides to go quickly or to quickly go."

Infinitives are not the only form of verb in the English language that consists of two words, but they are the only form about which anyone ever worries whether it is permitted, or advisable, or whatever, to separate the two words. I can't find anything about infinitives that logically makes them any different from the other verb forms in this regard. For example, no one concerns himself with whether it is more "correct" to say "I have gladly donated" than to say "I have donated gladly"; he simply uses one or the other on the basis of style, stress, or his mood at the moment. "Splitting" or not never enters his mind.

Even those of us who say we don't give a damn whether we split infinitives or not subconsciously bear the detritus of the old saw "Yes, it's all right to split an infinitive once in a while, provided that you know that you're doing it and have a good reason for doing it." Why do I need a good reason for doing it?

Albert Kreindler
Bronx, New York

You seem to suggest that the choice between better to equip, to better equip, and to equip better depends only on the matter of a split infinitive or no.

It is not as simple as that. There are three separate meanings here.

"Better to equip" has the sense of making it easier to take the action of equipping, as in the sentence, "It was arranged that way the better to equip the men." Here there is no thought of how easily or quickly the equipping is done, nor of the quality of the resulting equipment.

"To better equip" has the sense of improving the action of the equipping. This does not imply that the resulting equipment will be of any particular quality, but simply means that the equipping has been facilitated.

"To equip better" means that the result of the equipping is of higher quality than if it were done poorly.

Pedantry should not be allowed to obstruct the full scope of the language.

Harvey M. Templeton
Winchester, Tennessee

My understanding is that split infinitives were first proscribed in our language because early attempts to standardize English grammar, in the eighteenth century, were based on theories of Latin grammar. Latin was considered a superior and logically perfect language, the model for all others, and its infinitives simply cannot be split because they are single words.

The English double negative is also illegal because it was forbidden in Latin although quite acceptable in classical Greek.

Thomas J. Snow
New York, New York

Dear Bill:

No, no, no, and again: no on the split infinitive. All you need to know about the infinitive is that it functions as a single word. *Now a case can be made for splitting up a single word now and then. Literate people find themselves saying: "That's a whole nother matter." Characters in George Higgins novels say things like, "He spent the whole fuckin' weekend in Hono-fuckin'-lulu." That's all right, too. Samuel Goldwyn knew how to split a word when he answered somebody's request, "In two words: im possible." Equally, the best writers find it effective now and then to split an infinitive. But it still works—in the rule book, in the language, in good speech —as* one word.

Chris [Lydon]
Boston, Massachusetts

I thought I would share with you an unforgettable experience I had as an undergraduate at Yale College on this subject. While watching the beginning of Star Trek *in the Common Room, I heard Captain Kirk state the mission of the Starship* Enterprise: *"These are the voyages . . . to* boldly go *where. . . ." Such a grammatical faux pas did not go unnoticed. There was such an outcry of "Split Infinitive," the Doppler effect took on a new meaning.*

H. Alford Johnson
New York, New York

Sir, you protest too much about the inappropriateness of the Soviet delegation sailing "into the sunset" from New York. I think that the metaphor is apt.

For freighters, no. But passenger liners, including the Maxim Gorky *and* Alexander Pushkin, *use the Municipal Passenger Ship Terminal on the Hudson River. Most cruise ships depart in the late afternoon. In autumn and winter, when the sun is considerably to the south of New York, after backing up with tug assistance into the Hudson, a ship will steam off southward. To an observer on or near the West Side Highway, it will indeed appear that the ship is steaming into the sunset. Try it yourself, while you still have the opportunity!*

William E. Thoms
Grand Forks, North Dakota

When You Say That, Resile

"Regarding its position in Lebanon," asked the foreign minister of Pakistan, Yaqub Khan, "do you think the United States will resile?"

Heads snapped around at the Jockey Club in Washington. Columnists and editorialists who had been ostentatiously looking the other way, pretending not to listen so as not to poach on a competitor's interview, dropped all pretense and gaped. *Resile?*

"Did you say *resign?*" I inquired for myself, the others in the room and generations yet unborn.

"Resile," the diplomat repeated, adding graciously, "Perhaps I have misused the word. Is it intransitive?"

I said I thought so and perhaps he should try the verb in an intransitive form in a sentence.

"I hope you will not resile from your ideological position," the hyperarticulate foreign minister offered, adding, "which has become, if I may say so without offending an old friend, somewhat eschatological."

That last word was an old friend: Eschatology is the branch of theology concerned with ultimates, like heaven and hell, and people in the pundit dodge are frequently accused of seeing finality in tea leaves. Joe Alsop was especially good at that. Diplomacy is the branch of nontheology dealing with ambiguities and ambivalences, and diplomats deride the tendency of pundits to leap to conclusions. (When Southern columnists sneeze, their companions say, "E-scat!").

I took a shot at *resile:* "It's a recent back-formation from *resilient* and means 'to snap back.' "

The consummate diplomat did not deride my guesswork, murmuring only: "I would have thought it was older than that. And perhaps I am mistaken about the meaning."

Back to the office and into my *Oxford English Dictionary*. Yaqub Khan was right: *Resile* turns out to be an old word, chiefly in Scottish use, from the Latin *resilire*, "to leap back." First recorded use was in 1529, in the state papers of Henry VIII, when King Henry said of one of his wives that he wished she "wold herafter resile and goo back from that." In the old days, if the queen failed to resile when she was told, she lost her head.

It means "to retract, draw back," is both transitive and intransitive, and is most often used with *from:* To resile from is to recoil from, or back away from, and is a perfect diplomatic term, since so many nations resile from agreements when their interests change.

In 1708, a scientist in Britain's Royal Society used the verb to describe the return of contracted fibers to their original position. That was applied to all elastic bodies, and the action of snapping back gained the adjective *resilient*. Today, a resilient politician is one who can make a comeback, and the word has a pleasing connotation of toughness; its verb root, however, has a craven meaning, and when I run into the foreign minister again, I will assure him that the United States will not resile from its commitment to Lebanon. (Never say "never"—that's being eschatological.)

". . . do you think the United States will resile?"

From the dialogue that followed the quotation above, it seems that Yaqub Khan believed that he had used resile *as a transitive verb, and you apparently thought so, too—"I said I thought so and perhaps he should try the verb in an intransitive form in a sentence." (He had done just that.) Later you state that* resile *"is both transitive and intransitive, and is most often used with* from.*"*

In the sentence quoting Yaqub Khan, resile *is an intransitive verb; it does not involve, or* pass over to, *an object. And in that respect Yaqub Khan used the word correctly. Both Merriam's* New International Dictionary *and the* Oxford English Dictionary *define* resile *as an intransitive verb, and not as a transitive verb. Indeed, the etymology of the verb (* re + salire = *to spring back) corroborates its intransitive nature.*

Edward C. Schneider
New York, New York

The Foreign Minister of Pakistan, Yaqub Khan, and I have one thing in common: we both resile.

In fifth-year Latin, I recall being taught the great vowel shift:

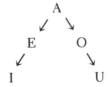

The best example I ever found for remembering the A-E-I side was:

salio *in the Latin means "to dance, to leap";*
in a Romance language, such as French, it goes to selio;

in English, we have resile *from a position or the spatula has resilient qualities.*

The interstices of my mind are filled with verbs such as ensile. *A classical education does wonders for the vocabulary, but little for the pocketbook.*

Alice Coyle Lunn, Ph.D.
Olmsted Falls, Ohio

Who's a Patsy?

"It is appalling," snorted James Buckley, president of Radio Free Europe, "that any American should allow himself to act the patsy in forwarding such obvious Soviet objectives."

Mr. Buckley was excoriating an American member of the International Olympic Committee for joining in a Russian-sponsored resolution to deny the American broadcaster press credentials.

Reporters at his press conference in Washington naturally turned from the substance of the issue to the meaning of the word *patsy*, proving again that what counts ain't what you say; it's the way that you say it.

"A patsy is simply a by-stander," responded Mr. Buckley, the former New York senator, indicating that he understood the word not to imply moral culpability, "someone who advances someone else's cause, not because he intends to."

Back at R.F.E. headquarters in Munich, Mr. Buckley writes, "I tried to see how close I was to the mark, but there is a dearth hereabouts of reference books on American slang. I write to you in your capacity as America's premier popular etymologist: What does *patsy* mean?"

Accepting the put-down in his qualifying "popular" and assuming a question directed to an etymologist to be primarily "Where does it come from?" I can report that two provenances are suggested. One is from the Italian *pazzo*, meaning "fool." The other is that *Patsy*, as the diminutive of the name *Patrick*, was originally an underworld adjective for "all is well," which when turned into a noun came to mean "sucker," in the sense of one being born every minute.

The term has been tracked by Merriam-Webster to 1903, but the popularization was helped by John O'Hara in 1939's *Pal Joey*, when the charmingly sleazy hero says, "I do not pretend I am some kind of a patsy."

Turning now from etymology to semantics, the study of meaning, especially the changes in the meaning of words: A *patsy* is currently best defined as "a dupe; a fool easily victimized or a naïve person readily manipulated."

Does it imply moral guilt? No, except to the extent that all that is needed for the triumph of evil is for good men to do nothing, which Edmund Burke never said. If you go along with the commies when they're undermining freedom of expression, you're a patsy—one not expected to understand how you're being used. Perhaps that explains the decline of the diminutive *Patsy* as a girl's name.

The word patsy *as a noun, as in "The Patsy," was made known in the theatre well before the line in* Pal Joey.

In 1925 a play by Barry Connors called The Patsy *opened at the Booth Theatre in New York and ran for 245 performances.*

While the heroine's name was Patricia (played by Claiborne Foster), the use of the word patsy *to describe her seemed to mean that she was blamed for everything— all that happened was her fault, making her "the patsy."*

Not a bad play, for its time, either.

Helen G. Levine
Cincinnati, Ohio

Dear Bill,
Being a patsy, in the sense of acting as a cat's paw, was widely current in the 1920's. I heard my father use the expression many times.

Its familiarity, in fact, was such that a Broadway play was entitled The Patsy *and was made into a silent movie as a vehicle for Marion Davies. Historically, the film was an attempt to rival Constance Talmadge's success in* Dulcy. *On a personal basis I happen to recall it vividly, because Marion Davies, along with Charlie Chaplin, Harold Lloyd, Douglas Fairbanks, Mary Pickford and Jackie Coogan, was one of a very select group of stars whose pictures I was allowed to see in my then tender years.*

Ira [Avery]
Stamford, Connecticut

You neglected the chess epithet "patzer."

One definition of a patzer (sometimes pronounced PATS-er, *sometimes* POTS-er*) is a player whose moves are so transparent that his opponent sees through his every intention. It is not uncommon to roam the corridors at chess tournaments and see a chessplayer (yes, even occasionally a master) with palm to his forehead bemoaning the fact that he is playing "like a patz."*

It is often used in conjunction with its pejorative cousin "fish" to form the ultimate chess put-down: "patzer fish" (roughly the equivalent of calling a baseball player "ya bum").

James R. West
Kearny, New Jersey

The Wicked Which and the Comma

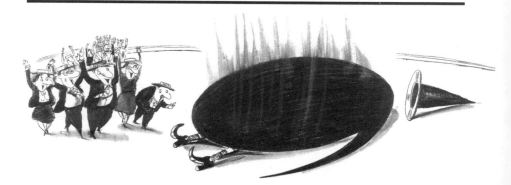

"G.O.P. Tax Battle Over a Comma" was the front-page headline of Long Island's *Newsday*. Over the story on an inside page, the headline writer had a little fun with the verb: "Comma Punctuates Debate on G.O.P.'s Tax Hike Policy."

This is the story of a truly needy *dependent clause*, a poor *relative pronoun* and a heroic—or villainous—*comma*. Before dealing with the plot at the Republican convention in Dallas in August 1984, let us first consider the cast of characters.

A *dependent clause* is like a dependent child: incapable of standing on its own but able to cause a lot of trouble. You can recognize these lovable but troublesome clauses because they begin with a *relative pronoun*, such as *that, which, who, whom, whose*—words that stand in for nouns.

These clauses come in two types: Fowler, the great grammarian whom sensible people follow on *that vs. which*, called them *defining* and *nondefining* clauses.

Here is a *defining* dependent clause: The President gave an acceptance address *that was a sure sign he would run an aggressive campaign*. The clause in italics defines, or limits, its antecedent, "address"; as such, it began with *that*, which is the best way of beginning a defining dependent clause.

Here is a *nondefining* dependent clause: The President gave an acceptance address, *which was a sure sign he would run an aggressive campaign*. Catch the difference? In the earlier example, the defining clause began with *that* and dealt strictly with that particular address. But in this example, the nondefining clause begins with *which*, is separated by a comma, and says something different: By giving an acceptance address—any old acceptance address—he signaled his intention of running an aggressive campaign. Had he not given an acceptance address and merely said, "Gee, O.K., I'll do it," that would have meant he intended to be nonaggressive.

Let's hit that notion again, harder: "He deep-sixed the evidence that was incriminating." (Defining clause, beginning with *that*, no commas; it is "the evidence" that was incriminating.)

Try that sentence this way: "He deep-sixed the evidence, which was incriminating." (Nondefining clause, beginning with *which*, separated by a comma; it is the fact that he deep-sixed it, not the evidence itself, that was incriminating. You think grammarians are splitting hairs? A person could go to jail on the difference.)

Now to the Republican platform-writers in Dallas. The fight on the tax plank pitted the hot-eyed antitax-increase crusaders against the laid-back pragmatists, led by Senator Bob Dole of Kansas, who did not want to say "never" to future increases. Both sides wanted to give the impression they looked on tax increases with disfavor, but the hard-liners wanted to say "positively."

"We therefore oppose any attempt to increase taxes which would harm the recovery . . ." went the early draft. That was deliberately confusing: The laid-back pragmatists looked at *which would harm the recovery* as a defining clause, unseparated by a comma, directed to the word *taxes*. They were against increases in only those "taxes which would harm the recovery," not taxes that would help the recovery by reducing the deficit.

The confusing part was the misuse of *which:* The pragmatists did not insist on *that*, which would have been the better choice to introduce a defining clause, but rested their defining case on the absence of commas.

The antitax crowd saw through that. Representative Tom Loeffler of Texas proposed the shortest amendment in political history: the insertion of a comma before the "which." Pragmatists objected, but Representative Vin Weber of Minnesota warned, "We'll take that comma to the floor."

The prospect of commas all over the convention floor evidently dismayed the platform committee, which voted to put the comma before the dependent clause. That made the clause unmistakably nondefining—not limited to specific taxes, but applied to the whole idea of taxing.

(Not since Richard Nixon referred to "the great Republican Chief Justice Earl Warren" had there been such a ruckus over a comma; had Nixon put a comma after "Republican," he would not have been accused of politicizing the Supreme Court.)

Senator Dole was wryly philosophical about the antitax crowd's comma-kaze attack. Said the man who would head the Finance Committee when tax-writing began after the election: "We'll just say it was a typo." (He must be privy to The Secret Plan.)

At the risk of an accusation of which-hunting, I must point out that Republicans seem to have an unfortunate aversion to *that*. In his off-the-record thigh-slapper before a radio broadcast, President Reagan said, "My fellow Americans, I am pleased to tell you I just signed legislation which outlaws Russia forever." In that sentence, "which outlaws Russia forever" is a defining clause referring to the particular legislation and should be introduced by the relative pronoun *that*. Otherwise, if the clause were led by *which* and separated by a comma, the sentence would mean that, by virtue of the act of signing any legislation, he had outlawed Russia. ("I just signed legislation, which outlaws Russia forever." Quite different, and not what he meant.)

President Reagan, whose comment was noted around the world, may consider this complaint as a kind of late hit, but in future off-the-record outlawings, he should introduce his defining clauses with *that*. That will keep him out of trouble with grammarians.

Dear Bill:

In your remarks on the distinction between restrictive and nonrestrictive clauses, you barely touched on an important question that is equally important in interpreting your examples, namely the question of what the antecedent of the relative clause is.

Restrictive and nonrestrictive clauses differ in what they allow as an antecedent, and many examples that are unambiguous as to which kind of relative clause they have are ambiguous as to what its antecedent is. For example, in your sentence "He deep-sixed the evidence, which was incriminating," the antecedent could be either the noun phrase "the evidence" or the clause "he deep-sixed the evidence"; thus, in addition to the difference that you cite that can determine whether someone goes to jail, we have a difference that could determine which *person goes to jail.*

Even in your corrected version of the sentence that figured in the dispute at the Republican convention, there is an ambiguity as to the antecedent: "We therefore oppose any attempt to increase taxes that would harm the recovery . . ." allows either taxes *or* attempt to increase taxes *as the antecedent. While you take the former to be the antecedent, the latter seems equally plausible to me. Actually, on reflection I find the latter considerably more plausible than the former: With* taxes *as the antecedent, the sentence presupposes that there are taxes that would harm the recovery and taxes that wouldn't harm it and suggests that it would be all right to increase the latter kind of taxes (e.g., inheritance taxes wouldn't harm the recovery, so maybe we can increase inheritance taxes), while the other interpretation presupposes that some attempts to raise taxes would harm the recovery and other attempts wouldn't, a much less bizarre presupposition.* *

If you want to avoid an ambiguity as to what the antecedent of a relative clause is, you have to resort to the same sorts of dodges that allow you to avoid ambiguity as to the antecedent of a personal pronoun. For example, you can choose your words in such a way that only one of the potential antecedents has the appropriate number or gender. In this case, the two potential antecedents differ in number, but the would *of the relative clause leaves it unclear whether the underlying subject of the relative clause is singular or plural. The following revision resolves the ambiguity:*

> *a: . . . any attempt to increase taxes which are likely to harm the recovery*
> *. . . b: . . . any attempt to increase taxes which is likely to harm the recovery . . .*

(Substitute that *for* which *if you like—it doesn't affect this point.) The antecedent in* a *is unambiguously* taxes *and that in* b *is unambiguously* attempt to increase taxes. *In* a, *even if you stick with* which, *no monkey business with commas could give the interpretation that Tom Loeffler wanted: If the antecedent is a clause, the relative pronoun must be singular.*

Earlier in the column, you said that that *was "the best way" of beginning a restrictive clause. I can be expected to disagree with any statement of the form "the best way of doing X is Y" (indeed, making such a statement may be the best way of stimulating me to write a letter of disagreement)—what is "best" always depends on your goals and the constraints under which you're operating, and any "best"*

---

* Cf. taxes *is the antecedent,* would *doesn't make much sense.*

method is sure to subvert your goals or be ruled out by your constraints, at least some of the time.

English provides its users with both that *and true relative pronouns as means of introducing relative clauses. (I have argued that* that *in relative clauses is not a relative pronoun but is rather the "complementizer"* that *of such sentences as* I doubt that Mondale will carry Arizona.*) Each of these two devices is subject to some restrictions that the other is not subject to; for example,* that *cannot introduce nonrestrictive clauses and cannot combine with other words into complex relative expressions the way that relative pronouns can* (the person to whom/that I sent the letter), *but it can be used in certain cases where no relative pronoun exists* (the way that/how I feel). *Thus,* that *and relative pronouns have similar functions but are not available in the same classes of cases. There is a large class of cases where both seem perfectly normal to me* (the book that/which I was reading), *though for reasons I find unfathomable, Fowler and other prescriptive grammarians have decided to favor one of the two forms in those cases. Since speakers and writers are perpetually in the position of choosing among expressive devices that have overlapping domains of applicability, I don't see any reason why in this particular case such a choice should be resolved in advance for them.*

Jim [James D. McCawley]
Department of Linguistics
The University of Chicago
Chicago, Illinois

If you will read the article in Fowler again, you will see that the distinction he proposes between the relative pronouns that *and* which *is not an infallible rule but a guiding principle. You violate the spirit of his proposal when you erect it into a dogma. Fowler argues that to observe this distinction would increase lucidity and ease, but concedes that "it would be idle to pretend that it is the practice either of most or of the best writers."*

Michael Kowal
New York, New York

One corrective note on the third paragraph of your welcome piece on limiting and unlimiting relative clauses:

You equate relative clauses with dependent clauses. In fact, a relative clause—so named because it is introduced by a relative pronoun, it functions as an adjective—is only one of several kinds of dependent clauses. Others are: noun clauses (I don't know what you mean; Let me know *when you are coming), introduced by interrogative pronouns or interrogative adverbs; and adverbial clauses, introduced by subor-*

*dinating conjunctions (*When I read that, *I was amused; He stopped reading* because he was annoyed*).*

The notion of "limiting" and "unlimiting" (also called "restrictive" and "non-restrictive") seems, logically, "limited" to relative clauses, even though I have a feeling one could dream up adverbial clauses with analogous options.

Eva Schiffer
Amherst, Massachusetts

I believe that your column contains a small error: You state that dependent clauses can be recognized "because they begin with a relative pronoun, . . . *" Although many dependent clauses do, of course, begin with a relative pronoun, at least an equal number begin instead with a subordinating conjunction such as* after, until, when, *or—as in the dependent first clause of this sentence—*although*.*

Aaron Schneider
New York, New York

I'm sure to be one of dozens responding to your brave attempt to clarify the difference between defining and nondefining clauses, and one of dozens pointing out that "He deep-sixed the evidence, which was incriminating" can be read in at least two ways.

In your reading, which *refers to the entire preceding clause: [The fact that] he deep-sixed the evidence was incriminating.*

Now try this: He deep-sixed the evidence.

The evidence was incriminating.

And compare that with: He deep-sixed the incriminating evidence (i.e., the evidence that was incriminating).

The difference between the defining (limiting) that *and the nondefining* which *is the difference between some and all. Obvious enough, but devilishly difficult to explain by traditional grammatical analysis. The newer, transformational technique calls upon the writer to use substitutions (as I've done here).*

Alan Stern
Hastings-on-Hudson, New York

I can't resist joining the hundreds of retired English teachers who are doubtless writing you to point out an error in your analysis of the sentence "He deep-sixed the evidence, which was incriminating."

Which refers solely to the word *evidence, not to the clause as a whole. The man doing the deep-sixing may or may not have known that the evidence was incriminating; he may or may not have had a criminal purpose; all the sentence says is that he deep-sixed it, adding in a lightly marked parenthesis that it was incriminating evidence.*

Without the comma, with either that *or* which *as the connective, the reference is still solely to the word* evidence, *and the meaning of the sentence is "He deep-sixed that portion of the evidence which was incriminating."*

Using relative pronouns to refer to an entire clause was one of the many errors we English teachers used to try to correct, insisting that only a noun could properly refer back to a clause. To get one meaning you might want, we'd have said, you must write, "He deep-sixed the evidence, an act which was incriminating."

> *F. G. Schoff*
> *Minneapolis, Minnesota*

I'm troubled by one thing: the sentence "He deep-sixed the evidence, which was incriminating." You say that here, "which . . . [refers to] the fact that he deep-sixed it, not to the evidence itself. . . ." I have been taught that which *must refer to a specific noun in preceding material, not simply to an idea that is expressed in that material in some other form. By that standard, you don't have an antecedent for your* which, *or at least not one that is related to your thought.*

And by that standard, this is the distinction I would make: "He deep-sixed the evidence that was incriminating" means that he got rid of only some of the evidence—the incriminating evidence. There may have been other evidence, with no taint of incrimination (which latter could be expressed as "There may have been evidence that was not incriminating"). "He deep-sixed the evidence, which was incriminating" means that he had a whole collection of evidence, all of which was incriminating and all of which he deep-sixed.

To make your point—that deep-sixing is incriminating—calls for something like this, I believe: "His deep-sixing the evidence was incriminating." Or "The fact that he deep-sixed the evidence was incriminating." Or "The simple act of deep-sixing the evidence was incriminating." And you never come near the Wicked Which!

> *Mendelle T. Berenson,*
> *Chief, Economic Editing Section*
> *Board of Governors of the Federal Reserve System*
> *Washington, D.C.*

Your "wicked which" may be more wicked than you realize. One of the rules that I as an English teacher have always insisted upon is that the antecedent of a pronoun be a noun—not a general idea. In your nondefining dependent adjective clause which was a sure sign that he would run an aggressive campaign, *the* which *does not stand for* address; *it stands for his action of making the address.*

In Manter Hall and Warriner, both of which we use in my school, your sentence would be identified as grammatically incorrect because of the general reference of the pronoun which. *To correct your sentence, our students would insert a noun in front of the* which. *They would write the following: The President gave an acceptance address, an* action *which was a sure sign that he would run an aggressive campaign.*

The difference between the restrictive and the nonrestrictive adjective clauses or, as Fowler calls them, the defining and nondefining clauses, is that in the restrictive clause the information is necessary while in the nonrestrictive clause the information is incidental.

Here is a sentence with a restrictive adjective clause: The tests that were unsatisfactory *were returned to the students. In this sentence only some tests were returned. Here is a sentence with a nonrestrictive adjective clause: The tests,* which were unsatisfactory, *were returned to the students. In this case all of the tests were returned. In both cases the pronoun following* tests *clearly refers to it. In your example about the acceptance address, the* which *refers to the whole action of making an acceptance address, not incidentally to the address itself.*

The same error is present in your "deep-sixed" sentence. The which *stands for his action, not for the evidence even though* evidence *precedes the offending* which. *Our students would correct your sentence in this way: "He deep-sixed the evidence, an action which was incriminating." As you wrote it, the sentence means that he deep-sixed* all *of the evidence.*

Please reassure me that I am right, or I shall have to revise my reference rule, an action which would be traumatic for me at my age.

Ruth M. Thompson
English Department
Boston Latin Academy
Boston, Massachusetts

You write, ". . . , but applied to the whole idea of taxing."

Would not taxation *have been a better or clearer word than* taxing, *which can imply stress and not tax.*

I must say I am confused. Taxing *made the sentence unmistakably less defined—not limited to specific grammatical vexes, but applied to the whole idea of vexation.*

Robert Saigh
Chicago, Illinois

Speaking of commas, and their placement, there is a famous—or infamous— example which happened more than 600 years ago, and resulted in the gruesome death of an English king.

Edward II wasn't much of a king, even though he was the image of his Plantagenet father Edward I. But the son didn't like his job and much preferred work with his hands. Also he probably was what we now call gay, though much of his life was far from gay in its original meaning. His wife, Isabella of France, bore him a fine family, the first of whom was the great Edward III. But her husband preferred the boys and meanwhile Isabel fell in love with Roger de Mortimer, who became her close personal friend and bore the distinction of being the first prisoner who ever escaped from the Tower of London.

The people as well as Isabel became fed up with Mortimer, who simply took over the country. It was Mortimer who decided that Edward would be better off with his Plantagenet ancestors and arranged for his removal to Berkeley Castle. Isabel knew he was not off on a jolly weekend trip, but history does not indicate that she was a conspirator in his murder.

Now about that comma: One of Edward's keepers, Adam of Orleton, received a note, probably from Mortimer, which read in Latin "Edwardum occidere nolite timere, bonum est," which translated reads, "Edward to kill be unwilling to fear, it is good." The meaning could have been changed by placing the comma after the word unwilling, *but his captors took it from the first version and proceeded with the grisly plan.*

Thomas B. Costain, in The Three Edwards *writes that this phrase has appeared in many histories, but he for one does not believe it. Who would put such a damning statement in writing, and who among the thugs who held Edward captive knew Latin? Nevertheless this story appears whenever Edward II is written about. So, watch those commas!*

Jean Van Evera Markle
Haverford, Pennsylvania

Did you know that before the GOP had its battle over a comma, the Democrats had had theirs?

The issue was over quotas. The Mondale people were determined, at least before the convention proper, to be on record clearly opposing quotas. So the Arrington drafting committee came in with this language: "The Democratic Party opposes quotas, which are inconsistent with the principles of our country." There then ensued a battle with Jackson forces over the central issue, and the latter then suggested a compromise, just delete the comma. This was adopted after a hectic debate and a final comment from Arrington that he wasn't going to have the convention battle over a comma! But, of course without the comma—but with the which *retained—the resolution was then opposing only quotas that somebody would decide are not inconsistent with the principles of our country.*

As you know, this battle over the comma never reached the convention floor when all sides agreed not to mention quotas at all. Somebody suggested the phrase "verifiable measurements" which (that?) was accepted by the convention after one speaker favoring the compromise said it would permit quotas and one other delegate who also favored the compromise said it would not. All clear?

Hyman Bookbinder
Washington, D.C.

Wiggle Room

"The conservatives in Congress," wrote Steven V. Roberts in *The New York Times* from the Democratic convention, "tried to make the 'wiggle room' as small as possible."

"White House officials contend," wrote Hedrick Smith of *The New York Times* in a follow-up story, "that . . . Mr. Reagan has plenty of 'wiggle room' on the tax issue."

Wiggle room has become the Star Chamber in the tax legislators' boarding-house. The expression is a favorite of Senator Robert Kasten Jr., Republican of Wisconsin, who was quoted on April 19, 1983, as saying: "It's clear we have the votes. But we're going to try to give the White House some wiggle room." Two years before, Representative James Jones, the Oklahoma Democrat who heads the House Budget Committee, said for the record that after talking with governors and business leaders about deficit disputes, he sensed "some wiggle room."

The term is evidently new; the first use I have been able to find is in the September 11, 1978, issue of *Business Week:* "Congress has drafted regulatory legislation in a way that gives agencies . . . as little 'wiggle room' as possible." Neologism-hungry *Newsweek* followed a week later with "When it came to plugging Democratic candidates, Rosalynn Carter was sensitive enough to give each a little wiggle room—to dodge clear of her husband's political liabilities."

From these pioneer uses, the meaning becomes evident: *wiggle room,* noun, space in which to turn around; an implicit opportunity for later flexibility; a political position permitting interpretation leading to modification. Not quite an *escape hatch* or a *way out.*

The usefulness of such a phrase in a campaign year cannot be overstated. The muddying of clear commitment—the deliberate compromise in favor of vagueness, designed to prevent future embarrassment—is part and parcel of the process of comity and amelioration in the midst of political strife. The object is to get your hook into somebody in such a way as to let him get off the hook later, a nonpartisan concept encapsulated in *wiggle room*.

The phrase is too new for the dictionaries, although the *Second Barnhart Dictionary of New English* has *wiggle seat*, defined as "a lie detector fitted into a chair to measure physiological changes and movement of the occupant." At *Webster's New World*, David Guralnik was not able to flog his citators (a better name than cite-seers) into coming up with anything and tries to get out of this lapse by suggesting that "a much more apt term would be *wriggle room*, since *wiggle* is not quite the precise word."

Wiggle, a verb moving to and fro for seven centuries, means "to move from side to side, usually jerkily," akin to the Old English *wegan*, "to move." *Wriggle* means "to squirm" or "to proceed with twisting and turning movements" and is related to the Old English *wrigian*, "to turn," which is also the root of *wry* and *awry*. The meanings of the verbs have merged, but some hint of difference of emphasis remains: You can *wiggle* a portion of your anatomy, but you *wriggle* your whole body; by metaphoric extension, you can *wiggle* your way out of a tight spot, but you really have to *wriggle* to squeeze out of a trap.

Yes, *wriggle room* seems more colorful and has the benefit of alliteration, but the language is the way it is and not the way it should be. The term is *wiggle room*, and there is just no way out of it.

As you suggested on the subject of "wiggle room," we might wiggle a toe, while a whole worm wriggles altogether.

The distinction, which has tended to disappear in our grammar classes, is between a transitive and an intransitive verb. While both wiggle *and* wriggle *may be used transitively or intransitively, that is with or without an object,* wiggle *is mainly transitive (we wiggle something), and* wriggle *intransitive (we just wriggle).*

When belly dancer Gloria wriggles, she wiggles everything. Therefore we may say appreciatively, "Sic transitive Gloria."

> Art J. Morgan
> New York, New York

Wired!

Wired is the title of a book by Bob Woodward; its subtitle is *The Short Life and Fast Times of John Belushi*. This illustrates the latest use of an electrifying word on which a great many people have been strung out.

In underworld slang use, *wired* has for years meant "clandestinely carrying a recording device." Merriam-Webster's earliest citation for a person being *wired* this way was in *The Atlantic* of February 1972. Richard Dougherty reported on the Knapp Commission's use of an informant to uncover graft among New York police: "To make sure that they would get more than uncorroborated testimony . . . the Commission wired him for sound after he agreed to become an informant."

F.B.I. informants are often *wired* for sound, with tiny *bugs*, or transmitters, implanted in their lapel or tie clasp or hairpiece; others carry briefcases with recording machines or umbrellas that catch the pitter-patter of conversation. That repugnant practice has a new verb: *body-mike*. When a private detective taped conversations of the chief investigator in the office of the Senate Labor Committee, the shamus boasted, "I body-miked the [deleted] out of him."

Another meaning, perhaps growing out of the sense of being *set up* by someone who is *wired*, is "all set." When a deal is wired, it is in such closable shape that only an idiot can fail to bring it to fruition. Florida Representative Dan Mica, looking into the possibility of White House pressure on a government agency to blacklist politically unsavory speakers, discovered a tape of one official saying to another, "This can be prewired." The meaning was: "This can be arranged in advance." (*Prewired* is like *prerecorded*—a silly redundancy. Bureaucrats bastardize simon-pure street slang.)

The meaning that has taken over slang primacy is "high on alcohol or drugs." The term *strung out* is metaphorically related, as is the picture of an addict cruelly bound with wires. That is the sense used by Bob Woodward in his book on John Belushi, who died of an overdose of heroin and cocaine.

In slang, however, no word's meaning remains the same for long. Outside the drug culture, *wired* is coming to mean "tense, nervous, keyed up," which is also the state of mind of the informant doing a body-mike job.

Wired may indeed first have come to your knowledge due to FBI personnel wearing body mikes. I do not know any FBI agents, so this is terra incognito as far as i'm concerned. On the other hand, i know the word wired *had reference to the sensation produced by prolonged amphetamine abuse as long ago as the 1960s. "He was wired on speed," was a common phrase, as was "He's been up for three days and he's really wired." You say wired means "high on alcohol or drugs." This is NOT the way it is intended. It carries more than a statement about a person's current state of intoxication—it implies the deleterious effects of drugs which act as central nervous system stimulants by making the user nervous, irritable, insomniac, edgy, paranoid, and, in short, strung out. It is NOT the image of being "cruelly bound by wires" which is invoked here, despite what you say. It is the image of one's own nervous system as a high tension electrical system carrying peak loads through uninsulated wires.*

Catherine Yronwode
Editor in Chief
Eclipse Comics
Forestville, California

The use of the word "wired" to describe someone or something high on alcohol or drugs, or at least unnaturally nervous or active, has been associated with the show horse circuit for decades.

The term dates back to at least the last century when it was closely associated with show quality Tennessee Walkers. To accent the peculiar gait of these horses, stable managers would commonly burn the tender inner tissues of the front hooves of the horses with mustard oil or carbolic acid.

When this practice was rightfully banned for its cruelty, people shifted to less easily detectable methods of irritating the front legs. One of the most effective and most common techniques was to tighten a thin strand of wire around the leg just above the hoof so tightly that it would cut its way into the flesh. After the resulting wound healed, the buried wire was difficult to detect. The irritation was still great enough to make the horse prance around and refuse to put weight on the front legs for any period of time.

A horse treated in this way was "wired up" or "wired." The term came to be more generally used for any horse that acted excessively nervous with a lot of prancing and a demonstrated unwillingness to stand still, especially in the show ring.

More recently (the last 40 ± years), the term also specifically referred to those gaited horses that were drugged with "uppers" to enhance their nervousness in the final line-up. Wild eyes, spookiness, and nervous prancing are considered desirable traits for certain types of events and breeds (five-gaited Thoroughbreds, for example).

While the advent of urine tests has greatly reduced the use of actual drugs, many horses are still given a quart or two of good black coffee before show time to "get 'em properly wired up" for the show.

The circuit that I was briefly associated with actually made a distinction between the use of "wired up," which was used as a general term for any high-strung animal, and "wired" (without the "up"), which was used only to refer to animals that looked as if they were actually drugged (with something stronger than coffee). I don't know if this differentiation was a widespread usage or whether it was limited to a narrow area.

Finally, I know that the term "wired up" was commonly used by parents in eastern Pennsylvania and New Jersey in the late 1940's and early 1950's to refer to children who had a little too much energy for their own good. I heard the phrase: "Boy, you sure are wired up today" from my own mother more often than I care to remember; and her only contact with horses was with the police horses we used to see in the city park.

Our family still uses both terms that way today. While our three boys are often "wired up," I hope they never come home "wired."

Andrew D. Skibo
Danville, California

On the use of the term "prerecorded," which you labeled "a silly redundancy":

Neither silly nor redundant, the "pre" provides a clear signal to those readers concerned with such matters that the audio or audio/video content of the tape has been *commercially* duplicated. *This distinction is helpful when a home recordist in conversation seeks to differentiate a commercially produced audio or video cassette recording from tapes that have been dubbed off-the-air or copied from discs or other tapes.*

The question is far from trivial, since the Supreme Court was asked to judge whether those who duplicated (rerecorded) prerecorded material for private use were flouting the copyright laws.

As the technical editor/director of Stereo Review *magazine for about 20 years, I had a hand in popularizing the "pre" prefix, since that was the sort of tech-lish decision I was frequently involved in.*

Larry Klein
Dobbs Ferry, New York

With Coolness Toward None

"That's cool."

When the first word of that phrase is emphasized—*"That's* cool"—the slang term means "O.K., I'll go along, no big deal, I won't get lathered up about it."

When the second word is stressed—"That's *cool*"—the phrase means "That's far out, man; that's one dynamite set of wheels, wowie, hoo-ha!"

When neither word is stressed, the phrase can have this meaning, as listed in Merriam-Webster's Third Unabridged: "marked by deliberate unabashed effrontery, presumption or lack of due deference." A slang near-synonym is "That's rich." The coolness in this is a laid-back, unconcerned contempt for what others might get all worked up over.

Since this department sometimes deals in unlikely coinages—those voices in history that come up with "the right stuff" or "do your own thing"—Michael Ticktin of Roosevelt, New Jersey, submits this bit of Lincolniana:

"But you will not abide the election of a Republican President!" orated Lincoln in his 1860 speech at Cooper Institute in New York. "In that supposed event, you say, you will destroy the Union; and then, you say, the great crime of having destroyed it will be upon us! That is cool. A highwayman holds a pistol to my ear and mutters through his teeth, 'Stand and deliver, or I shall kill you, and then you will be a murderer!' "

No candidate, even those who travel on envelopes, should fear to use the latest hip expression.

The Woid on -Oid

"Whether these Reaganoid Democrats actually vote" was a clause used by columnists Evans and Novak. They used the *-oid* suffix to create an adjective. Is it correct?

We all know that the use of *-oid* to create a noun has been growing by leapoids and bounds. Among the earliest were *android*, or "automaton in human form," created in 1727, and *asteroid*, "small body like a star," in 1802. Scientists and mathematicians were especially attracted to the ending, juggling their *cylindroids, globoids* and *spheroids*.

Lately, thanks to science fiction and "Star Wars," the noun *android*—in a more familiar form as *droid*—has been losing some of the old, sinister connotations once attached to it because the robot was a soulless creature. Still, some inherent disparagement remains in the suffix: A *philanthropoid* is a put-down of one active in foundation management—meaning "one who makes a living helping philanthropists."

In creating nouns, then, the *-oid* suffix is useful to scientists who need to give names to things with specific characteristics and to laymen who like to jab at people who have certain weaknesses.

However, in creating adjectives, we have a problem of confusion. Take a name like Reagan: How do you make it into an adjective? "By far the most common adjective ending applied to names of persons in English," responds Fred Mish at Merriam-Webster, "is the *-an* or *-ian* or *-ean* set *(Churchillian, Jacksonian, Debussyan, Shakespearean)*. But *-esque* is also found, not only in your suggestion of *Kafkaesque*, but in *Dantesque, Rembrandtesque* and *Lincolnesque*. One also finds a few other forms in occasional use, such as *-ic* in *Platonic, Byronic* and *-ine* in *Bernardine*."

That means we have the choice of *Reaganan, Reaganian, Reaganean, Reaganesque, Reaganic* and *Reaganine*. Of those, I'd pick *Reaganesque* as the most natural, just as I'd say *Mondalean, Glennic, Cranstonesque, Jacksonian, Hollingslike, Askevian* (with a *v*, as in "Shavian"), *McGovernesque* and *Hartfelt*. Matter of personal taste, but my old girlfriend Norma Loquendi and I would agree most often on these.

Most native speakers would resist *Reaganoid, Mondaleoid* or *Glennoid*, etc. That's because the ending is confusing—noun or adjective?—as well as pejorative. *-Ite* is confusing enough—*McGovernite* is more likely a noun for "supporter" than an adjective to describe "plan"—but *-oid* could go either way.

Therefore, although it is not for anyone to say *-oid* is "incorrect" as an adjective, it is surely a happier suffix for a noun. *Reaganoid*, noun, is a derogation of those people who like to call themselves *Reaganauts* and are most often called *Reaganites*. Same with *Glennoids* and *Jacksonoids*. To create adjectives out of names, let us stick to the *-ians* and the *-esques*. (For attorney general, however, I would go for the offbeat *Meesine*.)

A human being is a human. A humanoid being is not human. It is akin to a human, like a human, an imitation of a human.

A Reaganite Republican is valid. He is of the same political "species" (i.e., party) as Reagan. But a Reaganite Democrat is a contradiction in terms. A Reaganoid Democrat is valid. He is an artificial Reaganaut, akin to but certainly not a true Reaganite.

It's seldom I agree with Evans and Novak, but in this case I think they were seeking to give an implication that was warranted.

Richard P. Wilson
Mobile, Alabama

-oid! Oi! Could you have leapt into print without benefit of counsel, or are you having us on? My Webster's Unabridged defines -oid as a suffix meaning "like,"

derived from a Greek word for form or shape. Nothing there says celluloid cannot be an adjective as well as a noun; nothing derogatory in rhomboid, trapezoid, anthropoid, Mongoloid, humanoid, schizoid, Polaroid, all of which are adjectives as well as nouns. Even typhoid can be used adjectivally, as in "West Africa is a typhoid area." Lots of others, no doubt.

Evans and Novak are following form, so to speak; Reaganoid Democrats are Democrats who (whose views) resemble Reagan('s). Reaganesque seems to me to lean more to style than form, so perhaps Evans and Novak chose -oid for a precise purpose.

Will you give us further woid?

> *Ewen Gillies*
> *New York, New York*

On the topic of suffixes meaning "like" (Reaganoid et al.), I was surprised that you did not mention ly *and* ish *(perhaps because they are rarely used to modify proper names). Still, I like the ring of Reaganly, which, like womanly or kingly, implies a sort of compliment both to the original and to the person who is like the original. The suffix means not only "like" but also "befitting." (A friend of mine once suggested a "teacherly" outfit in response to a question about how substitute teachers ought to dress.)*

Ish, on the other hand, has a touch of derision about it when added to a noun referring to a person (when tacked onto an adjective—"coldish"—it is slangish and means "sort of"). "Mannish," for example, almost invariably refers to a woman (or her clothes) and suggests a certain inappropriateness, a vain imitation. I opt for Reaganish in the context here—Reaganish Democrats would be like Reagan but they are not the genuine article, not being Republicans.

> *Elizabeth Ladd Glick*
> *Holliston, Massachusetts*

As a self-appointed member of the Etymological Irregulars, Mathematics Branch, I submit that you missed the snooker in your discussion of the suffix -oid.

Mathematicians and scientists, who are pretty picky about agreed terminology, use -oid in the sense of "it may look like one but it really ain't." Furthermore, the "ain't" is the dominant feature of the coinage. Thus, an "android" is demonstratively non-human, and "oblate spheroid," a favorite term of pompous sportswriters, means a football doesn't roll so good. Any punt returner or fumble recoverer will attest to a football's non-sphericity.

Therefore, I think your "Reaganoid" bad example was actually pretty good, at

least in meaning. Whether it started and ended in the proper forms of speech I'll leave to the Nitpicking Branch of the above learned society.
    Your respectful criticoid,

                                                                J. R. Foley
                                                                Vernon, Connecticut

Did you purposely neglect -ish in your woids on adjectival suffixes? Or were you just being Safiresque?

                                                                Claire Gerber
                                                                Port Republic, New Jersey

Would That Mine Adversary . . .

"There has to be an *adversarial* relationship between press and candidate," Richard Nixon told the American Society of Newspaper Editors in 1983. "There has to be an *adversarial* relationship between the press and whoever is in an office. . . ."

That's not what he used to say. "The press is the *enemy*," Mr. Nixon used to say when President, and he used to say that a lot. Between *enemy* and *adversary* lies a world of difference.

"Did President Nixon invent a new word, *adversarial*," asks William Doerrier of New York, "the way President Eisenhower did when he used *finalize* a long time ago?"

With *finalize*, President Eisenhower popularized a term that had been growing in use for more than half a century, but Mr. Nixon's choice of *adversarial* was more up-to-date: That adjective has been in use only since the 1960's. (Ixnay on the letters about not putting an apostrophe before the *s* in 1960's. This is my style; you do it your way.)

Curious, isn't it? *Adversary* has been in use since the thirteenth century, but *adversarial* is relatively new. *Adversary* was frequently a synonym for the Devil; in the King James translation of the Bible, Job is quoted as saying, "Would . . . that mine adversary had written a book." (The afflicted Job, atop the ash heap of his life, did not know who his adversary was and meant that he wished that whoever had it in for him would submit a written indictment, or bill of particulars.) The noun *adversary* is old, but the need for the adjective *adversarial* did not crop up until recently.

The reason for the late blooming of the adjective will be preceded by this brief rundown of the history of the noun, because etymologies based on the Latin verb *vertere*, "to turn," should follow in turn. *Adversus* means "turned opposite to," and the related English verb, *advert*, means "to turn attention to," a meaning that clearly led to the noun *advert* as a British shortening of *advertisement*.

The Latin *adversarius* means "turn toward or against," and I am not averse (people are *averse*, things are *adverse*) to pointing out that the only adjectival use of *adversarious* in the *Oxford English Dictionary* or its supplements is in an 1826 letter by Robert Southey: "I am not sensible of any adversarious feeling." In grammar, *adversative* is an adjective describing words that show opposition, like *but* and *although*.

Now to the new word, *adversarial*. The noun *adversary* lost its devilish connotation in its frequent use in law, as the *adversary system:* That is the basis of our trials, out of which the truth is supposed to emerge. From the positive connotation of that phrase, I think, *adversary* became identified with rational opposition rather than unbridled hostility.

In 1961, *adversary* got its big break. Speechwriter Ted Sorensen, working on the inaugural address of President John F. Kennedy ("Let the word go forth," "Ask not," etc.), had the word *enemy* in the speech a few times. "One of the changes in the final drafts," he informs me, "was to replace *enemy* with *adversary*. It was a suggestion made by Walter Lippmann—practically the only change he suggested—when I showed the draft to him. He felt that *adversary* would have a less harsh and permanent ring to it than *enemy*. *Adversary* would be a way of defining those in the opposition and would still leave the door open for them to agree with us later."

"If memory serves," continues Mr. Sorensen, whose memory serves, "that was the point that *enemy* became *adversary*, and it stayed that way through the Kennedy Administration."

In 1968, Mr. Nixon remembered that difference in nuance and, in his "era of negotiation" address, talked of the Russians as *adversaries* rather than *enemies*. (Later, he came to call the North Vietnamese forces "the enemy.") Since that time, the use of *enemy* has been frowned upon as unnecessarily provocative; Mr. Reagan, even in his "evil empire" characterization, prefers *adversary* as his name for the Soviet Union.

With all that emphasis on using the noun as a term of art in diplomacy, it was only a matter of time before the adjective showed up. *Adversarial* it was, not *adversarious* or *adversative*, and a cliché soon emerged: *adversarial relationship*.

Outside the courtroom, even this mildly confrontational attitude was not considered healthy by people who put amelioration before all.

Of late, even *adversarial* is being treated as too tough. In the report on the relationship between the military and the press issued in August 1984, Major General Winant Sidle concluded: "An *adversarial*—perhaps *politely critical* would be a better term—relationship between the media and the Government, including the military, is healthy. . . ." He skillfully juxtaposed *adversarial* against a more hostile term: "However, this relationship must not become *antagonistic*, an 'us versus them' relationship."

That's the term standing between *adversary* and *enemy:* The Greek *anti* means "against" and *agon* means "struggle, contest." An *adversary* stands opposite to you; an *antagonist* struggles with you; an *enemy* is not an *amicus*, not a friend, and is not likely to shake hands with you when the contest ends.

Had Walter Lippmann chosen *antagonist* rather than the milder *adversary*, the adjective *adversarial* might have had to wait another century before coinage. A generation ago, columnists made things happen; not now. I'm an unreconstructed hawk, and I cannot think of a different adjective form for *enemy*.

You stated that the word adversarial *"has been in use only since the 1960's." By typing this term into the LEXIS computerized legal research system, however, I found that the term was in use at least as far back as 1949, when a United States District Court opinion (*Brooks v. *United States) included the sentence, "This clearly shows an adversarial element which appears to have been entirely absent in the Rainger case." LEXIS retrieved a number of other occurrences in pre-1960 judicial opinions, indicating that the adjective was part of legal terminology prior to John Kennedy's inaugural use of* adversary.

> Fred R. Shapiro
> Head of Reference Services and Adjunct Assistant Professor
> New York Law School
> New York, New York

We enjoyed your comments on "adversary" and "adversarial."

You state that "adversarial" has been in use only since the 1960s, but that is not correct.

Chief Judge Paul J. McCormick used the word on 20 June 1949, in the U.S. District Court for the Southern District of California, in the case of Brooks v. United States *(84 F. Supp. 622, at p. 629).*

And District Judge Waldo H. Rogers used the word on 6 October 1954, in the U.S. District Court for New Mexico, in the case of Your Food Stores of Santa Fe v. Retail Clerks' Local No. 1564 *(124 F. Supp. 697, at p. 700).*
It seems that "adversarial" entered American English from the west.

Lance E. Dickson
Librarian and Professor, Law Center
Louisiana State University
Baton Rouge, Louisiana

Isn't "enemial" the logical extension of your learned discourse on "adversarial"? Logical, perhaps, but not practical because the almost homonym that precedes "enemy" in the Random House College Dictionary *would preclude that extension.*

Irving Kellogg
Los Angeles, California

When you write "people are averse, *things are* adverse," *you are quite wrong because you are confusing two entirely different Latin prefixes: the "ab-" prefix, meaning "away from," and the "ad-" prefix, meaning "toward." The "ab-" prefix is shortened to "a-" before a consonant, as in "averse."*
This is further complicated by the Greek "Alpha Privative" prefix, which implies simple negation of what follows, as in the words "a-phasis," "a-pathetic," etc.

José de Vinck
Allendale, New Jersey

The Writer's Art

James J. Kilpatrick, my colleague in columnizing (but never in calumniating), has written a delight of a guide to the expression of thoughts in words called *The Writer's Art* (Andrews, McMeel & Parker, $14.95).

Kilpo and I have jousted about *hopefully*— he is still it-is-to-be-hoping on the burning deck while almost all the rest of us have fled—but in the eternal battle between impossible-to-maintain standards and impossible-to-stand maintenances, his trumpet is certain.

We are liable to disagree on *parameter*, which I have been too quick to tolerate as a synonym for "guideline," "perimeter" and "range"—none of which mean the same. The word means "variable constant" and to hell with it. As Kilpatrick writes: "My own thought on the subject of *parameter* is to ship this poor damaged noun back to the mathematicians and to forswear its use hereafter." Good idea. He's wrong about *hopefully*, because there is no *hopably* (as there is a *regrettably* alongside *regretfully*), but as he writes, "When it comes to words, nobody has the last word."

One paragraph upward, I misused *liable*, which is liable to bring an angry torrent of letters. (Just misused it again.) The Word According to Kilpo: "In precise usage, *liable* should be reserved for those contexts in which some adverse contingency is implied. Thus we are *liable* to be stung by a hornet if we get too close to a hornet's nest. In view of that prospect, we are *likely* to stay a good distance away." In the future, when happy contingencies are in mind, I'll choose *likely* or opt for *apt*.

More important (not *importantly*, although I have nothing against sentence adverbs), he shows present and future writers how to let a simile be their umbrella: "There was a time when sly fellows nipped tiny bits of gold or silver from coins in circulation," writes the writer, "until at last the coins lost much of their value. Then a diemaker invented the milled edge, and the practice ceased. All I am saying is that words have milled edges too, and we ought to keep them that way."

Good grief, Bill Safire—

I said, when I caught the confession that you had misused "liable." It was as (it would be) if you had used "disinterested" for "uninterested." To my rising, increasing, deepening (?) incredulity, when you were all through, both you and Kilpo were still using it wrong. Seems to me I learned, once for all, in grammar school that "liable" never goes to an infinitive but always to a noun: e.g., liable to a fine, liable to prosecution, etc. I've always said "likely to misuse liable" or "apt to misuse."

In complete confidence I turned to my original Fowler and then to Gowers' update. Damme if they don't make my point at all, at all. Nor does my Fowler primer (The King's English—Abridged for School Use), to which I was introduced in 1923. Where did I pick up the nice notion? I don't know. But it's too late to change. I will (not shall) never say or write "liable to change" or even "liable to break his neck."

Am only slightly less shocked by your misuse of "parameter." (See "Eternal

Vigilance—By Whom?," Oct. 19, 1969, in The Americans *by A. Cooke.) To be exact, dear friend, a parameter is a quantity constant* in a given case, *but one that varies in different cases.*

A.C. *[Alistair Cooke]*
New York, New York

Your discussion of Mr. Kilpatrick's distinction between liable *and* likely *overlooked an important point: If* liable *implies an element of risk, then the word cannot be used correctly with an inanimate subject. Thus your misuse of the word makes it likely that readers will send you angry letters; you are liable to receive them.*
   Perhaps (not a bad substitute for hopefully*) this will clarify the issue.*

Gladys Topkis
Senior Editor
Yale University Press
New Haven, Connecticut

If you opt for apt, you will not be opting aptly!
   Although "apt" may mean "likely," it is only the second meaning listed in Webster. The main sense is explained clearly in the list of synonyms: suitable, qualified, disposed, inclined, prone, dexterous—all of which indicate that the subject is properly fit for action.
   In your favor, there is this: Webster continues: "But apt *and* likely *are often interchanged," but not by purists such as*

José de Vinck
Allendale, New Jersey

Yawners and Sleepers

Target: the new word *yawner*. The earliest citation churned out by Nexis, a computerized newspaper morgue run by Mead Data Central that makes life easier for new-word hunters, was dated January 14, 1983: "Normally, the Continental Basketball Association's all-star game is a midseason yawner." That was the lead of a *New York Times* sports story by Neil Amdur and Michael Katz.

"Until the leaders' last six holes," states the next citation, from an August 8, 1983, *Times* story by John Radosta, "the final round of the championship had looked like a yawner. . . ."

The hot, lively new word is *yawner*. Yes, you can find it in old dictionaries, in its ho-hum meaning of "one who yawns" or "something that yawns; a chasm." That's passé. *Yawner*'s new meaning is, in teen-agers' parlance, "bor-ring"—more formally, "sleep-inducing; a subject, event, or person that has a soporific effect on an audience."

The word, evidently begun in the sports world, has crossed into politics. In *Near East Report*, a Washington newsletter, M. J. Rosenberg criticized *Newsweek* magazine in January 1984 for what he believed to be its fascination with "soft" news: "[Fritz] Hollings' detailed budget plan is a yawner. Or so *Newsweek* thinks."

Yawner, in its new meaning, should not be confused with *sleeper*, a racetrack term for a horse that has not been doing its best in previous outings so that it can win unexpectedly at high odds.

From that shady origin, *sleeper* has come to mean any previously unimpressive person or object that suddenly blossoms or may be expected to attract wide attention at any moment. In the stock market, it is an undervalued security that the investment adviser likes; in the publishing trade, a *sleeper* is a book that sells well for years without being advertised; in the military, it is a delayed-action bomb; in the movie business, it is a film that unexpectedly grabs audiences, and in politics, a *sleeper* is an unimportant-seeming amendment that, when tacked onto a bill, would have far-reaching effect if not spotted by its opponents.

Most uses of *sleeper* have that larcenous or surprising connotation; even in children's sleepwear, it describes a garment that amazes tots by prohibiting access to toes. In Herbert Burkholz's and Clifford Irving's recent novel *The Sleeping Spy*, readers were provided with this definition of the term in spook-speak: "In the parlance of their trade, a sleeper was an agent who had been introduced into a target territory for an unspecified purpose in the future . . . and, as the name implied, a sleeper was expected to remain in place for long periods of time—half a lifetime if necessary—before becoming operational."

A *yawner*, however, has no such sinister overtones. I predict a good future for the word because it responds to a felt need (I have a snap-brim fedora made of a felt need) for a short word to describe a person lacking in charisma or an issue lacking in gutsiness. Until now, we had to make do with *MEGO*, an acronym for "my eyes glaze over."

Politicians like to use new words, thereby appearing to be *au courant*, but sometimes find themselves snoozing at the linguistic switch. Consider this exchange about the federal deficit and other issues between Senator Paul Laxalt, chairman of the Reagan 1984 campaign, and CBS reporter Lesley Stahl:

STAHL: "How big of an issue is that going to be?"

LAXALT: "On the deficits? Standing alone? I think it's a sleeper."

STAHL: "What about the fairness issue? Well, you think it's a sleeper—"

LAXALT: "Yes, it's a sleeper."

STAHL: "You think it will come back?"

LAXALT: "No, no, I don't mean it in that respect." The President's campaign chairman paused, gave the matter of with-it lingo some careful thought and came to this conclusion: "I think that maybe I should have said 'a yawner.'"

Your statement, "The earliest citation [for yawner*] churned out by Nexis . . . was dated January 14, 1983," was especially interesting to me, since I myself have been investigating the utility of on-line data bases as tools for historical lexicography.*

Your Nexis terminal may be in need of some repairs. When I searched for the term yawner *on my terminal, Nexis gave me citations for the meaning "something that has a soporific effect on an audience" dating back to 1976. The earliest usage was* Newsweek, *October 25, 1976: "NBC's other new hit, a detective yawner called 'Quincy' . . . merely proves that Jack Klugman is an actor who can survive burial in the deadliest of plots." The first sports citation was "Ali had just won a yawner by decision after 15 rounds" (*Washington Post, *May 18, 1977). All the other early examples were from entertainment or publishing contexts, suggesting that the term may not have originated in the sports world after all.*

Fred Shapiro
New York, New York

You are correct that the NEXIS *service makes life easier for new-word hunters. But your description of* NEXIS *as a "computerized newspaper morgue" was incorrect.* NEXIS *is a research service that includes much more than newspapers. The earliest use of the word "yawner" found by* NEXIS *was in* Newsweek *(October 25, 1976), in which television critic Harry Walters described "Quincy" as a "detective yawner." New-word hunters who use* NEXIS *(and there are several who do) use* all *of* NEXIS.

F. D. Reed
NEXIS Product Manager
Dayton, Ohio

We at Merriam-Webster thought you might like to know that our non-computerized citation file yields six citations for the use of the word yawner *in the sense you discussed, all six antedating the example you give. The earliest is from* The New York Times, *19 November 1972, Section 2, page D18, and the latest is from the* Wall Street Journal, *24 June 1982, page 1. In addition, this sense of* yawner *was entered in* Webster's Ninth New Collegiate, *published in 1983.*

Kathleen M. Doherty
Merriam-Webster, Inc.
Springfield, Massachusetts

How big of an issue are you willing to make of the use of that "of" after "big"? Is Stahl a Middle Westerner? I ask because I find this usage most common in that area: "How good of a day will it be?" "How bad of a cold do you have?" etc.

Barbara S. Wright
Amston, Connecticut

There are two solecisms that I have been hearing more and more frequently, both of them involving the preposition of. *One of these appeared in your column—* "STAHL: *'How big of an issue is that going to be?'* " *To her credit, Miss Stahl corrected herself later in the interview when she said, "How big an issue. . . ." My favorite example of this usage is the sportscaster who said, "He's not that good of a batter."*

The other mistake I often hear, from people who should know better, is "that kind of a man." (Even worse: "Those kinds of a man.") This is not only ungrammatical, it is also illogical!

When I was in school (many years ago when grammar was still taught), I learned two rules: 1. The preposition of *is not used after an adjective except poetically (fair of face, for instance) and 2. An article is not used after any synonym of category of (such as kind, sort, type, etc.).*

I believe that there is room for change in the English language, but not in the rules of grammar. Syntax is the skeleton supporting the body of language, in which we think. When the skeleton is abused, the body is crippled, and so is our thinking.

The same rules govern both syntax and logic that, in turn, govern the scientific method. If our children are ever to become educated in the sciences, there is no better place to start than in the study of grammar.

Margaret O. Ablitt
Westport, Connecticut

Yip, Yap, Yumpies

Presidential aide Richard Darman was described by a Washington seer recently as "king of the yumpies." (Actually, I was the one who labeled him that way, because the acronym *yumpie* was called to my attention by *New York Times* White House correspondent Steven Weisman, and I had not seen the new word in print. Now there is a printed citation, and I can comment on it; this is an advantage I have over other language scholars.)

Yumpies—the singular, *yumpie*, takes the diminutive ending *ie*, on the analogy of *yippie* and *preppie*, because the early spotter gets to lay down the rules—are "Young Upwardly Mobile Professionals." These are the people who used to be called *comers*, with all the advantages of youth and talent and education that made them "likely to succeed."

In an earlier form, *yuppie*—for "Young Urban Professional"—spawned *The Yuppie Handbook*, by Marissa Piesman and Marilee Hartley, a spoof similar to the handbook on *preppies*. They defined the yuppie as a fast-track baby-boomer between twenty-five and forty-five, residing in or near a major city and living on aspirations of glory and power, or "anyone who brunches on the weekend or works out after work."

The use of the initial *y* in this gentle put-down of upcomers is partly from a play on the 1960's term *yippie*, which itself was derived from *hippie*. (That's it! The diminutive ending of this series of words began with the noun *hippie*, to differentiate scruffy youths from the adjective *hippy*, which is what most of their parents were.) More specifically, the 1970's forerunner of *yuppie* and *yumpie* was *yavis*, psychotherapeutic jargon for "Young, Attractive, Verbal, Intelligent, Successful." In 1979, a *New York Times* article used the word: "Those who derive the most benefit from psychoanalysis have frequently been dubbed 'yavis.' "

The yumpies climbing the ladder of success with great agility can be described as *upscaling*.

As a candidate member of your Lexicographic Irregulars, let me suggest the following etymology for the words hippie *and* yippie.

Hep was, of course, the ancestor of both terms, but by the late Forties, hip *had replaced* hep *among jazz musicians, who viewed with scorn anyone who used the latter term.* Hip *was a verb as well as noun and adjective. You could* hip *someone to the fact that Bird would be sitting in at Bop City, say.*

Mailer and others used hipster *in a complimentary way. This was before that word came to mean a kind of jeans or ladies panties. By the late Fifties, I recall that* hippie *had become a put-down term in the coffee bars and jazz joints of Grant Avenue. A* hippie *was a faker, someone trying to be* hip *but not making it (viz.,* beatnik *for* beat*).*

By '66 it was a portmanteau word for longhaired acidheads in the Haight. Hep, *meanwhile, had been forgotten by everyone but Lawrence Welk.*

Yippie was, I think, coined by Paul Krassner, an acronym out of Youth International Party, which pricked some balloons at the '68 Democratic Convention in Chicago.

Traveling in Brazil a month ago, it amused me to discover that hippie *has taken on yet another meaning there. Every Sunday there's a* hippie *fair in Ipanema, for example, and at the foot of the TV tower in Brasília, but all they are are flea markets.*

> Maitland Zane
> San Francisco, California

The word yumpies *has another, and earlier, meaning than the one cited.*

In the late 1960's, the sport of international rally driving (and the allied sports of Autocross and Rallycross) was dominated by Finns and Swedes, although the predominant language of the sport remained English. As you are no doubt aware, Scandinavians generally pronounce the letter "j" as a "y" and consequently the word "jump" would be pronounced "yump." At this time, the speed and durability of the cars used for this sport had reached a point at which allowing the car to become airborne when negotiating hills and bridges became both safe and practicable. This practice became known as "yumping" and those who made a habit of it were known as "yumpers" or, less frequently, "yumpies." More often than not, the latter word was applied in a negative sense in that a driver whose nerve did not allow such auto-gymnastics or a navigator with a sensitive stomach was referred to as having "a touch of the yumpies." Alas, I can recall no driver or navigator ever being referred to as "king of the yumpies (or yumpers)."

Cris Whetton
Levittown, Pennsylvania

Zapmanship

"Zapping," writes columnist Ellen Goodman of the *Boston Globe* in applauding the Supreme Court decision to permit home video recording, "is what we in the shadowy world of VCR owners do to commercials. We push the fast-forward button right through the buggers."

Miss Goodman's paragraph illustrates two points: First, the word *bugger* has lost its original pejorative meanings, which included an ethnic slur on "Bulgarian," and later came to mean "sodomite" and, finally, in its most loathsome incarnation, "one who implants secret listening devices." Today, *bugger*—meaning "gizmo, whatchamacallit, unidentified sitting object" as well as an intensified "thing"—has become an acceptable noun in family newspapers.

Second, the headline for her column—"The Right to Zap"—elevates a slang term to the honor of best describing an activity newly protected by the United States Constitution.

According to the novelist Ray Russell, the word *zap* was coined by Philip Francis Nowlan, creator of the character of Buck Rogers, who was introduced in the August 1928 issue of *Amazing Stories*. Mr. Nowlan teamed up with artist Dick Calkins the next year to produce the science-fiction comic strip, and used the onomatopoeic word *zap* to simulate the sound emitted by a "paralysis gun."

The sound soon became a verb, and *to zap* has turned into a major slang coinage. At Oxford, England, the world's most influential lexicographer, Robert Burchfield, editor of the *Supplement to the Oxford English Dictionary*, was working on the final volume of his monumental effort, which appeared in 1986. On the assumption that he was already well into *z*, I called him at his office (this department spares no expense) to find out the lineage of *zap*.

"Primarily the word means 'to point a weapon at somebody, to kill, to shoot, to hit,' " reports Mr. Burchfield. "It can also mean 'to pretend to kill,' as in saying, 'Zap, you're dead.' In later contexts, the verb has been weakened to mean 'to attack, to argue with, to confront.' "

The earliest usage found is American, although serious research into comic-book linguistics is scandalously slight; the British have adopted it in both science fiction and spy fiction.

In a different semantic direction, the scholarly trackers of our lingo note that the verb has come to mean "to move quickly." "In this case," says my friend, "*zap* is an intransitive verb." He adds, with his usual generosity of spirit, "which means, as you know, that it takes no object." He may have heard that I have had some difficulty with intransitives lately.

"Often the word is used as an interjection," Mr. Burchfield finds, "followed by an exclamation point and spelled with an uppercase zed: *Zap!*" He notes that a 1962 issue of *American Speech* magazine cites an Arkansas student, pretending to be a space creature, pointing his finger at another student and saying, "Zap! You're sterile."

"By 1969," the lexicographer continues, "*zap* was being used as a noun meaning 'a blow' or, less often, 'an argument,' and then it develops into 'energy' or 'power.' One citation offers the phrase, 'the zap of his language,' and another in a 1979 Canadian journal is 'lost some of her old zap.' There is the related noun *Zapper*, which is a registered trademark for a machine that uses microwaves to destroy unwanted insects, pests, or weeds."

If the noun is here, can the adjective be far behind? "From 1969 on there has been the adjective *zappy*," reports New Zealand's successor to Sir James Murray, "which means 'lively, amusing, energetic.' In a British newspaper in 1972, there appeared an advertisement for an energetic young man that stated, 'We badly need some zappy young editor.' "

In the United States, I have used the noun interchangeably with *zoosh*, to mean "piquancy," perhaps influenced by *zest* and *zip*; the adjective *zappy* is rarely used here because of the confusion with *sappy*.

More serious than any misuse of language is the misunderstanding of the Supreme Court revealed by your characterization of home videotaping as "an activity newly protected by the United States Constitution." This is the common error of thinking that whatever the Supreme Court allows is constitutional and whatever it forbids is unconstitutional. Those who comment on public issues should understand that this is not necessarily so. What the Court decided in the Betamax case was that the pertinent statute—the Copyright Act—did not prohibit home videotaping. The Court did not have to consider whether there is a constitutional right to videotape at home; that question would arise only if Congress amended the Copyright Act and tried to prohibit home videotaping. Federal courts spend most of their time (remaining after writing usage dictators) trying to determine what Congress has allowed or prohibited. That type of decision is entirely different from a decision as to what the Constitution allows or prohibits.

> *Jon O. Newman*
> *United States Circuit Judge*
> *Hartford, Connecticut*

Dear Bill,

Perhaps you had a bad connection on that transatlantic call, because I can hardly imagine Robert Burchfield making the egregious error of saying that zap *"can also mean 'to pretend to kill,' as in saying, 'Zap, you're dead.' " It no more means that than it means "to pretend to sterilize" in the anecdote that you quote three paragraphs later. The meaning of* zap *in such sentences is like that of* bang, pow, *etc.: it denotes the sound of some event that is being represented (the firing of a pistol or a ray gun, the impact of a fist against a jaw, the impact of Sylvester the Cat against the sidewalk), and it is immaterial whether that event is being represented as part of a pretense, in the telling of an anecdote, or in the giving of advice ("You should sock him one, pow, right in the kisser!"). It is also immaterial whether the represented event is an event of killing—*zap *is equally appropriate when the victim is sterilized, maimed, or turned into a mindless vegetable.*

You and Burchfield do much better with the uses of zap *as a verb. In "Zap, you're dead/sterile/liquid,"* zap *is not a verb but one of several kinds of words that have been lumped indiscriminately under the label "interjections" (only a wastebasket category could accommodate* zap, hello, *and* ouch*), and only when lexicographers come to appreciate how different such things are from nouns, verbs, and adjectives can we expect to find accurate entries for them in dictionaries.*

I turn from the main order of business to the less pressing matter of bugger, *which you take up briefly in the same column. While* bugger *for most Americans "has lost its* original *pejorative meanings," I dispute your implied claim that it has lost its status as a pejorative. Have you ever seen it used in a context where it was unambiguously non-pejorative? If you happen not to remember the word* artichoke, *you aren't going to compliment your hostess's cooking by saying, "Those buggers were delicious." It may now be a virtually contentless pejorative, but a pejorative it remains.*

Jim [James D. McCawley]
Department of Linguistics
The University of Chicago
Chicago, Illinois

Re "Zapping," you do not mention the meaning which I have most often heard— i.e., to win (an argument, a game, an election, etc.) by a wide margin. For instance, if you beat me at tennis 7–6, 6–7, 7–6, I might say, "Well, you finally won this match." But if you took the match 6–0, 6–0, I might say, "Wow! You really zapped *me that time."*

Robert O. Vaughn
West New York, New Jersey

You may be interested to know that, in medical circles, zapping *means "to deliver radiation therapy." It is slang if not a somewhat pejorative term.*

William D. Bloomer, M.D.
Professor and Chairman, Department of Radiology
Mt. Sinai Medical Center
New York, New York

According to Karen R. Wagner, postmaster of Zap, North Dakota (founded May 29, 1913; incorporated 1917), "Zap was named after a coal mining hamlet by that name in Scotland. The choice was made because of the lignite coal mines in the vicinity."

Fleming Meeks
New York, New York

Last week my wife had her hair done by Zap Coiffeurs. I can't say her hair was standing on end when she came home, but the name reminded me of your column.

I remember seeing "zap" used as both a verb and a description of a sound in the Buck Rogers comic strips when I was a kid. I agree that the origin was in those strips or in the stories published in Amazing, *the science fiction magazine. I also believe the word is onomatopoeic. It sounds like an electric spark.*

I have, in my work in radiation protection, more than once said to heating and ventilating engineers, "You can't put that air duct there! Anyone outside it is going to get zapped from the stuff in that tank."

When talking about γ-radiation from radioactive material "zap" is an appropriate word.

James H. Ray
Irvington, New York

Your mentioning of the word bugger *brings to mind the English slang expression* bugger all, *which means, I believe, "nothing." For example, if I were asked, "What did you give your wife for Valentine's Day?", I could reply "bugger all." I am curious about the origin of this expression.*

As an illustration of its usage, in a public TV series, Rumpole of the Bailey, *Rumpole's client was just found guilty and the following took place:*

ELDERLY JUDGE: "Before I pass sentence, do you have anything to say?"
PRISONER (almost inaudibly): *"Bugger all."*
JUDGE: "Rumpole, what did your client say?"
RUMPOLE: " 'Bugger all,' Your Grace."
JUDGE: "That's funny, I never saw his lips move."

Michael S. Martus, P.E.
Chappaqua, New York

You referred to the usage of the term bugger. *A reference that fairly sprung to my mind, and which you did not cite, is from the classic Hemingway story "Fathers and Sons"—one of what is commonly referred to as the Nick Adams stories.*

I give you the quotation:

"The little bugger," Nick said.
"Do you know what a bugger is?" his father asked him.
"We call anything a bugger," Nick said.
"A bugger is a man who has intercourse with animals."

"Why?" Nick said.
"I don't know," his father said, "but it is a heinous crime."

Adam Hanft
New York, New York

Zap, You're Alive

Zap has done it again.

This major slang coinage, the emergence of which has been tracked in this space, is pressing ahead in its fight to become standard English. (You don't think an imitative sound can make it? What about *crunch*, the sound of an icebreaker moving through ice? That made it from an imitative sound to a standard verb and now has spread to notoriety as a noun, as in "Zap is coming to the crunch.")

To recap (*itulate* has been scratched): *Zap* was coined by Philip Francis Nowlan, the creator of Buck Rogers, in the late 1920's to describe the sound made by his character's paralysis gun. During the Vietnam War, this example of onomatopoeia was adopted by soldiers as a verb for "to destroy or kill with a burst of gunfire, flame or electric current," as the *American Heritage Dictionary* defined it. It then made its way back to children's usage as in a kid's pointing a finger, cocking a thumb and announcing happily, "Zap, you're dead!"

In the 1980's, owners of video recorders began using the word as a verb with a meaning particularly appropriate to its paralysis-gun origin: "to avoid, erase or stop the recording or playing back of a commercial."

Under the headline "Fighting Television 'Zapping,' " Philip Dougherty, advertising columnist of *The New York Times*, brought the term up-to-date: "Zapping, originally meant to describe the use of a TV remote-control device to skip around the dial during commercial messages, now has become a generic word to cover all use of technological advancement to escape the advertising."

Consumers, armed with a Buck Rogers weapon to defend themselves against advertising saturation by Wilma the spokesperson and TV's grand viziers, can hit their "fast forward" buttons when playing back a sponsored program and thereby zap the commercials.

"The ultimate defense against being zapped," says adman Kenneth Roman, speaking to a war council of his peers, many of them worried about the end of advertising's era of uninterrupted intrusiveness, "is to involve the viewer."

Many of us are already involved and are just waiting for him to come on the screen. We have the weapon and, thanks to Buck Rogers, the verb to immortal-ize it.

Ringing Rhetoric: The Return of Political Oratory

The following essay on political rhetoric was the cover story of The New York Times Magazine *on August 19, 1984.*

The halls are alive with the sound of oratory. Democrats assembled in conven-tion last month hurled a challenge to tight-lipped Republicans in the form of five goose-bumping speeches that shivered the presidential timbers.

Now we are on the eve of the Republican reply, to come in the form of convention oratory that will thunder out of Dallas. Ringing rhetoric is reborn.

Put another way:

I stand before you, my friends, to hail the renaissance of a great art form.

How long have we put up with the mealy mouthings of politicians incapable of lifting our hearts and making our pulses quicken?

How long—oh, how long!—have we waited for glorious Oratory, that sonorous instrument used by Churchill and Roosevelt to dispel debilitating despair, to rise up, like the Phoenix, from its own ashes to blaze forth once again on its mission of inspiration, castigation and fabrication?

Not too long. Only twenty-three years ago, oratory was in. John F. Kennedy asked not what he could do for the spoken word, but what oratory could do for him; in his inaugural address, following on the heels of a surprisingly strong farewell to the military-industrial complex by Dwight D. Eisenhower, President Kennedy made listeners and viewers feel like audiences again.

In the mid-1960's, speechmaking fell relatively silent. Lyndon B. Johnson's Texas twang got in the way. Hubert H. Humphrey was a real orator, far more than Adlai E. Stevenson (who was a fine speechwriter and speechmaker, but no orator), but he lost to Richard M. Nixon, whose resonant voice lacked the dramatic intensity to deliver what he called "the lift of a driving dream."

Audiences hungry for the red meat of passionate partisanship were fed for a time by Vice President Spiro T. Agnew, but with his disgrace the whole field of speechifying underwent a decline. Presidents Ford and Carter were poor orators; besides, we were told, "old-fashioned oratory" had no place in the cool electronic wavelengths. No longer would statesmen thrill us in the crowd; the crowd had become a family in a living room, and instead of messages being thundered, thoughts were to be shared.

The new speechmaking of the 1970's went like this:

Let me take these few brief moments to share my thoughts with you on a subject close to my heart.

The other day I received this letter (HOLD UP LETTER, DISSOLVE TO HANDWRITING) *from an eleven-year old girl in Grosse Pointe, Michigan. "Mr. President," she writes, "how come I never see you standing on a stump, bellowing out your speech to the multitudes, like the pictures of William Jennings Bryan in olden times? How come you're always sitting at your desk, all cool and collected, sharing your thoughts with me alone?"*

To that little girl, and to all of you who would like a quick oratorical fix, I have to confide the simple truth: Nobody listens to a speech anymore. If I were to get up on a stump for an hour, you would see me on television for five seconds, and then you would see a reporter standing in front of me knocking down what I was saying for another thirty seconds, and that would be it.

I would like to make you a speech, little girl, but it requires a lot of work which turns out to be a waste of time. That is why I have to rely on question-and-answer sessions and these brief little episodes of thought-sharing. The director is already drawing his finger across his throat. Thank you and good night.

During the early years of the Reagan presidency, this low-key, talk-to-the-person-not-the-people technique—conscious anti-oratory—has reached its zenith. Mr. Reagan, trained as an actor, was able to add a new dimension to anti-oratory: When he spoke to a large audience, such as a joint session of Congress, he used it as a mere applause-line responder. The live audience in the hall was the satellite off which he bounced his message; his target was rarely the people in the hall, it was pre-eminently the camera and the person at home. The crowd was there for the camera to pan, but it was a stage set disguising the pitch to the tube.

Then came the Democratic convention of 1984. Suddenly, five big chunks of oratory boomed out into a hall filled with placard-waving people. This was not like the time in 1980 when earnest John Glenn, trying to be heard over the din with a serious, substantive visit to Dullsville, caused wags to say, "If he ever had to make a Fireside Chat, the fire would go out." Nor was this a setting for the speaker to talk over the heads of the people in the hall directly to the small audience at home.

No, my friends, this was Oratory. This was a speaker talking to a crowd.

This was drama on its feet, making a metaphor work until you could see the honest sweat on its face.

This was short sentences. This was give-and-take with the people in the hall. This was rock-'em-sock-'em use of rhythm and rhyme. This was a series of words starting off with the same letter—no, you won't hear me calling it by a $20 name like "alliteration," the way some people do to show off their education.

To those cynics who say the old-fashioned values of stem-winding are a thing of the past, I say—you ain't heard nothin' yet!

To those of faint heart and weak voice who say the Oratory that made this nation great is out-of-date, washed up, finished, I say—phooey!

Why this change? Why did Mario M. Cuomo, who most people outside of New York confused with a crooner of a previous generation, suddenly breathe life into a moribund art form?

I subscribe to the Political Pendulum Theory—that is, whoever or whatever is "in" now, will be "out" soon enough. The coolly warm style so admired in thought-sharers of the past decade was "in" long enough; the audience was ready for something different. *(Had enough, my friends? It's time for a change!)*

Deeper thinkers will say that the urge to be part of a large audience never really disappeared in the American electorate. Although television delivery, person-to-person, suppressed this desire for a while, the latent urge reasserted itself. Kids who buy records of groups like "The Truly Needy" to play in the privacy of earphones also go in droves to their concerts; adults who listen dutifully as a single target have a need to respond as part of a large group.

A third reason is the Demosthenes Factor. As one of the ancients said of Athens' greatest orators: "When Pericles spoke, the people said, 'How well he speaks.' But when Demosthenes spoke, the people said, 'Let us march!' " One or two good speeches, given wide dissemination, quickly give oratory back its good name.

The speeches made at the Democratic convention last month married some good speechmaking to the return of interest in speaking at a moment when the red lights of television cameras were on. Not all the speeches there rated as good oratory. The boring bombast of Tip O'Neill and Ed Koch made conventioneers' eyes glaze over. (Ted Kennedy's barnburner introduction of Mondale accomplished its purpose of whipping up enthusiasm, but had no lasting impact and has all but slipped into oblivion.) But five are worth study.

First, a grading of The Big Five on oratorical style and rhetorical technique, not on content:

Mario Cuomo, the keynoter, delivered a stunner. Remarkable use of hands and body English to control crowd reaction in delivery. Superb modulation of speed and tone, with the exception of a demagogic use of murdered nuns. Nice rejection of rhetorical devices while using them. Grade: A.

Jesse Jackson delivered an emotional sermon-on-the-stump. Intensely personal content, riveting delivery after nervous start. Overuse of rhyme to make phrases, but wise use of repetition to drive home "our time has come." Big speech, could have been a great speech if length cut by half. Grade: A minus.

Gary Hart put forward a speech to be played back in four years which was unsatisfying now; he tried to get in too many of his stump themes. Speech delivered at a constant pace and without break in tone, making delivery monotonous. "Nostalgia is not a program," a good shot; but old-fashioned slams at a "gang of greedy polluters" and "toxic terrorists" marred the cerebral yuppie approach. Grade: B minus.

Geraldine A. Ferraro was skillful in evoking origins, but banal in the "To those who say . . . we say" device. No dramatic modulation in delivery, but no stumbling, either. Her writers could have done better in such a dramatic moment. Grade: B.

Walter F. Mondale suffered in emotional comparison to Jackson and Ferraro and the new-face appeal of Cuomo, but deserves a "medium hello" for a verge-of-tears delivery of a solid speech. Excellent on antithesis, sloppy on parallel structure, good use of short sentences—"He won't tell you. I just did."—and strong on vision of America. Grade: B plus.

Will Republican speeches this week match this standard? The emotional charge of blacks and a woman candidate will be absent, and the response is rarely as good as the attack (although Daniel Webster did well in his "Second Reply to Hayne"). The styles of the scheduled speakers in Dallas vary from the cracker-barrel even-handedness of Howard Baker to the enthusiastic economics of Jack Kemp, who rides supply-side saddle to suggest a new cross of gold. Although former President Ford and Vice President Bush are not expected suddenly to bloom as orators, Ambassador Jeane Kirkpatrick's didactic hawkishness might provide some diversion, and it will be interesting to see if Ronald Reagan, the master of the person-to-person technique, can adapt to the new interest in a person-to-people-in-the-hall approach.

Republican oratory tends to be more flag-waving and God-fearing than Democratic oratory, and speeches by Democrats reflect an institutional grumpiness about that. This year, however, the Democrats made a point of God, Jesus and St. Francis and of physically waving flags at the conclusion of their convention, and Republicans may try to grab the clothes of compassion the Democrats left by the riverbank.

Let us examine both the tried-and-true and tried-and-false tricks of the oratorical trade to see how they were employed by the Democrats last month, occasionally sprinkling in a few examples from speeches of some of the Republicans scheduled to give the nation a quick transfix next week.

Antirhetoric rhetoric. "Please allow me to skip the stories and the poetry and the temptation to deal in nice but vague rhetoric," began Governor Cuomo, staking his claim to the fed-up-with-schmaltz crowd. (We shall return to his rhetoric under "metaphor.") Republican Howard H. Baker Jr. likes to work that same vein, deriding "the same acrid rhetoric which befouls our domestic politics."

This exploits the antipolitician resentment, treating the word *rhetoric*—once a definition of rational argument—in its newer sense of artificial eloquence: mere words. "Oratory" is the spoken form of rhetoric, now with a bombastic connotation, forever belittled by Wendell Willkie's postelection derogation of his own spoken stands as "just campaign oratory."

Governor Cuomo played off President Reagan's frequent evocation of "a shining city on a hill," an image often used in the Camelot days of John F. Kennedy, taken from John Winthrop's line in establishing the Massachusetts Bay Colony in 1630: "We shall be a city upon a hill. The eyes of all the people are upon us." Using a rhetorical device the Greeks called *apostrophe*—addressing a person not present—Governor Cuomo declaimed, "There is despair, Mr. President, in faces you never see, in the places you never visit in your shining city."

In the same way, when Gary Hart said "rhetoric about jobs and fairness is but sound and fury signifying nothing," the senator was using the device of *allusion*, quoting Shakespeare's *Macbeth* without belaboring the listener with attribution. (Geraldine Ferraro used the same allusive technique in paraphrasing John Kennedy: "The issue is not what America can do for women, but what women can do for America.")

Antirhetoric rhetoric is best used by the extremely skillful rhetorician or the hopelessly uninspired speaker. One can effectively admire the city's shine or deplore its glitter; optimism and realism both work.

Alliteration.   This is probably the easiest device for orators and their writers, although it was in the doghouse immediately after the Agnew era. (I was the author of "nattering nabobs of negativism," an updating of Adlai Stevenson's derogation of pessimists as "prophets of gloom and doom." I also submitted "hopeless, hysterical hypochondriacs of history," but when the 4-H Clubs objected, the Vice President dropped it. I now profess to scorn the technique, but began this article with "ringing rhetoric is reborn.")

"My constituency is the damned, disinherited, disrespected, despised," cried Jesse Jackson, later deploring the "sadness, sacrifice and suffering" caused by Reaganomics. He dreamed of artists "who will convey music and message, rhythm, rhyme and reason."

Edward Kennedy chimed in, praising Walter Mondale's "chance for change," demanding a "spirit of sacrifice" and deriding the "California Coolidge" whose advisers "practice polarization politics." Mario Cuomo preferred "reasonableness and rationality" lest the nation be divided "into the lucky and the left-out, the royalty and the rabble."

We can look for an alliterative counter-barrage when the Republicans convene.

Katherine D Ortega, the Treasurer of the United States and the keynoter, has in previous speeches extolled "peace, prosperity and progress," hardly an original formulation. President Reagan has already labeled his target pessimists as "sour souls." (Tradition uses alliteration to excoriate pessimists, who are also known as "those who." Just as the Washington Generals are a basketball team organized for the sole purpose of losing to the Harlem Globetrotters in exhibitions, "those who"—and their sneering sidekicks, "some," as in "some say"—are always wrong.)

Humble origins.   Big this year. "I watched a small man with thick calluses on both hands work fifteen and sixteen hours a day," remembered Mario Cuomo. "I saw him once literally bleed from the bottoms of his feet." Geraldine Ferraro identified herself as "the daughter of working Americans" and "the daughter of an immigrant from Italy." Gary Hart pointed out that he "was raised in a Kansas family that was poor on resources . . . but rich with confidence and love." Walter Mondale improved on that with, "We never had a dime. But we were rich in the values that are important."

The Republicans may come back strong on humble origins. Ronald Reagan's father was fired during the Depression, and his mother went to work in a dress shop for $14 a week. Katherine Ortega, youngest of nine children, tells audiences that her father was a blacksmith who augmented his income "by nailing together custom-made coffins."

Of all current leading orators, Senator Kennedy is the one most handicapped in using this theme.

Rhyme.   This can be effective on occasion in making a point, but it is a dangerous device because it often borders on the banal. "They lavish tax breaks on the greedy and deny bread to the needy," said Senator Kennedy, and it didn't fly. That was reminiscent of Richard Nixon's "the wealthiest nation in the world should be the healthiest nation in the world." It looked all right on paper as an applause line, but it didn't sing.

Jesse Jackson overdid rhyme: "Young America . . . don't put dope in your veins, put hope in your brains." "Jesus said that we should not be judged by the bark we wear but by the fruit we bear." "Small farmers . . . will either have 90 percent parity or 100 percent charity." These strained for effect; more subtle and more effective was "for friends who loved and cared for me, and for a God who spared me."

Alan Dundes, professor of anthropology and folklore at the University of California at Berkeley, points to a long-standing tradition in Afro-American culture in which young men use rhyme in argument: "It is common for young men to try to put down their opponents in rhyme, in what is called 'playing the dozens.' Muhammed Ali used it, too." But rhyme is the most obvious of all rhetorical tricks; it is the way children can remember instructions—*i* before *e*, except after *c*—and strains too much to make a political message memorable, "I like Ike" to the contrary notwithstanding.

Repetition. Called *anaphora* in rhetoric classes, it can work well if the orator knows just how far to take it. Jackson's "our time has come," repeated three times, was just right. Gary Hart began five sentences with "At issue in this campaign . . ." and I thought it began to wear. Geraldine Ferraro used "It isn't right" to begin six sentences, and what began as a strongly moral series took on a whining quality about the fifth time. The only place that such frequent repetition seems to be sustainable is in a "Vision-of-America," for which see below.

Metaphor. This gives a knockout figure to speech. "The Republicans believe the wagon train will not make it to the frontier," said Governor Cuomo, "unless some of our old, some of our young and some of our weak are left behind by the side of the trail." He rode that wagon through his speech, recalling the image gracefully at the end not with a wagon but with words like "pioneer" and "new frontier."

Jesse Jackson used metaphor both beautifully and badly. "If there were occasions when my grape turned into a raisin and my joy bell lost its resonance, please forgive me." That was fresh. "In 1980, many . . . saw a light at the end of the tunnel in Reaganism. But in 1984, we now know it was not sunshine, but a train coming this way." That was stale.

John Kennedy said memorably that "the torch has been passed to a new generation of Americans," and Gary Hart picked up that flaming metaphor: "Today the torch has been taken down from the Statue of Liberty. And if our government continues to replace the words 'Give me your tired, your poor, your huddled masses yearning to breathe free' with 'What's in it for me . . . tighten your belts . . . and show us your identification card'—then they might just as well leave that torch on the ground." That complex sentence required careful delivery, and was the high point of Hart's oratory.

Ronald Reagan is no fizzle when it comes to torches, either. "For those who yearn to be free," he said on this Fourth of July about the persecuted of the world, "for those who fight for the right to worship . . . for all those people, America is not just a word, it is a hope, a torch shedding light to all the hopeless of the world."

The President added another metaphor that day: "The totalitarian world is a tired place held down by the gravity of its own devising. And America is a rocket pushing upward to the stars." His torch works better than his rocket; John Kennedy showed how a new-age metaphor could exalt with "America has tossed its cap over the wall of space." That evocation of a small boy challenging himself was a great metaphor.

So is the "safety net," first used by Winston Churchill, picked up by Jack Kemp, and popularized by President Reagan. Congressman Kemp, who will speak at the convention, has taken it further: "It's one thing to have a healthy and secure safety net, but it's also a requirement that we build a 'safety ladder,' a ladder of hope and opportunity . . ."

Perhaps Katherine Ortega will use her personal metaphor: "In the next year or so," she told a recent graduating class, "my signature will appear on $60 billion of U.S. currency. More important to me, however, is the signature that appears on my life—the strong, proud, assertive handwriting of a loving father and mother . . ." Some will call it cornball; I think that metaphor works because her claim to fame is the signature on the money we carry.

Invocation. This, or some reference to the Deity, is traditional in American political rhetoric, although Abraham Lincoln had to be prodded by his pious Treasury secretary to include a reference to Divine Providence in his Emancipation Proclamation. Mario Cuomo concluded with, "for the love of this great nation, for the family of America"—based on Lincoln's "family of man"—"for the love of God." Jesse Jackson, as might be expected of a minister, spoke most easily and personally of God, as in "God is not finished with me yet."

No politician has incorporated God into his speech endings more than Ronald Reagan. Like Jimmy Carter, he signs off with "God bless you," and it is not that the nation is sneezing. Ronald Reagan is among those who believe it quite appropriate to deliver a layman's blessing in a political context; other speakers consider it presumptuous or out of place.

Of the Democrats, Gary Hart and Jesse Jackson—not Walter Mondale or Geraldine Ferraro—blessed us at their conclusion; of the Republicans, Howard Baker and Ronald Reagan are regular blessers.

Vision of America. This is the now-mandatory positive, idealistic side of even the most slashing ripsnorter. It consists of a series of sightings of an America in the future, shimmering, if Governor Cuomo will permit, like a city on a hill in the sunlight.

"I see an America where greed, self-interest and division are conquered by idealism, by the common good and by the national interest," said Gary Hart. "I see an America too young to quit . . . an America with unmet dreams that will not die." His ardent followers saw a vision of Gary Hart in that as well, as the orator had intended.

For Walter Mondale, the vision came in a series of six sentences beginning, "By the start of the next decade," and including, "I want to ask our children their dreams, and hear not one word about nuclear nightmares," and "I want to point to the Supreme Court and say 'Justice is in good hands.' "

That construction will be familiar to Old Nixon Hands who recall his acceptance at the 1968 Republican convention: "I see a day when Americans are once again proud of their flag . . . I see a day when we will again have freedom from fear . . . I see a day when our nation is at peace and the world is at peace."

I had a hand in that Nixon draft, stealing the device from a 1940 F.D.R. speech: "I see an America where factory workers are not discarded after they reach their prime . . . I see an America whose rivers and valleys and lakes . . . are protected as the rightful heritage of all the people . . . I see an America devoted to our freedom."

After the Nixon convention speech, I called F.D.R.'s speechwriter, Judge Samuel I. Rosenman, to apologize for lifting his technique. He sent me a speech by Robert Green Ingersoll, who called James G. Blaine "the Plumed Knight" at the 1876 Democratic convention: "I see a country filled with happy homes . . . I see a world where thrones have crumbled . . . I see a world at peace." Rosenman didn't know where Ingersoll had taken it from.

These lessons in current rhetoric could go on, but as Hubert Humphrey used to say when he talked too long, "I am reminded of the little girl who said she knew how to spell *banana*, but never knew when to stop." Other devices, such as the *rhetorical question*—from Mr. Reagan's famous, "Are you happier today than when Mr. Carter became President?" to Mr. Mondale's, "Why can't we reach agreements to save this Earth?"—will not be mentioned here. (That old trick is called *apophasis*, saying something by artfully declining to say it; nobody's pulled that yet this year.)

Will the current interest in oratory turn out to be a blip on the public's attention spanner, or is the long self-consciousness of public speakers coming to an end? Can the Republicans match the Democrats in convention oratory, forcing television producers to run great chunks of speeches, treating them as events to be covered rather than meaningless burbling requiring interpretive "voice over"?

I see an oratory that appeals to the heart as well as the head, that speaks to the people as well as the issues, neither pompously programmatic nor mawkishly cornball.

I see an oratory that affirms a party's roots, that allows Democrats to quote F.D.R. and Republicans to quote Lincoln, and not vice versa.

I see an oratory that celebrates the unity of an idea, marching logically from a beginning to a middle and end with no dribbling off.

I see an oratory that takes an audience through an entire speech without mentioning family values.

I see an oratory delivered by the same person who writes the lines—the way Cuomo, Jackson and Hart did, and Reagan and Kirkpatrick can do—willing to stand before the public without benefit of ghosts.

I see an oratory that lets a person feel like part of a great audience, an enthusiastic

*member of a diverse and participating community of listeners, rather than a lonely
viewer with a six-pack and a grudge.*

  I see an oratory that uplifts a heart and upholds a principle.
  I see an oratory that ends when it is finished.

Acknowledgments

As Casey Stengel said, "You could look it up"—or so everyone thought, until a Lexicographic Irregular's tip helped to verify that James Thurber's title for a 1941 short story is the source. In Thurber's baseball story, the team manager, Squawks Magrew, hires a midget as a pinch hitter. Magrew's pal Doc insists on the veracity of this tale by repeatedly saying, "You could look it up."

Our words *verify* and *veracity* come from the Latin *verus*, "truth," and we should all be grateful to the many lexicographers who seek the truth on language: John Algeo, Clarence Barnhart, Robert Barnhart, Jacques Barzun, Robert Burchfield, Ronald Butters, Frederic Cassidy, Willard Espy, Stuart Berg Flexner, David Guralnik, Frederic Mish, Victoria Neufeldt, Mary Gray Porter, Allen Walker Read, Norman Schur, Anne Soukhanov, Sol Steinmetz and Laurence Urdang.

Those who help me "look it up" at *The New York Times* include my editing colleagues Lynn Karpen and Condon Rodgers at *The New York Times Magazine* and Steve Pickering and Mary Drohan at the Op-Ed page. In the Washington bureau, I count on my assistant, Ann Elise Rubin; my research associate, Jeff McQuain; and chief librarian Nancy Ganahl and her successor, Barclay Walsh, with added assistance from Jean Smith at the Library of Congress. For help at Times Books, I'm grateful to Sarah Trotta, Beth Pearson, Charlotte Gross, Gary Huffman, Amy Robbins, Victoria Mathews, and Laura Ogar.

Then there's the veritable legion of Lexicographic Irregulars and Gotcha! Gangsters to thank. (*Veritable*, also from *verus*, is an adjective meaning "actual," to describe something "in truth.") They're the ones who, red pen in hand, read "On Language" carefully enough to send in their corrections and gleefully add, "You could look it up."

Index